D0857716

Communism and the Dilemmas of National Liberation

James E. Mace

Communism and the Dilemmas of National Liberation

National Communism in Soviet Ukraine, 1918-1933

Distributed by Harvard University Press
for the Harvard Ukrainian Research Institute
and the Ukrainian Academy of Arts and Sciences in the U.S.

Publication of this book was made possible in part by the generous donation of Dr. and Mrs. Jerry Mihaychuk.

The Harvard Ukrainian Research Institute was established in 1973 as an integral part of Harvard University. It supports research associates and visiting scholars who are engaged in projects concerned with all aspects of Ukrainian studies. The Institute also works in close cooperation with the Committee on Ukrainian Studies, which supervises and coordinates the teaching of Ukrainian history, language, and literature at Harvard University.

4-6-85

Preface

THIS BOOK WAS originally a dissertation written at the University of Michigan, and thanks are first of all due to those who helped see it through this initial stage. Professor Roman Szporluk, the chairman of my dissertation committee, gave generously of his time, effort, and profound knowledge of the history of twentieth-century Ukraine. Professor Assya Humetsky was also helpful, particularly in dealing with questions of Ukrainian literary life during the period. Professor Alfred G. Meyer was unfailingly enthusiastic, encouraging, and helpful in explaining problems of Marxist-Leninist theory. Professor Stephen Tonsor, the lone non-Slavicist on the committee, did much to strengthen the work by his insistence that the writing be understandable, insofar as possible, to the non-specialist.

Others also greatly aided the author at this initial stage: among them are Professor George Luckyj, Yury Boshyk, Roman Solchanyk, Hryhory Kostiuk, Jurij Lawrynenko, and Myroslav Yurkevych. The historian's craft is inevitably and happily dependent upon the librarians who preserve, catalog, and guide the scholar to the sources that are the raw material of history. Mr. Joseph Placek of the University of Michigan Library, Dr. Dmytro Shtohryn of the University of Illinois, Dr. Roman Ilnytzkyj of the New York Public Library, and the staff of the Library of Congress were all extremely helpful. The dissertation would also have been impossible were it not for the generous financial assistance provided by the University of Michigan Center for Russian and East European Studies, Department of History, and Rackham School of Graduate Studies.

A dissertation, however, is one thing, and a book quite another. It would scarcely have been possible to accomplish the transformation without the financial support, encouragement, and atmosphere of constructive criticism provided by the Ukrainian Research Institute at Harvard University. Professor Omeljan Pritsak, Dr. Donald Ostrowski,

S. Maksudov, and Kazuo Nakai were extremely helpful, as were the staff of Widener Library, particularly Dr. Hugh Olmsted and Oksana Procyk. The author's deep appreciation must also be expressed to Professors Manoly Lupul, Bohdan Krawchenko, and John-Paul Himka of the Canadian Institute of Ukrainian Studies, as well as to Professor Stephan Horak and the editorial board of *Nationalities Papers,* who agreed to publish the major findings of the chapter on Ukrainian Soviet historiography on the understanding that it would also appear in this work.

Last, but certainly not least, profound gratitude must be expressed to Brenda Sens, who completed typing the revised manuscript.

Glossary of Terms
and Abbreviations

Borotbisty- offshoot of the Ukrainian Socialist Revolutionaries formed in 1918; favored an independent Ukrainian Soviet Republic. Most of the Borotbisty were admitted into the KP(b)U in 1920.

Central Rada- the Ukrainian national council established in 1917 that proclaimed and governed the independent Ukrainian People's Republic. The Rada was replaced by the Hetmanate in the spring of 1918, but its traditions were later continued by the Directory.

Cheka- Bolshevik political police of the War Communism period (1917–1921).

Directory- Ukrainian government led by Vynnychenko and Petliura; overthrew the Hetmanate at the end of 1918 and fought the Bolsheviks until 1921.

Federalist Opposition- a group within the KP(b)U led by Georg Lapchinskii in 1919–1920, demanding an independent Soviet Ukraine.

Gosplan- the economic planning agency of the Soviet state.

GPU- Bolshevik political police during the 1920s and early 1930s, replaced the Cheka and was replaced by the NKVD.

Hart- "Tempering," a union of Ukrainian proletarian writers led by Vasyl Ellan-Blakytnyi.

Hetmanate- a restorationist Ukrainian government sponsored by the German Army in 1918.

Istpart- Commission on the History of the Communist Party.

Kolkhoz- collective farm. This more familiar Russian term had been used in preference to the Ukrainian term *kolhosp.*

Kombidy- committees of poor peasants, the Ukrainian counterpart to the Russian *kombedy;* disbanded and replaced by *komnezamy* in Ukraine in 1920.

Komnezamy- short for *komitety nezamozhnykh selian,* committees of non-wealthy peasants that replaced the *kombidy* in 1920. These committees functioned in a manner identical to the *kombidy* except for the fact that they included some middle peasants in their membership. In 1925 they were reorganized and state power was taken away from them, but they were retained in Ukraine until 1933.

KP(b)U- initials of *Komunistychna Partiia (bilshovykiv) Ukrainy,* the Communist Party (bolshevik) of Ukraine.

KPZU- Komunistychna Partiia Zakhidnoi Ukrainy, the Communist Party of Western Ukraine, an autonomous section of the Communist Party of Poland until 1938.

Kulak- rich peasant. This more familiar Russian terms has been used in preference to the Ukrainian terms *kurkul* and *hlytai.*

Narkomos, Narkomosvity- People's Commissar (or Commissariat) of Education in Ukraine. *Narkomos* had broad authority over all spheres of cultural life.

NEP- Novaia Ekonomicheskaia Politika, the New Economic Party, a policy of limited free enterprise and toleration pursued by the Soviet government, 1921–1928.

NKVD- People's Commissariat of Internal Affairs, assumed political police functions under Stalin, successor of GPU and ancestor of KGB.

Oblast- region, a unit of administration below the level of the republic and above that of the *okruh.*

OGPU- see GPU.

Okruh- circle, a unit of administration between *oblast* and *raion.*

Otamanshchyna- regime of the *otamany* or warlords, a period of chaos during the revolution when large areas of Ukraine were under the sway of warlords independent of the control of the Directory, the Bolsheviks, or the Whites.

Piatakovshchyna- 1919 Soviet Ukrainian regime headed by Iurii Piatakov and Khristian Rakovskii; notorious for its hostility to Ukrainian aspirations.

Pluh- "Plow," a union of peasant writers headed by Serhii Pylypenko.

Rada- council; the Russian counterpart is *sovet.*

Raion- district, unit of Soviet administration below the *okruh.*

Revkom- revolutionary committee, a unit of government during the period of War Communism appointed by an army or Party committee and exercising supreme power.

RKP(b)- Rossiiskaia Kommunisticheskaia Partiia (bolshevikov), the Russian Communist Party (bolshevik), later renamed the All-Union Communist Party (bolshevik) [VKP(b)], then the Communist Party of the Soviet Union.

RSDRP- Rossiiskaia Sotsial-Demokraticheskaia Rabochaia Partiia, Russian Social Democratic Workers Party, which in 1903 split into Bolshevik and Menshevik wings.

RUP- Revoliutsiina Ukrainska Partiia, the Revolutionary Ukrainian Party, first mass Ukrainian political party in Eastern Ukraine; after splitting in 1904, one faction became the Ukrainian Social-Democratic Spilka and became affiliated with the Menshevik wing of the RSDRP, while the other changed its name to the USDRP.

Sekretni sotrudnyky- secret collaborators recruited by the Soviet political police.

Silrada- village council or soviet.

Sovnarkom- Council of People's Commissars, used in preference to the Ukrainian counterpart *radnarkom.*

Spilka- union. The Ukrainian Social-Democratic Spilka was an autonomous part of the RSDRP during and immediately after the Revolution of 1905. The Ukrainian *Selianska* (Peasant) Spilka was a rural network associated with the Central Rada during the Revolution of 1917.

SVU- Spilka Vyzvolennia Ukrainy, Union for the Liberation of Ukraine, an imaginary conspiracy "uncovered" by the GPU for the purpose of a 1930 show trial designed to discredit the Ukrainian intelligentsia and, indirectly, the policies of Mykola Skrypnyk.

UIML- Ukrainskyi Instytut Marksyzmu-Leninizmu, the Ukrainian Institute of Marxism-Leninism, replaced in 1931 by VUAMLIN.

Ukapisty- members of the *Ukrainska Komunistychna Partiia* or Ukrainian Communist Party; sought to replace the KP(b)U as the ruling party in Soviet Ukraine. Organized in 1920 as a Left wing offshoot of the USDRP, the Ukapisty's positions were similar to those of the Borotbisty. The group was disbanded on orders from the Comintern in 1925, and most of its members were admitted into the KP(b)U.

UPSF- Ukrainska Partiia Sotsiialistiv-Federalistiv, the Ukrainian Party of Socialist-Federalists; represented the Right wing of the Ukrainian revolution in 1917. Although they used the word "socialist," their social policies were basically like those of the Russian Kadety.

UPSR- Ukrainska Partiia Sotsiialistiv-Revoliutsioneriv, Ukrainian Party of Socialist Revolutionaries, agrarian socialists and the largest party in the Central Rada.

USDRP- Ukrainska Sotsiial-Demokratychna Robitnycha Partiia, Ukrainian Social-Democratic Workers Party, the Marxist wing of the Ukrainian revolutionary movement after 1905.

Vaplite- Vilna Akademiia Proletarskoi Literatury, the Free Academy of Proletarian Literature, the followers of Mykola Khvylovyi, disbanded by the Party in 1928.

Vesenkha- Supreme Council of People's Economy.

VKP(b)- Vsesoiuznaia Kommunisticheskaia Partiia (bolshevikov), the All-Union Communist Party (bolshevik), successor of the RKP(b), later renamed the Communist Party of the Soviet Union.

VUAN- Vseukrainska Akademiia Nauk, the All-Ukrainian Academy of Sciences.

VUAMLIN- Vseukrainska Asosiiatsiia Marksystsko-Leninskykh Instytutiv, the All-Ukrainian Association of Marxist-Leninist Institutes, a federation of autonomous institutes, which was created when UIML was split up in 1931.

War Communism- Bolshevik Policy preceding the NEP; based on wholesale nationalization of industry, rationing, and compulsory requisition of agricultural produce from the peasantry.

White Guards- Russian counterrevolutionary army; those active in Ukraine were led by Denikin and later Wrangel.

Note on Transliteration

The author has used the following system for Ukrainian:

А a	I i	Т t
Б b	Ï i	У u
В v	Й i	Ф f
Г h	К k	Х kh
Ґ g	Л l	Ц ts
Д d	М m	Ч ch
Е e	Н n	Ш sh
Є ie	О o	Щ shch
Ж zh	П p	Ю iu
З z	Р r	Я ia
И y	С s	Ь deleted

This is basically a simplified adaptation of the Library of Congress system. An exception was made in cases during the discussion of whether Ukrainians should adopt the Latin alphabet when some authors published Ukrainian language materials in their own versions of the Latin script. In those instances the original system has been retained.

Place names have been rendered according to the Russian form if they are currently within the borders of the RSFSR, and according to the Ukrainian form if they are currently within the Ukrainian Soviet Socialist Republic, except when there are universally accepted English forms, such as Kiev. Hard and soft signs have been deleted throughout.

Various orthographic systems were in use during the period, and the author has transliterated them all directly according to the above system. Thus, for example, the daily organ of the Soviet Ukrainian state is rendered *Visty VUTsVK* until January 1, 1929, in conformity with the VUAN orthography and as *Visti VUTsVK* thereafter in conformity with the Skrypnyk orthography officially adopted on that date, as well as with the Stalin-Postyshev-Khvylia orthography adopted in 1933 and still in use.

Table of Contents

Introduction

NOT LONG AFTER Tito broke with Stalin, Milovan Djilas, then the chief ideologist of Yugoslavia's budding quest for its own road to socialism, published an article designed to justify the break by showing how Lenin himself had guaranteed nations the right to seek their own roads to socialism. Called "Lenin on the Relations Between Socialist States," it consisted largely of Lenin's assurances to the Ukrainians that their rights and aspirations would be respected.[1] It was quite appropriate that the Yugoslavs turned to Ukraine for a precedent, for it was the Ukrainians who first attempted to find their own national road to socialism. What follows is an attempt to trace this aborted Ukrainian road to socialism, how it came to be, what the Ukrainian communists tried to achieve, what measure of success was temporarily theirs, and how their quest was ended. It shows that, while what Soviet Ukraine achieved fell considerably short of anything that could plausibly be portrayed as "national liberation," the regime was profoundly influenced by the national aspirations it sought to placate, and that these aspirations were expressed through the Communist Party (bolshevik) of Ukraine during the formative, pre-totalitarian period of Soviet history.

The present study falls into three discrete but interconnected parts. The first two chapters explore the development of nationalism and socialism in what would become the Soviet Ukraine of the interwar period, the problem of Ukrainian national liberation as it manifested itself during the revolution and Civil War, and the process by which the Bolshevik Party came to realize the need for a reversal of its nationality policy. The next three chapters deal with the question of how the Bolshevik search for Ukrainian national legitimacy led to the expression of Ukrainian national aspirations within the communist movement and how these aspirations were expressed by the so-called national

---

[1] Milovan Djilas, *Lenin on the Relations Between Socialist States* (New York, n.d.).

1

deviationists, Oleksander Shumskyi, Mykola Khvylovyi, and Mykhailo Volobuiev. The final section deals with the distinctive Ukrainian communist orthodoxy associated with the name of Mykola Skrypnyk and how Stalin suppressed it.

During the Russian Revolution of 1917 the old empire simply disintegrated. The Ukrainians were led by their national intelligentsia, most of which was organized into socialist parties. Soon after the tsar's abdication the Ukrainian socialist parties organized a national council, the Central Rada, which the Russian Provisional Government was ultimately forced to recognize as the political organ of Ukrainian autonomy. The Ukrainian movement enjoyed widespread popular support, which is demonstrated by the fact that Ukrainian socialist parties participating in the Rada polled 80% of the votes cast in the election to the Russian Constituent Assembly in Ukraine. In early 1918, the Ukrainian Central Rada declared its independence from Russia, and a Ukrainian national government continued to exist in one form or another until 1921.

The Ukrainians were unable to maintain their political independence against the Poles, the Bolsheviks, and the Whites. Ukraine was one of the main theaters of the civil war, changing hands a dozen times or more and undergoing tremendous devastation. Early Bolshevik policy was hostile to the Ukrainian national liberation movement, and Ukraine's peasant majority was more than willing to pay the Russian Bolsheviks back in their own coin. At first, the Bolsheviks ignored those who called for them to come to terms with Ukrainian aspirations, but by the early twenties even the Bolshevik leaders themselves realized that rural resistance in Ukraine could never be overcome without concessions to the peasantry and the national intelligentsia, which had led it in 1917.The Ukrainian Borotbisty were admitted into the official Communist Party (bolshevik) of Ukraine in 1920, but a real reversal of the Party's nationality policy came only in 1923 at the Twelfth Party Congress.

By 1923, a number of communists had denounced the tendency of the Bolsheviks to cast themselves in the role of imperialists who were intent on reuniting the old empire against the wishes of its non-Russian inhabitants. A Muslim Bolshevik, Sultan-Galiev produced the most systematic indictment of Red imperialism.[2] Yet, similar views were expressed even earlier in Ukraine: by Shakhrai and Mazlakh in late 1918

---

[2] On Sultan-Galiev, see Alexandre A. Bennigsen and S. Enders Wimbush, *Muslim National Communism in the Soviet Union: A Revolutionary Strategy for the Colonial World* (Chicago and London, 1979), pp. 39–47ff.

and early 1919, by the Federalist Opposition in the KP(b)U, as well as by indigenous pro-Soviet Ukrainian groups such as the Borotbisty and Ukapisty.

The Twelfth Party Congress partially vindicated these critics when it officially committed the regime to a policy of indigenization (*korenizatsiia*), adopted in hopes of giving the non-Russian Soviet republics some measure of national legitimacy. The indigenization policy involved recruiting non-Russians into the Party and state administration, encouraging Party members and state employees to learn the local language and integrate themselves into the local national life, and fostering indigenous national cultural development. Ukrainization, the Ukrainian version of this policy, went farther than any of its counterparts and enabled the Soviet Ukrainian government to seek and receive the support of a substantial part of the formerly hostile national intelligentsia.

Ukrainization succeeded in giving Soviet Ukraine a measure of national legitimacy, but this success was achieved only at the cost of legitimizing Ukrainian national aspirations within the Party itself. Communists began to raise questions that Moscow found exceedingly awkward. Oleksander Shumskyi, the former Borotbist leader who was made Commissar of Education, argued that national liberation was somewhat less than complete if Soviet Ukraine was not allowed its own national political leadership. Mykola Khvylovyi, the most popular Ukrainian communist writer of the day, argued that Ukraine had to emancipate itself culturally from its former colonial oppressor, Russia. The Russian-born Mykhailo Volobuiev, who was head of political education in Soviet Ukraine and who represented the new generation the Party itself had reared, published an impressive treatise designed to show that the Soviet system had not overcome the economic legacy of colonialism because Soviet Ukraine was being exploited under the Soviets no less than it had been under the tsars. Moscow felt threatened to the point that Stalin himself intervened against Shumskyi and Khvylovyi, denouncing their "national deviations" from the Party line. Their colleagues duly condemned them, and the issues they raised were never more than partially addressed.

Yet, Soviet Ukraine did succeed in evolving its own national road to socialism under Mykola Skrypnyk, the Old Bolshevik who in 1927 replaced Shumskyi as Commissar of Education. The secondary rank of his title is belied by his serving as *de facto* minister of the nationality question, ideology, culture, and Soviet Ukraine's most effective lobbyist in Union councils. Skrypnyk pursued Ukrainization as a policy of nationbuilding and attempted to consolidate a Ukrainian nation-state within the framework of the USSR in anticipation of Ukraine's entry into a future world socialist commonwealth as an equal to the advanced nations of Europe. Perhaps one could view him as a Gomulka or a Tito, except that he lacked the crucial levers of power, a national army and police force, that could have enabled him to defy Moscow successfully. Yet, while it lasted, Skrypnyk's Soviet Ukraine for all its authoritarian and totalitarian elements was not a wholly unattractive surrogate for national independence. In any case, it was far preferable to the regime of complete national suppression that followed it.

The Soviet flirtation with this surrogate for national liberation within its borders came to an end during the course of the first Five-Year Plan. The full extent of the suppression—the destruction of the national intelligentsia and new political elites associated with Skrypnyk, the *de facto* restoration of serfdom through forced collectivization of agriculture, the deliberate creation of mass starvation in the Ukrainian countryside, which cost millions of lives—would require a separate study in order to be treated and explained fully. This study can only portray those events in broad outline.

A number of valuable studies by scholars outside the Soviet Union were essential to the present study. Jurij Lawrynenko's bibliography of Ukrainian communism and Panas Fedenko's survey of Ukrainian nationalism in the twentieth century remain the inevitable points of departure for any excursion into modern Ukrainian history.[3] Histories of Soviet Ukraine and its Communist Party by Basil Dmytryshyn, V. Sadovskyi, Vsevolod Holubnychy, Iwan Majstrenko, and Robert Sullivant were equally indispensible.[4] John Reshetar's classic study of the Ukrainian revolution remains the standard treatment of the subject, although it has been supplemented in a number of respects by the collection recently edited by Taras Hunczak.[5] Jurij Borys' study of the establishment of

---

[3] Jurij Lawrynenko, *Ukrainian Communism and Soviet Russian Policy Toward the Ukraine: An Annotated Bibliography* (New York, 1953); Panas Fedenko, *Ukrainskyi rukh u 20 stolitti* (London, 1959).

[4] Basil Dmytryshyn, *Moscow and the Ukraine, 1918–1953: A Study of Russian Bolshevik Nationality Policy* (New York, 1956); V. Sadovskyi, *Natsionalna politika Sovitiv na Ukraini* (Warsaw, 1937); Vsevolod Holubnychy, "Outline History of the Communist Party of the Ukraine," *Ukrainian Review,* no. 6, 1958, pp. 68–125; Iwan Majstrenko, *Storinky z istorii Komunistychnoi Partii Ukrainy* (Munich, 1969); Robert S. Sullivant, *Soviet Politics and the Ukraine, 1917–1957* (New York and London, 1962).

[5] John Reshetar, *The Ukrainian Revolution, 1917–1920: A Study in Nationalism* (Princeton, 1953); Taras Hunczak, ed., *The Ukraine, 1917–1921: A Study in Revolution* (Cambridge, Mass., 1977).

the Soviet Ukrainian state has recently appeared in a new edition.[6] Iwan Majstrenko's monograph on the Borotbisty and Arthur Adams' study of the Piatakov regime of 1919 are also useful.[7] Valuable studies of the so-called national deviations in the Communist Party (bolshevik) of Ukraine and the Communist Party of Western Ukraine have been written by Janusz Radziejowski, Vsevolod Holubnychy, and Roman Solchanyk.[8] Works by George Luckyj, Myroslav Shkandrij, and Jurij Lawrynenko are indispensible for understanding the literary trends and politics of the period.[9] Iwan Koszeliwec has published an extremely interesting biography of Mykola Skrypnyk.[10] The more specialized but nonetheless crucial topic of Soviet Ukrainian historical writing has been surveyed by Myron Korduba, Borys Krupnytskyi, and Olexander Ohloblyn.[11] Hryhory Kostiuk's study of the decade of mass terror (1929–1939) in Soviet Ukraine is indispensable for understanding how Ukrainian national communism was suppressed.[12]

Some of the Soviet secondary literature has also proved to be useful, in spite of the official preoccupation with "Party mindedness" that gives even the best of it a tendentious character. Of the official histories of the KP(b)U, those by Moisei Ravich-Cherkasskii and Nikolai Popov

---

[6] Jurij Borys, *The Sovietization of Ukraine 1917–1923: The Communist Doctrine and Practice of National Self-Determination* (Edmonton, Alberta, 1980).

[7] Iwan Majstrenko, *Borot'bism: A Chapter in the History of Ukrainian Communism* (New York, 1954); Arthur E. Adams, *Bolsheviks in the Ukraine: The Second Campaign, 1918–1919* (New Haven and London, 1963).

[8] Janusz Radziejowski, "Kwestia narodowa w partii komunistycznej na Ukrainie radzieckiej (1920–1927)," *Przegląd historyczny*, 1971, no. 3, pp. 477–498; *idem.*, *Komunistyczna Partia Zachodniej Ukrainy, 1919–1929: Węzłowe problemy ideologiczne* (Cracow, 1976); Vsevolod Holubnychy, "The Views of M. Volobuyev and V. Dobrohaiyev and Party Criticism," *Ukrainian Review*, no. 3, 1956, pp. 5–12; Roman Solchanyk, *The Communist Party of Western Ukraine, 1919–1938* (Ph.D. dissertation, University of Michigan, 1973).

[9] George S. N. Luckyj, *Literary Politics in the Soviet Ukraine, 1917–1934* (New York, 1956); Myroslav Shkandrij, *The "Literary Discussion" in Soviet Ukraine, 1925–1928* (Ph.D. dissertation, University of Toronto, 1980); Jurij Lawrynenko, *Rozstriliane vidrodzhennia: Antolohiia, 1917–1933* (Paris, 1959).

[10] Iwan Koszeliwec, *Mykola Skrypnyk* (Munich, 1972).

[11] Myron Korduba, *La littérature historique soviétique-ukrainienne: Compte-rendu 1917–1931* (Munich, 1972); Borys Krupnytskyi, *Ukrainska istorychna nauka pid sovietamy (1920–1950 roky)* (Munich, 1957); Olexander Ohloblyn, "Ukrainian Historiography, 1917–1957," *Annals of the Ukrainian Academy of Arts and Sciences in the U.S.*, vol. 6, 1957, pp. 307–456.

[12] Hryhory Kostiuk, *Stalinist Rule in the Ukraine: A Study in the Decade of Mass Terror (1929–1939)* (London, 1960).

are both the earliest and the most informative.[13] Ukrainian communists who were condemned as national deviationists in the 1920s have never been rehabilitated, and later Soviet historians have been able to publish little more than empty denunciations of everything they said and did. Mykola Skrypnyk was more fortunate, thanks to his temporary and selective posthumous rehabilitation, at which time a rather informative official biography appeared.[14]

Those scholars who went before must be given a great deal of credit for whatever usefulness this work might possess. For whatever errors remain, the author alone is responsible.

[13] M. Ravich-Cherkasskii, *Istoriia Kommunisticheskoi Partii (b-ov) Ukrainy* (Kharkiv, 1923); M. M. Popov, *Narys istorii Komunistychnoi Partii (bilshovykiv) Ukrainy* (Kharkiv, 1928).

[14] Iu. Babko and I. Bilokobylskyi, *Mykola Oleksiiovych Skrypnyk* (Kiev, 1967).

PART ONE

From Russian Colony to Soviet Republic

CHAPTER ONE

Nationalism and Socialism in Ukraine

BOTH NATIONALISM AND socialism represent conflicting world views that attempt to explain human society in terms of a group to which the individual owes allegiance. Nationalism focuses upon the nation and advocates the collaboration of different social classes within a given language community. Socialism takes class conflict as its point of departure and calls for the cooperation of working people across national lines against the bourgeoisie of all nations. Nationalism usually seeks to avoid class conflict because it weakens national unity, while socialism has historically viewed nationalism as a species of bourgeois false consciousness serving only to hinder the struggle for social justice. The two rival views would seem to be irreconcilable, but the history of this century provides numerous examples of their merging.

Ukrainian national communism was in a sense the successor of a particularly national brand of socialism that had evolved long before the revolution of 1917. Such an ideology, first systematically expressed by Mykhailo Drahomanov in the 1870s and later cast in a Marxist framework, arose in response to the particular situation of the Ukrainian nation.[1] The propertied classes in pre-revolutionary Ukraine were overwhelmingly non-Ukrainian, while the Ukrainians were almost wholly a nation of peasants who were not yet free of the vestiges of serfdom and who lived under a government that promulgated laws against printing materials in the Ukrainian language. The Ukrainian peasantry thus provided a natural constituency for those who could articulate both their national and social grievances. The Ukrainian national intelligentsia created an amalgam of nationalism and socialism capable of expressing

---

[1] On the development of the Ukrainian national movement, see Ivan L. Rudnytsky, *Mizh istoriieiu i politykoiu* (Munich, 1973); Iuliian Okhrymovych, *Rozvytok ukrainskoi natsionalno-politychnoi dumky (Vid pochatku XIX stolittia do Mykhaila Drahomanova* (New York, 1965); Panas Fedenko, *Ukrainskyi rukh u 20 stolitti* (London, 1959).

the aspirations of the nation's rural majority, enjoyed widespread popular support, and was able to establish an independent Ukrainian Peoples Republic. Although Ukrainians were unable to maintain their political independence, they could effectively block the establishment of any regime that did not take into account their aspirations for national liberation.

Marxism and the Nationality Question

Before the development of political movements in what would later become Soviet Ukraine can be traced, the ways in which Marxists attempted to come to terms with national aspirations must be briefly examined. Marxists refer to this problem as "the nationality question."

Marx and Engels did not produce any systematic theory of nationalism, nor did they provide any clear prescriptions regarding what ought to be done about it. They did, however, enunciate certain principles, which can be summarized as follows:

1) *Proletarian internationalism.* Marx held that the workers have no fatherland and considered the very idea that workers owed loyalty to a common fatherland with the bourgeoisie to be a fraud aimed at seducing the workers into collaboration with their exploiters. The workers' real interests, in the Marxist view, lie in the international solidarity of all workers regardless of nationality. Nationalism thus becomes a species of bourgeois false consciousness serving to divide the workers along national lines, to divert their attention from their class enemies, and thereby to inhibit the struggle for socialism.

2) *National equality.* Opposition to national oppression, discrimination, and inequality is merely a corollary of proletarian internationalism. It would be the height of inconsistency for the proletariat to proclaim the solidarity of the workers of all nations and simultaneously sanction the oppression of one nation by another. As a resolution of the First International put it in 1870: "The people which oppresses another is forging its own chains."[2]

3) *Preference for large political units.* Other things being equal, Marx and Engels favored large states as more conducive to more rapid economic development, which, they assumed, would bring closer the attainment of socialism. They did not, however, consider this a hard

---

[2] As quoted by Horace B. Davis, *Nationalism and Socialism: Marxist and Labor Theories of Nationalism to 1917* (New York and London, 1967), p. 66.

and fast rule, and in certain individual cases favored the break-up of existing states.

4) *The progressive significance of small nations' assimilation.* Marx and especially Engels thought in terms of "historical" and "non-historical" nations, as did most nineteenth-century European philosophers. The former, it was assumed, had proven their right to political independence by having maintained it in relatively recent times. The latter, having failed to do so, were assumed to be proven incapable of it and destined for assimilation.[3] The assimilation of such peoples was also assumed to be progressive in that it removed barriers to economic intercourse. In *The German Ideology,* a manuscript that Marx and Engels wrote in the mid-1840s but never published, they indicated that socialism would ultimately lead not only to the elimination of social classes, but of nationalities as well.[4]

The specific cases of Ireland and Poland deserve attention, because the statements that Marx and Engels made concerning them would have an important impact on later Marxists who attempted to deal with the nationality question. Marx was particularly concerned with the Irish question because of its importance to the English working-class movement: he believed that the possibility of Irish revolt gave the English ruling class their only excuse to maintain a large standing army that could be used against the English proletariat. For this reason he came to see the Irish question as a life-or-death matter for the English workers. He favored Irish independence as the most desirable solution to the question, although he held out the hope that independence might later be followed by an Anglo-Irish federation.[5]

Marx's advocacy of Polish independence should be attributed to his fear of Russia, for he believed it likely that any socialist revolution in Europe would face Russian intervention similar to the one that crushed the Hungarian revolution in 1849. The Poles, Russophobic Slavs and a large historical nation, which had over the years provided more than

---

[3] See Roman Rosdolsky, *Zur nationalen Frage: Friedrich Engels und das Problem der "geschichtlosen" Völker* (Berlin, 1979); Jósef Chlebowczyk, "Marks i Engels a problem małych narodów w Europie śródkowo-wschodniej (W kwestii genezy i rozwoju tzw. narodów niehistorycznych)," *Z pola walki,* 1970, no. 2, pp. 15–43.

[4] They described the proletariat as a class that "is in itself the expression of the dissolution of all classes, nationalities, etc., within present society." K. Marx, F. Engels, V. Lenin, *On Historical Materialism* (Moscow, 1972), p. 38.

[5] Davis, *Nationalism and Socialism,* p. 66; Solomon F. Bloom, *The World of Nations: A Study of the National Implications in the Works of Karl Marx* (New York, 1941), p. 39.

its share of revolutionaries, seemed a natural buffer against a reactionary Russian autocracy. Marx and Engels championed the cause of Polish independence eloquently and often.[6]

After Marx and Engels died there were three particularly noteworthy attempts to deal with the nationality question. One attempt was made by the Austrian Marxists Otto Bauer and Karl Renner. Another, probably closer to the spirit of the original doctrine, was made by Rosa Luxemburg. A third attempt, decisive for the object of this study, was Lenin's.

The nationality question was particularly urgent for the Habsburg Empire, which contained over a dozen nationalities, each with its own emergent aspirations. One concession that Austrian socialists made was to sanction the idea that geographically compact nationalities be given territorial autonomy. Another concession was to restructure the party as a federation of national socialist parties. In order to deal with the problem of members of a given nationality who lived outside their ethnic territory, or who, like the Jews, had no compact territory but constituted a nationality nonetheless, Bauer and Renner proposed that each nationality within the empire be recognized as a self-governing corporate entity that would have responsibility for education in the native language as well as for other activities broadly defined as cultural. Every member of a given nationality would be a member of his national corporation regardless of his or her place of residence. The distinction between historical and non-historical peoples was transformed into a historico-sociological category. Bauer argued that peoples considered non-historical also had their histories and possessed the same rights as others.[7]

Luxemburg completely rejected the distinction between historical and non-historical peoples. Nationalism was reactionary, as far as she was concerned, and she dismissed all national aspirations as a non-issue. A native of Poland, she opposed what she saw as the excessive nationalism of the Polish Socialist Party and rejected Marx's claim that Poland should be an independent state. Times had changed since Marx's day, she argued, and the various parts of Poland had become integrated so thoroughly into the economies of the states holding them that a

---

[6] For a selection of their writings on the Polish question, see Paul W. Blackstock and Bert F. Hoselitz, eds., *The Russian Menace to Europe* (Glencoe, Ill., 1952), pp. 91–120.

[7] See the selections from Bauer and Renner in Tom Bottomore and Patrick Goode, eds., *Austro-Marxism* (Oxford, 1978), pp. 102–125.

reconstituted Poland would simply not be economically viable.[8] Luxemburg also argued against national self-determination on principle because she believed that capitalism was the root cause of national oppression: overthrow capitalism and the problem will be solved; let it survive and national oppression is inevitable. For many, the word "Luxemburgism" became synonymous with "national nihilism," that is, complete disregard for the problem of nationality.[9]

Lenin's goal, preserving international proletarian unity in the struggle against capitalism, was the same as Luxemburg's, but his strategy was considerably more sophisticated than hers.[10] As early as 1903, he opposed the Jewish Bund's bid for autonomy within the RSDRP, and he never altered his belief that the workers of a multinational state ought to be united in a single socialist party.[11] But he made a fundamental distinction between the nationalism of peoples that oppress other peoples and peoples that are oppressed. While the former was reactionary, the latter should be seen as a defensive reaction against imperialist oppression and might even be marshalled for the struggle against international capitalism. They had only to be shown that they had nothing to fear from the proletariat and the socialists of the oppressor nation. Once this was accomplished, they would then be able to see the advantages of unity and even assimilation.[12] The Russian Social Democrats had long recognized the right of nations to self-determination, but they had limited it to regional self-government, not complete independence. Lenin wanted to go farther, to recognize the right of nations to secession and independence.[13] The breakdown of the old distinction between historical and non-historical peoples allowed him to find sanction for his position

---

[8] This is the thesis of her dissertation, which is available in English as Rosa Luxemburg, *The Industrial Development of Poland* (New York, 1977).

[9] See Rosa Luxemburg, *The National Question: Selected Writings,* ed. Horace B. Davis (New York, 1976). A more concise exposition of her views on the nationality question may be found in J. P. Nettl, *Rosa Luxemburg* (London, 1966), vol. 2, pp. 842–862.

[10] Lenin's views on the nationality question have been analyzed by a number of authors. See, for example, Alfred D. Low, *Lenin on the Question of Nationality* (New York, 1958); Davis, *Nationalism and Socialism,* pp. 187ff.

[11] Lenin held this view as early as 1903 when he opposed the Jewish Bund's attempt to gain sanction for its autonomous status within the RSDRP. See V. I. Lenin, *Polnoe sobranie sochinenii (PSS)* (Moscow, 1960–1965), vol. 7, pp. 254–246, 266–269, 300, 322–325.

[12] *Ibid.,* vol. 24, pp. 123–130; Lenin, *Collected Works (CW)* (Moscow, 1960–1970), vol. 20, pp. 27–33.

[13] František Silnický, *Natsionalnaia politika KPSS v period s 1917 po 1922 god* (Munich, 1978), p. 34.

even in the classics: he had only to cite Marx's and Engels' statements on Ireland and Poland.[14] When, in 1913, Lenin first argued for extending the right of nations to self-determination, he did so to the point of granting their rights to secession and independence, as he put it,

> not because we have dreamt of splitting up the country economically or of the ideal of small states, but on the contrary, because we want large states and the closer unity and even fusion of nations, only on a truly democratic, truly internationalist basis, which is *inconceivable* without the freedom to secede.[15]

To further prevent the nationalities from exercising their right to self-determination Lenin argued that, while socialists of an oppressor nation ought to champion the right, socialists of an oppressed nation ought to oppose its exercise and advocate unity. Should the latter advocate independence, it would become the involuntary ally of the national bourgeoisie, which would inevitably betray it.[16] The right to national self-determination thus became a right recognized in the hope that it would never be exercised. Lenin remained adamantly opposed to anything that threatened to hinder assimilation as did the Austrian plan of national cultural autonomy.[17] His goal was identical with Luxemburg's. Only his tactics differed.

Near the end of his life, the experience of the Russian Revolution and the resistance of non-Russians to anything smacking of Russian domination would lead Lenin to modify his views on the nationality question. But before this final evolution of his thought can be understood, it is first necessary to explore what it was that forced him to rethink the issue of how non-Russians ought to be treated by a socialist government that was, by and large, a Russian creation.

Ukrainian Socialism in the Russian Empire

In 1917 the Ukrainians were still overwhelmingly a peasant people for the most part little touched by the rapid industrial development of their country that had taken place over the last half-century. Ukraine, on the eve of the Russian Revolution of 1917, was still "the breadbasket of Europe," producing, between 1909 and 1913, 98% of the Russian Empire's wheat, 75% of its rye, and 27% of its oats. Its eastern area

---

[14] Lenin, *PSS,* vol. 27, p. 64; *CW,* vol. 21, p. 409.
[15] Lenin, *PSS,* vol. 27, pp. 67–68; *CW,* vol. 21, pp. 413–414.
[16] Lenin, *PSS,* vol. 27, pp. 63–64; *CW,* vol. 21, p. 409.
[17] Lenin, *PSS,* vol. 24, pp. 313–315.

had become transformed into an industrial and mining region that produced 68% of the empire's cast-iron, 77% of its iron ore, 87% of its
coal, and 82% of its raw sugar.[18] Economic development had been so
rapid that one writer described Ukraine as an "El Dorado" attracting
job-seekers from all parts of the empire.[19] Yet, what there was of a
Ukrainian working class was, by and large, either assimilated or confined to the lowest paying and least skilled jobs. The trade unions and
the Social Democratic movement, which dominated them, were led by
Russians or by those who had adopted the Russian language and culture.[20]

The development of Ukrainian national consciousness had been
severely hampered by the ban on Ukrainian literary and cultural activities that was enacted in the Russian Empire in 1863 and broadened in
1876.[21] While it became possible to publish Ukrainian language books
and periodicals in the aftermath of the 1905 revolution, a new round
of piecemeal oppression soon attempted to restore the situation to the
status quo ante. After World War I began, nothing could be published
in Ukrainian beyond an occasional pamphlet on improving farm techniques or similarly non-political topics.[22] Mykola Kovalevskyi, a man
of long-standing service to the Ukrainian movement, recalled that the
movement obtained a mass following only in 1912.[23]

The fact that class and nationality coincided made it seem only natural
that Ukrainian nationalism would go hand in hand with agrarian
socialism. The danger against which Lenin had warned, betrayal by the
national bourgeoisie, did not exist: the Ukrainians had no national
bourgeoisie to speak of. From the turn of the century to the revolution
of 1917 one encounters one word again and again in the writings of
Ukrainian socialists, *bezburzhuaznist*, literally, the "bourgeoislessness"
of the Ukrainian nation. Some Ukrainians blamed Ukrainian *bezbur-*

---

[18] Jurij Borys, *The Sovietization of Ukraine 1917–1923: The Communist Doctrine and Practice of National Self-Determination* (Edmonton, 1980), pp. 54–56.

[19] Mykola Porsh, "Vidnosyny Ukrainy do ynshykh raioniv Rossii na robitnychomu rynku na osnovi materialiv pershoho vseliudskoho perepysu," *Literaturno-naukovyi vistnyk*, 1912, no. 3, p. 525.

[20] On the RSDRP in Ukraine before World War I, see Ralph Carter Elwood, *Russian Social Democracy in the Underground: The RSDRP in the Ukraine, 1907–1914* (Assen, 1974).

[21] John Reshetar, *The Ukrainian Revolution*, p. 7.

[22] D. Doroshenko, *Moi spomyny pro davnie-mynule* (Winnipeg, 1949), pp. 75ff. Doroshenko, "Voina i revoliutsiia na Ukraine," *Istorik i sovremennik*, vol. 1, 1922, p. 216.

[23] Mykola Kovalevskyi, *Pry dzherelakh borotby: Spomyny, vrazhennia, refleksii* (Innsbruck, 1960), p. 101.

zhuaznist for the weakness of Ukrainian nationalism, and others rejoiced in it because they believed it fostered greater national unity. But regardless of how they viewed the phenomenon, they were unanimous in recognizing its existence.[24]

The first attempt to combine Ukrainian nationalism with agrarian socialism was made in the 1870s by M. P. Drahomanov. Drahomanov's socialism was to be based on self-governing and independent local peasant communities (*hromady*), which would cooperate with one another as the need arose. Ukraine, in Drahomanov's anarchist vision, was to be "a society of societies, of free communities, free in all their affairs." Ukraine would become a member of a world federation of socialist nations, the elected representatives of which would meet in congresses. As Drahomanov himself indicated, it was a vision that owed more to Proudhon and Bakunin than to Marx.[25]

The first real political party of Ukrainians in the Russian Empire was formed only at the turn of the century.[26] Founded in 1900 as a radical nationalist group, the Revolutionary Ukrainian Party (RUP) quickly came under Marxist influence and moderated its nationalism quite substantially. Less than five years after RUP was founded, one wing of its leadership went so far as to proclaim nationality a "non-existent question" and made an unsuccessful bid to lead the entire party into the Russian Social Democratic fold. The result was that the party split in two.[27] One wing joined the RSDRP *en masse,* took the name Ukrainian Social

---

[24] For the optimistic view, see Vynnychenko's June 1917 speech to the Second All-Ukrainian Military Congress in S. M. Dimanshtein, ed., *Revoliutsiia i natsionalnyi vopros: Dokumenty i materialy po istorii natsionalnogo voprosa v Rossii i SSSR v XX veke* (Moscow, 1930), vol. 3, pp. 157–158. Several years earlier a Ukrainian activist wrote, "Our Ukrainian movement is weak and feeble because we do not have our own bourgeoisie." K., "Klasova borotba y natsionalna solidarnist," *Ukrainska khata,* 1909, no. 7–8, p. 383.

[25] M. P. Drahomanov, "Peredne slovo do Hromady 1878," in Mykh. Hrushevskyi, ed., *Z pochyniv ukrainskoho sotsiialistychnoho rukhu: Mykh. Drahomanov i zhenevskyi sotsiialistychnyi hurtok* (Vienna, 1922), pp. 103–150, especially p. 121. This article is perhaps Drahomanov's most concise statement of his views.

[26] True, a group called Ukrainian Social Democracy pre-dated the RSDRP by a year, but it never had more than a few adherents and ceased to exist after a few years. A valuable study of this group is Jurij Lawrynenko, "Ukrainska sotsiial-demokratiia (hrupa USD) i ii lider Lesia Ukrainka," *Suchasnist,* vol. 11, 1971, nos. 5, 6, 7–8.

[27] On the history of RUP, see George Y. Boshyk, *The Rise of Ukrainian Political Parties in Russia, 1900–1907: With Special Reference to Social Democracy* (D. Phil. Thesis, University of Oxford, 1981) and Osyp Hermaize, *Narysy z istorii revoliutsiinoho rukhu na Ukraini* (Kharkiv, 1926).

Democratic *Spilka,* and became something like a Ukrainian section of the RSDRP charged with carrying on Social Democratic propaganda in Ukrainian. Although the Spilka foreswore national demands, it had its own Supreme Committee. The Spilka played a substantial role in the RSDRP's victories in the 1907 election to the Second Imperial Duma, and seems to have briefly had more adherents than what was left of the old RUP, which now called itself the Ukrainian Social Democratic Labor Party (USDRP).[28] The USDRP also petitioned for admission to the RSDRP, asking only that it be allowed to continue its advocacy of Ukrainian autonomy by leaving the question open pending the next RSDRP Congress.[29] The rebuff that the Ukrainian Social Democrats received was fortunate. Had they been accepted into the RSDRP their organization might well have joined the Spilka in the oblivion to which it was condemned after being crippled by a wave of arrests in 1908. Because of the parent organization's apathy, confusion over its role, and the tendency of local Russian Social-Democratic organizations to exclude the Spilka from the towns and factories, the Spilka soon virtually ceased to function, although its organizational shell survived until 1912.[30]

Although the USDRP survived, and the 1917 revolution made a number of its leaders ministers of state, its pre-1917 survival was as precarious as that of all revolutionary parties during the period, and the organization was twice forced to suspend operations for lack of funds. Both times the party was rescued by Lev Iurkevych, a young man of means whose polemical talents catapulted him to party prominence.[31] During the war Iurkevych crossed polemical swords with Lenin. Iurkevych declared that Ukrainians were not much impressed with the fact that Lenin had granted them a right that they were not supposed to exercise; a right that nobody is supposed to exercise seemed to him a contradiction in terms. He warned that the Ukrainian masses wanted national self-determination as well as socialism and that if Russian socialists should prove recalcitrant in granting Ukraine self-government, Ukrainians would fight for it.[32]

---

[28] Arnold Rish, "Ocherki po istorii 'Spilki'," *Letopis revoliutsii,* 1925, no. 2, pp. 134–149, 167–173.

[29] Published in full in M. Ravich-Cherkasskii, *Istoriia KP(b)U,* p. 189.

[30] Rish, "Ocherki . . . ," *Letopis revoliutsii,* 1925, no. 3, pp. 92–107; Boshyk, *The Rise of Ukrainian Political Parties,* pp. 320–334, 380.

[31] D. Doroshenko, *Z istorii ukrainskoi politychnoi dumky za chasiv svitovoi viiny* (Prague, 1936), pp. 26–29ff.

[32] Rybalka (Iurkevych), *Rosiiski sotsiial-demokraty i natsionalne pytannia* (Munich, 1969). See also, Doroshenko, *Z istorii ukrainskoi politychnoi dumky,* pp. 67–86.

The other Ukrainian socialist party that would be prominent in the 1917 revolution was the Ukrainian Party of Socialist-Revolutionaries (UPSR). In 1903 or 1904 a few members of the Revolutionary Ukrainian Party had split off and formed a Ukrainian SR circle as part of the Russian SRs, but almost no one knew of its existence until 1905. The police learned of it only in 1907. Consisting of young Ukrainians who attempted to reconcile Russian Socialist-Revolutionary doctrine with the teachings of Drahomanov, the UPSR had few adherents and little importance until the fall of autocracy. During the First World War, members of this group published an illegal paper in Kiev. The paper was entitled *Borotba* ("The Struggle").[33]

The Revolutions in Ukraine

The division between town and country in Ukraine was such that it is perhaps best to follow the Bolshevik historian Ravich-Cherkasskii and describe what occurred as two revolutions that took place simultaneously. These revolutions were not separated by place as much as they were divided by nationality. For the Russian cities, mines, and factories, what took place was but a regional part of the Russian Revolution. But it was quite different with the Ukrainians; their revolution was national as well as social and developed quite differently from its Russian counterpart.[34] What took place in Ukraine was in essence a struggle between the Russian and Ukrainian revolutions for control of a country that both the urban Russian and rural Ukrainian revolutionaries had good reason to consider theirs. The Soviet Ukraine of the mid-1920s would be based on the *modus vivendi* worked out between these two sets of revolutionaries.

On March 13, 1917 (February 28, according to the Julian calendar then still in use), news reached Kiev that the tsar had fallen, and within a week a Ukrainian national council, the Ukrainian Central Rada, and a predominantly Russian workers' council, the Kiev Soviet of Workers' Deputies, were formed. While the Soviet was not unlike similar organizations set up in other parts of the empire, the Rada was something of a national clearinghouse for Ukrainian activities. It united the Ukrainian Scholarly Society, the Ukrainian Technico-Agronomist Society, the

---

[33] Ark. Zhyvotko, "Do istorii Ukr. Partii Sotsiialistiv-Revoliutsioneriv," *Vilna Spilka: Neperiodychnyi organ UPSR*, no. 3, 1927–1929, pp. 128–132; Pavlo Khrystiuk, *Zamitky i materiialy do istorii ukrainskoi revoliutsii, 1917–1920 rr.* (Vienna, 1921–1922), vol. 1, pp. 35–125; Juryj Borys, "Political Parties in Ukraine," in Hunczak, ed., *The Ukraine, 1917–1921,* p. 135.

[34] Ravich-Cherkasskii, *Istoriia KP(b)U*, pp. 3–11ff.

Ukrainian Pedagogical Society, the Ukrainian National Union, cooperatives, student societies, and the like, on the basis of one demand upon which they all agreed: Ukrainian territorial autonomy with safeguards for the rights of national minorities.[35]

The Ukrainian Central Rada was transformed by degrees from a clearinghouse to a political body, then to the recognized organ of the Provisional Government, and finally to a full-fledged government of an independent Ukrainian Peoples Republic. Early on, it became a body of Ukrainian socialist parties, and after the revolution all Ukrainian figures proclaimed themselves to be socialists. In the popular mind "socialist" had come to mean "for the people." If a Ukrainian figure failed to identify himself with socialism, he was instantly identified with "reaction" and effectively excluded from political life.[36] The three principal parties in the Ukrainian Central Rada were the Ukrainian Party of Socialist-Revolutionaries (UPSR), the Ukrainian Social-Democratic Workers' Party (USDRP), and the Ukrainian Party of Socialist-Federalists (UPSF). After Ukrainian independence was proclaimed in January 1918, the Ukrainian Party of Socialist-Independents (UPSS, formerly the radical nationalist Ukrainian People's Party, which had been the only party to advocate Ukrainian independence on principle from the start) emerged from the shadows of semi-legality and joined the Central Rada.[37]

The UPSR, by far the largest and most popular of Ukrainian parties, was, at least in the early phases of the revolution, the most radical as well.[38] At its founding congress, held in April 1917, it passed resolutions calling for the transformation of the Russian Empire into a democratic federation, including an autonomous Ukraine, and for the socialization of the land. By socialization, the UPSR meant some sort

---

[35] V. Manilov, ed., *1917 god na Kievshchine: Khronika sobytii* (Kiev, 1928), pp. 1–6; Oleh S. Pidhainy, *The Formation of the Ukrainian Republic* (Toronto and New York, 1966), pp. 33–43; Reshetar, *The Ukrainian Revolution*, p. 48.

[36] "From the moment the revolution broke out, all conscious Ukrainians proclaimed themselves to be socialists, and those who had the courage not to number themselves among the socialists were eliminated from political life. It was not even possible to imagine a Ukrainian patriot who was not also a socialist." M. Zabarevskyi, *Viacheslav Lypynskyi i ioho dumka pro ukrainsku natsiiu i derzhavu* (Kiev-Vienna, 1920), p. 5.

[37] On the UPSS, an official account is Ukrainska Partiia Samostiinykiv-Sotsiialistiv, *Ukrainska Revoliutsiia (1917–1919): Diialnist partii S.-S. v zviazku z polítychnymy podiiamy na Ukraini za chas 1901–1919: Ideologiia, prohram i statut partii* (Kiev-Vienna, 1920), p. 5.

[38] Khrystiuk, *Zamitky i materiialy*, vol. 1, p. 35.

of redistribution among individual peasant households to be supervised by an elective Ukrainian Land Reserve Board. The Ukrainian peasantry had no tradition of common tenure similar to the rural commune (*mir*), which the Russian SRs had long hoped to use as a basis for agrarian socialism. Beyond that, however, the UPSR's plans were vague. What sort of autonomy Ukraine was to have was a question that the Constituent Assembly would decide; the UPSR Congress merely expressed "the opinion that the rapid establishment of Ukraine's territorial autonomy with protection of the rights of national minorities is possible." The UPSR Congress also left undefined how much land an individual could keep and how much another might receive.[39] The UPSR had few leaders with significant political experience or national prestige, although it gained a few prestigious converts. Most notable among them were the Rada's President, Mykhailo Hrushevskyi, and the agronomist Mykola Kovalevskyi.[40]

The USDRP was poorer in mass support but richer in experienced leaders than was the UPSR. Due to the fact that the USDRP's natural constituency, workers of Ukrainian nationality, was a relatively small one, the USDRP was more a government party while the UPSR was more a mass party.[41] When it came time to set up a Rada executive in the form of the General Secretariat, it seemed only natural that it be headed by a Ukrainian Social-Democrat, the writer-revolutionary Volodymyr Vynnychenko. A party of committed Marxists whose social policies were rather similar to those of the Russian Mensheviks, the USDRP was less than comfortable with the UPSR as a coalition partner. The UPSR and its peasant constituency was thoroughly *petit-bourgeois* in the eyes of the USDRP. One USDRP spokesman, writing in the party organ, declared that "every peasant says he needs *land*, first land and then there will already be freedom. But what land and what freedom? Of this he has no understanding."[42] Land, the writer went on to state, must be collectively owned and worked in large collective units so that machinery out of the reach of the individual peasant could be employed. Land, he wrote, "cannot be the property of separate individuals; it belongs to all equally, to the whole people."[43]

---

[39] For the texts of these resolutions see Dimanshtein, ed., *Revoliutsiia i natsionalnyi vopros,* vol. 3, p. 137.

[40] Reshetar, *The Ukrainian Revolution,* pp. 51–52, 74.

[41] Khrystiuk, *Zamitky i materiialy,* vol. 2, pp. 117–119.

[42] Ol. Hrudnytskyi, "Choho treba selianam," *Robitnycha hazeta,* April 28, 1917, p. 1.

[43] *Ibid.,* May 5, 1917, p. 1.

When the Rada was established, the USDRP initially hesitated to take part, fearing association with the Society of Ukrainian Progressives, which had established it. Later they went so far as to propose a joint ticket with the local Bolsheviks in Kiev municipal elections, indicating they felt more at home with their future rivals than with the UPSR.[44] As for the latter, the USDRP's attitude was eloquently summed up in the title of an article that appeared in its daily organ: "What does the Ukrainian *Petit-Bourgeoisie* Want?"[45]

The UPSF had the most educated leadership but the smallest constituency of the major Ukrainian parties. Originally the Society of Ukrainian Progressives, the name of Socialist-Federalists was adopted in 1917, and the group's place on the Ukrainian political spectrum was roughly analogous to that of the Russian Kadety.[46] Officially opposed to all revolutionary experimentation, Vynnychenko later called them "also socialists" (*tezh sotsiialisty*), that is, socialists in name only.[47] The description was accurate.

By the time Lenin seized power in Petrograd, the Kiev Soviet of Workers' Deputies was securely in the hands of the local Bolsheviks, led by Iurii Piatakov and Evgeniia Bosh. Piatakov and Bosh had been among the leading Bolshevik adherents of Rosa Luxemburg's views on the nationality question. In 1915 they had joined with Nikolai Bukharin in issuing a platform that denounced national self-determination as reactionary and utopian, unattainable under capitalism and superfluous with the advent of socialism.[48] At the April 1917 empire-wide Bolshevik Conference, Piatakov led those who urged the Bolsheviks to drop their advocacy of the right to national self-determination, arguing that such

---

[44] V. Skorovstanskii (Vasyl Shakhrai), *Revoliutsiia na Ukraine* (2nd Russian edition, Saratov, 1919), p. 18. Evgeniia Bosh, *Natsionalnoe pravitelstvo i Sovetskaia vlast na Ukraine* (Moscow, 1919), p. 14.

[45] Oko., "Choho khochetsia ukrainskii dribnii burzhuazii?" *Robitnycha hazeta,* November 29, 1917, p. 1. Pidhainy (p. 43) emphasizes the unity of Ukrainian "bourgeois" figures and the socialists, claiming that it "explains to a great extent the rise and survival of the Ukrainian Republic." This is simply not true. In the first place, non-socialist Ukrainian figures and parties associated with the Central Rada all became socialists—if only in name—by the end of 1917. Those who did not, the Agrarian Democrats, were, in Pidhainy's words, "generally inimical to the Central Rada" (p. 56).

[46] Reshetar, *The Ukrainian Revolution,* pp. 51–52.

[47] Volodymyr Vynnychenko, *Vidrodzhennia natsii* (Kiev-Vienna, 1920), vol. 1, p. 250; vol. 3, p. 34.

[48] Text in M. Pokrovskii, ed., *Ocherki po istorii Oktiabrskoi revoliutsii: Raboty istoricheskogo seminariia Instituta Krasnoi professury* (Moscow-Leningrad, 1927), vol. 1, pp. 514–518.

a concession would inevitably play into the hands of "*petit-bourgeois* reaction" such as the USDRP.[49] His close contact with the Ukrainian national movement, which was centered in Kiev, convinced him that advocating the right to self-determination, while advising against its exercise, would only put his group in a ridiculous position. It was better to say that national oppression cannot be eliminated as long as imperialism exists because national oppression is a consequence of it.[50] Besides, the basic demands of the Ukrainian movement conflicted with the interests of the proletariat, he argued. Russia simply could not survive without Ukraine's sugar, coal, grain, and so forth. If the economic ties between Russia and Ukraine were severed, neither country would be economically viable, industry would come to a standstill, and workers would be left jobless.[51] The Party's rejection of his stand on the nationality question made silence his best public option. The Kiev Party organ hardly mentioned the issue.[52]

In any case, the Provisional Government was the main enemy for both the Bolsheviks and the Rada. Piatakov believed that the Rada could be supported in its conflicts with the Provisional government, and in August the Bolshevik contingent in the Central Rada went so far as to issue a declaration denouncing Russian imperialism and supporting broad territorial autonomy for Ukraine.[53] When the Provisional Government fell,

---

[49] *Sedmaia (aprelskaia) vserossiiskaia konferentsiia RSDRP (bolshevikov), aprel 1917 goda: Protokoly* (Moscow, 1958), pp. 212–216.

[50] In June 1917, Piatakov said: "We can't make up for this formula simply by saying to the oppressed nationalities: you have the right to self-determination but we do not recommend that you exercise it. We would put ourselves in a ridiculous position. There can be disagreement regarding democratization, but the elimination of national oppression is possible only with the elimination of imperialism because national oppression is a consequence of it. Therefore, the struggle for socialism is a struggle against national oppression: when class oppression is no more there will also be no national oppression." Quoted by I. Iu. Kulik, "Kievskaia organizatsiia ot fevralia do Oktiabria 1917 goda," *Letopis revoliutsii*, 1924, no. 1, pp. 201–202.

[51] Manilov, ed., *1917 god na Kievshchine*, p. 104.

[52] Kulik, "Kievskaia organizatsiia," pp. 197–198, states that the Kiev organization was totally unconcerned with national policy because it did not recognize "the danger to the proletarian revolution from Ukrainian chauvinist groupings." This should be taken with a grain of salt because there is clear evidence that Piatakov was very well aware of this danger. Kulik further notes that the Kiev Bolshevik organ was completely silent on the Ukrainian question except for "two notes in Ukrainian signed 'Ukrainets' which reflected their author's position and not the position of the Bolshevik committee."

[53] Text in Evgeniia Bosh, *God borby: Borba za vlast na Ukraine s aprelia 1917 g. do nemetskoi okupatsii* (Moscow and Leningrad, 1925), p. 240.

the Bolsheviks joined the Rada in a joint Committee for the Defense of the Revolution in Ukraine and fought side by side against the local garrison troops loyal to Kerenskii. But once the common enemy was defeated, the temporary allies fell out.[54]

The Ukrainian socialists, in conformity with the conventional wisdom of the day, expected the Bolsheviks to suffer a rapid defeat, which might well open the door to counterrevolution. *Robitnycha hazeta,* the USDRP organ, began its report of events in Petrograd with the words: "That which we feared so much and so wanted to escape has come to pass."[55] Two days later, it described the October Revolution as a "great tragedy."[56] The Central Rada issued its Third Universal, proclaiming the autonomous Ukrainian Peoples Republic to be part of a non-Bolshevik Russian democratic federation and promising land and social reforms.[57] At the same time, various prominent USDRP spokesmen began to make overtures to the proprietary classes. They assured them that the Third Universal did not violate the rights of property but only expressed the Rada's views on the matter pending the decision of the Constituent Assembly. They even promised to use troops to protect property in the interval.[58] This failure to go along with the tide of popular sentiment, especially the peasantry's desire for immediate land reform, was ultimately fatal to the Rada. When Russian Bolshevik forces began to invade Ukraine at the end of the year, the initially enthusiastic peasantry was at best neutral toward the Rada. Troops loyal to the Rada fell apart. The Bolsheviks won an easy victory, which only the intervention of the Central Powers could reverse.[59]

---

[54] Roman Ilnytskyi, "Shistdesiat dniv ukrainskoi polityky (lystopad-hruden 1917)," *Suchasnist,* vol. 12, 1972, no. 7–8, pp. 120–132; Roman Ilnytskyi, "Tsentralna Rada i bolshevyky voseny 1917 roku. Chomu Tsentralna Rada ne vyznala uriadu Lenina," *Suchasnist,* vol. 12, 1972, no. 10, pp. 57–66. Reshetar, *The Ukrainian Revolution,* pp. 82–85.

[55] "Spodivane stalosia!" *Robitnycha hazeta,* November 1, 1917, p. 1.

[56] F. Zadniprianskyi, "Khto taki bolshevyky?" *Robitnycha hazeta,* November 3, 1917, p. 1.

[57] The Third Universal appears in English in Hunczak, ed., *The Ukraine, 1917–1921,* pp. 387–391.

[58] Dmytro Doroshenko, *Istoriia Ukrainy, 1917–1923 rr.* (New York, 1954), vol. 1, pp. 189ff; I. V. Khmil, *Trudiashche selianstvo Ukrainy v borotby za vladu Rad* (Kiev, 1977), p. 69.

[59] Yaroslav Bilinsky, "The Communist Take-over of the Ukraine," in Hunczak, ed., *Ukraine, 1917–1921,* pp. 111–112. The Rada's loss of popular support has recently been analyzed by Stephen Guthier, "The Popular Base of Ukrainian Nationalism in 1917," *Slavic Review,* vol. 38, 1979, pp. 30–47.

The First Bolshevik Occupation of Ukraine

In the fall of 1917, the political situation in Ukraine was confusing. When it came time for a showdown between the Bolsheviks and the Rada, the hitherto vague distinction between Rada and Soviet had to be cleared up. After all, both words mean "council." Was not the Rada a "Soviet" organ of sorts? In November 1917 Mykola Porsh, a member of the USDRP Central Committee and Ukrainian General Secretary of Labor, indicated that "the Central Rada is by its composition a Soviet of Workers', Peasants', and Soldiers' Deputies which was elected at congresses of peasants, workers, and soldiers."[60] Not a few people were confused about who stood for what. Georg Lapchinskii later recalled that at any given meeting at which Bolsheviks spoke during the fall of 1917 there always seemed to be someone who would stand up and say that, while he was for the Bolsheviks, he was also a Ukrainian, and that while he was for Soviet power, the Rada was also a Soviet.[61] In order to appeal to those who felt this way, the Bolsheviks adopted the formula of recognizing the Rada's authority pending a congress of Soviets which would then "reconstitute" the Rada with a membership more to their liking.

In Ukraine as a whole, the Bolsheviks were a minority. This fact became quite apparent from the results of the election to the All-Russian Constituent Assembly, which took place shortly after Lenin's *coup d'etat* in Petrograd. In this election, the only free election in Russian history, Ukrainian parties polled 80% of votes cast in Ukraine, while the Bolsheviks received only 10%. In the January 1918 Ukrainian Constituent Assembly election, the Bolsheviks increased their shares of a considerably lighter turnout to 17.3%.[62] In any case, hopes for Ukraine's Bolsheviks to show strength sufficient to take power themselves proved illusory. Even among Ukraine's workers, the Mensheviks retained greater support than in Russia.[63]

---

[60] "Tekst razgovora po priamomu provodu predstavitelia S. N. K. I. Stalina s predstav. Ts. K. U. S. D. R. P. Porshem i oblastnoi org. R. S.-D. R. P. (b) Bakinskim 30 (17) noiabria," Manilov, ed., *1917 god na Kievshchine*, p. 532.

[61] Georg Lapchynskyi, "Z pershykh dniv vseukrainskoi radianskoi vlady," *Letopis revoliutsii*, 1927, no. 5-6, p. 56.

[62] Oliver H. Radkey, *The Election to the Russian Constituent Assembly of 1917* (Cambridge, Mass., 1950), pp. 29ff. Kazuo Nakai, "The Election to the Ukrainian Constituent Assembly" (unpublished paper, Harvard Ukrainian Research Institute, 1981). Borys, *The Sovietization of Ukraine*, p. 170.

[63] While Bolsheviks often argued that greater Menshevik strength among Ukraine's workers was due to the greater backwardness of the workers there, Isaak Mazepa argued

Still, the Kiev Bolsheviks pressed on with their plans for a Congress of Soviets. The first problem they faced was internal. Until December 1917, Ukraine's Bolsheviks were officially designated as members of the Russian Social Democratic Labor Party (bolshevik), but there is no Ukrainian equivalent to the word "Rossiiskaia" (Russian) in the Party's title. In Russian, *rossiiskaia* is a purely territorial designation without ethnic connotations: it refers merely to the empire as a whole. In Ukrainian, however, *rosiiska* means the same thing as the Russian *russkaia,* that is, Great Russian. And it would be difficult to prevent a struggle between the Ukrainian Rada and the Russian Bolsheviks from looking like a national struggle between an oppressed nation and the nation that oppressed it. Consequently, the Bolsheviks of the Southwest Regional Organization (Ukraine, less the industrial Donets Basin and Kharkiv) asked permission from the Russian Bolshevik leadership to call themselves "Social Democracy of Ukraine." Permission was granted, but Sverdlov warned on behalf of the Party leadership that, while the name change was acceptable, "the creation of a separate, Ukrainian, Party, whatever it might be called, whatever program it might adopt, we consider undesirable."[64]

The Kiev Bolshevik conference officially adopted the new name in December, although not without opposition from those like Evgeniia Bosh who considered even this an inadmissible concession to Ukrainian chauvinism.[65] The Bolsheviks also needed an issue that would allow them to oppose the Rada while sidestepping the national issue. The Poltava Bolshevik Vasyl Shakhrai argued that the refusal of the Rada to recognize the legitimacy of Lenin's regime while maintaining friendly relations with the anticommunist Don Cossack regime of General Kaledin showed that the Rada was on the side of the counterrevolution. He offered the following formula to capitalize on this:

> All Russia is divided into two parts, bourgeois and proletarian. One has its center in Petrograd and the other on the Don. The Rada has sided

---

that Ukraine had a larger proportion of "more cultured" laborers working in small establishments who were more attracted to "European" Menshevism than were the newer and more ignorant workers of large factories which provided the constituency for "Asiatic" Bolshevism in Russia proper. See I. Mazepa, *Bolshevyzm i okupatsiia Ukrainy* (Lviv-Kiev, 1922), pp. 28–37. Whether or not one accepts Mazepa's argument, all earlier sources concede the greater relative strength of Menshevism in Ukraine.

[64] Borys, *The Sovietization of Ukraine,* p. 143.

[65] *Ibid.,* p. 145. "Oblastnoi sezd RSDRP (b-ov) (Pervoe vseukrainskoe soveshchanie bolshevikov)," *Letopis revoliutsii,* 1926, no. 5–6, p. 76.

with the latter. We must unmask its reactionary nature and wean the soldiers, workers, and peasants away from it. When we succeed in defeating Kaledin, the Rada will also be beaten. In our resolution we must state 1) that the Rada betrays those masses in whose name it speaks, and 2) that we are not against the Rada in general, only this particular Rada with its reactionary membership.[66]

Shakhrai, who would later become one of the most outspoken advocates of an independent Soviet Ukraine and Ukrainian communist party, at this point argued that Ukraine's political separation from Russia required the establishment of a territorial Bolshevik organization. He went no further than proposing that it be called RSDRP(b) in Ukraine. It was Piatakov who, along with Zatonskyi and Gorvits, insisted that the word "Russian" be dropped from the Party's name and led the conference to adopt the designation "Social Democracy of Ukraine."[67] After the conference a document bearing the new name was issued over the signature of Zatonskyi, one of the few ethnic Ukrainians among the Bolshevik leadership. It announced that now there was a Bolshevik Party for Ukrainians and which Ukrainians could support.[68]

The All-Ukrainian Congress of Soviets, which opened just after the Bolshevik conference, was a victory for the Ukrainian socialists. While the Ukrainian socialists had at first denounced the idea of calling such a congress, they hit upon a way to translate their rural support into a majority at the meeting. After all, it was to be a congress of workers', soldiers', and peasants' deputies. Who represented the peasants if not the cooperatives and other rural organizations? The one organization that could mobilize large numbers of peasants on relatively short notice was the All-Ukrainian Peasant Spilka, which was extremely close to the UPSR and which, even Soviet sources concede, had a committee in almost every Ukrainian village.[69] The Spilka sent word to the villages that peasant organizations should send as many delegates to the congress as possible.[70] As a result, the largely Bolshevik delegations from

---

[66] *Ibid.*, p. 74.

[67] *Ibid.*, pp. 79–82. Borys, *The Sovietization of Ukraine*, pp. 144–145.

[68] Serhii Mazlakh and Vasyl Shakhrai, *Do khvyli: Shcho diietsia na Ukraini i z Ukrainoiu* (New York, 1967), pp. 236–237.

[69] A recent Soviet study declares that in 1917 "there was hardly a single village which did not have a Peasant Spilka." I. V. Khmil, *Trudiashche selianstvo Ukrainy v borotbi za vladu Rad*, p. 138.

[70] "Selianska Spilka pro Zizd Rad Rob., Sal., ta Sel. Dep. Ukrainy," *Robitnycha hazeta*, November 29, 1917, p. 3.

the urban Soviets found themselves literally swamped. Vynnychenko and other Ukrainian luminaries addressed the gathering and put the issue in purely national terms: Ukrainians against Russians. Hopelessly outnumbered, the Bolsheviks had little choice but to denounce the congress as unrepresentative and withdraw with a few sympathizers to hold a rump session in Kharkiv. The majority simply endorsed the Rada and adjourned.[71]

Meanwhile, the Bolshevik leadership in Russia despaired of the local Bolsheviks ever being able to take power on their own and sent an ultimatum threatening the Rada with war if it did not stop disarming Bolshevik troops and reverse its tilt toward Kaledin.[72] The Bolsheviks present at the Congress of Soviets when the ultimatum arrived tried to explain it away as a mistake that could be righted without bloodshed.[73] It was, however, no mistake.

Before he seized power, Lenin tried to use the Ukrainian question to weaken the Provisional Government and indulged in wishful thinking to the effect that Ukrainians would be less likely to seek separation from a Bolshevik government than from a "bourgeois" regime.[74]

After he seized power, Lenin disregarded all his statements on the right of nations to self-determination and began to take steps to extend his sway in Ukraine. By the end of 1917, he seems to have seen the conquest of Ukraine as the solution to all his problems: There he could obtain grain with which to feed Russia's hungry cities as well as coal and iron. One of Lenin's first official acts was to send Sergo Ordzhonikidze to Ukraine as an "extraordinary plenipotentiary commissar" charged with obtaining grain.[75] He can hardly be said to have taken Ukraine's right to self-determination seriously if he appointed a commissar to the region in defiance of the will of the local government.

Before Russian forces were sent to Ukraine, Ordzhonikidze's task was a difficult one. A member of the Katerynoslav food committee, who was present when Lenin's emissary addressed that body, later

---

[71] Borys, *The Sovietization of Ukraine*, pp. 182–188. Manilov, ed., *1917 god na Kiev-shchine*, pp. 434–436. *Robitnycha hazeta*, December 6, 1917, p. 1; December 8, pp. 2–3; December 9, pp. 2–3. Reshetar, *The Ukrainian Revolution*, pp. 93–95. Ravich-Cherkasskii, *Istoriia KP(b)U*, pp. 44–46.

[72] Reshetar, *The Ukrainian Revolution*, p. 93.

[73] *Ibid.*, p. 94.

[74] In the summer of 1917, Lenin criticized Kerenskii for acting in an undemocratic manner in not acceding to Ukrainian demands and declared that Ukraine would be more likely to separate from a "Kadet" government than from a Soviet regime. See Lenin, *PSS*, vol. 32, pp. 253–254, 341–342, 350–352.

[75] *Leninskii sbornik*, vol. 35, p. 11.

recalled that, in spite of accusations that the committee wanted to "starve the workers of Petrograd" and threats of the vengeance of the masses, Ordzhonikidze had to leave town empty-handed.[76] Once the Bolsheviks began their occupation of Ukraine, Lenin sent him telegram after telegram. One, dated January 15, 1918, and addressed to both Ordzhonikidze and the military commander Antonov-Ovseenko, is sufficient to indicate their tone and content:

> For God's sake, take the *most* energetic and *revolutionary* measures to send grain, grain and more grain!! Otherwise Petrograd may starve to death. *Special* trains and *detachments*. Collect and store. Escort the trains. *Inform* us every day.
> For God's sake![77]

In Bolshevik Russia, where Lenin's regime had precious little to offer the peasants in exchange for their agricultural produce, the Soviets set up ten-man requisition detachments, gun-toting workers who went into the villages and took the grain without ceremony. When the Bolsheviks invaded Ukraine, food detachments from the Petrograd Soviet went with them.[78] Obtaining food for Russia was a—if not the—primary consideration when Bolshevik Russia began its invasion of Ukraine. No attempt was made to come to terms with Ukrainian sensibilities. Military commanders held real power, and they showed little patience with the subtleties of the situation. When the Bolshevik commander Muraviev took Kiev in January he made it clear from the start that the regime being set up was to be a Russian one. In his first declaration to the city's inhabitants, he declared, "We took this power from the far North on the point of our bayonets."[79] Those found speaking Ukrainian in public were assumed to be nationalists and counterrevolutionaries subject to summary execution.[80] Practically everything of value that could be seized was taken for immediate shipment to Russia.[81]

---

[76] I. Mazepa, *Ukraina v ohni i buri revoliutsii* (n.p., 1950), vol. 1, pp. 44–45.

[77] *V. I. Lenin pro Ukrainu* (Kiev, 1959), vol. 2, p. 77.

[78] On January 15, 1918 (Old Style), the Presidium of the Petrograd Soviet ordered the district Soviets (*raionnye sovety*) subordinate to it to mobilize 5000 men in ten-man food detachments. Of these 190 men (19 detachments) were sent to Ukraine. V. M. Selunskaia, "Vedushchaia rol proletarskikh tsentrov v ustanovlenii vlasti sovetov na mestakh (oktiabr 1917 - vesna 1918 g.)" *Vestnik Moskovskogo universiteta,* 1967, no. 5, p. 31.

[79] V. Sadovskyi, *Natsionalna polityka Sovitiv na Ukraini* (Warsaw, 1937), p. 77.

[80] Khrystiuk, *Zamitky i materiialy,* vol. 2, p. 149.

[81] *Ibid.,* vol. 2, pp. 150–151. Some idea of the amount of grain sent to Russia can be gained from the fact that between February 18 and March 9, 1918, 1090 railroad cars of grain were shipped from Kherson Province to Russia. Partial figures from the

Social-Democracy of Ukraine was stillborn, and even the Soviet Ukrainian government had little real authority. When the Kiev Bolsheviks fled to Kharkiv with their sympathizers, they found an already functioning Soviet regime, the leaders of which wanted nothing whatsoever to do with Ukraine. The Kharkiv Bolsheviks refused even to provide accommodations for their Kievan comrades, offering them the choice of sleeping either in the hall where the rump Congress of Soviets was held or in one of the local jails. The Kievans chose the hall.[82] During the greater part of the first Soviet Ukrainian government's tenure, the Soviet Ukrainian regime elected in Kharkiv was only one of four Soviet governments operating in Ukraine. Only in March, after the Ukrainians had proclaimed their independence, made a separate peace with the Central Powers, and invited the latter to intervene, were the various Soviet governments unified and declared independent. Even then, the step was taken with the greatest reluctance.[83]

The formation of a Communist Party (bolshevik) of Ukraine was actually an afterthought, proclaimed at the April 1918 Taganrog Conference in the last Bolshevik stronghold in Ukraine. Simultaneously the Soviet government proclaimed itself dissolved.[84] The Bolsheviks were split into three mutually antagonistic groups. The ''Katerynoslavans,'' led by Emmanuil Kviring and probably smarting at the loss of their Donets-Krivoi Rog Republic, had little faith in Ukraine's indigenous revolutionary forces. They felt that the best strategy was to await the expected German revolution that would remove German troops from Ukraine and allow another Russian military intervention. In the meantime, they favored organizational work in the trade unions to planning revolts, which they believed were doomed to failure. If Ukraine had to have a separate communist party, they proposed it be merely a regional organization of the Russian party with the words ''in Ukraine'' tacked on. The ''Kievans,'' led by Piatakov, wanted immediate preparations for an armed uprising. They therefore wanted to make the party more

---

Kharkiv railroad station show that between February 19 to March 1, 1918, from two to as many as seven trains laden with grain were shipped daily to Russia. These figures are taken from *Peremoha velykoi Zhovtnevoi sotsialistychnoi revoliutsii na Ukraini* (Kiev, 1967), vol. 1, pp. 359-360.

[82] Yaroslav Bilinsky, ''The Communist Take-over of the Ukraine,'' Hunczak, ed., *The Ukraine, 1917-1921: A Study in Revolution,* p. 109.

[83] Bosh, *God borby,* pp. 255-256. M. M. Popov, *Narys istorii Komunistychnoi Partii (bilshovykiv) Ukrainy* (Kharkiv, 1928), pp. 145-148.

[84] Borys, *The Sovietization of Ukraine,* p. 146.

independent from Moscow and proposed the territorial designation Communist Party (bolshevik) of Ukraine (KP[b]U). A small "Poltavan" faction led by Vasyl Shakhrai proposed the name Ukrainian Communist Party (bolshevik). Mykola Skrypnyk, who had earlier been sent to Ukraine as Lenin's personal emissary, helped guide the deliberations. In accordance with his proposals, the name KP(b)U was adopted, and an organizational bureau headed by Piatakov was elected. The new party was even to be represented in the Comintern.[85] But the new KP(b)U was not envisioned as a truly independent political entity: the decisions of the Taganrog Conference had to be submitted to the Central Committee of the Russian Communist Party, which approved them on May 3.[86] A First Congress was held in Moscow in July; Piatakov retained control, and plans were made for an armed uprising, which was to be launched under the slogan of the revival of Soviet Ukraine and its union with Soviet Russia.[87] Soviet Russia meanwhile used the "neutral zone" between it and the Ukrainian Hetman state to organize and arm two divisions for the planned rising.[88]

The uprising was attempted in August and ended in a complete fiasco. Except for a few sporadic and easily suppressed outbreaks, Piatakov's call for an uprising was ignored.[89] This led to the temporary eclipse of Piatakov and his Kievan cohorts at the Second KP(b)U Congress in October. The "Katerynoslavans" led by Kviring and Iakovlev-Epstein took over with Lenin's blessing. A "Kievan" minority was unwillingly included in the Central Committee by Kviring's faction. Realizing their minority status, Piatakov and his supporters had refused even to take

---

[85] M. Iavorskii, "K istorii KP(b)U," in *Oktiabrskaia revoliutsiia: Pervoe piatiletie* (Kharkiv, 1922), pp. 97–99. Bosh, *God borby,* pp. 218–220, 256–257. Ravich-Cherkasskii, *Istoriia KP(b)U,* p. 62. Popov, *Narys istorii KP(b)U,* pp. 150–151. In the account given by Borys (*The Sovietization of Ukraine,* 146–147) the distinction between the Kievans and Poltavans is unclear.

[86] M. I. Kulichenko, *Borba Kommunisticheskoi partii za reshenie natsionalnogo voprosa v 1918–1920 godakh* (Kharkiv, 1963), pp. 23–24.

[87] *Komunistychna Partiia Ukrainy v rezoliutsiiakh i reshenniakh zizdiv, konferentsii i plenumiv TsK* (Kiev, 1976), vol. 1, p. 12.

[88] Kulichenko, *Borba Kommunisticheskoi partii za reshenie natsionalnogo voprosa,* p. 30.

[89] At the Second Congress of the KP(b)U Mykola Skrypnyk spoke of the attempted uprising as follows: "What took place? Was there a general rising? No. We must recognize that there was no general uprising...there were only a number of individual outbreaks..." *Vtoroi sezd Kommunisticheskoi Partii (bolshevikov) Ukrainy (protokoly)* (2nd ed., Kharkiv, 1927), pp. 100–101.

part in the voting. All the resolutions adopted by the Congress had a"Katerynoslavan" orientation.[90] But the dominance of this Russophile faction was short-lived. In November 1918 came the Armistice ending the First World War in German defeat. The days of the German supported Hetmanate were clearly numbered, and it was time to make a revolution. Only the Kievans, for all their adventurism, seemed ready to do that. Piatakov was soon in charge once again.

The Piatakov Regime

The second Bolshevik government of Ukraine was popularly known as the *Piatakovshchyna*, the Piatakov regime. It began with popular enthusiasm and ended in a rout after being deserted on all sides. Later, Bolsheviks would remember it as a tragedy of errors in which practically every important segment of the population was alienated by policies that ignored the problem of nationality and peasant aspirations for land. During the *Piatakovshchyna*, the Luxemburgist position that the nationality and land questions could be handled without bending the theory to circumstances was given a try. The result was a complete fiasco.

The first Bolshevik occupation of Ukraine had ended because the Central Rada had purchased German military intervention by agreeing to sell huge quantities of grain to the Central Powers. But the peasantry proved far from eager to sell grain for currency that they considered worthless. The Central Rada—now led by an all-UPSR ministry—hoped to mollify the peasantry by obstructing German grain procurements. The Germans responded by engineering a *coup d'etat* that replaced the Rada with an aristocratic Ukrainian former general of the tsarist army, Pavlo Skoropadskyi, who proclaimed himself monarch with the old Cossack title of Hetman.[91] The Hetmanate seemed to many to be a restoration of the pre-revolutionary regime with its guarantees of private property and its sponsorship of the landlord's return to their former estates. Its only support—a firm enough one until the Armistice—was the German Army.[92] Thanks to the widely detested Hetman interlude, the idea of Ukrainian statehood lost much of its earlier mass appeal.[93]

[90] Borys, *The Sovietization of Ukraine*, pp. 148–149.

[91] Oleh S. Fedyshyn, *Germany's Drive to the East and the Ukrainian Revolution, 1917–1918* (New Brunswick, 1971), pp. 60–157.

[92] Taras Hunczak, "The Ukraine Under Hetman Pavlo Skoropadskyi," in Hunczak, ed., *The Ukraine, 1917–1921*, pp. 72–75.

[93] Iwan Majstrenko, *Borot'bism: A Chapter in the History of Ukrainian Communism*, pp. 91–92.

This led the Bolsheviks to believe that the problem of Ukrainian national aspirations would plague them no more. The Russian Bolshevik leadership had never reconciled itself to the loss of Ukraine, despite all the declarations recognizing Ukraine's right to self-determination and independence. In October 1918, Kamenev addressed the Second Congress of the KP(b)U on behalf of the Bolshevik leadership and outlined what was expected of Ukraine's Bolsheviks. He described Ukraine as "a big road for English and American imperialism to the East."[94] As for the tasks ahead, "These tasks at present consist in uniting Soviet Russia with a Soviet Ukraine. At the present time, we have no other tasks facing us."[95] All talk of national self-determination, he declared, had become impermissible; in Finland, Poland, and Ukraine, "the slogan of the self-determination of the nationalities has been turned into a weapon of the counterrevolution."[96]

Many KP(b)U members agreed with him. A few months earlier at the First KP(b)U Congress, Skrypnyk had declared,

Already at the time of the Brest negotiations the All-Ukrainian Congress of Soviets expressed its opposition to separation, and we are still against separation because independence has become a smokescreen (*shirma*) for the counterrevolutionary struggle against Soviet power.[97]

At this time the Bolsheviks fervently wanted to believe the Ukrainian problem solved, and the wish gave rise to the belief in its fulfillment. At the Eighth Congress of the Russian Communist Party, Lenin declared that whatever national feeling there might once have been in Ukraine had been knocked out by Germans. He even wondered aloud whether Ukrainian was in fact a mass language.[98] Some were eager to assure him that it was not. Most prominent among them was Khristian Rakovskii.

An émigré from the Balkans, Rakovskii was the personification of the revolutionary intellectual, ever ready to expound his own theory of the nationality question and the implications of the socialist revolution for its solution.[99] He had spent some time in Kiev negotiating with

---

[94] *Vtoroi sezd KP(b)U*, p. 118.

[95] *Ibid.*, pp. 123–124.

[96] *Ibid.*, pp. 123–124.

[97] As quoted by E. S. Oslikovskaia and A. V. Snegov, "Za pravdivoe osveshchenie istorii proletarskoi revoliutsii," *Voprosy istorii*, 1956, no. 3, p. 140.

[98] *VIII sezd RDP(b): Stenograficheskii otchet* (Moscow, 1919), p. 91.

[99] See Rakovskii, "Relations Between Soviet Republics: Russia and Ukraine," *The Communist International*, vol. 1, no. 11–12, 1920, columns 2321–2323. In this article,

the Hetmanate on behalf of Lenin's government, and it is doubtful that he had much direct contact with the Ukrainian countryside. Nonetheless, he returned to Moscow full of confirmation of everything that his comrades wished to believe. He suddenly became the Party's resident expert on Ukrainian affairs and published a series of articles full of glowing reports of revolutionary opportunities and confirmations that Ukrainian nationalism was dead except among a few misguided bourgeois intellectuals. One such article, published in *Izvestiia* on January 3, 1919, described the "Petliurist adventure" as a hopeless business that nobody wanted. Rakovskii told of Ukrainian peasants who upon receiving Bolshevik literature written in Ukrainian would throw it crumpled to the ground out of disgust at anything smacking of Ukrainianism, but would read it avidly when it was printed in Russian. To reach the Ukrainian peasantry, Rakovskii counselled, address it in Russian.[100] This was evidently just what Lenin wanted to hear, and it led him to make one of his rare political blunders. Two weeks after the Soviet Ukrainian government proclaimed its existence, Rakovskii was named Ukrainian head of state.[101]

The day after the Armistice, on November 12, 1918, a Ukrainian Military Revolutionary Committee had been formed, including Stalin, Piatakov, Zatonskyi, and Antonov-Ovseenko. On November 20, a Provisional Soviet Government of Ukraine was formed with Piatakov at its head, but the Russian Party leadership refused to allow these actions to be publicly announced. An agreement had been reached in October with Vynnychenko, by which Moscow agreed not to interfere in the affairs of the reborn Ukrainian Peoples Republic if the KP(b)U were allowed to function legally, and the Bolshevik leadership vacillated on whether to invade Ukraine until the end of 1918.[102]

Soon after the Armistice, the Hetmanate began to fall apart and was supplanted by a revived Ukrainian Peoples Republic under a Directory headed by Volodymyr Vynnychenko and with Semen Petliura as his

---

Rakovskii argued that the concept of exclusive citizenship was an outmoded notion derived from the idea of private property. In Soviet Ukraine, he stated, toilers from all lands were immediately accepted as full citizens. Soviet citizenship, in Rakovskii's view, was based solely on class; it had nothing to do with place of origin or nationality.

[100] Kh. G. Rakovskii, "Beznadezhnoe delo (O Petliurovskoi avantiure)," *Izvestiia,* January 3, 1919, p. 1.

[101] On January 25, 1919. Arthur E. Adams, *Bolsheviks in the Ukraine: The Second Campaign, 1918–1919,* p. 117.

[102] *Ibid.,* pp. 25, 55, 84–85, 99.

War Minister.[103] Petliura led a massive peasant revolt, which scattered the remnants of the Hetman's army. But after the removal of Skoropadskyi and the landlords, most of the Directory's armed villagers simply went home. Petliura had little choice but to put troops in the field any way he could. To do so, he appointed *otamany* (warlords), theoretically subject to his orders as supreme *otaman* but in fact subject to nobody. Vynnychenko did not exaggerate much when he later wrote that anybody could become an *otaman,* that one had only to express a desire to fight the Bolsheviks, and Petliura would send a title and a few million newly printed *karbovantsy* (Ukrainian rubles). The result was less a government than a regime of plundering warlords. It was known, in fact, as the "warlord regime" (*otamanshchyna*).[104]

The behavior of the Petliurist Otaman Balbachan greatly enhanced Bolshevik prospects in Ukraine. After occupying Kharkiv in mid-November 1918, Balbachan refused to permit the establishment of a local Soviet of workers' deputies. When such a body was formed without his permission, he attempted to suppress it. The workers responded with a general strike and briefly took control of the city. When Balbachan retook Kharkiv in mid-December, he shot what ringleaders he could find and forced the workers' movement underground.[105] His heavy-handed methods created such disaffection among the workers and other radical elements that, as Vynnychenko put it, "This open and conscious Ukrainian reactionary rapidly undermined and even killed the Directory's influence throughout Left Bank Ukraine."[106]

The Bolshevik invasion began ostensibly as a civil war between Piatakov's regime and the Ukrainian Directory. After the Directory declared war on Russia on January 16, however, there was little point in pretending this was anything but a war to extend Soviet Russia's borders. Ukraine was treated simply as a province. As early as December 9, 1918, the RKP Central Committee telegraphed its KP(b)U counterpart, then in Kursk, that it would send orders directly to Ukrainian state organs rather than go through the KP(b)U.[107] On December 24, *Isvestiia* published a statement of the Russian Commissariat of Foreign Affairs, stating that with the annulment of the Treaty of Brest-Litovsk, the RSFSR

---

[103] Reshetar, *The Ukrainian Revolution,* pp. 211–218.

[104] Vynnychenko, *Vidrodzhennia natsii,* vol. 3, p. 352.

[105] Adams, *Bolsheviks in the Ukraine,* pp. 82–84.

[106] Vynnychenko, *Vidrodzhennia natsii,* vol. 3, pp. 145–146.

[107] Kulichenko, *Borba Kommunisticheskoi partii za reshenie natsionalnogo voprosa,* p. 231.

ceased to recognize Ukraine as an independent state.[108] And once Piatakov's regime was established in Ukraine, its officials were directly subject to decrees of the Russian *Sovnarkom* as well as to those of the Ukrainian Soviet government.[109]

Piatakov and Rakovskii cannot be accused of Russian imperialism or even nationalism in any conventional sense. Piatakov was a follower of Rosa Luxemburg who saw all manifestations of national aspirations as equally counterrevolutionary, and Rakovskii had no sentiments that could properly be called imperialistic. Yet, even if they were not Russian imperialists by sentiment, their refusal to recognize the legitimacy of Ukrainian aspirations forced them to play roles indistinguishable from that of the Russian imperialists. Perhaps they should be described as imperialists by default, for their every action reeked of hostility toward the Ukrainian nationality in general and its peasantry in particular. Rakovskii publicly declared that recognition of Ukrainian as an official language in Ukraine would be a "reactionary" measure of benefit only to the kulaks and nationalist intelligentsia.[110] Ukrainian political parties, including those that adopted the Soviet platform and welcomed the arrival of the Red Army, were excluded from political participation and forced into open revolt.[111] Only the Borotbisty, a Ukrainian socialist group whose policy was collaboration with the Bolsheviks at any price, were able to function legally.

The Soviet regime's agricultural policies could not help but alienate the peasantry. One of its first pronouncements declared that "cultured" estates, that is, those where the former lords had made significant improvements, were to be kept intact for collective use.[112] In March 1919, the Third KP(b)U Congress declared that the Party's main task in the countryside was to promote the transition from small individual farms to "comradely" agriculture.[113] Such actions constituted a slap in the face to the land-hungry peasants who could see little difference between the old estates and the new communes, since often the one became the other by simply changing the name. On the local level,

---

[108] Quoted in Khrystiuk, *Zamitky i materiialy,* vol. 4, p. 32.

[109] Khmil, *Trudiashche selianstvo,* p. 119.

[110] See Rakovskii's February 1919 statement to the Kiev Soviet in Khrystiuk, *Zamitky i materiialy,* vol. 3, pp. 172–173.

[111] Vynnychenko, *Vidrodzhennia natsii,* vol. 3, 344.

[112] *Sobranie Uzakonenii i Rasporiazhenii Raboche-Krestianskogo Pravitelstva Ukrainy,* no. 4, January 25–31, 1919, p. 49.

[113] *Komunistychna Partiia Ukrainy v rezoliutsiiakh i rishenniakh,* vol. 1, pp. 45–46.

overzealous Bolsheviks sometimes countered peasant reluctance to joining the communes by employing coercion.[114] Even after the leadership managed to put an end to such politically suicidal behavior, a pro-Soviet speaker had only to mention the word "commune" to a peasant audience to find himself in immediate peril of being lynched.[115]

Most galling of all, Ukraine was treated primarily as a source of food for Russia. In contrast to Russia, where *kombedy* (committees of poor peasants) existed alongside village Soviets and exercised primarily economic power, Ukrainian *kombidy* served as independent organs in the absence of local Soviets and "for some time held all power in the villages in their hands."[116] Also, Lenin sent his most efficient requisitioner, Aleksandr Shlikhter, to Ukraine with orders to send back fifty million *pudy* (one *pud* is just over 16 2/3 kg.) of grain to Russia. Instead, as Shlikhter himself later recalled, only 8.5 million *pudy* could be requisitioned and two-thirds of that had to stay in Ukraine to feed the cities and the Red Army. As for the difficulties in getting grain from the peasants, he wrote, "Figuratively speaking, one could say that every *pud* of requisitioned grain was tinged with drops of workers' blood."[117] Food detachments, *kombidy,* forced collectivization of agriculture, and demands for inductees into the Red Army all gave the peasants reason to hate the Soviet regime. The number of rural revolts increased steadily from month to month.[118]

---

[114] V. Kachinskii, "Zemelnaia politika sovvlasti na Ukraini v 1919 g.," *Litopys revoliutsii,* 1929, no. 1, pp. 21–30. For a general study of how Bolsheviks throughout the former empire overcame such "leftist errors," see V. M. Selunskaia, "Preodolenie Kommunisticheskoi partii levatskikh oshibok v stroitelstve pervykh kolkhozov i sovkhozov," *Vestnik Moskovskogo universiteta,* 1965, no. 6, pp. 3–19.

[115] When the Borotbist, Oleksander Shumskyi, addressed the peasant troops of the pro-Soviet Otaman Hryhoriiv and mentioned the word, only Hryhoriiv's personal intervention saved the unfortunate orator from a lynching. The incident was originally related in the memoirs of Antonov-Ovseenko and is retold by Adams, *Bolsheviks in the Ukraine,* pp. 272–274.

[116] P. S. Zahorskyi and P. K. Stoian, *Narysy istorii komitetiv nezamozhnykh selian* (Kiev, 1960), p. 17. In addition, M. I. Kulichenko, *Bolsheviki Kharkovshchiny v borbe za vlast Sovetov (1918–1920 gg.)* (Kharkiv, 1966), pp. 112–13, states that in many villages the *kombidy* fulfilled the function of a *revkom* and sometimes even usurped the powers of extant bodies. In other cases, however, Party cells assumed the role of the *kombidy,* or the *kombid* met only to proclaim itself dissolved.

[117] A. Shlikhter, "Borba za khleb na Ukraine v 1919 godu," *Litopys revoliutsii,* 1928, no. 2, p. 135.

[118] Rakovskii gave the following breakdown for "counterrevolutionary manifestations" occurring during the spring and summer of 1919: Of 93 revolts during the period April

Yet, the Piatakovshchyna had originally begun with mass enthusiasm. Almost everyone, it seemed, was enthusiastic for the coming of Soviet power.[119] After all, the system that Lenin had so recently described in his *State and Revolution* was profoundly democratic, almost anarchical. Not only did this work sanction federalism, it contained strictures against officials from the center being sent to impose their will upon local bodies.[120] This had obvious appeal to those who hoped for Ukrainian self-determination within the Soviet framework, and millions of people harbored such hopes.[121] However, Lenin's political behavior provides absolutely no evidence that he ever took such pledges seriously. If the decision of a given body went against him, he simply convinced himself that "counterrevolutionaries" had taken it over and acted accordingly. Nor did he ever show any qualms about telling local bodies what to do or in sending officials from the center in order to make sure it was done. Indeed, the survival of his government often depended on it. But in Lenin's Russia, Soviets did exist as organs of government, however circumscribed their authority might have become in fact. In Piatakov's Ukraine, elected Soviets were to replace revolutionary committees (*revkomy*) only after order had been established.[122] Outside of a few large cities and their environs, this never happened. On the eve of the March 1919 All-Ukrainian Congress of Soviets, elaborate regulations were published that set the norms of representation and fixed the

---

1–29, 29 were "kulak inspired," 21 were led by White guards, 14 were basically anti-semitic, 11 were military, 3 partisan, 6 against requisitions, and 2 against conscription. Of 28 risings during the first half of May, 6 were attributed to kulaks, 9 were partisan, one was against requisitions, and 6 were military. During the last weeks of Soviet rule (July 1–19), the number of risings was much higher. 25 were attributed to kulaks, 19 to anti-semitism, and 19 against conscription. Kh. G. Rakovskii, *Borba za osvobozhdenie derevni* (Kharkiv, 1920), pp. 37–38. While the various classifications used by Rakovskii probably serve more to confuse than elucidate, the number of revolts bear eloquent witness to the mounting dissatisfaction in the villages. One need only note that the first two and a half weeks of July had well over twice as many risings as did the whole month of April.

[119] Vynnychenko, *Vidrodzhennia natsii*, vol. 3, p. 328. Khrystiuk, *Zamitky i materiialy*, vol. 4, pp. 79–81.

[120] Lenin, *CW*, vol. 25, p. 448; *PSS*, vol. 33, p. 74.

[121] Not only the Borotbist wing of the UPSR and the Independent wing of the USDRP (Nezalezhnyky) accepted the Soviet platform in 1919; the UPSR (Central Course) did so as well. Inside the Directory, even Vynnychenko advocated the proclamation of a Soviet Ukraine led by Ukrainians; other members of the Directory settled for a quasi-Soviet solution in the form of the "toilers' republic."

[122] *Sobranie Uzakonenii i Rasporiazhenii*, no. 1, January 1–14, 1919.

number of delegates for various Soviets to send.[123] But, when the congress was convened, most of its delegates held mandates from *revkomy* appointed directly by Party organs because no Soviets existed to elect them.[124]

Having alienated the peasantry and lost all chance for a *modus vivendi* with Ukrainian groups other than the Borotbisty, it was probably inevitable that the second Bolshevik occupation of Ukraine would be of short duration. Its roots in the countryside were fragile, and its military survival depended upon the good will of indigenous military forces. In May the pro-Soviet warlord Otaman Hryhoriiv revolted against the Bolsheviks and called upon the people to take up pitchforks and whatever else they could lay hands on to "kill the hook-nosed commissars" who wanted to force the country folk into communes and to take their grain to supply "the feeding stalls of Muscovy." The Bolsheviks easily suppressed Hryhoriiv's revolt. The otaman had sent his troops off in all directions at once, and the Bolsheviks stopped them simply by blocking the main roads. Hryhoriiv himself was shot dead at the encampment of a rival otaman, Nestor Makhno. But the front was in disarray as a result of Hryhoriiv's revolt. General Denikin's Volunteer Army took advantage of the chaos and began its march toward Moscow.[125]

The *Piatakovshchyna* came quickly to an end. In August, the Bolsheviks evacuated Kiev. On October 2, the Soviet Ukrainian government, bypassed by the Whites in Chernihiv, declared itself dissolved. The KP(b)U proclaimed itself liquidated and directed its members to place themselves at the disposal of the RKP. For a time, it looked as though the Bolsheviks had written off Ukraine forever—at least that was how some Ukrainian Bolsheviks understood the move.[126]

---

[123] *Ibid.*, no. 9, February 12–14, 1919, pp. 133–135.

[124] At the III All-Ukrainian Congress of Soviets over two-thirds of the delegations of Chernihiv, Kharkiv, and Poltava provinces were sent by *revkomy*. Kulichenko, *Borba Kommunisticheskoi partii za reshenie natsionalnogo voprosa*, p. 318. See also, Vynnychenko, *Vidrodzhennia natsii*, vol. 3, pp. 315–319; Shlikhter, "Borba za khleb...," pp. 121ff.

[125] On the Hryhoriiv revolt and the collapse of the *Piatakovshchyna*, see Adams, *Bolsheviks in the Ukraine*, pp. 278–404; "Grigorevskaia avantiura (mai 1919 goda)," *Letopis revoliutsii*, no. 3, 1923, pp. 152–159.

[126] Georg Lapchinskii, a member of the first Soviet Ukrainian government and leader of the so-called Federalists in the KP(b)U, described the dissolution of the KP(b)U as a decision to give up all possibility of future revolutionary struggle in Ukraine. G. Lapchinskii, "Gomelskoe soveshchanie (vospominaniia)," *Letopis revoliutsii*, 1926, no. 6, p. 37.

*   *   *

The protracted struggle between Russian Bolshevism and Ukrainian socialism was rooted in the reluctance of both groups to satisfy the aspirations of Ukraine's rural majority. Russians, including both workers and Bolshevik Party cadres, were in the habit of considering Ukraine an integral part of Russia, and Russia as the world had hitherto known it would indeed have been inconceivable without Ukraine's agriculture and industry. Yet, Ukraine had by 1917 become a nation that demanded political recognition—autonomy at first, then complete independence from Russia.

Ukrainian socialism extended its roots far back into the preceding century, evolving a synthesis of socialism and national aspirations that in 1917 appealed to most of the country's inhabitants. The results of the Constituent Assembly election left no doubt on that score. The collapse of the Central Rada in early 1918 was primarily due to Ukrainian socialism's hesitation to satisfy the peasantry's demand for land reform rather than any lack of popular enthusiasm for Ukrainian national demands.

The leaders of Ukrainian socialism were repeatedly forced to resort to courses of action that alienated their rural constituency. Like most other socialists in the Russian Empire, they saw the fall of autocracy in terms of the so-called bourgeois revolution and tried to defer all questions of social transformation to the Constituent Assembly. This enabled the Bolsheviks to take credit for sanctioning the peasants' seizures of gentry estates. The Bolsheviks defeated the Rada in 1918 as much due to rural enthusiasm for Lenin's land decree as to Russian Red Guards. The Rada purchased German intervention at the cost of obligating the peasants to sell large quantities of grain for paper money that was considered worthless in the countryside. When the Rada tried to stand up to its foreign allies, it found itself replaced by a German sponsored military *coup*. Petliura was able to mobilize the peasants against the Hetmanate, but his troops largely went home once the immediate task was accomplished. The Ukrainian People's Republic was thus at the mercy of the *otamany*, warlords beyond any political control, at a time when the country was surrounded by hostile foreign powers.

The Bolsheviks possessed little understanding or sympathy for Ukrainian aspirations. Lenin saw the question of national aspirations as a purely tactical matter that had nothing to do with principle. He went further than other Russian socialists in defending the right of oppressed peoples to create independent states so long as he did not have power. He initially indulged in the wishful thinking that Ukrainians would voluntarily join a unitary Bolshevik state. When they did not, he sent in the Red Guards and took whatever Ukrainian grain could be found.

Other Bolsheviks did not necessarily share Lenin's views on what ought to be done about the colonies. The Kievan faction of Ukraine's Bolsheviks were followers of the theory of Rosa Luxemburg and opposed any concession to national aspirations on principle. The Katerynoslavan wing shared with the Donbas workers a general antipathy toward the Ukrainian movement. The early attempts to create a Soviet Ukrainian government were characterized by a tendency to equate Ukrainian aspirations for national liberation with counterrevolution. It is a moot question whether this or the Bolshevik's radically anti-peasant agrarian policies did more to undermine their popular support in Ukraine. The collapse of the Piatakov regime, begun under the most favorable of political circumstances, showed that Bolshevik policies were inherently self-defeating in Ukraine. By mid-1919 it was clear that a stable Soviet Ukrainian state was impossible without the acquiescence of the Ukrainian peasantry, and such acquiescence would be possible only if Ukrainian aspirations were taken into account.

CHAPTER TWO

The Road to National Communism

THE COLLAPSE OF the Piatakov-Rakovskii regime in Ukraine and the dissolution of the KP(b)U made evident the inadequacies of previous Bolshevik policies that ignored national and agrarian aspirations. Clearly Ukraine could be ruled only by a regime that was acceptable to the Ukrainian countryside and to the armed peasant followers of at least some of the *otamany*. This realization raised the question of the participation of indigenous Ukrainian radicals in any future Soviet Ukrainian government and ultimately of their admission into the Party. The minimum condition for a workable *modus vivendi* between the Bolsheviks and Ukrainians was Bolshevik recognition of the fact that Ukraine was a separate country and ought to be treated as such.

Shakhrai and Mazlakh

Even before the Piatakov episode, there were Bolsheviks who demanded that the party adapt its policies to Ukrainian realities. Vasyl Shakhrai, first Soviet Ukrainian Commissar of Foreign Affairs and leader of the "Poltavan" faction in early Party controversies, upon hearing of Germany's collapse, which in turn implied the speedy fall of the Hetmanate, joined forces with a less well-known collaborator, Serhii Mazlakh, in writing detailed analyses of the situation and critiques of previous Bolshevik policies in Ukraine. The first of Shakhrai's two pamphlets, *Revolution in Ukraine,* appeared shortly after the Armistice, and its sequel, *Concerning the Moment: What is Happening to and in Ukraine?* was published at the beginning of 1919.[1] Both were ignored

---

[1] The preface to the first Ukrainian edition of *Revolution in Ukraine* is dated November 20, 1918. Internal evidence, such as newspaper articles cited, indicate that *Concerning the Moment* was written in mid-January 1919. An English translation of the latter pamphlet is available as Serhii Mazlakh and Vasyl Shakhrai, *On the Current Situation in the Ukraine* (Ann Arbor, 1970). Unfortunately, the translator evidently did not unders-

40

in Party councils, but their ideas would later become the unacknowledged source of the line that would be given the stamp of orthodoxy less than half a decade later.

Shakhrai joined the Bolsheviks in February 1917, shortly after graduating from the local military academy, which had been moved from Vilnius to Poltava for the duration of the war. There he came in contact with Serhii Mazlakh (Robsman), an Old Bolshevik of Jewish origin who had six years in the underground and four years as a political émigré to his credit. They worked together to oust the Mensheviks from the local RSDRP organization and, after succeeding, were elected to the editorial board of the local Party organ in August. By this time Shakhrai had become a defender of the Ukrainian national movement, and his Bolshevik comrades saw no reason to contradict him, given the strong Ukrainian sentiment in the region.[2] As Mazlakh later recalled, the official Bolshevik position of advocating the right to national self-determination while opposing its exercise made little political sense given local conditions:

> But in Poltava Province in the heart of Ukraine, where everything Russian had been completely discredited by the tsarist-landlordist regime and even the names *"rossiiskii," "rossiiskaia," "rossiiskoe"* called forth the fullest possible distrust, which everything done by the Provisional Government served only to confirm, the position of our organization with its name RSDRP (bolshevik) was rather ticklish. The Russian Bolshevik line on the nationality question was in its pure form unsuitable for us. The general politico-economic slogans of the Bolsheviks were difficult for the entire toiling masses to comprehend, but to agitate for the closest possible union of Ukraine and Russia while bourgeois-capitalist relationships survived both here and there would have meant agitating in the presence of the masses *against* the autonomy and *against* the independence of Ukraine, agitating *for* the continuation of Russia's colonial policy in Ukraine.

Poltavan Bolsheviks addressed queries to the Party Central Committee in Petrograd, hoping for guidance on how to deal with this ticklish situa-

---

tand the ironic use of quotation marks so extensively used in the polemical style of the day and by dropping them sometimes has the authors stating the opposite of what they intended. All quotations are my own translation, although reference is also made to this translation. All emphasis is in the original. For *Revolution in Ukraine* the second Russian edition, a copy of which is located in the New York Public Library, has been used.

[2] Michael Martin Luther, "Introduction," Serhii Mazlakh and Vasyl Shakhrai, *On the Current Situation in the Ukraine* (Ann Arbor, 1970), pp. xv–xvi.

tion, but they received no answer beyond a letter referring them to earlier—and, in the minds of the Poltavans, clearly outdated—Party resolutions on the nationality question.[3] This left them essentially on their own, and for a brief moment on the eve of the Russian invasion it seemed as if Shakhrai's pro-Ukrainian sentiments might prevail. They did not, although Shakhrai himself became a member of the first Soviet Ukrainian government. When the Bolsheviks were driven from Ukraine by the Germans, Mazlakh and Shakhrai went to Saratov rather than to Moscow as did most of their colleagues. It seems that they had lost all hope of changing what they saw as the misguided policies of their comrades, and of all the cities then held by the Bolsheviks, Saratov was closest to Ukraine.[4]

The defeat of Germany meant that Hetman Skoropadskii, whose name literally means "quickly fall," would live up to it. To emphasize this point Shakhrai published his first pamphlet under the pseudonym Skorovstanskii, "quickly stand up." With the imminent fall of the Hetmanate the road to Ukraine was again open to the Bolsheviks. Formulating the correct policy was imperative. Shakhrai hoped to provoke his fellow Bolsheviks into facing squarely the question of what to do about Ukraine, and that meant understanding what they had done wrong in the past.

Revolution in Ukraine was, for the most part, written in July 1918 as an attack on the Katerynoslavan wing of the KP(b)U and was hastily completed in November 1918.[5] Shakhrai made it clear that he was not attempting to solve the nationality question in general, but rather to contribute to its solution in Ukraine. Nevertheless, he pointed out that those who thought socialism would instantly and automatically solve the problem by rendering it obsolete were dead wrong:

> A people that oppresses other peoples cannot be free, nor can a people that is oppressed by another people be free. The socialization of the means of production *eo ipso* still does not eliminate the rule of the one and the enslavement of the other nation; it does not eliminate, does not solve, does not "render obsolete" the national question. The national question remains; the socialization of the means of production creates only the most favorable conditions for its solution. And so long as the national

---

[3] Sergei Mazlakh, "Oktiabrskaia revoliutsiia na Poltavshchine," *Letopis revoliutsii,* no. 1, 1922, pp. 127–128.

[4] Luther, "Introduction," *On the Current Situation,* p. xviii.

[5] V. Skorovstanskii (pseudonym of Vasyl Shakhrai), *Revoliutsiia na Ukraine* (2nd Russian edition, Saratov, 1919), p. i.

question is not solved, so long as one nation rules and another is forced to be subordinate to it, what we have is still not socialism but only the socialization of the means of production. . . . the national question simply cannot be proclaimed solved "on the second day" after the socialist revolution. It can and must be solved *before, during, and after* the socialist revolution. "First the social question and then the national question" is just as false and hypocritical as the opposite formula, "first the national and then the social question". . . . [6]

In other words, the Bolsheviks had to understand and actively take measures to solve the questions raised by non-Russian national aspirations, or else all their socialist aspirations would remain no more than a jumble of empty phrases.

Shakhrai began the main body of his pamphlet by noting that many Russians had been shocked by the strength of the Ukrainian movement in 1917 and that this made it necessary to survey briefly Ukraine's territory, population, and history. He pointed out that under the cossack regime from the fifteenth through seventeenth centuries the country had had a strong political life complete with complicated relations with neighboring states and that, despite its division between the Austrian and Russian empires at the end of the eighteenth century, Ukrainians on both sides of the border remained conscious of their kinship. Because of national oppression, illiteracy had become higher among Ukrainians than among Russians, and the cities had become Russified to the extent that the Ukrainian countryside confronted the towns of their own country as alien entities: "the city is the pans', foreign, not ours, not Ukrainian. Great Russian, Jewish, Polish—only not ours, not Ukrainian."[7] He traced the beginning of Ukrainianism to the remnants of the cossack *starshyna* as represented by Kotliarevskyi at the end of the eighteenth century, extending through Shevchenko and the Cyril-Methodius Brotherhood of the 1840s, which created the central Ukrainian political idea surviving to his own day, that of a Ukrainian republic in a Slavic federation. Although the language bans of 1863 and 1876 had moved the center of the Ukrainian movement to Galicia, Ukrainianism began to revive in the East at the turn of the century and later grew into a viable movement:

From these tightly knit and small circles of the Ukrainian intelligentsia, literary figures, publicists, poets, artists, students of the problem

---

[6] *Ibid.*, pp. xi–xii.
[7] *Ibid.*, pp. 1–8. Quotation from p. 8.

of national rebirth and political formation went out onto the broad field
of the class struggle of the proletariat and peasantry. Various political
parties with deeply democratic political content and tinges of socialism
began to rise up and take shape because no other kind of political party
could take advantage of the aspirations of the workers and the landless
and smallholding peasants. For this reason everyone in Ukraine became
a "socialist," (saying) "We have no bourgeoisie, only socialists."

Beginning as non-party circles, some Ukrainians formed political parties: RUP, the more nationalistic elements of which split off to form
the Ukrainian Peoples Party, the more socialistic elements of which
became the Social Democratic Spilka, and the rest of which became
the USDRP. In 1905 Ukrainian activists had called for autonomy, and
the language ban was lifted. After the 1907 Stolypin *coup* only literary
work remained possible, and even that ceased at the beginning of the
World War.[8]

Shakhrai then pointed to the extraordinary strength the Ukrainian
movement showed immediately after the fall of the autocracy. As early
as March 19, 1917, a Kiev demonstration of 100,000 participants passed
a resolution calling for a constituent assembly that must establish broad
autonomy for Ukraine and demanded that the Russian Provisional
Government recognize the need to establish such autonomy. Since full
independence was associated in many minds with reaction, he stated,
most Ukrainians rallied around the USDRP and UPSR, which stood
for autonomy, but when the Provisional Government hesitated to
recognize Ukrainian autonomy, sentiment for full independence began
to grow. Asking why Ukrainians had been overwhelmingly hostile to
the slogan of Soviet power after the Bolshevik *coup d'ètat* in Petrograd,
Shakhrai pointed to the central fact that the Soviets were isolated from
the Ukrainian movement, represented the country's non-Ukrainian
minority, and were opposed by Ukrainians above all because they were
Russians. Ukrainians might accept Soviet power for Russia, but he believed that "here there could not even be any talk of transferring power
to the Soviets because the Soviets represented only Russian democracy,
which in Ukraine was a minority and was hostile to the national demands
of Ukraine." In explaining the deterioration of Russo-Ukrainian relations leading to war, Shakhrai emphasized Bolshevik cooperation with
the Rada in the October conflict with troops still loyal to Kerenskii and
blamed the growth of "Ukrainian chauvinism" at least as much as the

---

[8] *Ibid.*, pp. 8–19. Quotation from p. 15.

Bolsheviks, especially the fact that by supporting Kaledin "the Central Rada stood . . . on the side of the counterrevolution, perhaps against the will of its leaders." After describing the First All-Ukrainian Congress of Soviets in Kiev and the establishment of a Soviet government in Kharkiv, he explained the loss of mass support for the Rada as largely motivated by the land bill, which would have allowed individual farmers to keep up to 40 desiatynas of land as private property. Shakhrai admitted that the Rada's loss of support did not translate into support for the Soviets, but merely into a widespread attitude that there was no difference between them.[9]

Shakhrai becomes critical of Bolshevik chauvinism when he turns his attention to the first Soviet occupation of Kiev and its aftermath, arguing that the quarrelsomeness of the relations between the Soviet Ukrainian regime and the local Soviets was not the product of simple ambition but the result of fundamental attitudes toward the Ukrainian question. When a Soviet Ukrainian government was formed not a single responsible Bolshevik opposed it. While the workers of the Donbas were hostile to the idea of being politically subordinate to even a Soviet Ukrainian government, most Bolsheviks were quite willing to accept a Soviet Ukrainian government in theory. But it soon became clear that they considered themselves responsible only to Moscow and not to any Ukrainian political center. The reason for this was that non-Ukrainian workers had no interest in the creation of a separate Ukrainian political center. The result was the anarchy of several overlapping Soviet governments competing for men, food, and other resources. This administrative chaos was an important factor in alienating the Ukrainian masses from Soviet power. Still, in spite of their disorganization, the Bolsheviks had been able to resist the Germans for three months.[10]

Shakhrai described the Hetman regime as a cross between counterrevolution and comic opera, with "all the Russian patriots and eaters of Germans" taking shelter under the troops of the German Kaiser, and the sovereign of an independent Ukrainian state locking people up for their excessive zeal in Ukrainizing Ukraine's schools. In his view, the Hetmanate was a farce, but it presented the Bolsheviks with an extraordinary revolutionary opportunity if they would join with the Ukrainian masses and help establish a genuinely independent Soviet Ukraine. As he put it,

---

[9] *Ibid.*, pp. 19–80. Quotations from pp. 70, 78.
[10] *Ibid.*, pp. 81–125.

The current "independent" Ukraine, the Hetmanate, is a nest of the
Russian counterrevoluion, which like black ravens has covered
Ukraine and drinks the blood of the Ukrainian people. The current Hetmanate is the prison of the Ukrainian people. The Ukrainian people
must still fight for its fatherland, its Ukraine. Only Soviet Russia, only
the international proletariat, is capable of being its ally. Hand in hand
with the latter it will fight for a real independent Ukraine. [11]

Shakhrai concluded by examining the Ukrainian national question
within the context of the larger Russian revolutionary movement.
Geopolitically, it was flanked by the Central powers in the West and
Soviet Russia to the North. Although the Germans had used Russian
counterrevolutionaries to create the Hetmanate, it refused to support
the latter's striving for the creation of a one and indivisible Russia, and
this had given the Ukrainian National Union (Petliura, Vynnychenko,
and co.) some hope that Germany would end up helping to create a real
Ukrainian state. However, with the Central Powers collapsing, the wind
was changing, and the Entente, led by the USA, was in favor of a united
and restored Russia. This meant that the capitalist states provided absolutely no basis for Ukrainian hopes. On the other hand, Ukraine had
all the resources for independence. In 1917–1918 it had undergone a
profound experience of state building in which even the Bolsheviks had
participated by creating a Soviet Ukrainian government. Both the Rada
and the Soviet regime had come to the state of independence, and both
had entered the international arena by going to Brest-Litovsk. Now,
with the collapse of Germany and Austria, the way opened for union
between Greater Ukraine and Eastern Galicia. Ukrainian independence,
Shakhrai argued, in no way conflicted with Bolshevik doctrine or the
program of the Comintern, while the forcible establishment of
Russo-Ukrainian unity could only serve to divide the proletariat along
national lines and weaken the revolution. The lack of any other ally
that could help establish Ukrainian independence provided the Bolsheviks
an opportunity to extend the proletarian revolution by aligning itself
with the aspirations of the Ukrainian people. The Ukrainian movement
had shown its strength; its entire tendency had been toward independence.
Marxism also calls for national self-determination as a matter both of
general principles and of the general tendency for national movements
to develop under imperialism. Both pointed in the same direction:

> . . .both principles and facts clearly, definitely, and necessarily *dictate*

---

[11] *Ibid.*, pp. 125–135. Quotation from p. 136.

only one way out: Ukraine must and will be (if the socialist revolution and socialism are not to be just phrases and chicanery) *united and independent.* . . . Victorious socialism absolutely must realize complete democracy and, it follows, not only establish the complete equality of nations but *also realize* the right of oppressed nations to self-determination, *i.e.,* the right to free political secession.

Socialist parties that do not show by their actions *now, during the revolution, and after its victory* that they will liberate the enslaved nations and establish relations with them on the basis of a free union—and free union is only a false phrase without freedom to secede—such parties would be traitors to the cause of socialism.

. . . the international revolution is the only path to a really free, really independent Ukraine.

The international revolution is a fact of today. Independent Ukraine is a fact of tomorrow. And after today tomorrow will come.

Long live the independent Worker-Peasant Soviet Ukraine![12]

Concerning the Moment, this time published by Mazlakh and Shakhrai under their real names, appeared in January 1919. Precious weeks had passed, and the Bolsheviks in Moscow seemed to have learned absolutely nothing. The Bolshevik press was publishing articles by Khristian Rakovskii to the effect that the Ukrainian movement was dead and that Ukrainians desired nothing more than to be ruled by Red Moscow. Lenin's government had even announced that it no longer recognized Ukrainian independence, whether it be Hetmanite, Petliurist, or Soviet. Therefore, this pamphlet was written in a far more polemical tone and its points made far more forcefully than had been the case with its predecessor. Both the Bolsheviks and their Ukrainian opponents were denounced in far stronger terms than before. Mazlakh and Shakhrai were writing as revolutionaries who believed that if war is the continuation of politics by other means, then "revolution is the continuation of previous politics and of the war 'by other means.'. . . Revolution is a war against the old society and for a new socialist society. . . ."[13] For them the USDRP was but a den of counterrevolutionaries who had consorted with the Hetmanate.[14]

Although they had no love for the various Ukrainian socialist parties, Mazlakh and Shakhrai stressed that they were writing as men devoted

---

[12] *Ibid.,* pp. 136–150. Quotation from pp. 149–150. Parentheses and emphasis in the original.

[13] Serhii Mazlakh and Vasyl Shakhrai, *Do khvyli: Shcho diietsia na Ukraini i z Ukrainoiu* (New York, 1967), p. 26; *On the Current Situation,* p. 5.

[14] Mazlakh and Shakhrai, *Do khvyli,* pp. 51–53; *On the Current Situation,* pp. 22–24.

both to socialism and to Ukraine; they wanted above all to demonstrate that the two were not incompatible. Far from it, they argued, the vast majority of Ukrainians were toilers who wanted socialism as much as anyone. But the Bolshevik Party had to recognize that Ukrainians also constituted a nation with its own political movement, the whole historical tendency of which pointed toward independence. And the fact that Shakhrai had helped represent Soviet Ukraine at the Brest-Litovsk negotiations lent their words particular authority when they wrote, "the Central Rada was led to independence, not by conscious leaders, but by the logic of the facts themselves."[15]

The question of whether Ukraine ought to be independent no longer existed, they argued; there was only the question of whether the Bolsheviks would recognize the fact of Ukrainian independence. The pressures of the Russian counterrevolution and foreign intervention were inexorably pushing the Ukrainian masses toward an alliance with the Russian workers. The main obstacles to such an alliance came not from the Ukrainian side but from the Bolsheviks in the form of pseudo-experts like Rakovskii, the blatantly chauvinistic "Katerynoslavan" wing of the KP(b)U, and the pseudo-internationalist "Kievans" whose policy was objectively more imperialistic than that of their rivals. To achieve such an alliance with the people of Ukraine Bolsheviks had only to recognize that

> Ukraine is a country just like Russia, Germany, France, Italy, Norway, England, and the rest. Like them it not only has a "right" but is in fact already as sovereign and independent as they are... *And* when the Russian proletariat approaches Ukraine...sincerely, openly without any "ulterior motives," and without any "adaptations to local conditions," the sympathies of Ukraine, of the worker-peasant Ukraine, will be with Russia "to the end of time."[16]

Mazlakh and Shakhrai called for the creation of a new Ukrainian Communist Party (bolshevik). The KP(b)U as it then existed could not do what needed to be done for the simple reason that it was not even a political party in its own right, only a regional section of the Russian parent organization.[17] The first thing that they hoped such a new party would do would be to fight energetically against the various forces of counterrevolution, be they of Russian, Ukrainian, or foreign origin. It

---

[15] Mazlakh and Shakhrai, *Do khvyli*, p. 96; *On the Current Situation*, p. 51.

[16] Mazlakh and Shakhrai, *Do khvyli*, pp. 222–223; *On the Current Situation*, p. 132.

[17] Mazlakh and Shakhrai, *Do khvyli*, p. 242; *On the Current Situation*, p. 146.

should fight those advocates of independence who were willing to accept the sponsorship of a foreign power and thus open the door to foreign occupation like the one just ending. It must educate the Russian and Russified proletariat to the fact that Ukraine exists as a country, nation, language, and culture, that the Russian tongue is no more "international" than its Ukrainian counterpart and has no special rights over the latter. It must make the democratic slogan of the power of the workers and peasants a reality through the Soviets. It must make Soviet Ukrainian independence a reality and not just a propaganda ploy. This, they argued, need not imply an attack on other nationalities. All nationalities ought to be granted equal rights along the line set forth in Paragraph 19 of the Austrian constitution, which guaranteed all nationalities within the state the right to use their own language in schools, the administration, and social intercourse and guaranteed to all the right to education in their mother tongue.[18]

Although they facetiously called one chapter "We are Nationalists. We are Chauvinists," they called for a party that would fight both Russian and Ukrainian chauvinism, clearly seeing Russian chauvinism as the greater danger.[19] A few years later this idea would be enshrined as Party orthodoxy, but for the moment their ideas were ignored. Mazlakh and Shakhrai did not mount an organized opposition aimed at taking over the Party. They evidently hoped only to convince leading Bolsheviks that the policies currently in force were mistaken. When they published their pamphlets, however, the leadership was clearly not ready to be convinced. It would take much bitter experience before even a few of the ideas first advocated by Mazlakh and Shakhrai would be reconsidered.

Georg Lapchinskii and the Federalist Opposition

A more formidable challenge to Communist policy in Ukraine was mounted by what came to be known as the Federalist Opposition within the KP(b)U. This group began to take shape during the final weeks of the Piatakov regime, when a group of disaffected Bolsheviks led by Petro Slynko held a series of meetings in Kiev. Georg Lapchinskii, who would later emerge as the leading Federalist, summarized their views as follows:

the need for the total independence of the Soviet Ukrainian state, which must command its full measure of power, including regional military and

---

[18] Mazlakh and Shakhrai, *Do khvyli*, pp. 256–260; *On the Current Situation*, pp. 154–156.

[19] Mazlakh and Shakhrai, *Do khvyli*, p. 263ff; *On the Current Situation*, pp. 158–159.

economic authority as well as an independent Party center in no way
subordinate to the RKP Party center and having a free hand in policy
and in selecting its leading Party apparatus from among the internal forces
of the country.

After the evacuation of Kiev in the late summer of 1919, Lapchinskii
went to Moscow, where more meetings were held. These émigré gather-
ings charged Lapchinskii and Slynko with the task of drawing up a
memorandum that was then presented to the RKP Central Committee.[20]
The memorandum began with a short sketch of Ukraine's economic
development and argued that Ukraine was fundamentally different from
Russia in that the countryside was a far more decisive factor there. The
basic shortcoming of past Bolshevik policies in Ukraine arose from the
fact that the KP(b)U was not really a Ukrainian political force that could
see things from the viewpoint of Ukraine's revolutionary masses. Rather,
it had seen everything from the viewpoint of the Russian center. The
Federalist memorandum argued for creating a Party organization able
to unite the proletarian masses of Ukraine's cities with their rural counterparts. Such a center would have to lead in its own right, not just take
orders from Moscow as had been the case in the past. Ukraine's masses,
the Federalists declared, had a right "to their own revolutionary creation" both in the realm of the Party and the state. Any future Soviet
Ukrainian state ought to be federated with Soviet Russia, but it must
be a real federation "on the basis of the equality of all Soviet republics"
and not just a territorial extension of Moscow's sway.[21]

Meanwhile, a number of profoundly disturbing events had taken place.
On June 1, the Russian Central Executive Committee proclaimed a
federation of all Soviet republics, which was ratified by Soviet Ukraine
on June 14 and Soviet Belorussia on June 20. This federation, as the
Belorussian government officially declared, actually meant the creation
"from all Soviet republics of a single socialist federative republic." On
October 2, the remnant of the Soviet Ukrainian government, which the
advancing Whites had bypassed in Chernihiv, proclaimed itself dissolved,
and the the KP(b)U Central Committee did likewise. These moves, taken
on Moscow's orders, seemed to imply giving up forever on the idea
of Ukraine as even a quasi-separate Soviet republic. But they also left

---

[20] G. Lapchinskii, "Gomelskoe soveshchanie (vospominaniia)," *Letopis revoliutsii,*
1926, no. 6, pp. 37–41; quotations from p. 41.

[21] Excerpts from this document are quoted by M. Ravich-Cherkasskii, *Istoriia Kommunisticheskoi Partii (b-ov) Ukrainy,* pp. 137–138.

the Twelfth Red Army and its *revkom,* which still held parts of three provinces, on their own. Cut off and seemingly forgot by Moscow, the Twelfth Army *revkom* was still a *de facto* Soviet government in Ukraine. Lapchinskii immediately saw the possibilities offered by the existence of a Bolshevik regime unhampered by RKP directives; it was what he had called for all along and gave him a chance to put his ideas into practice. As a first step, he arranged that the memorandum be published in territory under the Twelfth Army's control. The document bore the imprimatur of the "Organizational Bureau of the Group of Federalists, Members of the KP(b)U," although, as Lapchinskii later admitted, there was as yet no formally organized "Group of Federalists" and certainly no Orgburo.[22]

Lapchinskii returned to Ukraine hoping to create a new Ukrainian Communist Party (bolshevik) from what he considered to be healthy elements of the now defunct KP(b)U and unite them with two indigenous Ukrainian radical groups, the Borotbisty and Ukapisty. Upon arriving in Volyn Province, he learned that the situation had become quite complicated. The Bolshevik regime in Chernihiv had declared itself part of Soviet Russia and was trying to carry on as best it could. In Volyn and the small corner of Kiev Province left unoccupied by Denikin, the Bolsheviks had opted for the idea of an independent Soviet Ukraine and abandoned previous policies that they judged ill-suited to local conditions. Though most of the Volyn Bolsheviks did not speak Ukrainian, they had been impressed by the fact that the Borotbisty had managed to gain the allegiance of a prominent Petliurist commander, Otaman Polokh. They were further impressed by the fact that a number of the Borotbisty's most prominent leaders had opted to remain in the area and were organizing troops that could serve as the nucleus for a Ukrainian Red Army.[23]

In mid-November at Lapchinskii's prompting the Gomel Provincial Party Committee (*gubkom*) issued a call for a Party conference, named a committee to organize it, and sent word to certain former leaders of the KP(b)U then in Moscow. Despite a telegram from Moscow declaring the conference illegal and ordering its cancellation, the KP(b)U sent such luminaries as Kosior, Zatonskyi, and Manuilskyi to take part, and the Gomel Conference was held on November 25–26, 1919.[24] Opponents

---

[22] Lapchinskii, "Gomelskoe soveshchanie . . . ," pp. 41–42; quotation from Kulichenko, *Borba Kommunisticheskoi partii za reshenie natsionalnogo voprosa,* p. 267.

[23] *Ibid.,* pp. 42–44.

[24] S. Ia. Sluchevska, "Do pytaniia pro homelsku naradu partiinykh orhanizatsii ta

of Lapchinskii expressed trepidations concerning the illegal nature of the meeting, but enough of them took part to prevent passage of the resolutions he offered. His resolutions called for the creation of a new Communist Party (bolshevik) of Ukraine that would include Borotbisty and Ukapisty as well as Bolsheviks, an independent Soviet Ukraine that was to be free from all outside interference, and a separate Ukrainian Red Army. A more moderate proposal presented by D. Z. Manuilskyi carried the day. This resolution called for the reestablishment of Soviet Ukraine in military and economic union with Soviet Russia, reestablishment of the KP(b)U as it formerly existed, and the rejection of any talk of merging with the Borotbisty and Ukapisty until these groups dropped their demand for a separate Ukrainian Red Army.[25] At about the same time as the Gomel Conference, another Federalist, P. Popov, was invited to a meeting of the RKP Central Committee and explained his group's views on what Russo-Ukrainian relations should be. While the RKP officially rejected the Federalists' views and declared the Gomel Conference illegal, Moscow was changing its attitude.[26] Even before the Gomel meeting, Lenin had written the draft of his famous resolution on Soviet Rule in Ukraine. A few weeks later the KP(b)U was revived with a three-man Party Center consisting of Manuilskyi, Zatonskyi, and Kosior. A Soviet Ukrainian government was established under a *revkom* subordinate to Moscow.[27]

Lapchinskii was not finished yet. In March 1920 the KP(b)U held its Fourth Conference in Kharkiv, and Lapchinskii arrived with a printed platform of eighteen points and the support of a majority of the Volyn delegation.[28] By this time, however, the Borotbisty had already reached agreement with the Bolsheviks on terms for a merger with the KP(b)U and would have nothing further to do with Lapchinskii and his group. This left the Federalists in the embarrassing position of appearing to be more nationalistic than those whose "nationalism" the Party had long condemned. In any case, the conference was controlled by another opposition, the Democratic Centralists (Detsisty) led by T. V. Sapronov

okremykh vidpovidalnykh pratsivnykiv (25–26 listopada 1919 r.), *Ukrainskyi istorychnyi zhurnal*, 1965, no. 10, p. 79.

   [25] Lapchinskii, "Gomelskoe soveshchanie...," pp. 36, 44–48.

   [26] Ravich-Cherkasskii, *Istoriia KP(b)U*, pp. 138–140; Kulichenko, *Borba Kommunisticheskoi Partii za reshenie natsionalnogo voprosa*, pp. 426–427.

   [27] M. Pohrebinskyi, *Stanislav Vikentiiovych Kosior* (Kiev, 1967), pp. 170–173.

   [28] V. Sukhyno-Khomenko, "Problemy istorii KP(b)U," *Bilshovyk Ukrainy*, 1928, no. 13, p. 75.

who had been exiled from Russia to Ukraine for his previous opposition activities. The Detsisty took control of the Central Committee and went on to challenge Lenin at the Ninth RKP congress where they were defeated. After their defeat Lenin simply declared the Fourth Conference of the KP(b)U invalid, disbanded its Central Committee, and appointed one more to his liking.[29] As for Lapchinskii, he created a *cause célèbre* by leaving the Party, joining the Ukapisty, and publishing a letter which was sharply critical of the KP(b)U and outlined his reasons for leaving it.[30]

Ukrainian Communism: The Borotbisty

The Borotbisty, many of whom would rise to prominence in the KP(b)U during the 1920s, took shape as the Left wing of the UPSR. During the first Russo-Ukrainian War in early 1918, a number of future Borotbisty were briefly jailed for planning a *coup d'état* aimed at overthrowing the Central Rada. As the German occupation increased the revolutionary fervor of the UPSR's rural constituency, its Left wing gained in strength. This gain resulted in a Leftist majority at the UPSR's Fourth Congress held illegally near Kiev in May 1918. The Fourth UPSR Congress gave the Left control of the Central Committee and the UPSR's official organ, *Borotba* (The Struggle). Those sympathetic to the former UPSR leadership split off and took the name UPSR (Central Course), and the Left gradually came to be known as the Borotbisty after their newspaper. Soon thereafter, the Borotbisty began to debate among themselves whether they in fact had anything in common with the old nationalistic UPSR or were a wholly new party committed to the radical transformation of society. Either way, the name Borotbisty stuck, and before long the party officially began to use the name UPSR (borotbist).[31]

From the start, the Borotbisty condemned other Ukrainian parties for excessive nationalism and the tendency to see political independence as an end in itself. They denounced artificial borders between states

---

[29] Ravich-Cherkasskii, *Istoriia KP(b)U,* pp. 149–65. Robert V. Daniels, *The Conscience of the Revolution: Communist Opposition in Soviet Russia* (New York, 1960), p. 102.

[30] The letter is published with a gloss explaining the circumstances surrounding it in the pamphlet, *Revoliutsiia v nebezpetsi! (Lyst Zak. Grupy U.K.P. do komunistiv i revoliutsiinykh sotsiialistiv Ievropy ta Ameryky* (Vienna-Kiev, 1920), pp. 73–82.

[31] Iwan Majstrenko, *Borot'bism: A Chapter in the History of Ukrainian Communism,* pp. 36–88. Pavlo Khrystiuk, *Zamitky i materiialy do istorii Ukrainskoi revoliutsii,* vol. 3, pp. 19–25, 99–101. See also H. Ovcharov, "Z pryvodu vysvitlennia pytaniia pro borotbyzm," *Komunist Ukrainy,* 1958, no. 2, pp. 36–47.

and saw absolutely no reason why the toilers of Russia and Ukraine should be fighting each other. But they also took it for granted that association with Soviet Russia should be based on the principle of equality and that Soviet Ukraine should be Ukrainian, the product of and organically tied to the forces of the Ukrainian revolution. Soon after the fall of the Hetmanate the Borotbisty attempted to set up their own Soviet Ukrainian regime backed by the troops of Otaman Hryhoriiv, thus hoping to present the Bolsheviks with a *fait accompli*. But when the Bolsheviks refused to recognize the Borotbist *revkom*, the Borotbisty and Hryhoriiv had no other choice but to revolt or submit. They chose the latter and offered their services to the Piatakov regime. In March 1919 the UPSR (borotbist) moved closer to the Bolsheviks by changing its name to UPSR (communist-borotbist) and requesting admission into the KP(b)U, but the latter, flushed with its initial success in taking Ukraine, refused. It was only at Lenin's personal insistence that the Borotbisty were allowed to participate in the government; Lenin realized that widespread rural support for the Borotbisty made them a group that the Bolsheviks could ill afford to ignore. During the *Piatakovshchyna* the Borotbisty were docile allies of the Bolsheviks even after the revolt of their erstwhile military backer, Hryhoriiv.[32]

During the final days of the Piatakov regime in August 1919, the Borotbisty merged with a small group of Marxist intellectuals, the Left-Nezalezhnyky. The Nezalezhnyky had split off from the USDRP at the beginning of 1919, adopted the Soviet platform and welcomed the establishment of a Soviet Ukrainian state. When this group revolted against Bolshevik excesses in May, a small number of its members refused to go along and split off, calling themselves the Left-Nezalezhnyky. Given the fact that the Borotbisty were a far larger party than this tiny splinter group, one might expect the Borotbisty to absorb them but hardly to accept a merger. This, however, is precisely what happened. A merger gave the Borotbisty the opportunity to repudiate their narodnik heritage and to officially adopt Marxist ideology, a step that they hoped would give them a measure of ideological legitimacy which they had hitherto lacked. At the same time, the party once again changed its name, and the new Ukrainian Communist Party (borotbist) applied for admission to the newly established Third International.[33]

On August 7 Oleksander Shumskyi, the Borotbist leader who had been

---

[32] Majstrenko, *Borot'bism*, pp. 74–76, 89–135.
[33] *Ibid.*, pp. 136–140.

given the post of People's Commissar of Education in the government, presented a draft decree on the nationality question to the All-Ukrainian Central Executive Committee (VUTsVK), and on August 28 the party presented a detailed memorandum to the Comintern executive. While both appeals were rejected, they provide the best indication of Borotbist aspirations and, in the case of the nationality resolution, the unacknowledged basis of cultural policy during NEP. Each must be briefly considered.

The Memorandum of the Ukrainian Communist Party (borotbist) to the Executive Committee of the Third Communist International is a thoroughly Marxist document designed to demonstrate that the Borotbisty were orthodox and revolutionary Marxists, the legitimate leaders of the Ukrainian revolution, and had the best chance of leading Ukraine to communism. It begins with a review of the events that culminated with the August 6 merger. The result, the Ukrainian Communist Party (borotbist), represented "the organized kernel of Ukrainian communism," which had crystallized from revolutionary elements that had split off from the UPSR and USDRP and which were impelled by the force of the Ukrainian revolutionary process itself. These revolutionary elements, the memorandum claims, had led the Ukrainian revolutionary masses against both monarchist Hetmanate and "bourgeois" Directory. Finally they had united in a single party in order to bring together all communist elements in Ukraine around a single center. The KP(b)U, as a regional section of the Russian Communist Party, was alien to Ukraine and incapable even of recognizing the need to create a Ukrainian center.[34]

The bulk of the memorandum is taken up by a detailed analysis of the Ukrainian revolution and the ways the Bolsheviks had unintentionally hampered it by bringing in people who knew nothing about the Ukrainian nation and "the natural course of its revolutionary development." Ukraine, the memorandum argues, was markedly different from Russia. It was "a particular and, to a substantial degree, independent national-economic organism with its own structure of economic life and exceedingly complex configuration of social relationships." It was an agrarian country in which the industrial proletariat constituted at most 15% of the population, and while much had been done to organize the urban proletariat, very little had been done to organize the proletarians

---

[34] *Memorandum Ukrainskoi Komunistychnoi Partii (borotbystiv) do Vykonavchoho Komitetu III-ho Komunistychnoho Internatsionalu* (Kiev, 1920), pp. 3–6.

and semi-proletarians of the countryside. The poor and middle peasantry, the document points out, together constituted a substantial majority of the country's population, but these strata possessed deeply rooted
proprietary instincts. Circumstances dictated that agrarian revolution
be the "inevitable consequence of Ukraine's economic structure."
Hence, for the Ukrainian revolution to succeed it had to base itself on
rural proletarians and semi-proletarians who were not yet conscious of
the need for socialism. The KP(b)U, with its blatant antipathy for all
things rural and Ukrainian, had shown itself incapable of gaining the
support of those rural elements that were crucial to the revolution's success. The ephemeral nature of past attempts to build a Soviet Ukraine
is explained by this failure to base itself on the rural as well as urban
elements, which by their class nature should have been the strongest
supporters of a Soviet regime.[35]

If the KP(b)U's tendency to alienate the peasantry constituted one
obstacle to Soviet power, its hostility to the Ukrainian nationality was
another. The memorandum points out that the KP(b)U's attempt to base
Soviet power solely on urban workers who were culturally alien to the
countryside could not fail to harm the natural course of the Ukrainian
revolution. Long experience of national oppression and artificial
Russification had served to make Ukrainians naturally suspicious of
everything Russian. The Bolsheviks' own tendencies toward Russification
had not helped matters; they had further alienated rural proletarian
elements from their urban counterparts. The Ukrainian revolution could
be led only by those who recognized the national form of Ukrainian
culture. Without cultural equality for rural proletarian elements and
without recognition of their national needs and aspirations, the growth
of rural proletarian consciousness itself and its consciousness of the need
for unity of all proletarian elements, rural and urban, would be inconceivable. Only real cultural equality could make the rural proletarians
immune to the counterrevolutionary slogans of the Ukrainian bourgeois
nationalists, and this raised the question of what kind of Soviet republic
Ukraine should be. The Borotbisty believed that Ukraine's particular
socio-economic and national features dictated that Ukraine had to have
its own independent Soviet republic, bound organically to the Ukrainian countryside and an equal member of the future world federation of
Soviet republics. The nationality question, the memorandum declares,
was a tactical question, to be sure, but it made tactical sense to establish

---

[35] *Ibid.*, pp. 7–12. Quotations from pages 9 and 10.

a Soviet Ukraine that would be capable of harnessing the indigenous forces of the Ukrainian revolution. Tactical errors regarding the nationality question only made it more difficult to implant proletarian consciousness in those rural elements that had to be mobilized if the revolution were to succeed. The errors of the KP(b)U served only to focus rural attention on the nationality issue, bringing it to the fore and helping it to overshadow the class struggle. The international struggle between the revolution and the counterrevolution on a world scale, the memorandum concludes, demanded that the Ukrainian proletariat be included in the ranks of the world proletariat. This in turn required the leadership of a Ukrainian communist center that had grown out of the socio-economic and national-cultural soil of Ukraine, a role that only the Borotbisty could play.[36]

The other major Borotbist statement made at this time is a pamphlet entitled *Concerning the Solution to the Nationality Question,* which contains the text of the resolution presented by Shumskyi to the Soviet Ukrainian government and a long preface arguing for its adoption. The pamphlet begins by attempting to redefine the terms in which the nationality question ought to be replaced by "the question of raising the level of culture in national forms."[37]

Revolutionaries should take the slogan, "culture in the mother tongue," out of the hands of Petliurist reaction and make it their own. The document argues in orthodox Marxist fashion that capitalism was responsible for the systematic enslavement of nations as well as the enforced ignorance of stateless peoples, but thus far the bourgeois intelligentsia, the kulaks, the middle peasants, and even backward segments of the working class had united around the slogan of national independence to the detriment of the cause of socialism. Borotbisty applauded the Russian Communist Party for its opposition to national privileges, but they saw this as only the passive side of the solution. An active solution must also be pursued by realizing that culture, including national culture, is a weapon of the class struggle. If this weapon is to be used in the fight for socialism, stateless nations must see their proletarian vanguard encouraging and promoting their national culture.[38]

Describing past Bolshevik policies, the pamphlet declares, "In Ukraine

---

[36] *Ibid.,* pp. 12–22.

[37] Ukrainskaia Kommunisticheskaia Partiia (borotbistov), *K razresheniiu natsionalnogo voprosa* (Kiev, 1920), p. 5.

[38] *Ibid.,* pp. 6–10.

we see an example of how not to solve the 'nationality question.' '' The years of forced Russification by the tsarist regime had made the cities into centers of Russian culture, cut off from the surrounding countryside by barriers of nationality. After the revolution came, its leaders looked to the cities. Recruits for the state apparatus came mainly from the *petit-bourgeois* Russified intelligentsia, while those who knew the language and culture of the countryside were ignored and their efforts sabotaged. The practice of concentrating power in the hands of representatives of the Russian or Russified urban proletariat *"de facto* creates a privileged position for Russian national forms of culture'' and, in spite of fine words about national equality, resulted in fanning the flames of national tagonism in the countryside. Elimination of national oppression, the Borotbisty argued, was not enough. The cultural level of less developed nationalities had to be raised as quickly as possible to the level of their more highly developed counterparts so that they could participate in social life on an equal basis. This seemed to be only the logical extension of the RKP's own slogan of national equality, an extension dictated by the urgent need "to take the slogan of national liberation out of the hands of reaction and by attaining real equality of national forms of culture to clear a broad path for the socialist development of Ukraine's masses of toiling people. . . . '' The socio-economic conditions that first promoted Russification might have disappeared, but the legacy of Russification clearly had not. The resulting "inertia of life" still held Ukrainians back; Soviet power would have to break it by providing "broad and planned aid for the development of Ukrainian forms of culture.'' The Commissariat of Public Education should take the lead in combatting simultaneously the legacy of Russification and deviations toward Ukrainian chauvinism. It must above all realize that formal recognitions of equality are in themselves insufficient. The state itself must assume the burden of fostering the cultural development of those nationalities that had been held back by past injustice, and the means for doing just that were outlined in the attached decree.[39]

The issue raised sixty years ago by the Borotbisty is a complicated one and raises questions that remain unresolved to this day. If simple legal equality is not enough to overcome the legacy of past injustice and previously oppressed groups must be actively helped to *make* them equal, does not this imply discrimination against those who had no hand in the oppression but who happen to belong to the same race as the

---

[39] *Ibid.*, pp. 10–24. Quotations from pp. 10, 12, 13.

previous oppressors? Is it not unjust to discriminate against those who are personally guiltless? It shall be seen below that after such a policy was adopted in Soviet Ukraine, voices were raised which would argue precisely that.

The Borotbist attempt to win the confidence of the Comintern was unsuccessful. In any case, they were faced with the more immediate problem of fighting the White occupation, which supplanted the Bolsheviks. Denikin did not recognize the existence of a Ukrainian nationality or even that of Ukraine. Ukrainian language schools, cultural organizations, publications, and bookstores were closed down. The term "Little Russia" (*Malorossiia*) was used in preference to Ukraine in referring to the region. Denikin's aim was quite simply to restore the situation that had prevailed before the revolution. Even the landlords returned to claim their former estates. It was not a popular regime, but neither was it easy to fight. The Borotbisty lost some of their best leaders to Denikin's firing squads.[40]

The Borotbisty were extremely effective as underground fighters. M. S. Hrushevskyi, former leader of the Central Rada and then still a leader of UPSR (Central Course), could not be accused of partiality toward the Borotbisty who had at one time plotted his overthrow and had later split his party. Yet, in 1920 he wrote that

> when during Denikin's offensive in August of last year the Left Ukrainian Socialist-Revolutionaries (the so-called "Borotbisty") and Left Independent Social Democrats united, took the name Communist, and led an uprising under the slogan of a Ukrainian Republic that would be independent yet Soviet and friendly toward the Bolsheviks and Soviet Russia, the masses flocked to their banner...[41]

Whether the Borotbisty enjoyed mass support because their slogan offered a way out of a difficult situation, as Hrushevskyi argued, or whether their slogans were genuinely popular is a matter that is open to dispute. Either way, the fact that the Borotbisty enjoyed substantial support in the Ukrainian countryside is indisputable. The Borotbisty cooperated against the Denikin regime with the Russian Left SRs (known as Borbisty in Ukraine) and the Bolsheviks. The Bolsheviks benefited greatly

---

[40] Most notably Vasyl Chumak and Hnat Mykhailychenko. The latter was to become something of a cult figure among Ukrainian poets in the succeeding decade.

[41] Mykh. Hrushevskyi, "Mizh Moskvoiu i Varshavoiu," *Boritesia-poborete! Zakordonnyi organ Ukrainskoi Partii Sotsiialistiv-Revoliutsioneriv*, no. 2, October 1920, pp. 6–7.

from such cooperation because, while they had money and weapons, they had virtually no contacts in the countryside where resistance was most effective and where the Borotbisty had their basis of support. The Borotbisty survived the trials of the White occupation with a record of unblemished support for the idea of Soviet power. In Bolshevik eyes, their principal sin lay in their continued attempts to create a Ukrainian Red Army, which would have threatened to preclude any future Bolshevik attempt to regain a monopoly of political power in the country.[42]

Lenin's attitude toward the Borotbisty was ambivalent. He recognized their usefulness, but he also saw them as potentially dangerous rivals whom he hoped to eliminate by absorbing what he considered to be their best elements and dispersing the rest. During the Piatakov-Rakovskii regime he seems to have wanted to use the Borotbisty to infuse the KP(b)U with new blood, while earmarking the party for liquidation as a separate political entity. However, the collapse of Soviet Ukraine in the summer of 1919 forced him to abandon such plans for the time being.[43]

In November 1919, the Comintern sponsored the opening of negotiations between Borotbist and KP(b)U representatives on the question of merging the two parties on the basis of the rule of one communist party per country. Despite Zinoviev's recommendation that terms be speedily agreed upon, the talks began in an atmosphere of deep mutual hostility. Immediately before the negotiations were to begin, the Borotbisty sent Lenin a letter containing a scathing critique of the entire history of the defunct Soviet Ukraine and blunders of the KP(b)U.[44]Rakovskii, who

---

[42] Majstrenko, *Borot'bism,* pp. 133–188.

[43] For Lenin's attitude toward the Borotbisty during the Piatakov regime, see the documents from the Trotsky archives first published by Bertram D. Wolfe, "The Influence of Early Military Decisions Upon the National Structure of the Soviet Union," *American Slavonic and East European Review,* vol. 9, 1950, pp. 174–178. Among other things, Lenin clearly stated that he was awaiting only the proper moment for the liquidation of the Borotbisty.

[44] This letter deserves to be reproduced at length:

"Soviet troops reached Kiev itself and occupied the entire Left Bank with the support of the local population. The Soviet troops were themselves Ukrainians. The proletariat and, most importantly, the peasants staunchly supported Soviet power. There were *uezdy* through which Soviet troops passed without a shot being fired (You know this from Piatakov's report). The will of the toilers was completely evident. The link-up with Hungary drew near. . . .

"Then 'Soviet' construction began. At first the long-awaited Soviet regime was getting used to the business of Soviet power, and much was pardoned it; the dictatorships of ignorant foreigners rejected indigenous communist forces and did absolutely nothing

was one of the KP(b)U negotiators, was absolutely livid upon learning of the letter and attempted to counter it by charging that the Borotbisty were a *petit-bourgeois* party by virtue of the fact that they were based in the countryside—the charge itself speaks volumes about why Rakovskii's earlier tenure as a head of state had ended in fiasco—and that they were "making themselves a center in Ukraine around which *petit-bourgeois* counterrevolution is being organized." He also obtained a letter from Manuilskyi accusing the Borotbisty of having connections with Petliura and recommending that the lot of them be turned over to the Cheka for execution. Hryhorii Hrynko, one of the Borotbist negotiators, defended his comrades from the charge of nationalism by

---

themselves. Then—revolt. Then the Soviet regime set fire to the whole countryside and began shooting Red Army men of the Tarashchanskyi division and poor peasants. Then everything got mixed up, and the Kiev proletariat greeted Comrade Trotsky in a not quite comradely manner. . . .

"Soviet power in Ukraine has fallen. Those who took part in it have now gone on to spread it to Turkestan, Siberia, and so on. But Soviet power still lives in Ukraine. And it will be there if the Russian Communist Party displays real internationalism and stops trying to implant 'Red' imperialism in Ukraine.

"Comrade Petrovskyi has stated in the press that the Ukrainian movement (*ukrainstvo*) is supported by kulaks and rascals. Comrade Rakovskii, while President of the Council of People's Commissars, demanded the dictatorship of Russian culture in Ukraine. This is very far from an internationalist understanding of communism. This is very close to the tsarist dictum that there never was, is not, and never can be a Ukrainian language.

"And if the leaders view the matter this way, what is the wonder that the gang of Johnny-Come-Latelys from Russia shoot members of their own party, seasoned revolutionaries who are known in the poor peasant districts, for no other reason than that they expressed their Ukrainian sympathies. (Zenkov, Poltava Province. Shot or more probably tortured to death was Comrade Rudenko, a member of a local KPU group, by the decision of a general meeting of the group without any semblance of a trial after a simple show of hands). . .

"It is not clear what they wanted. If it was Soviet power as we understand it, then why fight the poor peasants? . . . Why treat the toilers caddishly with insults and humiliations? . . . The desire to make Ukraine a colony doesn't jibe with the appearance of Soviet power as a historical phenomenon. How then can this be explained to the local revolutionary forces, which are the sole basis for Soviet power?

"A number of economic measures are along the same lines (Shlikhter: You can't stand on ceremony with a *khokhol*). The results are horrible, both in the mass of needless victims and in its consequences for the overall development of the socialist revolution. I cannot explain what created this malicious intent, but it was created just as if the Soviet regime in Ukraine had been led by experienced Black Hundreds laying the groundwork for the counterrevolution.

"You know that many who saw the disgraceful things done in the name of Soviet power in Ukraine protested that it was a mistake, that the 'center' did not know what

declaring that his party favored the complete economic unity of Ukraine and Russia:

> Only we understand this unity not in the sense of there being two entities and then one of them disappears, but rather as there being some sort of federally constituted Council of People's Economy. We think it necessary that in Ukraine, if we are talking about independence (*samostoiatelnost*) of the Ukrainian republic, there be created a Ukrainian economic center, because the simple extension of organs, the organs of the RSFSR, to the Ukrainian provinces irrationally will lead to bad results.[45]

The negotiations dragged on from November 6 to December 26, 1919, and, after being suspended for a time, from February 5 to April 22, 1920. After the reestablishment of Soviet power in Ukraine, the Borotbisty campaigned in the March 1920 elections to the Soviets on a platform of Soviet Ukrainian independence, and the KP(b)U responded by excluding them from the government at all levels.[46] On February 26, 1920, the Comintern officially refused the Borotbisty admission and charged them with "national deviations," not the least of which remained their advocacy of a separate Ukrainian Red Army.[47] In the end, however, Moscow ordered that the Borotbisty be admitted to the KP(b)U, a step that was officially taken at the Fourth KP(b)U Conference on March 20, when the Borotbists Shumskyi and Blakytnyi were elected to the Central Committee. A joint Bolshevik-Borotbist screening was set up to pass on who would be admitted, and those who were accepted had their Party seniority (*partstazh*) listed as the date they had joined the Borotbisty.[48] Of approximately 5000 Borotbisty, about 4000 were admitted into the KP(b)U.[49] A few days later the Borotbist Central Committee met for the last time to declare the party dissolved and direct its membership to apply for admission to the KP(b)U.[50]

---

was really happening. In particular, many have much faith in your authority. Answer. Much depends on your answer. What is needed now is the voice of a real revolutionary. "5.11.1919. Moscow. Signature illegible." Archival document first published by Frantíšek Silnický, "Lenin i borotbisty," *Novyi zhurnal*, no. 118, 1975, pp. 230–231.

[45] Silnický, "Lenin i borotbisty," 232–233. Quotation from p. 233.

[46] *Ibid.*, pp. 233–235.

[47] Text in *Kommunisticheskaia Partiia—Vdokhnovitel i organizator obedinitelnogo dvizheniia ukrainskogo naroda za obrazovanie SSSR: Sbornik dokumentov i materialov* (Kiev, 1962), pp. 167–169.

[48] Majstrenko, *Borot'bism*, pp. 188–189.

[49] P. Bachynskyi, *Panas Petrovych Liubchenko*, (Kiev, 1971), p. 25.

[50] On March 24, 1920, the Borotbist Central Committee adopted its final resolution, "On the Liquidation of the Party":

"1. The Ukrainian Communist Party (borotbist) proclaims itself no longer in existence,

The Bolsheviks in Search of a Policy

The merger of the Borotbisty with the KP(b)U could not have occurred had there not been a major shift in Bolshevik policy from that which was followed during the *Piatakovshchyna*. Indeed, even the government of Piatakov and Rakovskii had paid some lip-service to Ukrainian aspirations by promising everyone the right to get an education in one's native language or making official preparations for the celebration of Shevchenko Day.[51] After Denikin began his retreat in late 1919, the Ukrainian problem again became urgent as the Red Army advanced, and the Bolsheviks responded with statements promising that Ukrainian rights would be respected. Most notable among these statements were the RKP Central Committee resolution "On Soviet Rule in Ukraine," Lenin's "Letter to the Workers and Peasants of Ukraine Concerning the Victory over Denikin," and Trotsky's statement to the Red Army at the time it entered Ukraine.

Lenin personally drafted the resolution "On Soviet Rule," which was adopted by the RKP Central Committee and the Eighth Congress. While reaffirming the federation of Soviet republics, which had been proclaimed on June 1 and which was tantamount to the absorption of Ukraine and Belorussia by Russia, the resolution also demanded that Communists take all possible measures to eliminate anything hindering the development of the Ukrainian language and culture, that Ukrainians be able to get an education in Ukrainian and use their native tongue in dealing with state institutions, and that no effort be spared in the attempt to win over the Ukrainian poor and middle peasants.[52]

Lenin's "Letter to the Workers and Peasants of Ukraine," published December 28, 1919, was meant for the consumption of Ukrainians and glossed over a number of issues such as those that divided the Bolsheviks and the Borotbisty. Lenin defended the idea of a Russo-Ukrainian federation while indicating that Russian Communists would work to overcome their own nationalism. Communists, he wrote, were internationalists

---

and its members are prepared to join the KP(b)U in accordance with the directives of the Central Committee.

"2. The Central Committee of the UKP(b) dissolves itself." O. Iurchenko, *Chetverta konferentsiia KP(b)U* (Kiev, 1961), p. 100.

[51] The former pledge was made on January 26, 1919, and the latter decision was taken on February 27. *Kulturne budivnytstvo v Ukrainskii RSR: Vazhlyvishi rishennia Komunistychnoi partii i Radianskoho uriadu, 1917–1959* (Kiev, 1959), vol. 1, p. 31. Evhen Kyryliuk, "Zhovten i literaturna spadshchyna ukrainskoho narodu," in *Zhovten i ukrainska kultura: Zbirnyk z mizhnarodnoho sympoziumu* (Presov, 1968), p. 13.

[52] *V. I. Lenin pro Ukrainu*, vol. 2, pp. 359–361.

who opposed all nationalism in the name of internationalism. They committed themselves to complete national equality. The Soviet Ukrainian government, Lenin explained, was headed by a *revkom,* which contained both Communists and Borotbisty. The difference between the two groups, as he saw it, was that while the Borotbisty were committed to the idea of an independent Ukraine, there were Communists who supported the idea and Communists who did not favor it. According to Lenin the latter were determined not to let the issue divide revolutionaries from one another, but just how it could be settled in a manner acceptable to all was left vague.[53]

Trotsky's address to the Red Army declared that a "fraternal country" was being liberated: "Ukraine is the country of the Ukrainian workers and toiling peasants." Only the Ukrainian worker and peasant, he wrote, "possess the sole right to rule their own country." Trotsky warned against anyone offending them. He also indicated that Ukraine would be an independent Soviet state. The message seemed to have been intended more for Ukrainian consumption than for the instruction of those to whom it was formally addressed.[54]

Such statements as these were not just propaganda but represented a real shift in Lenin's attitude. His later insistence that the republics have rights guaranteed in the Soviet constitution showed that the change extended beyond the cultural sphere to that of politics. Yet substantive policy changes were delayed first by the victory of Sapronov's Democratic Centralists at the Fourth KP(b)U congress in March 1920. After the opposition-dominated leadership was replaced with another more to Lenin's liking, the Poles drove the Bolsheviks out of Ukraine once again. Nothing could be done until it was regained.

The Polish invasion was the product of a temporary alliance between the formerly bitter enemies. After the Armistice the West Ukrainian People's Republic was established in Eastern Galicia, and the Poles invaded. Formally united, the Ukrainian People's Republic and its West Ukrainian counterpart maintained separate governments, the former socialist and the latter farther to the Right. In August 1919 Petliura sent a peace mission to Warsaw, and the Galicians feared he would make peace at their expense. In the Fall, the Galicians made peace with Denikin, and Petliura made peace with the Poles, agreeing to their annexation of Eastern Galicia. In the Spring of 1920 the Poles and Petliura

---

[53] *Ibid.,* vol. 2, pp. 403–410.
[54] Vynnychenko, *Vidrodzhennia natsii,* vol. 3, pp. 494–495.

began a joint offensive that briefly drove the Bolsheviks out of Ukraine.[55] Then the tide turned, and the Poles were driven back to the outskirts of Warsaw before they again took the offensive. The result was the partition of Ukraine between the Poles and the Bolsheviks. This, along with the final defeat of the remnants of the Volunteer Army in November 1920, ended the Russian Civil War. But for Ukrainians, it meant only the end of the set-piece phase of their war of national liberation (if one may be pardoned for using a term more common to our own day). There the situation remained far from peaceful.

According to two separate but entirely consistent sources there were an estimated 102 armed anticommunist bands operating in Ukraine and Crimea as of April 1, 1921. Each band had from twenty or thirty to as much as 500 armed men, and a few had as many as 800. In addition, the anarchist forces of Nestor Makhno still contained from 10,000 to 15,000. Excluding Makhno's men, there were at least 10,000 armed "kulak bandits," as the Bolsheviks dubbed them.[56] Some were peasant anarchists, a few were still loyal to the Volunteer Army, but most were nationally conscious Ukrainians whether or not they supported Petliura. "Kulak banditism" was for a time the Bolsheviks' most pressing concern. All available forces were pressed into service against them—the Red Army, Cheka, worker-peasant militias, Special Assignment Sections of the Party and Komsomol, and the *komnezamy*.[57]

The basis of "kulak banditism," although the proportion of real kulaks among the so-called bandits is questionable, was the mass disenchantment of the countryside with Bolshevik policies.[58] Although peasants were no longer forced into communes, the policy most galling to them, forced requisitions of foodstuffs at nominal fixed prices, was enforced and even intensified right up to 1921 when the New Economic Policy

---

[55] The basic documents on this "divorce" between the UNR and its Western counterpart may be consulted in Mykhailo Lozynskyi, *Halychyna v rr. 1918-1920* (reprint, New York, 1970), pp. 170-201 and I. Mazepa, *Ukraina v ohni i buri revoliutsii*, vol. 3, pp. 201-207.

[56] The figures are given by O. O. Kucher, *Rozhrom zbroinoi vnutrishnoi kontrrevoliutsii na Ukraini u 1921-1923 rr.* (Kharkiv, 1971), p. 18. These figures are broadly consistent with more detailed documents published in the Ukrainian émigré press in 1932. These documents, the authenticity of which Kucher unintentionally confirms, were published as "Protybolshevytski povstannia na Ukraini v 1921 (Na osnovi ofitsiialnykh bolshevytskykh zvidomlen i inshykh nepublykovanykh materiialiv sot. N. P-pa)," *Litopys chervonoi kalyny*, vol. 4, 1932, no. 6, pp. 19-23 and vol. 4, 1932, no. 9, pp. 6-7.

[57] Kucher, *Rozhrom zbroinoi vnutrishnoi kontrrevoliutsii*, pp. 97-127.

[58] *Ibid.*, p. 28, where he admits that there was "mass dissatisfaction of the peasants with the policy of War Communism."

was implemented. In Ukraine the implementation of the NEP was delayed for several months later than in Russia.[59] The state of affairs in the Ukrainian countryside is reflected in the measures to which the Bolsheviks resorted in order to maintain a foothold there.

The *kombidy*, which had been established in Ukraine just as they were being merged with village and *volost* Soviets in Russia, were replaced in May 1920 by the *komnezamy* (committees of non-wealthy peasants), which had no counterpart in Russia. In fact, the two organizations were identical in regard to function: they were "militant class organizations" established to organize communes, requisition grain, and fight the "kulak" with expropriation as well as with gun in hand.[60] The only difference between *kombid* and *komnezam* was that the latter were to include some members of the lower stratum of the middle peasants as well as the impoverished and thereby put up a stronger front against the kulaks.[61] For years they remained the main organ of Soviet rule in the countryside.

An excellent portrait of the *komnezamy* is provided by a communist writing in 1923. He saw them as necessary because, as he put it, the kulak too often tried to "put the village Soviet in his pocket"—a line of argument suspiciously akin to saying that the peasants could not be trusted to order their own affairs because the "class enemies" would take over. The only other organization upon which the Party could rely, the union of agricultural workers (*Vserabotzemles*), was too weak. At the time of his writing, he estimated that the *komnezamy* controlled half the Soviet administration in the villages despite the crisis into which they had been thrown by the NEP. Earlier they had been far more powerful: "In reality during 1920 power in the villages was almost completely in the hands of the *komnezamy* such that it was extremely difficult in practice to distinguish clearly between the powers of the *komnezamy*

---

[59] Alec Nove, *An Economic History of the U.S.S.R.* (Baltimore, 1975), p. 54. In Ukraine, six times as much grain was requisitioned during the last half of 1920 as in all of 1919, and since the amount requisitioned during the first three months of 1921 was only 40% of what the state called for, the introduction of the New Economic Policy was delayed there until the summer and fall of 1921. V. P. Iubkin, "Zdiisnennia prodovolchoi polityky na Ukraini (hruden 1919–1920 rr.)," *Ukrainskyi istorychnyi zhurnal*, 1961, no. 1, p. 30; Iu. I. Tereshchenko, "Polityka 'voiennoho komunizmu' na Ukraini," *Ukrainskyi istorychnyi zhurnal*, 1980, no. 10, p. 85.

[60] P. S. Zahorskyi and P. K. Stoian, *Narysy istorii komitetiv nezamozhnykh selian* (Kiev, 1960), pp. 22–26.

[61] Kulichenko, *Borba Kommunisticheskoi partii za reshenie natsionalnogo voprosa*, p. 400.

and those of the Executive Committees (of the Soviets.)''[62] They seem
to have functioned as so many petty tyrannies with no interference whatsoever from the outside world:

> Who guided the work of the *komnezamy*? Formally the actions of the
> *volost* and village *komnezamy* were regulated by *uezd* and provincial
> *komnezam* subsections under responsible subsections of the Soviet
> (*Ispolkom*) administration. *In fact the komnezamy were left to themselves
> and were guided in all their actions by their "revolutionary" self-
> consciousness.*

Membership in such practically omnipotent bodies, he added, brought
"real privileges and advantages to members." Occasionally there was
a congress or conference on the *uezd* or province level, and these served
to give the *komnezamy* whatever instruction or supervision they got.
Both the Party and state were, as our witness put it, "extremely hesi-
tant" to look into the operations of these bodies.[63] A fear that many
of the *komnezamy* had been taken over by more prosperous villagers
led to a purge of many members, but afterwards the *komnezam* leadership still left much to be desired. An order from an *uezd komnezam*
official of May 22, 1922, given in response to a query about how to
deal with those who protested the way in which a local body did its
work, is illustrative of how these bodies dealt with disagreements. If
"kulak counterrevolution interferes with your work," the *uezd* official
counseled his village friend, lock those responsible up for 15 days; if
that does not suffice, "shoot them."[64]

The reliance upon rough and ready expedients like the *komnezamy*
is less an indication of malicious intent than a symptom of the pervasive
rural hostility toward the regime, a "united front in the villages against
Soviet power," as one writer dubbed it.[65] The *komnezamy* continued
to function as *de facto* organs of power side by side with the village
Soviets until this situation of "dual power" was ended by the 1925
reorganization of the *komnezamy* into "voluntary social organizations,"
that is, when political power was taken away from them.[66] Such policies
doubtless helped produce the famine of 1921–22 in which, according

---

[62] S. Kagan, *Agrarnaia revoliutsiia na Kievshchine: K voprosu o sotsialnykh i
politicheskikh protsessakh na seli* (Kiev, 1923), pp. 31–34. Quotation from p. 14.

[63] *Ibid.*, p. 15.

[64] *Ibid.*, p. 17.

[65] Ravich-Cherkasskii, *Istoriia KP(b)U*, p. 170.

[66] Popov, *Narys istorii KP(b)U*, pp. 284–288; Zahorskyi and Stoian, *op. cit.*, pp. 88–94.

to Soviet figures, Russia had 23 million hungry at the end of 1921, and Ukraine had an additional four million hungry in the following spring.[67]

By the end of 1919, the KP(b)U had dropped its earlier opposition to the Ukrainian language as such. No longer did figures like Rakovskii denounce Ukrainian as a "kulak" tongue. Rather, there was a growing realization, as a Bolshevik publication put it in 1920, that

> the Ukrainian language is not a Petliurist language, but just a language, and like all languages it is only a means by which the toilers may be organized. To think otherwise means being naive, falling prey to Russian chauvinism, and forced assimilation.[68]

While the above realization was a step forward, it would not in itself suffice to overcome the legacy of hostility to which past Bolshevik errors had given birth. The KP(b)U could not reach the Ukrainian peasantry unless it could provide literature in Ukrainian, but the boycott of the regime by the Ukrainian intelligentsia guaranteed that the Party's Ukrainian language publications were, as a Bolshevik put it, "a torture to read."[69]

Mykola Skrypnyk was the most thoughtful of the Old Bolsheviks in reappraising the nationality question. In 1920 he published an article entitled "Donbas and Ukraine," in which he analyzed what he saw as the greatest obstacle to establishing a stable Soviet government in Ukraine, the estrangement of the Ukrainian peasantry from the Russian proletariat. Skrypnyk pointed out that Ukraine differed from Russia in several important respects: its peasantry was more important politically, its "kulaks" were stronger and better organized, and its towns were divided from the countryside by barriers of language and culture. The KP(b)U, he argued, had echoed the Russian proletariat's prejudice against things rural and Ukrainian. The fall of the autocracy had brought the Ukrainian masses to national and political life under the UPSR and USDRP. "But," he wrote,

> our Communist Party was from the very beginning of 1917 hindered in its attempt to influence the peasantry by the Russian chauvinist (*rusotiapskymy*) prejudices of backward segments of Ukraine's urban workers. Our tragedy in Ukraine lies in the very fact that we had to rely on the support of a working class, Russian by nationality or assimilation, which

---

[67] *Ibid.*, p. 54.

[68] *Kommunist*, January 24, 1920, as quoted by S. K. Hutianskyi, *V. I. Lenin i kulturne budivnytstvo na Ukraini* (Kiev, 1965), p. 65.

[69] E. Kasianenko, "Kriza movy i shliakh ii rozvytku skriz sotsiializmu," *Komunist*, no. 1, August 1920, p. 9. The title is itself indicative of the problem.

despised the least hint of the Ukrainian language and Ukrainian culture,
to impose ourselves with the support of it and its forces upon the peasantry
and rural proletariat; and those who were of Ukrainian nationality, owing
to complex historical circumstances, approached with suspicion and
mistrust everything Russian—"Muscovite".[70]

The only solution, Skrypnyk believed, lay in establishing real linguistic
equality and aiding the development of Ukrainian culture: "to raise the
Ukrainian peasant to the level of the proletarian city."[71]

Skrypnyk was not alone in thinking along such lines. Even a former
leader of the Russophile "Katerynoslavan" wing of the Party like
Iakovlev-Epshtein argued the same lines. He declared that the lack of
real equality of the Russian and Ukrainian languages in state institutions created "at every step estrangement of the rural population from
our Soviet organs, which [estrangement] is used by our enemies, the
Petliurists." Only by carrying on agitation and propaganda in Ukrainian, by opening Ukrainian schools and bookstores, and by publishing
more Ukrainian books, pamphlets, brochures, and textbooks could the
Ukrainian masses be raised "to the level of conscious, revolutionary
activity." Only by giving the Ukrainian language equality in Party and
state institutions and not just by passing decrees to that effect could the
Bolsheviks "bring these institutions truly close to the overwhelming
majority of the poor peasantry and proletariat."[72] The issue of linguistic
equality became especially important when confronting the issue of
"kulak banditism." At the November 1920 Fifth KP(b)U Conference,
Iakovlev ended his report on the question with the words: "Transforming the Ukrainian language into our weapon—this is the task we must
never forget when we talk about banditism."[73]

Meanwhile, the former Borotbisty were becoming more assertive in
the Party. At the Fifth Conference there was a Borotbist-led opposition
known as the Autonomists. On the eve of the conference Blakytnyi wrote
an article entitled "The Communist Party of Ukraine and the Way For
It To Be Strengthened," restating the old Borotbist position that Ukraine
ought to be more independent.[74] At the conference, he complained that

---

[70] Mykola Skrypnyk, *Statti i promovy z natsionalnoho pytannia* (Munich, 1974), pp.
9–18. Quotation from p. 11.

[71] *Ibid.*, p. 12.

[72] Ravich-Cherkasskii, *Istoriia KP(b)U,* p. 171.

[73] *Ibid.*, p. 180.

[74] H. Ovcharov, "Z pryvodu vysvitlennia pytannia pro borotbyzm," *Komunist Ukrainy,*
1958, no. 2, p. 40.

in the months since the merger of the Borotbisty with the KP(b)U, a "complete welding together" had not come to pass. In terms not calculated to flatter his Russian comrades, he declared, "That portion of the communists that came to communism through the channel of the Ukrainian revolution remains isolated from the portion that travelled the path of the bourgeois-national Russian revolution." Both wings, he said, ought to strive to overcome their respective nationalism. He stated that all power in the KP(b)U must reside in its representative Central Committee, not in Moscow, that the proletariat must be Ukrainized if it is to lead the countryside, and that communists coming from Russia to Ukraine must "assimilate themselves into the basic cadres of the KP(b)U, . . . throwing off their specifically Russian characteristics."[75]

Still, the KP(b)U continued to take steps designed to place Ukrainian on an equal footing with Russian. A decree of February 21, 1920, declared Ukrainian equal with Russian in all civil and military institutions in Ukraine.[76] A decree of September 21 of the same year directed the Commissariat of Public Education to work out a plan for introducing Ukrainian in all educational institutions and organize evening courses in each province and *povit* town to teach Ukrainian to civil servants. The decree also directed the State Publishing House to publish more textbooks in Ukrainian and ordered that Ukrainian be used in all government offices.[77]

The Tenth Congress of the Russian Communist Party in March 1921 took the first tentative step toward guaranteeing national equality by committing the Party to take active steps to foster the development of non-Russian cultures. Largely as a result of the arguments of non-Russian communists, the final resolution adopted by the congress went considerably farther than the original draft presented by Stalin. As adopted, the resolution condemned Russian "great power chauvinism" as a greater danger than local nationalism and ordered communists to take active measures aimed at helping formerly oppressed nationalities overcome the legacy of national oppression and illegality.[78] Soon thereafter, an all-Ukrainian Party conference was held to discuss ways of carrying out the Tenth Congress resolutions, especially the transition from War

---

[75] Ravich-Cherkasskii, *Istoriia KP(b)U,* p. 174.

[76] *Kulturne budivnytstvo v Ukrainskii RSR,* vol. 1, p. 63.

[77] *Ibid.,* vol. 1, pp. 71–72.

[78] *Desiatyi sezd RKP(b), mart 1921 goda: Stenograficheskii otchet* (Moscow, 1963), pp. 182–213, 598–704; final resolution, pp. 598–607.

Communism to the NEP and the new nationality policy. Stalin, who attended as Moscow's representative, urged those present to recognize that Ukrainians would ultimately become dominant in the cities of Ukraine and that communists should do everything in their power to help Ukrainians develop their national culture:

> the Ukrainian nationality exists and the development of its culture is the obligation of communists. You cannot go against history. It is clear that if Russian elements have hitherto been dominant in the cities, with the passage of time these cities will inevitably be Ukrainized.[79]

This was a far cry from past policies. At the Eighth Congress in 1919, it had been all Lenin could do to prevent the Party from repudiating the slogan of national self-determination.[80] Now the Party was committed to actively fostering national equality. But would even that be enough?

Meanwhile, the question of the nature of the Soviet federation had to be answered. Until 1923 the various Soviet Republics were united in a *de facto* union sanctioned by bilateral agreements with the Russian federation, in Ukraine's case the Russo-Ukrainian Military and Economic Union of 1920.[81] Under such treaties, military and economic unity gradually led to greater political centralization, reinforced all the while by a centralized communist party of which the non-Russian communist parties were considered regional organizations subject to directives from the center.[82] The Military-Economic Union checked the earlier policy of merely extending Russian organs to Ukraine by establishing a number of joint commissariats, but such joint commissariats were far more responsive to directives from Moscow than to Ukrainian priorities.[83] The centralization of authority also subtly changed the ground rules of politics in the non-Russian republics. It became impossible for a regional group even to hope to win a victory without support from Moscow.

---

[79] Ravich-Cherkasskii, *Istoriia KP(b)U*, p. 181. Stalin said the same thing in almost the same words earlier at the Tenth Congress. *Desiatyi sezd RKP(b)*, p. 213.

[80] *VIII sezd RKP(b)*, pp. 40–92. Bukharin and Piatakov opposed Lenin.

[81] Jurij Borys, *The Sovietization of Ukraine*, pp. 300–312.

[82] The process of political centralization has been traced by Richard Pipes, *The Formation of the Soviet Union: Communism and Nationalism, 1917–1923* (New York, 1968), pp. 242–255 and by František Silnický, *Natsionalnaia politika KPSS*, pp. 199–217.

[83] At the Twelfth Congress, Rakovskii declared that the Union commissariats were taking too much power and that nine-tenths of their authority should be returned to the national republics. *Dvenadtsatyi sezd RKP(b), 17–25 aprelia 1923 goda: Stenograficheskii otchet* (Moscow, 1968), p. 573.

Both in Party and state affairs, Moscow remained the final arbiter of disputes. Even national communists would have to appeal to Moscow for support. Autonomy was possible only if and only to the extent that the center allowed it.

By 1922 it was decided that a more formal union was desirable. For one thing, ideological imperatives seemed to demand greater centralization, and Lenin saw autonomy as a temporary expedient, "a transitional form to the complete unity of the workers of various nations."[84] In Ukraine, however, Rakovskii and Skrypnyk were trying to halt the process of centralization or at least to keep such a union as decentralized as possible. Perhaps Rakovskii was trying to insulate his own position as a head of state for the uncertainties that lay ahead as Lenin grew more feeble, but Skrypnyk seems to have been genuinely converted to the idea that Ukraine ought to be as autonomous as possible. At the Eleventh RKP Congress in 1922, Skrypnyk denounced unchecked centralism as a manifestation of Russian chauvinism and identified it with *smenovekhovstvo,* that is, support of the Soviet regime on the grounds of Russian nationalism and not out of a desire for socialism.[85] In the discussions concerning the form that the new Soviet Union would take, Skrypnyk and Rakovskii advocated broad rights to non-Russian republics. Rakovskii opposed the idea that the USSR even have a constitution, preferring to leave all questions to be worked out individually as the need for cooperation arose on specific issues. Skrypnyk wanted the Commissariats of Foreign Affairs and Foreign Trade to be jointly controlled by the republics and the Union rather than by the All-Union authority. These points he failed to win, but one important feature of the Soviet Constitution was proposed by Skrypnyk and adopted at Lenin's insistence: that the All-Union legislature be bicameral with a Chamber of Nationalities.[86]

A thoroughgoing reappraisal of Bolshevik nationality policy took place in 1923. In March of that year, the RKP Central Committee made public

---

[84] "Federation is a transitional form to the complete unity of the workers of various nations. In practice federation has already displayed its expediency both in the RSFSR's relations with other Soviet republics (Hungary, Finland, and Latvia in the past as well as Azerbaijan and Ukraine in the present) and also within the RSFSR (for example, the Bashkir and Turkestan autonomous republics in the RSFSR, created in 1919 and 1920)." Lenin, *PSS,* vol. 41, p. 164. "Tezisy ko II. Kongresu Kommunisticheskogo Internatsionala" (1920).

[85] Skrypnyk, *Statti i promovy z natsionalnoho pytannia,* p. 21.

[86] Koszeliwec, *Mykola Skrypnyk,* pp. 86–87.

a lengthy document that was to be adopted the following month by the Twelfth Party Congress in the form of a new resolution on the nationality question. The Seventh KP(b)U Conference, held in early April in anticipation of the Congress, heard Trotsky who addressed the body on behalf of the RKP Central Committee. Trotsky expressed shock that many communists thought of the nationality question as solved and emphasized the connection between the nationality and peasant problems. He counseled communists in Ukraine to avoid antagonizing the peasantry along national lines and warned against attempting to force the Russian language on rural Ukrainians. Trotsky's words were echoed by N. N. Popov, a Secretary of the KP(b)U Central Committee, who published an article on the opening day of the Conference. Popov assailed Party members who suggested Russification as a method of conquering the Ukrainian countryside, who denied the existence of Ukrainian culture and the need for Ukrainian propaganda and institutions, and who recognized the existence of a Ukrainian culture but strove to prevent its spread to the cities. Peasant nationalism, Popov concluded, was a potent force, and the party had to come to terms with it by learning to conduct Party and cultural work in the Ukrainian language.[87]

The Twelfth Congress resolution on the nationality question committed Party organizations in the non-Russian parts of the USSR to a policy that became known as "indigenization" (*korenizatsiia*). In Ukraine it was known as Ukrainization and was designed to do exactly what the name implied: make the KP(b)U more Ukrainian and thereby cloak it in an aura of national legitimacy. The Twelfth Congress resolution committed the Party to the recruitment of non-Russians who knew the local language and way of life, to insure that Party and state organs functioned in the local language rather than in Russian, and to take all possible measures to foster the development of the local language and culture.[88] Resolutions had encompassed some of these ideas before. By the Twelfth Congress everyone knew, as Skrypnyk put it, "Passing resolutions is not important; what is important is carrying them out."[89] Ukrainization was carried out. Rakovskii was transferred from Ukraine a short time later, no doubt for his allegiance to Trotsky in the developing struggle for power. In 1925, Kviring was replaced as head of the KP(b)U by Lazar Kaganovich, a loyal Stalinist who was committed to carrying

---

[87] Dmytryshyn, *Moscow and the Ukraine, 1919–1953*, pp. 57–60.
[88] Text of the resolution is in *Dvenadtsatyi sezd RKP(b)*, pp. 57–60.
[89] *Ibid.*, p. 573.

out Ukrainization according to Moscow's dictates. Ukrainization would become the central issue in Soviet Ukrainian political cultural life for a full decade after the Twelfth Congress.

Ukapism—The Last Soviet Party

At the time of the Twelfth Congress, Soviet Ukraine had one thing that Soviet Russia lacked, a legal opposition party. The Ukrainian Communist Party, known as the Ukapisty after its initials, was almost the last non-Bolshevik "Soviet" party to be eliminated in the USSR.[90] Only in 1925 was it abolished and most of its members incorporated into the KP(b)U. For most of its existence it played a role like that which the Borotbisty once had: a loyal opposition, committed to Soviet power but critical of Russian domination of Ukraine through the KP(b)U.

The Ukapisty were an offshoot of the USDRP, which had split after the German occupation into a Petliurist Right wing and a pro-Soviet Left. The Left was known as the Nezalezhnyky (Independents), and as early as December 1918 a Nezalezhnyk Organizational Bureau was set up in Kiev. Its principles were summed up in the title of its printed organ, *The Ukrainian People's Socialist Republic:* replacement of the Ukrainian Directory by an independent Soviet Ukrainian government composed of Ukrainians who were equally committed to building Ukrainan independence and a socialist society. At the same time, the Nezalezhnyk Orgburo resolutely opposed the KP(b)U as an anti-Ukrainian organization that had consistently violated Ukrainian national rights, perverted the idea of the dictatorship of the proletariat to mean the dictatorship of their Party, and been obsessed with violence as a solution to every conceivable problem. The split in the USDRP became official at the party's Sixth Congress in January 1919, when the Nezalezhnyky walked out after the congress rejected a Nezalezhnyk resolution that called for the transformation of the Ukrainian People's Republic into a socialist state. Soon the USDRP Nezalezhnyky were functioning as an independent party with its own official organ, *Chervonyi prapor* (Red Banner).[91]

---

[90] It has often been mistakenly stated that the Ukapisty were the last legal opponents of the Bolsheviks in the USSR. There was, however, a Jewish Communist Workers Party (Poalei Tsion), which was allowed to exist legally as a non-Bolshevik political organization until 1928. On this group, see Baruch Gurevitz, *National Communism in the Soviet Union, 1918–1928* (Pittsburgh, 1980), pp. 42–64; 94–109.

[91] Khrystiuk, *Zamitky i materiialy,* vol. 4, pp. 49–56, 69–73; V. A. Chyrko, "Krakh ideolohii ta polityky natsionalistychnoi partii Ukapistiv," *Ukrainskyi istorychnyi zhurnal,* 1968, no. 12, pp. 24–27.

Like the Borotbisty, the Nezalezhnyky initially adopted the Soviet platform and tried to work through the Soviets and other political institutions officially sanctioned by the Piatakov regime. But the mounting intensity of official oppression soon made it virtually impossible for them to function legally. The Nezalezhnyk leadership came to the conclusion that the only way to prevent the Bolsheviks from turning Ukraine into a Russian colony was to fight them on the battlefield. Their leader, Iurii Mazurenko set up a Nezalezhnyk *revkom* in Kiev Province under the protection of Otaman Zelenyi. Mazurenko sent the Bolsheviks an ultimatum stating that the Nezalezhnyky would fight for Soviet power, national self-determination, and against the "plunderers of the toiling masses," that is, for Bolshevik principles, which the Bolsheviks had violated.[92] The revolt spread, attracting a number of other *otamany* and the remnants of Hryhoriiv's army. The Bolsheviks were less than pleased at the prospect of having their officially enunciated principles turned against them. One member of the Soviet Ukrainian government rather unaesthetically equated the uprising with a case of syphilis.[93] Nezalezhnyk participation in the revolt of Otaman Zelenyi soured relations between the future Ukapisty and the Bolsheviks for a long time to come and is probably the single most important factor explaining why the Ukapisty would never attain the respectability in Bolshevik eyes that the Borotbisty ultimately gained.

When Denikin's Volunteer Army supplanted the Bolsheviks in Ukraine, it became apparent to the Nezalezhnyky that effective opposition to the new regime required collaboration with some larger political force. Since the Nezalezhnyky had already broken with the Bolsheviks and no political party could expect cooperation from the anarchist Makhnovists, Petliura's Directory was the only possible ally. While Petliura was far too "bourgeois" for Nezalezhnyk tastes, he was at least Ukrainian and went to considerable lengths to reach a *modus vivendi* with the Nezalezhnyk *revkom*. The association was short-lived due to Petliura's reluctance to militarily oppose the Whites. After the Nezalezhnyky learned that Petliura had surrendered one position after another to Denikin's forces without a fight, they repudiated their agreement with Petliura and declared that they would fight both the Directory and the Volunteer Army. Militarily they could not long hold out against two vastly more powerful forces. In October 1919 two

---

[92] The text of this ultimatum is in Vynnychenko, *Vidrodzhennia natsii,* vol. 3, pp. 346–347.

[93] *Ibid.,* vol. 3, p. 347.

Nezalezhnyk leaders, Mazurenko and Tkachenko, fled to Moscow in hopes of finding some basis for cooperation with the Bolsheviks.[94]

In January 1920 the Nezalezhnyky imitated the Borotbisty in holding a congress, which changed their name to Ukrainian Communist Party, thereby raising the number of Ukraine's communist parties to three. Known by their initials as the Ukapisty, they were stronger in their public criticism of the KP(b)U than the Borotbisty had been, while they followed the Borotbist example of petitioning the Comintern for admission as the sole representative of the Ukrainian proletariat. In order to buttress their claim to represent a full-fledged alternative to the KP(b)U, the Ukapisty also published a detailed program that contained proposals on everything from the treatment of religion to public health, along with a theoretical discourse on the function of law.

The central concern of the Ukapisty was, of course, the nationality question. It is in reference to this question that the Ukapisty made their case most forcefully. Their basic argument may now seem rather commonplace for anyone familiar with anti-imperialist arguments made by Third World thinkers today, but it was quite original for 1920. According to the Ukapist program, imperialism is in a crisis that, on the one hand, threatens colonial peoples with "the destruction of their national-political life as well as their national culture." On the other hand, it simultaneously raises the economic level of colonial peoples, thereby stimulating them to consolidate their economic powers and strive for national liberation. Since imperialism creates an abnormally weak native bourgeoisie, the national struggle overlaps with the struggle against capitalism. This gives communists the opportunity to lead the national liberation struggle and harness it to the cause of socialism. In backward countries like Ukraine, this means that the national liberation struggle, once it has accomplished its strictly national tasks, will tend to be transformed into a communist revolution by the force of its own internal dynamics. All that is needed is a party capable of leading it to communism. Not surprisingly, the Ukapisty proclaimed themselves ready and able to perform this task. However, they further claimed that it was not merely a question of whether the RKP would recognize the national aspect of the Ukrainian revolution. The Ukapisty argued that revolutions take place within given national-territorial entities and that refusal to recognize the national aspect of a given revolution could only harm its chances for success. The Ukapist view of the national and social

---

[94] Ravich-Cherkasskii, *Istoriia KP(b)U*, pp. 142–143.

aspects of revolution was dialectical: while revolution must grow organizationally from the internal forces of a given nation, the in- interdependence of the world capitalist system precluded the achieve- ment of the national and social liberation of the, workers except on a world scale. The goal, the Ukapisty argued, must be an independent socialist republic for every nation, albeit associated in "close comradely alliance" (*soiuz*) with others.[95]

The Memorandum of the Ukrainian Communist Party to the Congress of the Third Communist International set forth the Ukapist case for recognition as the sole representative of the Ukrainian proletariat. The document begins with a historical sketch of the Ukrainian revolution designed to show why a Ukrainian Communist Party was needed when the KP(b)U already existed as a regional organization of the RKP. The Ukapisty argued that the legacy of colonial oppression in Ukraine had brought about a distinctly Ukrainian revolutionary process, led first by revolutionary *intelligenty* like Shevchenko and Drahomanov, by the RUP at the turn of the century, and later by the USDRP. In 1917, the Ukapisty stated, the USDRP had been the most active party in the Ukrainian Cen- tral Rada, possessed a membership in the tens of thousands, and exerted much influence over the Ukrainian proletariat. By contrast, the Rus- sian Bolsheviks of the KP(b)U had played no part in the national revolu- tion and refused to recognize that the Ukrainian masses aspired to national as well as social liberation. The Bolshevik view of the Ukrainian move- ment as simple chauvinism had led them to exclude themselves from the Ukrainian revolution. Despite the fact that they occasionally recog- nized positive aspects of the Ukrainian revolution, they set out to destroy everything Ukrainian when they got control of Ukraine. Still, the revolu- tion's internal forces continued to develop and crystallize, leading the split in the USDRP when its most revolutionary elements left their former comrades to form the Nezalezhnyky. The Zelenyi-Nezalezhnyk revolt against the Bolsheviks in no way diminished the revolutionary creden- tials of the Ukapisty, the memorandum argued; it was the inevitable result of the KP(b)U's policies, which were a holdover from tsarist days of national oppression. In January 1920 the Nezalezhnyky completed their evolution toward communism, took the name Ukrainian Communist Party, and began to lead Ukrainian workers and peasants toward com-

---

[95] *Prohrama Ukrainskoi Komunistychnoi Partii* (Vienna-Kiev, 1920). In addition to this version published by Vynnychenko's Foreign Group of the UKP, an earlier version was published in Kiev on the "Chervonyi prapor" typography. While pagination dif- fers, the text is identical.

munism. As a regional organization of the RKP and because of its old imperialist habits, the KP(b)U was incapable of doing this, the Ukapisty argued. For this reason, the Comintern should admit the Ukapisty as the sole recognized leaders of all proletarians in Ukraine.[96]

The memorandum then turned to the problem of colonial revolution in general, arguing that it was a question that the world communist movement could ill afford to ignore, for capitalism and imperialism have made inevitable the struggle of oppressed peoples for national liberation and political independence. Taking as their starting point Lenin's argument that imperialism exports its surplus capital to the colonies, the Ukapisty argued that this influx of capital had the unintended effect of fostering the consolidation of a given colonial people as an economic organism based on its own natural economic and geographical conditions. The result of this process, they maintained, was that the colonial nation develops a tendency to seek liberation from its colonial oppressors. The world communist movement then is faced with the problem of what to do about these colonial movements that arise as an inevitable concomitant of the transition from capitalism to socialism.[97]

The memorandum then turned to analysis of the Ukrainian revolution as a particular manifestation of these processes. Ukraine, they pointed out, was a colony of Russia, which had in turn been a semi-colony of Western European capitalism. At the same time, Ukraine was also a national-economic organism that had developed even faster than had the empire of which it was a part. The Russifying policies of tsarism had led to the preponderance of Russians among skilled workers in Ukraine, while Ukrainians had been relegated to the less skilled strata of the proletariat largely owing to official encouragement of the emigration of skilled workers from Russia proper. When the revolution came, the Russian proletariat in Ukraine followed the lead of its counterpart in Russia proper and followed a path of revolutionary development completely independent of the Ukrainian revolution. The Russian proletariat had failed to understand Ukrainian aspirations and the fact that the Ukrainian masses also needed to carry through the bourgeois revolution to its socialist culmination.[98]

The memorandum concluded by arguing that the internal logic of class forces in Ukraine required the establishment of an independent Soviet Ukraine with its own economic, political, and party centers. The

---

[96] *Memorandum Ukrainskoi Komunistychnoi Partii Kongresovi III. Komunistychnoho Internatsionalu* (Vienna-Kiev, 1920), pp. 3–17.

[97] *Ibid.*, pp. 18–22.

[98] *Ibid.*, pp. 22–33.

KP(b)U's failure to understand this fact, the Ukapisty argued, had been objectively responsible for strengthening the counterrevolution. The formation of the Borotbisty as a self-proclaimed communist party was one product of the simultaneous Ukrainian strivings for national independence and Soviet-style socialism. But, according to the Ukapisty, the Borotbisty had been imprisoned by their narodnik heritage, which had been responsible for their ideological weakness and for the irresolution of their cadres. This weakness had in turn led the Borotbisty to join the KP(b)U, while the best "proletarian" cadres of the Borotbisty had come over to the Ukapisty. Even within the KP(b)U, the memorandum noted, there were Russian Bolsheviks who had come to see that a separate Ukrainian revolutionary center was necessary and who realized that the KP(b)U's dependence on Moscow rendered it incapable of playing this role. The resulting schism in the KP(b)U had gone deep and had led those in control to purge many of their new Borotbist compatriots and to rely more and more upon opportunistic elements drawn from Ukraine's Russified cities or simply imported from Russia proper. Only the Ukapisty, the document added, could be a real Ukrainian communist party able to lead all Ukraine's communist forces and take its rightful place in the Comintern alongside the communist parties of other countries.[99]

The Ukapist memorandum was a plea to treat Ukraine like a separate nation and is reminiscent of arguments made earlier by those who supported Soviet rule but not Russian domination. Moreover, by presenting its own schema of the forces leading to colonial revolutions in Ukraine and elsewhere, the Ukapisty put the Ukrainian question in the larger framework of a universal process, the struggle of colonial peoples for national liberation. The Comintern was not yet ready for the idea that communism and national liberation might have something in common. While today communist support for national liberation struggles outside the Soviet sphere of influence (undoubtedly, in the hope of expanding that sphere) has become almost axiomatic, in 1920 the Comintern was still committed to the classical Marxist notion that the transition from pre-capitalist colonial existence to socialism was impossible. It is illustrative of Bolshevik attitudes toward the Ukapisty that on July 19, 1920, the KP(b)U politburo ordered that the Ukapist organ *Chervonyi prapor* be immediately closed down in view of what was called its "clearly chauvinist character."[100]

---

[99] *Ibid.*, pp. 33–36.

[100] Kulichenko, *Borba Kommunisticheskoi partii za reshenie natsionalnogo voprosa*, p. 429.

Volodymyr Vynnychenko, who had parted company with the Directory in early 1919 and drifted toward the left, saw agreement with the Bolsheviks as the sole hope for Ukrainian statehood and saw the Ukapisty as a logical vehicle for such an arrangement. Vynnchenko had been convinced by the ease with which the Bolsheviks had driven the Directory out of Kiev at the beginning of 1919 that Ukrainians could not maintain their independence by relying solely on their own forces.[101] They needed an ally, but what kind of ally depended on what kind of Ukraine was to exist. Vynnychenko came to the conclusion that neither the monarchist Ukraine of the Hetmanate nor a bourgeois Ukraine would be able to retain its Ukrainian character, because the Ukrainians lacked both a gentry and a bourgeoisie. Any Ukraine except for a Soviet one would have to rely on non-Ukrainians for support and inevitably lose its Ukrainian character. Only a socialist Ukraine, a state based on the workers and peasants, could retain its national character.[102]

That made the Bolsheviks natural allies. While other Ukrainians had attempted to come to terms with Lenin, none of them possessed the prestige of the former Ukrainian prime minister. The basis for agreement would have to be an independent Soviet Ukraine led by Ukrainians, in other words, the Ukapist platform. In February 1920 Vynnychenko organized a "Foreign Group of the Ukrainian Communist Party" in Vienna, sponsored similar groups in other European cities, got the Ukapisty to accept him as one of their own, and set up his own organ, *Nova doba* (New Era). The Bolsheviks, immediately recognizing the propaganda value of having the former head of the Directory in a Bolshevik government, held out the possibility of an accommodation. In May 1920 Vynnychenko set out for Moscow hoping to achieve a fully independent Soviet Ukraine led by the Ukapisty.[103]

After arriving in Moscow on June 3, Vynnychenko met with a series

---

[101] Vynnychenko expressed the idea as early as August 1919 in an outline for an unfinished pamphlet: "It is now impossible for us to build Ukrainian statehood with our own forces." Archive of Volodymyr Vynnychenko, Ukrainian Academy of Arts and Sciences in the U.S., document group 3, part 1, 2, folder K2e, p. 3. The same document also states that "the defeat of the Bolsheviks is the defeat of Ukrainian statehood and labor."

[102] This argument is developed in V. Vynnychenko, *Ukrainska derzhavnist* (Vienna-Kiev, 1920).

[103] V. A. Chyrko, "Krakh ideolohii ta polityky natsionalistychnoi partii Ukapistiv," *Ukrainskyi istorychnyi zhurnal*, 1968, no. 12, pp. 28–35. Hryhory Kostiuk. *Volodymyr Vynnychenko ta ioho doba: Doslidzhennia, krytyka, polemika* (New York, 1980), pp. 49–50.

of snubs and delays, which forced him to conclude that the Bolsheviks were serious neither about a merger with the Ukapisty nor about allowing a genuinely independent Soviet regime to exist in Ukraine. He began a campaign designed to convince Bolshevik leaders that the excessive centralism of the RKP structure was detrimental to the cause of the revolution. At the end of June he travelled to Kharkiv and for a few weeks held the posts of Deputy Head of the Council of People's Commissars and Commissar of Foreign Affairs in the Soviet Ukrainian government. But it became clear that he was to be treated as a mere figurehead. This propaganda coup enabled the Bolsheviks to boast of the "bankruptcy" of Ukrainian nationalism as evidenced by the defection of one of its most prominent leaders. Vynnychenko returned to Moscow, where he received word that the Ukapisty had disowned him. On August 25 he was given permission to leave for the West.[104] In a draft letter intended for the RKP Central Committee, Vynnychenko rather melodramatically described his fate: "I have decided to leave Russia and go abroad. If not forever, at least for a long time to come, I have ended my political career by committing suicide."[105]

The failure of Vynnychenko's mission had consequences beyond the fact that it brought to an end the career of one of the Ukrainian revolution's most colorful and mercurial figures. It demonstrated that, while the Bolsheviks were ready to make use of any individual or group that could help strengthen their position, they would share power with no one. Had the Ukapisty merged with the KP(b)U in 1920 as did the Borotbisty, they would still have been unable to change the situation without the support of Moscow, for that was where the final power of decision remained. The RKP leadership was clearly unwilling to change this crucial circumstance.

The failure of Vynnychenko's mission also had another consequence. For a few months during 1920 the Ukapisty enjoyed a favored position. Not only had they been legalized, but the party was even briefly subsidized by the Bolsheviks. This came to an end with their prospects of joining the government.[106] The Ukapisty were reduced to the status of a legal but impotent opposition.

---

[104] *Ibid.*, pp. 49–56, 210–225; Melanie Czajkowskyj, "Volodymyr Vynnychenko and His Mission to Moscow and Kharkiv," *Journal of Ukrainian Graduate Studies*, no. 5, 1978, pp. 6–24.
[105] Archive of Volodymyr Vynnychenko, gr. 3, pt. 1, 2, K5b, 2, "Nedokladnaia zapiska, a pismo TsK RKP."
[106] Chyrko, "Krakh ideolohii ta polityky," pp. 28–35.

The Ukapisty became ever more outspoken opponents of "Red imperialism," attacking the Russo-Ukrainian military-economic union as a continuation of colonialism and the product of a tradition of Russian chauvinism, which the Bolsheviks had never been able to overcome.[107] At times, various Ukapisty made statements that sounded downright treasonous to Bolshevik ears. For example, the Ukapist Oliinyk declared that Russia was exploiting Ukraine mercilessly:

> ...industry in Moscow and Leningrad uses Ukrainian coal and Ukrainian metal. We also have factories working, but they don't profit the workers and peasants much because the iron pots they make are all sent to Great Russia.[108]

Another Ukapist was even more outspoken, declaring in public, "Down with the KP(b)U!" and "Tsar Nikolai built monuments, and they are gone. Lenin's monuments will go, too."[109] Never numerous, the Ukapisty were no political threat to the Bolshevik regime in Ukraine.

In August 1924 the Ukapisty applied for admission to the Comintern one last time, and on December 17, 1924, a special commission on the Ukrainian question was appointed. Representatives of the KP(b)U, the Ukapisty, and the so-called Ukapist Left Fraction, a small group of Ukapisty who had been recruited by the regime to undermine the party from within and who had been expelled by the main body of the party in 1923, were given one final opportunity to present their respective cases.[110] Of the Bolshevik representatives, only the former Borotbist Oleksander Shumskyi would admit that the Ukapisty had fought for the revolution and played only an "objectively counterrevolutionary" role by appealing to peasant backwardness and bourgeois nationalism.[111] More typical of the KP(b)U view was Skrypnyk, who charged:

> In the initial period of the NEP, when we had not yet overcome many of our shortcomings, they came to the workers and said, "If you live badly, it is because Moscow rules." They go the prosperous peasants and tell them: "They rob you. Bread is sent from Ukraine to Moscow."

---

[107] An Ukapist pamphlet denounced the resolution of the Fourth All-Ukrainian Congress of Soviets in precisely these terms. V. Levynskyi, *Iedyna nedilyma Sovitska Rosia? (Na pravakh rukopysu)* (Kiev-Vienna, 1920).
[108] As quoted by M. Halahan, "Likvidatsiia U.K.P.," *Nova Ukraina*, vol. 4, 1925, no. 1, pp. 33–34.
[109] *Ibid.*, p. 32.
[110] *Kak i pochemu Ispolkom Kominterna raspustil UKP* (Kharkiv, 1925).
[111] *Ibid.*, pp. 90–96.

That is their program in practice. Allow me to ask, how the propaganda of these "communist" statements by this "communist" party differs from the counterrevolutionary propaganda carried on by our enemies? There is no difference. The Ukapisty oppose Russia to Ukraine. So do the Petliurists. Both the Ukapisty and the Petliurists play on the proprietary instincts of the peasants. In what is the difference? In the fact that the Ukapisty conceal their activities under the name of communists.[112]

As for the Left Fraction, the vehemence of their attacks on the Ukapist majority for the latter's "nationalism" and "counterrevolutionary activities" gave credence to Richytskyi's charge that the Fraction was only a group of provocateurs organized by the GPU.[113] In any case, the conclusion was foregone from the beginning, and the Comintern Executive Committee ordered the Ukapisty and its Left Fraction to disperse and mandated the KP(b)U to establish joint commissions with both groups to pass on the admission of Ukapisty and members of the Left Fraction into the KP(b)U.[114] In January 1925 the Ukrainian Communist Party officially dissolved itself.[115] A few weeks later, the Left Fraction did likewise.[116]

*   *   *

Ukrainization was part of the all-Union program of indigenization adopted at Moscow's insistence and pushed through despite the opposition of many members of the still preponderantly Russian KP(b)U. Ukrainian communists were always dependent upon Moscow's favor because while popular democracy in Ukraine would in all likelihood have ended the rule of the KP(b)U, Party democracy would in all likelihood have imperiled the position of non-Russian figures in the KP(b)U. This is seen from the fact that, although about 80% of Soviet Ukraine's inhabitants were Ukrainians, Ukrainians remained a minority in the KP(b)U until 1927.[117] For the time being, however, the position of Ukrainians in the Party and state was assured because Moscow saw that it was in the interests of stable Soviet rule to accord non-Russian regimes as much

---

[112] *Ibid.*, p. 67.

[113] *Ibid.*, pp. 55–60.

[114] *Ibid.*, pp. 145–149.

[115] Halahan, "Likvidatsiia U.K.P.," pp. 26–38; Chyrko, "Krakh," pp. 28–35.

[116] "Likvidatsiinyi zizd livoi fraktsii UKP," *Visty VUTsVK,* March 14, 1925, p. 4; "Likvidatsiia livoi fraksii UKP," *Visty VUTsVK,* March 15, 1925, p. 3.

[117] For figures on the national composition of the KP(b)U, see Basil Dmytryshyn, "National and Social Composition of the Membership of the Communist Party (bolshevik)

national legitimacy as possible. As Kalinin put it in 1926, the government realized that it was in its interest to maintain the national feeling of non-Russians in the USSR. ''Only under such conditions . . . will each nationality consider the Soviet Union its fatherland.''[118]

The Twelfth Party Congress resolution on the nationality question represented at least a partial vindication of those who had long argued to the effect that a stable Soviet Ukraine was impossible unless it was willing to assume a Ukrainian national character. The decision to adopt a policy of Ukrainization was above all a promise that the regime in Soviet Ukraine would not only foster Ukrainian cultural development but also gradually transform itself into a Ukrainian regime. It was an attempt to give Soviet Ukraine some measure of national legitimacy.

To be sure, it was a gamble for the Soviet Union to bank on stability through the recognition and encouragement of the national diversity of its inhabitants. The gains it promised were tremendous, because it would not only guarantee the stability of the Soviet regimes in the so-called borderlands, but also raised the possibility that kindred peoples bordering on the Soviet Union might begin to look to ''their'' national states inside the USSR. Yet, there was also the inherent danger that different nations inside the USSR might aspire to different paths of development and that this could lead to powerful centrifugal forces within the Union. How could the processes legitimized by the Twelfth Party Congress be kept in bounds? How far would this new Soviet surrogate for national liberation be allowed to go? These would soon become the central political questions for the Communist Party (bolshevik) of Ukraine.

---

of the Ukraine, 1918–1928,'' *Journal of Central European Affairs,* vol. 17, 1957, no. 3, pp. 243–258.

[118] Quoted by Zvi Gitelman, *Jewish Nationality and Soviet Politics: The Jewish Sections of the CPSU, 1917–1930* (Princeton, 1972), p. 417.

PART TWO

Ukrainization and Its Crisis

CHAPTER THREE

Oleksander Shumskyi and the Problem of Ukrainizing Soviet Ukraine

THE TWELFTH PARTY Congress adopted the indigenization policy in hopes of bringing the peoples of the Soviet Union closer together. The goal was for the regime to melt into the various non-Russian nations so as to lead them toward a *rapprochement* and a gradual withering of national division. The policy was based on the assumption that official encouragement of national cultural development would be received with gratitude, and that coming to terms with national diversity would ultimately foster international unity by demonstrating that such unity held nothing to fear.

Reality was quite different from Bolshevik assumptions. What if encouraging national diversity only stimulated people to aspire to be *more* different rather than less? What if they decided that they did not want Russian influence at all? What if they decided that they wanted more independence than Moscow felt it could allow? Such questions smacked of the conventional wisdom which Lenin had tried to refute in his writings on nationality. Leninists, therefore, assumed that Lenin would be proved correct, and the fears of his critics, unfounded. Unfortunately for them, just the opposite happened. Within three years after indigenization was introduced, Oleksander Shumskyi would call for the removal of the head of the KP(b)U sent by Stalin to push Ukrainization faster, and would demand that he be replaced by a Ukrainian. In literature, Mykola Khvylovyi would call for the total rejection of Russian cultural influence, and would demand that Ukrainian culture orient itself toward Western Europe. Within five years, Mykhailo Volobuiev would argue forcefully that Ukraine was being exploited by Russia and treated like a colonial dependency. Moscow would be shocked that such awkward questions were even being raised, and would intervene to stop such heresies.

Practically everything distinctive about Ukraine's brand of communism was directly or indirectly traceable to the Borotbisty, that group

86

of Ukrainian revolutionaries led by Oleksander Shumskyi and Vasyl Ellan-Blakytnyi that joined the KP(b)U in 1920. Before the Twelfth Congress, Shumskyi and Blakytnyi were in the forefront of those in the Party who pressed for concessions to the Ukrainian nationality. After the Twelfth Congress, they were in the forefront of the KP(b)U's attempt to gain some measure of national legitimacy through official sponsorship of national-cultural development. Shumskyi's so-called national deviation consisted in his pressing for more rapid Ukrainization and for it to be carried to the very summit of political authority. His demands were viewed by Moscow as a threat to the unity of the USSR; everything he had ever done was labelled "Shumskyism." Even the old idea of the KP(b)U as the product of a merger of Russian Bolshevism and Ukrainian Borotbism was rejected on the grounds that the Borotbist heritage was "un-Leninist". The campaign against Shumskyi caused a political crisis when it provoked an open schism in the Communist Party of Western Ukraine, which in turn cost the Soviet Government much of the support it enjoyed in the Ukrainian areas west of the Soviet Union's border. The campaign did not, however, mean abandoning the idea that Soviet Ukraine was following its own road to socialism, a notion that would survive until the regime's decisive break with the peasantry during the first Five Year Plan. The campaign against Shumskyi was merely a first step toward what would later become an organized effort to banish all national particularism from Soviet life. For the moment, it served only to mark the limits of how far Soviet Ukraine would be allowed to stray from the Russian model.

The KP(b)U and Ukrainization, 1923–1925

The basic outline of the Ukrainization policy and the reasons for its adoption have been explained by others in far greater depth than need be attempted here. Briefly, during the revolution the Ukrainians had been able to develop a variety of national institutions. The Bolsheviks, unable to reverse what the Ukrainians had achieved, attempted to place themselves at the head of the movement. The Bolsheviks recognized that Ukraine would never be pacified unless they came to terms with its national aspirations by adopting Ukrainian culture as their own and by overcoming the language barrier between the regime and those it ruled. Zatonskyi gave perhaps the best description of what Ukrainization basically involved when he explained it as not just the formal equality of the Russian and Ukrainian languages, but as an active policy of fostering the development of Ukrainian culture, Ukrainizing the Party and state administrations, and de-Russifying Ukrainians who had been Russified in the past.[1]

Ukrainization made itself felt in the cultural realm long before the political apparatus. Prominent members of the still predominantly Russian KP(b)U were far from eager to Ukrainize the regime itself. For one thing, it meant learning a new language, one that the Bolsheviks, like city-dwellers generally, tended to regard as a peasant tongue. To many it seemed that siding culturally with the Ukrainian countryside over the more advanced Russian-speaking urban centers was a step backward. Typical of the views held by many non-Ukrainian Bolsheviks in Ukraine were those voiced by Dmitrii Lebed, a secretary of the KP(b)U Central Committee. Shortly before the Twelfth Congress, Lebed expounded his "theory of the struggle of two cultures," arguing that a struggle between the Russian and Ukrainian cultures was inevitable in Ukraine, and that the Party should side with the Russian culture of the urban proletariat against the relatively backward Ukrainian countryside. His argument was in direct opposition to what would soon become known as Ukrainization. As Lebed himself wrote:

> To take upon ourselves the task of actively Ukrainizing the Party and, consequently, the working class (and in this matter the Party cannot avoid carrying its work over to the working class) at the present time would be reactionary from the standpoint of the interests of cultural development because nationalization, i.e., the artificial implantation of the Ukrainian language in the Party and the working class, given the present political, economic, and cultural relationships between town and country, would mean taking the position of the lower culture of the countryside in preference to the higher culture of the city.[2]

Lebed's idea of an inevitable struggle of national cultures in Ukraine was quickly cast beyond the pale, because such a struggle was precisely what the regime hoped to end. In fact, his "theory of the struggle of two cultures" achieved a sort of negative immortality in that the charge of reviving it was leveled against practically anyone who voiced an opinion out of step with the official Party line on the nationality question.

---

[1] V. Zatonskyi, *Natsionalna problema na Ukraini* (Kharkiv, 1927), pp. 3–4. The basic outlines of the Ukrainization policy are discussed by Basil Dmytryshyn, *Moscow and the Ukraine, 1918–1953: A Study of Russian Bolshevik Nationality Policy,* pp. 56–90.

[2] D. Z. Lebed, *Kommunist,* March 27, 1923, as quoted by E. F. Hirchak, *Na dva fronta v borbe s natsionalizmom* (Moscow-Leningrad, 1930), p. 20 and M. M. Popov, *Narys istorii Komunistychnoi Partii (bilshovykiv) Ukrainy,* p. 274n. Emphasis in the original.

But Lebed, and others who were willing to accept Ukrainization grudgingly, did not suffer much. After the Twelfth Congress, Emmanuil Kviring, leader of the Party's Katerynoslavan wing, became First Secretary of the KP(b)U. Lebed was Second Secretary and number two man in Ukraine's Party hierarchy.[3]

Kviring's record as First Secretary shows him as something less than an ardent Ukrainizer. The probable reason for this was that his tenure corresponded with the beginning of the struggle for Lenin's succession, and defeating "Trotskyism" had a much higher priority than pursuing Ukrainization. It may well have been that the two goals appeared to conflict: since the majority of the KP(b)U's members were non-Ukrainian, any attempt to proceed vigorously with the Ukrainization of the Party and State would have risked a Russian backlash and increased dissatisfaction with the RKP's ruling triumvirate.[4] Certainly, the KP(b)U leadership backed away from its early commitments in this area.

Immediately after the Twelfth Congress, before the rift inside the Russian Politburo became public, the KP(b)U and the Soviet Ukrainian government announced measures indicating a strong commitment to Ukrainization. A Central Committee resolution of June 1923 outlined a program of Ukrainization of the Party, and on August 1, the government published its first Ukrainization decree. The latter measure reasserted the regime's commitment to the right of all citizens to deal with state organs in their own language, recognized Ukrainian as the language of the overwhelming majority of citizens, and prohibited the state from employing any person not fluent in Ukrainian as well as in Russian. All state employees were to be completely bilingual within a year.[5] This noteworthy promise was not kept, although the shortage of available qualified personnel would have made it difficult to do so with even the best of intentions.

By the Eighth KP(b)U Congress in May 1924, the struggle against Trotskyism was at its height, and Ukrainization had clearly ceased to be a priority with Kviring. In his official report to the Congress, Kviring refrained from either supporting or rejecting the Twelfth Congress resolutions, but strongly hinted that the matter would not be pushed.

[3] Robert S. Sullivant, *Soviet Politics and the Ukraine, 1917–1957,* p. 107.

[4] The possibility of the Trotsky consideration slowing Ukrainization is mentioned by Vsevolod Holubnychy, "Outline History of the Communist Party of the Ukraine," *Ukrainian Review,* no. 6, 1958, p. 84.

[5] The texts of the Party resolution of June 22 and the state decree of August 1, 1923, are in *Kulturne budivnytstvo v Ukrainskii RSR,* vol. 1, pp. 229–232, 242–247.

He noted that the membership of the KP(b)U was already one-third Ukrainian and that there was much talk to the effect that Ukrainization had gone far enough. He explicitly condemned the "forcible Ukrainization of national minorities," particularly the Russian workers of Ukraine's cities.[6] Since there is no evidence of "forcible Ukrainization" whatsoever at this juncture, it can only be concluded that Kviring's attack upon this imaginary evil functioned as a coded reference for disapproval of Ukrainization as such.

Certainly, state employees who did not wish to trouble themselves with studying the language spoken in the countryside had little reason to fear enforcement of the Ukrainization decree. A report on the progress of Ukrainization, published after the end of Kviring's tenure, stated that few of those employed in the central offices of the various state agencies took seriously the requirement for studying Ukrainian until 1926.[7] That was a year after Kviring's removal. And Ukrainization of the party always lagged behind even the modest steps taken by state employees.

During the Kviring years Ukrainization was most obvious in the realm of culture; here the former Borotbisty were particularly prominent. Vasyl Ellan-Blakytnyi became editor-in-chief of the official daily organ of the state, *Visty VUTsVK,* and founded Hart (The Tempering), an organization to foster the development of Ukrainian writers of proletarian origin. Another former Borotbist, Serhii Pylypenko, was Blakytnyi's main assistant at *Visty* and headed Pluh (The Plow), Hart's far more active counterpart devoted to helping aspiring writers of peasant origins develop their skills. In 1925 Shumskyi became Commissar of Education, a post that placed him in overall charge of education and culture.[8]

In April 1923 a new journal appeared which gave visible proof of the opportunities which the Soviet government was prepared to grant the Ukrainian culture. *Chervonyi shliakh* (Red Pathway), edited by Shumskyi, was a Ukrainian counterpart to the Russian "thick journals" that had long been foci of intellectual life in Petrograd and Moscow. Advertised as a journal of cultural, social, and political discussion, *Chervonyi shliakh* published new Ukrainian writers committed to the revolution

---

[6] Holubnychy, "Outline," p. 84; Iwan Majstrenko, *Storinky z istorii Komunistychnoi Partii Ukrainy,* vol. 2, p. 27.

[7] "U Kharkovi. Stan ukrainizatsii ustanov mista i okruhy," *Visty VUTsVK,* June 10, 1927, p. 5.

[8] On the privileged position of the former Borotbisty in Soviet Ukrainian cultural life, see George S. N. Luckyj, *Literary Politics in the Soviet Ukraine, 1917–1934,* pp. 43–44.

as the sole hope for the national and social liberation of the Ukrainian masses. These new writers were usually of proletarian or peasant origin, and, as the dreary norms of socialist realism were not yet dreamt of, given broad scope for their talents. The new journal stood as visible proof that in collaboration with the Soviet regime, ample opportunities existed for the development of Ukrainian culture.

The editorial foreword to *Chervonyi shliakh's* first issue set the journal's tone by recognizing the Ukrainian revolution as a national as well as a social phenomenon, and by committing the journal to providing a "responsible orientation" to readers in a Ukraine that had been freed from its former colonial status and had entered upon the process of building its own national culture.[9] One of the basic themes which the journal attempted to hammer home was that Soviet Ukraine was truer to Ukrainian revolutionary traditions than the nationalist émigrés who had "sold out" to foreign imperialism. This argument was most forcefully made in an article by Shumskyi himself, in which he attacked the "new cossackdom" of the émigré nationalists, accusing them of having betrayed the tradition of Shevchenko's struggle against both national and social oppression. Shumskyi argued that the Ukrainian socialists had shown themselves impotent against class oppression, the elimination of which was as vital to the masses as was national liberation. According to Shumskyi, only Soviet power could accomplish both the national and the social liberation of the masses.[10] Such a line of argument is eloquent evidence of how radically things had changed in the half decade since the Piatakov regime, when the Bolsheviks equated Ukrainianness with counterrevolution.

The Quest for National Legitimacy

The ascendance of the Borotbisty in cultural affairs, and the official sponsorship and scope given to Ukrainian culture, led many Ukrainian émigrés to question the validity of continued opposition to the Soviet Ukrainian regime. Despite the fact that real power remained in Russian hands, the newfound benevolence toward things Ukrainian contrasted mightily with the anti-Ukrainian sentiments of the new nation states of Poland and Rumania. While tiny Transcarpathia lived under relatively benevolent rule of Czechoslovakia, Ukrainian schools and cultural institutions found it increasingly difficult to function in Poland

---

[9] "Vid redaktsii," *Chervonyi shliakh,* 1923, no. 1, pp. iii–iv.

[10] O. Shumskyi, "Stara i nova Ukraina," *Chervonyi shliakh,* 1923, no. 2, pp. 91–110.

and Rumania, as the new polities of East Central Europe were more interested in assimilating their national minorities than in placating them.[11] With constructive national activities becoming less possible in Western Ukraine, Soviet Ukraine seemed to show signs of gradual evolution in the direction of a Ukrainian national state. Ukrainian nationalism as it had grown up in Eastern Ukraine was also still socialist in orientation, and many émigrés saw the war and the revolution as the beginning of the end of world capitalism. Could not the undoubted shortcomings of Soviet Ukraine be overcome in time? Was not the Ukrainian nation, in the absence of any ruling class of its own, socialist by its very nature, and was the proletariat not its sole natural ally? Could not Soviet power provide a framework for a government of the peasants and workers? After all, even communist spokesmen predicted that Ukrainians would ultimately predominate in Ukraine's cities.[12] Given that, would not Soviet Ukraine inevitably become more and more a Ukrainian nation state as time passed? As rural "banditism" died out, it became obvious that armed opposition to Soviet Ukraine was hopeless. Ukrainization helped convince many prominent Ukrainians that Soviet Ukraine was the last best hope for their nation.

One by one prominent members of the nationalist emigration returned. Iurko Tiutiunnyk, the leader of Petliura's partisans in 1920–21, in 1923 returned to Soviet Ukraine and published an open letter urging his fellow exiles to follow. The following year Mykhailo Hrushevskyi, leader of the Central Rada and first President of Ukraine, did likewise.[13] Upon returning they found ample opportunities for cultural work. Hrushevskyi, his nation's most prominent scholar, took charge of the history section of the Ukrainian Academy of Sciences. Tiutiunyk turned his talents to writing.

Sometimes the Soviet press would refer to this movement of reconciliation to the Soviet regime as "Ukrainian *smenovekhovstvo*" (literally, change-of-landmarks-ism), thereby equating it with the Russian movement that argued for reconciliation with the Bolsheviks on grounds of Russian national interest. Ustrialov's Smena Vekh group believed that

---

[11] On the nationalities policy of interbellum Poland, see, for example, Stephan Horak, *Poland and Her National Minorities, 1919–1939* (New York, Washington, Hollywood, 1961).

[12] Stalin made such a prediction at the First All-Ukrainian Party *Soveshchanie* as well as at the Tenth RKP Congress. Stalin, *Sochineniia*, vol. 5, p. 49; Ravich-Cherkasskii, *Istoriia Kommunisticheskoi Partii (b-ov) Ukrainy*, p. 181.

[13] *Visty VUTsVK*, January 4, 1924, pp. 1–2; March 9, 1924, p. 1.

the Bolsheviks would inevitably assume the traditional roles of Russian statesmen simply because they ruled Russia; they had already united almost all the lands of the old empire in the USSR. Ustrialov predicted that their revolutionary aspirations would be far more transitory than the dynamics of their reconstituted empire. Many Ukrainians argued in similar fashion that the imperatives of ruling Ukraine would ultimately force the initially fictitious Soviet Ukrainian statehood to assume weightier content. This type of Sovietophilism became particularly widespread in Western Ukraine.[14] By early 1925, the strongest political party there, the *trudovyky,* could refer to

> the well-known and indisputable fact that the *Ukrainian national idea is developing, growing, and becoming stronger in Soviet Ukraine.* Side by side with the growth of this idea *the alien framework of a fictitious Soviet Ukrainian statehood* is being filled with the native content of genuine statehood. As Ukrainian nationalists, for us this is the crucial fact in the crystalization of our attitude toward Soviet Ukraine. The form which power takes and the people who exercise it are one thing; the nucleus of statehood as such is something quite different.[15]

The KP(b)U's attitude toward the phenomenon was ambivalent: it wanted and cultivated the support of prominent Ukrainians while protesting its own purity from any influences of such "bourgeois nationalism."

At the Eighth Congress of the KP(b)U in 1924, a declaration addressed to the Ukrainian Soviet intelligentsia and to Soviet society as a whole was presented. It bore the signatures of sixty-six prominent intellectuals, including former members of the UNR government such as Mykola Chechel, Pavlo Khrystiuk, and Mykola Shrah. Known as the Declaration of the Sixty-Six, it was printed in the official state organ, *Visty VUTsVK.* The declaration traced the process by which the intelligentsia had been won over to Soviet Ukraine and noted that only the Bolsheviks' earlier national nihilism had prevented reconciliation. It accepted the Twelfth Congress resolutions as a serious attempt by the Bolsheviks to overcome their past errors, and declared that with Ukrainization the Soviet Union had gained the opportunity to take Ukrainians beyond the borders under its protection. Those who felt qualified to speak for the Ukrainian nation were thus telling the regime that they

---

[14] Alexander J. Motyl, *The Turn to the Right: The Ideological Origins and Development of Ukrainian Nationalism, 1919–1929* (Boulder, 1980), pp. 57–60.

[15] Quoted by Roman Solchanyk, *The Communist Party of Western Ukraine,* p. 165.

would accept the Soviet regime because it held promise for the Ukrainian nation. They would accept it only on those grounds and only so long
as such was the case. Clearly, they intended their declaration to be a
covenant between rulers and ruled.[16]

The regime responded to the Declaration of the Sixty-Six by equating
it with views once expressed by Pitirim Sorokin and denounced by Lenin.
Those who had signed the document, argued a front page editorial in
Visty, were "bourgeois democrats" who placed the idea of the fatherland
above social class and the revolution.[17] This could be interpreted in a
dual sense. Party members should remain immune from temptations to
place national considerations above those of the working class, while
those outside the Party, for whom the national interest was paramount,
could best serve it by reconciliation with the Soviet regime.

Communists were certainly tempted by the prospect of assuming the
role of protector for Western Ukrainians and of making Soviet Ukraine
a magnet for their irredentist aspirations. In 1924 the Fifth Comintern
Congress, in its resolution on the nationality question in Central Europe
and the Balkans, ordered European Communist Parties to give full support to the aspirations of national minorities, and replaced the old slogan
of national self-determination with the more definite one of "the political
separation of the oppressed peoples from Poland, Rumania,
Czechoslovakia, Yugoslavia, and Greece." The Ukrainian question was
described as "one of the most important national problems in Central
Europe," the solution to which was dictated by the interests of the revolution in Poland, Czechoslovakia, and Rumania. The resolution declared
that the problem of the Ukrainian minorities "form(ed) one Ukrainian
national question, demanding a common solution for all these countries."
That solution was the separation of the Ukrainian territories from these
countries, "their union with Soviet Ukraine and through it, with the
Union of Soviet Socialist Republics."[18] Clearly, Ukrainian aspirations
were being recognized as one of the potentially most promising factors
for breaking down the *Cordon sanitaire* on the Soviet Union's Western
border, and for extending the Bolshevik revolution into Europe.

Soviet Ukrainian spokesmen waxed enthusiastic. Serhii Pylypenko,

---

[16] "Vidozva do ukrainskoi radianskoi intelihentsii ta vsoho radianskoho suspilstva,"
Visty VUTsVK, May 18, 1924, p. 2.

[17] "Uvahy spryvodu dekliaratsii 66," *Visty VUTsVK,* May 18, 1924, p. 1.

[18] "Resolution on National Question in Central Europe & Balkans," *The Communist
International,* no. 7, December 1924–January 1925, pp. 93–99. Quotations from pp.
93, 95, 96.

de facto editor of *Visty* during Blakytnyi's illness, wrote an editorial in which he spoke of a Ukrainian Socialist Federal Soviet Republic including all Ukrainian territories as "realistic dreams." [19] Vlas Chubar, Soviet Ukrainian head of government, later declared:

> The border with Poland was drawn in such a way that there are fathers who live on one side of the street as citizens of Ukrainian SSR, while their children on the other side of the street are under Poland... Those masses of Ukrainians who live under the yoke of the capitalist countries must learn from us that they must create their own regime and that they must break down the artificial borders. [20]

Soviet Ukraine was ready to do everything in its power to teach them.

Kaganovich and Shumskyi

If the Soviet Ukrainian regime was to retain the degree of national legitimacy that the beginnings of Ukrainization had given it, changes in the top leadership of the KP(b)U were imperative. As long as the Party was led by Kviring, Ukrainization was likely to remain confined to cultural affairs. But the balance of power within the KP(b)U changed abruptly in April 1925 when Kviring was replaced as First Secretary by Lazar Kaganovich, a trusted lieutenant of Stalin who was sent from Russia with orders to pursue vigorously the Ukrainization of the Party and state. [21] Although Kaganovich spoke Ukrainian fluently enough to use it in his public speeches, he was not an ethnic Ukrainian, but a Jew born in Ukraine. [22]

Kaganovich immediately began to press Ukrainization forward. In his first public statement, the new First Secretary demanded that Ukrainization be extended to the Party itself. [23] Shortly thereafter, Chubar defended the necessity for such a course by warning that the Party could hope to lead the Ukrainian cultural process, which it now was sponsoring, only if it Ukrainized itself, and that otherwise the Party risked

---

[19] S. Pylypenko, "USFRR (Realistychni mrii)," *Visty VUTsVK,* July 3, 1924, p. 1.

[20] "Vidchyt Ukrainskoho Uriadu na sessii TsVK SRSR. Doklad tov. Chubaria," *Visty VUTsVK,* April 17, 1926, p. 1.

[21] *Visty VUTsVK,* April 8, 1925, p. 3.

[22] Janusz Radziejowski, "Kwestia narodowa w partii komunistycznej na Ukraine radzieckiej (1920–1927)," *Przegląd historyczny,* 1971 no. 3, p. 458. Majstrenko, *Storinky z istorii KPU,* vol. 2, pp. 37–38.

[23] "Cherhovi zavdannia partii. Doklad tov. Kahanovycha," *Visty VUTsVK,* April 10, 1926, p. 3.

abdicating leadership of the movement to the ideologically alien Ukrainian national intelligentsia:

> Thus far we have failed to give sufficient attention to the matter of our Party gaining mastery over all those processes which are growing and developing in Ukrainian life on the basis of national tendencies. Our influence on the masses in this area of their life has been very weak. But the ideological influence of the Ukrainian intelligentsia which, of course, fosters nationalistic deviations among the masses and particularly among the peasantry, is constantly becoming more widespread, and an immediate danger of the possible alienation of the broad peasant masses and of certain segments of the proletariat from our Party will exist as long as the Party fails to follow the path marked out by the decisions of the Twelfth Congress on the nationality question.[24]

In other words, Bolshevik sponsorship of Ukrainian culture had helped to effect an outburst of national creativity over which the Party had no real control. In order to get control and to prevent such "processes" from getting out of hand, the Party had to fight the national intelligentsia on its own ground and to defeat it in its bid for the cultural leadership of the Ukrainian nation. The Party could not hope to do this unless it rapidly transformed itself into a Ukrainian force.

For this reason, the KP(b)U Central Committee ordered the Ukrainization of the Party and trade union apparatuses. At the same time, it set January 1, 1926, as the deadline for the complete Ukrainization of the state administration.[25] This would have meant that all Party, state, and trade union business in Ukraine would have been conducted exclusively in the Ukrainian language.

Kaganovich also pressed for the immediate Ukrainization of Red Army formations in Ukraine. A few days after the April Central Committee plenum, he addressed a conference of the Kiev Military District, arguing that rapid Ukrainization of the army was absolutely vital if Soviet rule was to avoid the appearance of a foreign occupation:

> if the Ukrainian peasant who joins the army sees people with bayonets speaking to him in a language other than his own and not taking his language seriously (and those who approach it with snickering irony are the guilty ones), then the peasantry will look at this army as an army of occupation instead of its own army.[26]

---

[24] V. Chubar, "Pro ukrainizatsiiu partii," *Visty VUTsVK*, April 17, 1925, p. 1.

[25] *Kulturne budivnytstvo v Ukrainskii RSR*, vol. 1, pp. 282–286.

[26] *Kommunist*, April 12, 1925, as quoted by Kyianyn, "Na Ukraini," *Nova Ukraina*, 1925, no. 1, p. 91. Parentheses in the original.

Clearly, Kaganovich was determined to see to it that the Ukrainian language would predominate in the major institutions of Soviet Ukraine. This development seemed the fulfillment of the fondest hopes of those who favored rapid Ukrainization; yet a year later, the KP(b)U began a campaign of character assassination against Shumskyi as a "super-Ukrainizer" and "national deviationist." The timing of the anathemas hurled against Shumskyi is significant because they coincide with the formation of the United Opposition against Stalin, a coalition of Stalin's former partners in the ruling RKP triumvirate with Trotsky.[27] We know that Stalin was sufficiently concerned with the possibility of such a coalition to make overtures to Trotsky in hopes of preventing it.[28] Was Shumskyi offered up to Russian Communists in Ukraine as a sop to the opponents of Ukrainization? A variety of important posts were held by those who opposed the policy, particularly in the Donbas and in the trade union apparatus.[29] Figures on the national composition of new candidate members of the KP(b)U indicate that efforts to recruit more Ukrainians into the Party were slowed down in the second half of 1926. In the second half of 1925, 54% of new KP(b)U candidates were Ukrainian; in the first half of 1926, 55.1% were; in the second half of 1926, the percentage of Ukrainians dropped to 52.6%, and in the first half of 1927, to 48.8%. During the same period, the percentage of new candidates who were Russians rose from 26.8%, in the first half of 1926, to 33.2% in the first half of 1927. A KP(b)U Politburo directive of May

---

[27] Stalin's letter to Kaganovich and the KP(b)U Central Committee denouncing Shumskyi, the beginning of the campaign against him, is dated April 26, 1926. The Russian Central Committee plenum of April 6–9, 1926, marked Trotsky's first active political foray in two years. It was at this meeting that Dzerzhinskii accused Trotsky and Kamenev of uniting in a new opposition. This was not yet the case, but it certainly became clear to Stalin at this time that such an alignment was in the making. Edward Hallett Carr, *Socialism in One Country, 1924–1926* (Baltimore, 1970), vol. 2, 289–292.

[28] According to the memoirs of one of Trotsky's leading followers, Stalin offered Trotsky the Commissariat of Industry. Victor Serge, *Memoirs of a Revolutionary, 1901–1941* (London and New York, 1963), p. 210.

[29] Majstrenko counts among such opponents of Ukrainization Radchenko, head of the Ukrainian trade union federation, two of the most influential *okrug* Party Secretaries in the Donbas, the head of the Kharkiv Party organization, the head of agitprop for the Kharkiv *okrug,* and a member of the KP(b)U Politburo. Majstrenko, *Storinky,* vol. 2, pp. 34–36. Later Party documents also allude to internal Party opposition to Ukrainization at this time. One of these mentions "serious obstacles" which the Party had to overcome in carrying out Ukrainization, including "a certain inertia with which a certain part of the Party *aktiv* met these directives" and Ukrainian chauvinism. *Dva roky roboty. Zvit Tsentralnoho Komitetu Komunistychnoi Partii (bilshovykiv) Ukrainy* (Kharkiv, 1927), p. 52.

9, 1927, contained an instruction that the admission of non-workers into the Party was to be halted until the next Party Congress. Since those barred were mostly non-Russians, the order had the effect of strengthening Russian preponderance in the KP(b)U.[30] In short, the campaign against Shumskyi was accompanied by a watering down of efforts to Ukrainize the Party. This would suggest that both actions were designed to increase the support of the Russian contingent in the KP(b)U for the ruling triumvirate.

In terms of the struggle against the United Opposition, there was little danger in alienating the Ukrainian contingent in the Party. The former Borotbisty had always been widely distrusted by Party members as representatives of an "un-Leninist" heritage.[31] Shumskyi's communist allies were in the Communist Party of Western Ukraine (KPZU) which had never been part of the Russian Communist Party and did not participate in the internal affairs of the VKP(b). Nor was there much chance of Ukrainian communists making common cause with the United Opposition, because the opposition advocated more rapid industrialization, to be financed by the peasants. Shumskyi, who had come to the Party as a leader of Ukrainian peasants, could never have joined those willing to sacrifice the interests of the peasantry on the altar of industrialization. Dissatisfaction with Ukrainization could help Stalin's opponents in the Party, but sentiments in favor of more rapid Ukrainization could not. To the meager extent that nationality policy became an issue in internal Party struggles on the Union level, it was the Opposition that criticized Ukrainization as a violation of the rights of Russians in Ukraine.[32] Sacrificing Shumskyi could only strengthen Stalin's position in the Party, however much it might weaken Soviet Ukraine's laboriously created aura of national legitimacy.

----

[30] Basil Dmytryshyn, "National and Social Composition of the Membership of the Communist Party (bolshevik) of the Ukraine 1918-1928," *Journal of Central European Affairs*, vol. 18, 1957, no. 3, pp. 253-254.

[31] Jurij Borys, "Who Ruled the Soviet Ukraine in Stalin's Time?" *Canadian Slavonic Papers*, vol. 14, 1972, no. 2, p. 219.

[32] The most vocal critic of Ukrainization was Iurii Larin, who attacked the policy in *Pravda* and in the All-Union Central Executive Committee, always drawing sharp rebuttals from KP(b)U spokesmen. See *Pravda*, May 12, 1925; *Visty VUTsVK*, May 22, 1925; *Soiuz Sovetskikh Sotsialisticheskikh Respublik: Tsent. ispolnytelni komitet, 3 sozyva, 2 sessiia. Stenograficheskii otchet* (Moscow, 1926), pp. 458-474, 499-500. Borys, "Who Rules," p. 224, claims that Larin's statements were "more or less sanctioned by Stalin" but offers no evidence to support a view which, upon close examination, seems little short of incredible. It is highly unlikely that Stalin would "sanction" criticism of Ukrainization six weeks after replacing the head of the KP(b)U for drag-

Shumskyi's "crime" evidently stemmed from a meeting that took place during the fall of 1925. Shortly after the Second Congress of the KPZU, a group of KPZU leaders accompanied Shumskyi on a trip to Moscow for a meeting with Stalin. According to a former member of the KPZU Central Committee interviewed by Janusz Radziejowski, Shumskyi broached the subject of why the KP(b)U should not be headed by a Ukrainian, especially since there were already sufficiently qualified Ukrainian Bolsheviks such as Skrypnyk and Chubar. At the time, Stalin answered only that such a step was not yet expedient.[33]

Stalin presented his own summary of Shumskyi's arguments in a letter of April 26, 1926, addressed to Kaganovich and the KP(b)U Central Committee Politburo. According to Stalin's account, Shumskyi had argued that Ukrainization was in difficult straits because it was being effected only reluctantly and with long delays. Ukrainian culture and the Ukrainian intelligentsia were growing rapidly; however, the Party was unable to assume leadership of this movement because leading elements in the Party and trade unions were deliberately hindering Ukrainization. According to Shumskyi, the Party could not hope to assert its leadership over the quickly developing national cultural movement, unless it were led by people who had direct ties to the Ukrainian culture. What ought to be done, Shumskyi was reported as saying, was to remove Kaganovich, replace him with Chubar, and name former Borotbist Hryhorii Hrynko to be head of government in Chubar's place. Shumskyi supposedly even threatened to be of no further use to the Party if these steps were not taken.[34]

---

ging his feet on the matter. Larin himself seems to have been a political maverick and was quite outspoken about the "kulak threat" in the mid-twenties and advocated a "second revolution" in the countryside at a time when Stalin condemned all those who wanted to fan the flames of class struggle in the countryside. See Isaac Deutscher, *Stalin: A Political Biography* (New York and London, 1966), p. 319; E. H. Carr, *Socialism in One Country, 1924–1926,* vol. 1, pp. 256, 259, 266, 283–284, 324, 346, 415, 490, vol. 2, pp. 343, 352. Among the leaders of the United Opposition, Zinoviev attacked Ukrainization at the April 24, 1927 meeting of the Presidium of the All-Union Central Executive Committee. "Natsionalne pytannia na Ukraini ta opozytsiia," *Bilshovyk Ukrainy,* 1927, no. 10, p. 4. Zinoviev was here quoted as having recalled how Lenin had disciplined Stalin on the nationality question and denouncing Ukrainization as a policy which "helps the Petliurists" and encourages chauvinism. Popov, in his history of the KP(b)U wrote that "Actually, in 1926–27, the Trotskyite opposition was the *de facto* representative of the Russian national deviation in Ukraine." Popov, *Narysy,* p. 293.

[33] Radziejowski, "Kwestia," p. 492.

[34] Stalin, *Sochineniia,* vol. 8, pp. 149–150. "Tov. Kaganovichu i drugim chlenam PB TsK KP(b)U."

The fact that Stalin addressed the letter to Kaganovich in particular, and to other Ukrainian Politburo members in general, left no doubt that the Ukrainian First Secretary enjoyed his total support. Still, Stalin conceded that Shumskyi had correctly pointed out the rapid growth of Ukrainian culture and the fact that it was absolutely vital for the Party to lead it. Stalin also agreed that those who were hostile to Ukrainization ought to be replaced by those who were committed to the program's success. Shumskyi's error, according to Stalin, lay in confusing the Ukrainization of institutions with an attempt to forcibly Ukrainize the proletariat. The Ukrainization of the working class could not be forced, Stalin wrote; it would take place only as a gradual process, as more Ukrainian peasants left the villages to take industrial jobs. Any attempt to force Ukrainian ways on Russian proletarians would serve only to alienate them from the Party, to foster anti-Ukrainian chauvinism, and would constitute a violation of their right to their own national culture. Stalin also accused Shumskyi of failing to see the "dark side" of the Ukrainian cultural life, as manifested in the desire of some Ukrainians for the estrangement of Ukrainian culture from cultural developments in other parts of the USSR and from Russian culture in particular. This, he warned, threatened to assume "the character of struggle against 'Moscow' in general, against Russians in general, against Russian culture and its highest attainment—Leninism." The young Ukrainian writer, Mykola Khvylovyi, was singled out for particular abuse from Stalin.[35]

Stalin also claimed to agree with Shumskyi that the KP(b)U leadership ought to become Ukrainian, but disagreed on the primary question of timing. Stalin argued that Ukrainians were still too weak in the KP(b)U for such a step to be taken immediately and scoffed at the idea of making Hrynko Ukraine's head of government, while pointing out that a number of Ukrainians were already in the leadership. He chose not to confront the issue of why they were unqualified to head the KP(b)U. Rather, he flattered them by referring to them as outstanding Old Bolsheviks, thereby implying that their loyalty might well be rewarded by higher posts in the future.[36]

The Campaign Against Shumskyism

The issue that Shumskyi had raised was an extremely sensitive one. After the dispute became public, an émigré Ukrainian journal character-

---

[35] *Ibid.*, pp. 150–153.
[36] *Ibid.*, pp. 153–154.

ized Shumskyi's position as arguing that "Ukrainization is not just a machination but the Ukrainization of the relations of power."[37] Phrasing the issue in these stark terms constituted the greatest imaginable embarrassment to the Soviet leadership. For this reason, the campaign against Shumskyi was continued in private until his removal could be accomplished by a swift stroke of political surgery. The campaign was similar to one later waged against Bukharin in Russia under the anonymous rubric of a "Rightist danger." In Ukraine, the campaign against Shumskyi was ostensibly about literature almost to the end. But then it spilled over into the KPZU and evolved into a scandal of international proportions.

According to Iwan Majstrenko, himself a former Borotbist, rumor once had it that Shumskyi had hatched a conspiracy to gain a majority on the KP(b)U Central Committee, overthrow Kaganovich, and effect the leadership changes which Stalin's letter credited him with having proposed. Andrii Khvylia, an ex-Borotbist, supposedly learned of Shumskyi's plans and reported them to Kaganovich, who, in turn, rewarded Khvylia by appointing him deputy head of Ukrainian agitprop.[38] When this alleged conspiracy was to be executed can only be a matter of speculation; whatever plans Shumskyi might have had were definitely cut short at the KP(b)U Politburo meeting of May 12, 1926.

Kaganovich laid the groundwork beforehand. A letter signed by him and Chubar, who would have been the chief beneficiary of Shumskyi's alleged conspiracy, was sent to all Central Committee members, thereby demonstrating that Kaganovich and Chubar stood together. This letter conceded the complex and difficult nature of the issues facing the Party but hinted that Shumskyi's motives had little to do with them:

> In Shumskyi's campaign (*vystup*) the subjective and like motives of Shumskyi himself must not be confused with the objective conditions of the country; the one must not be confused with the other by debasing the whole business to Shumskyi's acting peculiarly in a quarrel over a situation that he found disagreeable.[39]

Information on the May 12 meeting of the Politburo is extremely fragmentary. No minutes were ever published. That Shumskyi had to

---

[37] M. Sh., "Chudo sv. Antoniia i Oleksander Shumskyi," *Nova Ukraina*, 1927, no. 8–9, p. 72.

[38] Iwan Majstrenko, *Borot'bism: A Chapter in the History of Ukrainian Communism*, pp. 217, 250–251; Majstrenko, *Storinky z istorii KPU*, vol. 2, pp. 39, 65.

[39] *Ibid.*, vol. 2, p. 65.

defend himself at this time is evident from the scraps of his remarks
found in later articles. Perhaps his Borotbist past was attacked. At least,
he felt obliged to defend it in the following terms:

> I state that, aside from the struggle for the class and national liberation
> of the working class in union with the peasantry, there are no other tradi-
> tions in me. Throughout my entire revolutionary career, beginning in
> 1909, I have not retreated one iota from this. I renounce nothing in my
> past because I consider myself as having been an independent Bolshevik-
> Leninist in the conditions of Ukrainian realities, even though I had not
> yet entered Lenin's Party. I have no cause to renounce this, my past,
> but, on the contrary, I am proud of my past because in it there is nothing
> that would be unworthy of a Bolshevik revolutionary. From the first days
> of the revolution I was and now am a Ukrainian Bolshevik.[40]

What Shumskyi was saying was that the Borotbisty had been the Ukrainian counterpart to the Russian Bolsheviks and that therefore his revolutionary credentials were as good as those of any Old Bolshevik. Indeed,
the terms of the Bolshevik-Borotbist merger gave some support to such
a claim.[41] The earliest official history of the KP(b)U, written by Moisei
Ravich-Cherkasskii and published in 1923, argued that Ukrainian Communism was the product of "two roots" running through parallel Russian and Ukrainian revolutionary movements and culminating in the 1920
merger.[42] This remained the official view until 1927, when the "two
roots theory" was officially repudiated and labelled the basis of
"Khvylovyism" and "Shumskyism" in the KP(b)U.[43] Not until 1928,

---

[40] *Ibid.*, vol. 2, pp. 66–67.

[41] This was implicitly recognized by the fact that the *partstazh* of former Borotbisty
was listed as the date they had joined the Borotbisty or the date when the UPSR split
took place. See chapter two above.

[42] "The KPU is for us a great historical synthesis of the two great parallel movements
which embraced the huge masses of the workers of two nationalities: the Ukrainian and
the Russian." "Actually, *the merger of the Borotbisty with the Communist Party is the
end of the road along which two revolutionary forces in Ukraine travelled separately
for twenty years. One from the RUP to the KPU and the other from the first circles
of the RSDRP to the KPU.*" M. Ravich-Cherkasskii, *Istoriia Kommunisticheskoi Partii
(b-ov) Ukrainy,* pp. 5, 165. Emphasis in the original.

[43] D. Frid, "Do pytannia pro korinnia KPU," *Bilshovyk Ukrainy,* 1927, no. 10, pp.
39–50. Also condemned were the works of Osyp Hermaize, who traced the origins of
the Ukrainian revolutionary tradition to the RUP in a monograph on that group, and
Arnold Rish, whose monograph of the Ukrainian Social-Democratic Spilka also treated
it as an ancestor of the KP(b)U.

was Ravich-Cherkasskii's textbook replaced by a work of comparable scope.[44]

After joining the battle in the Politburo, Kaganovich took the issue before the entire Central Committee, which met on June 2–6, 1926. Ostensibly held to discuss Ukrainization, the plenum unanimously passed a resolution, "On the Results of Ukrainization." This resolution was to remain for several years the basic statement of communist nationality policy in Ukraine.

The resolution began in the customary fashion, with a historical summary of Bolshevik nationality policy, stating that it had always recognized the right of nations to self-determination without reservation, and that the October Revolution had given the Party the means to carry out this right in practice, while simultaneously paving the way for the international cooperation of the workers of different nationalities, a process which culminated in the creation of the USSR. Admitting early Bolshevik errors on the nationality question, the resolution gave the Borotbisty no credit for helping the KP(b)U overcome those errors. In fact, it never mentioned the Borotbisty, although the UPSR and USDRP were singled out for condemnation as representatives of the nationalist Ukrainian *petite bourgeoisie.* The Twelfth Congress of the Russian Communist Party was given complete credit for having set the Party on a correct course, and for decisively breaking with the "theory of the struggle of two cultures."[45]

The successes of Ukrainization were given unqualified praise. The resolution noted that 65% of the state's business was being executed in Ukrainian, as opposed to only 20% at the time of the previous year's April plenum. The state apparatus had largely switched to Ukrainization on the local level. Primary education had been completely Ukrainized; the 20% of schools which did not use Ukrainian were reserved for the national minorities. Middle schools and higher education were systematically being Ukrainized, and the Ukrainization of the press had reached 60%. In one year, the percentage of Ukrainians in the KP(b)U had risen from 37 to 47% and in the Komsomol from 50 to 61%. Aside from admitting that the trade unions had lagged behind, the resolution portrayed rapid and unprecedented strides made during the previous year.[46] Though Kaganovich was not mentioned by name, no one could fail to understand that the list of accomplishments since the April 1925

---

[44] M. M. Popov, *Narys istorii Komunistychnoi Partii (bilshovykiv) Ukrainy.*
[45] *Budivnytstvo Radianskoi Ukrainy* (Kharkiv, 1928), vol. 1, pp. 58–60.
[46] *Ibid.*, vol. 1, p. 61.

plenum meant those accomplished since he took charge of the Party.

At the same time, the resolution defended Kaganovich's tempo in carrying out Ukrainization. While the policy was necessary in order to bring the Party closer to the masses, pushing it more rapidly would have risked a rift between the Russian workers and the Ukrainian peasants. The implicit condemnation of Shumskyi could not have been more complete. Regarding the working class, the resolution defended the policy of concentrating the Party's efforts on de-Russifying non-Russian workers by urging those who spoke a Russo-Ukrainian *patois* to learn proper Ukrainian.[47]

The resolution then stated that the growth of capitalist elements in town and country under NEP had fostered the growth of both Russian and Ukrainian chauvinism in Ukraine. It claimed that Russian chauvinism had its social basis in the urban bourgeoisie and specialist intelligentsia, and that it manifested itself as national nihilism and passive opposition to Ukrainization. It declared that Russian chauvinism had to be fought by pushing faster with Ukrainization.[48]

As one might expect with a predominantly rural people, the social basis of Ukrainian nationalism was found in the villages as well as in the *petite bourgeoisie* and the intelligentsia. It had spilled over into literature, especially through the works of the Neoclassicist group led by the poet Mykola Zerov. It had infected communist writers like Mykola Khvylovyi, who was condemned for opposing the interests of Ukraine to those of other republics, calling for Ukrainian literature to free itself of Russian influence, and thereby implicitly advocating a "bourgeois" course of national development. The Party would oppose this call with its own plans for the development of Ukrainian culture. The Party declared that it would uphold the independent development of Ukrainian culture, its absorption of the highest world cultural values, its overcoming of all vestiges of provincialism, but that the Party could never sanction any attempt to oppose Ukrainian culture to the cultures of other nationalities of the Soviet Union.[49]

The resolution concluded that continuing the policy of Ukrainization, especially in the Party and the Komsomol, was the best way to fight both Russian and Ukrainian chauvinism. It called for the following specific measures: continuing Ukrainization, especially in the Party and Komsomol; explanation of the Ukrainization to the broad masses,

[47] *Ibid.*, vol. 1, pp. 61–62.
[48] *Ibid.*, vol. 1, pp. 62–63.
[49] *Ibid.*, vol. 1, pp. 63–64.

especially to the workers and in the trade unions; resolute opposition to all attempts to revive "the theory of the struggle of two cultures" from either the Russian or the Ukrainian standpoint; resolute unmasking of Ukrainian national deviations in the Party "with special attention and in a comradely way to comrades who err"; creation of more Party cadres able to do ideological battle in the field of Ukrainian culture; improvement of the highest Party institutions of scholarship, such as the Artem Communist University and the Institute of Marxism; the integration of more Ukrainian communists into state and Party work; endeavors to strengthen the work of Ukrainian intellectuals in the state apparatus; and, lastly, opposition to every tendency which might lead to a rift with other Soviet republics and nations in the USSR.[50]

The Central Committee resolution "On the Results of Ukrainization" contained no explicit attack on Shumskyi; in fact, he voted for it.[51] Aside from the vague call to unmask Ukrainian national deviations in the Party, whatever fire was directed at Ukrainians remained squarely aimed at writers such as the non-communist Zerov and the communist Khvylovyi, whose call for Ukrainian literature to orient itself toward Europe and away from Russia was the subject of a protracted literary discussion.[52] The danger to Shumskyi arose because, as Commissar of Education, he was responsible for keeping watch on cultural developments. His own autonomist aspirations could all too easily be linked with those of Khvylovyi, whose real or imagined sins could be used to bring Shumskyi down.

Although Shumskyi never wholly endorsed the views expounded by Khvylovyi, he defended him and the poet Volodymyr Sosiura, now also coming under attack, at the June Plenum. After a speech by Volodymyr Zatonskyi attacking these two writers, Shumskyi facetiously wondered how their work could ever have passed the censor if they had been even remotely as pernicious as Zatonskyi had portrayed them. The "individualism" of which both writers were guilty was, in Shumskyi's view, general in the Ukrainian literature of the time. If they had sinned, Shumskyi asked what could have caused it:

> Why, for what reason are the communist proletarians, Sosiura and Khvylovyi, thrust into the morass of nationalism? . . . Khvylovyi and

[50] *Ibid.*, vol. 1, pp. 64–65.
[51] M. Skrypnyk, "Khvylovyzm chy Shumskyzm?" *Bilshovyk Ukrainy*, 1927, no. 2, p. 33.
[52] See chapter four below.

Sosiura are the best representatives of contemporary proletarian literature.
Both were communist proletarians of the Donbas and are now outstand-
ing writers who went through the school of the Civil War in the Red
Army. What could have turned them into degenerates?[53]

The answer, Shumskyi argued, lay in the fact that the KP(b)U was still
a predominantly Russian body despite the decrees passed on Ukrainization. The literary discussion had broadened into "a discussion of the
whole socio-cultural process' and, in Shumskyi's view, would continue
whether the Party participated in it or not. To blame the rise of "national
deviations" in literature on the "growth of capitalist elements" during
the NEP, he argued, was to beg the question, because the real reason
the literary discussion might sometimes have gone astray lay in the Party's
refusal to give up its Russian culture, its continued practice of conduc-
ting its business in Russian, and its consequent isolation from the Ukrainian cultural process. Should this continue, he warned, it could lead to
abdicating the leadership of the cultural process to non-Party Ukrainian intellectuals like the scholar Hermaize and the Neoclassicist literary
critics who "are ideologically hostile to us and are struggling against
us for the leadership of the socio-cultural process."[54]

Shumskyi ended with a less than flattering comparison of the still
largely non-Ukrainized KP(b)U and the Russian Party leadership in
Moscow. In Russia, Shumskyi declared, "the Party embraces every pore
of social life and leads it by actively participating in its creative process." They could do so, he added, because there was no language barrier
between them and those doing creative cultural work. When a voice
from the audience interjected that the leadership in Moscow led the
cultural process for the entire Soviet Union, Shumskyi scoffed at the
idea, sardonically wondering whether it too should be Ukrainized. No,
Shumskyi concluded, the Ukrainian cultural process could not be led
from Moscow. "This leadership is our responsibility, the responsibility
of Ukraine's leaders, and it cannot be placed on the Union's shoulders."[55]

Other speakers at the June plenum took a different view. Chubar stated
that since the proletariat was still mainly of Russian culture, Khvylovyi's
slogans, "Away from Moscow!" and "Face to Europe," implicitly
threatened to isolate the proletariat from the process of building Soviet
Ukrainian culture.[56] Skrypnyk objected to the tenor of Shumskyi's

---

[53] *Budivnytstvo Radianskoi Ukrainy*, vol. 1, p. 27.
[54] *Ibid.*, vol. 1, p. 28.
[55] *Ibid.*, vol. 1, p. 29.
[56] *Ibid.*, vol. 1, pp. 38–39.

remarks on the grounds that they ostensibly, but did not actually, support the resolution.[57] Petrovskyi went so far as to accuse Shumskyi of being the leader of the "deviationists" Khvylovyi and Sosiura, and held him directly responsible for their errors.[58] Only Maksymovych, the representative of the KPZU in KP(b)U councils, defended what Shumskyi had said.[59] The official line, however, was most fully and authoritatively explained by Kaganovich.[60]

The KP(b)U First Secretary began by pointing out that the nationality question was of fundamental importance, not just in enabling the Russian proletariat to obtain the material, moral, and political support of non-Russians, but also in providing a model to oppressed peoples of how communism could satisfy their national aspirations:

> Just as for Eastern peoples we can and must present the examples of the Uzbek, Turkmen, Kazakh Republics, and so forth, for Western peoples Ukraine must serve as a model and example of the proletariat's solution to the problem of the national liberation of the oppressed masses, the problem of the political construction of nation republics within the confines of the Soviet system. We must show how it is possible to create a voluntary union of Soviet republics by bestowing on the formerly oppressed masses the maximum possibilities to manifest their own spontaneous creative work (*proiavy samodiialnosty*) in building their statehood, developing their economy, raising the cultural level of the country—in short, by drawing the masses numbering in the millions into socialist cultural construction.[61]

Referring to the transcript of the May Politburo session, which was never published but obviously circulated in the Central Committee, Kaganovich condemned Shumskyi for posing the question of Ukrainization in the wrong way. Instead of discussing policy questions, Kaganovich declared, Shumskyi had merely sought to stir up a heated atmosphere by using attacks of a personal nature. Kaganovich was quite willing to admit that difficulties existed and that the Party was currently unable to sustain the momentum of Ukrainian cultural development. Kaganovich drew an analogy between industrial and cultural development, stating that the revolution had set both processes in motion, but the Party was still unable to keep up with them. At present, he said, the Party could

---

[57] *Ibid.*, vol. 1, pp. 31–34.

[58] *Ibid.*, vol. 1, p. 56.

[59] Radziejowski, "Kwestia," p. 489.

[60] Although Kaganovich's speech was not actually the longest delivered at the plenum, it appeared that way in the printed record, thereby indicating its authoritative nature.

[61] *Budivnytstvo Radianskoi Ukrainy*, vol. 1, p. 41.

do no more than pose the question of taking over the cultural process. Just as there were economic difficulties, there were also difficulties in the realm of culture, especially "the activity of enemies" such as the nationalists. But this, Kaganovich claimed, did not mean that the Party's policy was wrong, merely that it would take a period of time to catch up with the demands made on it. The Party could draw closer to the Ukrainian masses only by understanding the Ukrainian language, culture, and psychology. The KP(b)U, as Kaganovich saw it, was on the right course; only by further Ukrainization and participation in the Ukrainian cultural process could shortcomings be overcome and errors corrected. While conceding that Great Russian chauvinism was still a greater danger than its Ukrainian counterpart, he condemned Khvylovyi for attempting to set the path of Ukrainian cultural development in opposition to Russia's at a time when a "united front" with the Russian proletariat was vital. He deftly touched on the issue of Shumskyi's Borotbist past by contrasting the "correct" attitude of Khvylia, a former Borotbist, with the errors of Khvylovyi, who was not, in such a way as to remind his listeners that it was an anomaly not generally encountered. Seconding Shumskyi's call for unanimous adoption of the resolution "On the Results of Ukrainization" as being in the interest of Party unity, he defended it as a continuation of his previous correct policies rather than a new departure. Both Great Russian and Ukrainian chauvinism, he concluded, were dangers which the Party had to oppose; unity behind the policy of Ukrainization was the way to avoid them.[62]

The basic arguments surrounding the Shumskyi controversy all emerged at the June plenum; little or nothing was added to them. Shumskyi was upbraided for his campaign against "personalities"; he was held responsible for the "national deviations" of writers with whom he did not completely agree, but whom he had still defended; the commitment to Ukrainization was reaffirmed along with opposition to "forced" Ukrainization of the proletariat; his Borotbist past was held suspect. Although no attempt to remove Shumskyi was as yet made, his virtual isolation was demonstrated to the point that he could be removed whenever his opponents chose to do so. For the moment, however, Party unity took priority over the "unmasking" of deviations. Whatever energy was devoted to such endeavors was in any case directed at writers, not politicians.[63] By pushing the heresy of "Khvylovyism" further and further beyond the Pale, the crime of political responsibili-

---

[62] *Ibid.*, vol. 1, pp. 40–54.
[63] See chapter four below.

ty for allowing the heresy to grow was made correspondingly greater, and the speakers at the June plenum had already held Shumskyi responsible. Meanwhile, Ukrainization, the success and shortcomings of which were alternately proclaimed with almost comic regularity, was strengthened by switching a number of Party journals to Ukrainian and by passing yet another resolution calling upon the trade unions to Ukrainize themselves.[64]

The first real action against Shumskyi was taken in November 1926, when he was replaced as editor-in-chief of *Chervonyi shliakh,* already criticized in an August Politburo resolution on the press.[65] After Khvylia attacked the journal for countenancing national deviations in literature, Shumskyi rose in defense of the writers described as deviationists. At one point Kaganovich interjected an accusation that Shumskyi had edited the journal in a manner unbefitting a Communist. As at the June plenum, the published resolutions made no mention of Shumskyi. The November resolution simply described and condemned the errors of certain writers and announced that Zatonskyi would become the new editor of *Chervonyi shliakh.*[66]

Shumskyi's last attempt to express his views publicly before they were hopelessly distorted by his opponents, was in a speech he made in his Commissariat of Education late in November. After refusing to revise what he had said, he published it verbatim in February 1927. In this speech, entitled "The Ideological Struggle in the Ukrainian Cultural Process," Shumskyi attempted to distance himself from Khvylovyi and the Neoclassicists. He did this by adopting the formulation of his opponents to the effect that Khvylovyi was guilty of reviving an inverted

---

[64] For example, S. Kasianiv in January 1926 announced that the Ukrainization of the state apparatus had been completed; in March of that year a commission headed by Chubar found this not to be the case. In January 1927 at the Fifth KNS Congress, Petrovskyi again announced the completion of the Ukrainization of the state apparatus only to be refuted by subsequent reports. Such premature announcements of the completion of Ukrainization seem to have been a way of suggesting that the process need be carried no farther. See S. Kasianiv, "Zakinchyty ukrainizatsiiu," *Visty VUTsVK,* January 9, 1926, p. 1; "Ukrainizatsiia radaparatu," *Visty VUTsVK,* March 5, 1926, p. 5; "V-i Vseukrainskyi Zizd Komitetiv Nezamozhnykh Selian. Mizhnarodnii i vnutrishnii stan SRSR. Doklad H. I. Petrovskoho," *Visty VUTsVK,* January 6, 1927, p. 2; "U Kharkovi. Stan ukrainizatsii ustanov mista i okruhy," *Visty VUTsVK,* June 10, 1927, p. 5. The resolutions made in the wake of the June plenum may be found in *Kulturne budivnytstvo v Ukrainskii RSR,* vol. 1, pp. 319–332, 336–337.

[65] *Kulturne budivnytstvo v Ukrainskii RSR,* vol. 1, pp. 329–330.

[66] *Budivnytstvo Radianskoi Ukrainy,* vol. 1, pp. 101–108.

version of Lebed's theory of the struggle of two cultures. "This theory," he declared,

> is foreign to the spirit of proletarian internationalism and exceedingly harmful to the cause of the proletariat's struggle for liberation because it disperses to the winds of national passions the brotherly solidarity of the toilers and works to the advantage of bourgeoisie, be they of the Russian or the Ukrainian camp.[67]

In terms reminiscent of those used by his opponents at the June plenum, Shumskyi attributed the rise of Khvylovyi's nationalistic "heresy" to the strengthening of the Ukrainian national bourgeoisie under NEP and to the return of the nationalist emigres. On the one hand, he explained, Ukraine had to deal with the Russian chauvinists of the *Zhizn isskustva* (Life of Art) group who protested the performance of Russian operas with Ukrainian libretti; on the other hand, it had Ukrainian chauvinists with their "zoological nationalism." That Khvylovyi had fallen in with the latter was amply demonstrated when he received the plaudits of the fascist Dontsov and the "bourgeois ideologue" Nikovskyi.[68]

Nor did Shumskyi have kind words for the returned émigré Hrushevskyi, who had sometimes hinted at similarities between the policies of the Soviet regime and its tsarist predecessor. Red Moscow, Shumskyi told his audience, was "the capital of the Union and the center of the world proletarian liberation movement," and any attempt to discredit it and the Union was impermissible. Neither the Russian nor the Ukrainian nationalists, he said, had anything in common with Marxism, and the slogan "Away from Moscow to Europe" had unintentionally but objectively led Khvylovyi to abandon the "proletarian class position" for the united national front of the bourgeois nationalists. Shumskyi expressed hope that Khvylovyi would recognize his errors and "with the whole Party become an active builder of Ukrainian literature and culture along the lines marked out by the June plenum." For Khvylovyi's Neoclassicist allies, however, Shumskyi extended no such hope. They were non-Marxist "internal emigres" who attempted to retreat from the present into the Graeco-Roman past. Those who prematurely concluded that Ukrainian literature was dead, however, were wrong. To those who bemoaned the fate of Ukrainian literature on the grounds that Ukrainians lacked a strong proletarian class, he opposed the literary dicta of

---

[67] O. Shumskyi, "Ideolohichna borotba v ukrainskomu kulturnomu protsesi," *Bilshovyk Ukrainy*, 1927, no. 2, p. 13.

[68] *Ibid.*, pp. 11–15.

Engels and Plekhanov, who held that the socio-economic determinants of art were decisive in the final instance but rejected any sort of mechanistic determinism. For the moment, he pointed out, Ukrainian literature had mainly the peasantry and the national intelligentsia for its audience. The proletariat, still predominantly Russian, would come to participate in the Ukrainian cultural process only with its gradual Ukrainization in the wake of industrialization. Shumskyi concluded by declaring his complete solidarity with the June plenum and current policy.[69]

Shumskyi's attempt to save himself by repudiating his political liabilities served only to enable his critics to berate him for inconsistency. The published text of his speech was immediately followed by an article written by Mykola Skrypnyk and accompanied by an editorial note which proclaimed the editors of *Bilshovyk Ukrainy* "in complete agreement with the criticism of Comrade Shumskyi's article which Comrade M. Skrypnyk provides." Skrypnyk accused Shumskyi of having revived the issues of the literary discussion after they had been settled by the June plenum. He accused *Chervonyi shliakh*, under Shumskyi's editorship, of having been the "incubator" of the heretical ideas of Khvylovyi and his group. According to Skrypnyk, the choice of capitalist Europe over proletarian Moscow by Khvylovyi and the Neoclassicists, a choice which Shumskyi had attempted to defend, was not just a question of Ukrainian rights but also an abandonment of communism. Skrypnyk, in fact, equated Moscow with communism by equating any attempt to create a rupture with Moscow as an objectively anti-communist position. According to Skrypnyk, Shumskyi had mingled his weak condemnation of Khvylovyi's errors with praise and attempted to dismiss the writer's deviations as an inevitable result of Russian intolerance. Lastly, Skrypnyk condemned Shumskyi's attempt to isolate the proletariat from Ukrainian literature and claimed that the Ukrainian proletariat is the motive force of Ukrainian writing. According to Skrypnyk, Shumskyi's heresy in literature provided the key to understanding "Shumskyism."[70] The coining of this new term of political abuse signaled Shumskyi's utter defeat. All that remained was his removal from his post.

---

[69] *Ibid.*, pp. 15–26.
[70] M. Skrypnyk, "Khvylovyzm chy Shumskyzm?" *Bilshovyk Ukrainy*, 1927, no. 2, pp. 27–36.

The Schism in the Communist Party of Western Ukraine

By March 1927, the stage was set for what the KP(b)U leadership obviously hoped would be the final act of the Shumskyi affair. A joint plenum of the KP(b)U Central Committee and Central Control Commission was held from February 26 to March 3; during its deliberations, *Visty* published a Politburo statement condemning Shumskyi's Commissariat of Education for having countenanced national deviations in the cultural sphere.[71] The resolution was adopted in January; on February 3, Shumskyi sent a letter to the Politburo, in which he blamed the policy of the current leadership for undermining the authority of Ukrainian communists with the masses by placing them under a cloud of suspicion. In the letter, Shumskyi denied charges that he had been in correspondence with other Ukrainian communists for disloyal ends, and charged that a generalized suspicion of Ukrainians in the Party had led to their complete demoralization.[72] By this time, Shumskyi had clearly given up any hope of saving himself by admitting past sins. His isolation in the KP(b)U leadership was completely evident to him.

At the March plenum, Kaganovich accused Shumskyi of a variety of "sins" and demanded his replacement by Skrypnyk as Commissar of Education.[73] Shumskyi also requested such a move.[74] In any case, Shumskyi was removed after various Central Committee members rose one by one to condemn him.[75] After the full members of the Central Committee and Central Control Commission voted, Shumskyi requested that candidate members also be polled.[76] When it came turn for Maksymovych, who represented the KPZU in the capacity of a candidate member of the KP(b)U Central Committee, he voiced doubts about the wisdom of removing Shumskyi and sending him to Russia on the grounds that such an action might well be misunderstood:

> At present the transfer of Comrade Shumskyi outside Ukraine could give rise to astonishment and misunderstanding among the KPZU Party mass in so much as it is difficult to find in what Shumskyi has done and on

[71] "Postanova Politbiura Tsk KP(b)U pro stan narodnoi osvity na Ukraini," *Visty VUTsVK*, March 2, 1927, p. 2.
[72] Text in *Budivnytstvo Radianskoi Ukrainy*, vol. 1, pp. 134–135.
[73] *Ibid.*, vol. 1, p. 123.
[74] M. Skrypnyk, *Natsionalistychnyi ukhyl v KPZU*, p. 218, as cited in Solchanyk, *The Communist Party of Western Ukraine*, p. 247.
[75] *Budivnytsvo Radianskoi Ukrainy*, vol. 1, pp. 121–134, 135–141.
[76] Solchanyk, *Communist Party of Western Ukraine*, pp. 247–248.

the basis of published materials where Comrade Shumskyi differs in principle from the Central Committee's line.

He warned that sending Shumskyi, "who from the first days of the revolution was one of the active leaders of the struggle against Ukrainian nationalism and for the regime of workers and peasants in Ukraine," might be used by Ukrainian nationalists and Polish "fascists" to disorient those who might otherwise support communism. While expressing his own and the whole KPZU's solidarity with the KP(b)U's nationality policy, he announced his opposition to approving Shumskyi's request for transfer outside Ukraine. Although Maksymovych assured Skrypnyk that he had spoken only for himself and not for the KPZU leadership as a whole, Skrypnyk demanded to know just where the KPZU stood on the matter, noting pointedly that it had been silent on Shumskyi's errors and had published one of Skrypnyk's articles on the struggle of two cultures in its organ with a statement which declared only that it had been written by a member of the KP(b)U Politburo and contained no expression of the KPZU's position.[77]

The extent of the KPZU's displeasure at Shumskyi's transfer soon became apparent. On March 26, Roman Turianskyi, a member of the KPZU Central Committee, berated the head of the Polono-Baltic Regional Secretariat of the Comintern when the latter charged that Shumskyi was sympathetic to Polish plans for creating a bourgeois Ukrainian state. The KP(b)U Central Committee then sent a letter to its West Ukrainian counterpart demanding to know what position the latter took regarding the actions of Shumskyi and Maksymovych. Skrypnyk, as the KP(b)U representative in the Comintern, was directed to look into the matter.[78]

At Skrypnyk's request, a special enlarged plenum of the KPZU Central Committee was held in April 1927, and Skrypnyk presented the case against Shumskyi and Maksymovych. A resolution condemning them was presented by Skrypnyk, but the KPZU Central Committee rejected it ten to two and passed an alternative resolution defending them. After Skrypnyk warned that the Comintern would look at such an act of defiance as a provocation, this resolution was withdrawn. The KPZU majority decided instead to send a delegation to the Comintern with instructions to explain that on the basis of the evidence which Skryp-

[77] *Budivnytstvo Radianskoi Ukrainy,* vol. 1, p. 209.
[78] Solchanyk, *Communist Party of Western Ukraine,* pp. 249–250; Janusz Radziejowski, *Komunistyczna Partia Zachodniej Ukrainy, 1919–1929: Węzłowe problemy ideologiczne,* p. 151; Radziejowski "Kwestia narodowa...," p. 494.

nyk had presented, they were unable to see any national deviation of which Shumskyi had been guilty. This delegation was also instructed to point out that Maksymovych's statement opposing Shumskyi's transfer was in no way intended to be a challenge to the KP(b)U's nationality policy. A few days after the plenum, the KPZU majority worked out a softened version of the resolution that had been passed, by incorporating some of the points Skrypnyk had made, most notably a strong condemnation of Khvylovyi as a national deviationist and a statement that the "fascist" regime in Poland was trying to discredit the KP(b)U's nationality policy.[79]

The KPZU majority thus upheld the understanding of Ukrainian communism that the Borotbisty had formerly represented in Eastern Ukraine. This is hardly surprising since the Borotbisty played a major role in the Communist Party of Eastern Galicia, the direct ancestor of the KPZU, and the latter had itself split over the national question from 1921 to 1923. Thereafter, neither the Polish Communist Party (KPP), to which it was formally subordinate, nor the KP(b)U fully trusted the KPZU as being free from nationalism.[80]

The KPP, in a resolution of its Central Committee, condemned Maksymovych's statement at the April KP(b)U plenum as "a political demonstration against the nationality policy of the KP(b)U and VKP(b) Central Committees." That the majority of KPZU Central Committee members had sided with him was simultaneously viewed as evidence of a deviation toward "national Bolshevism" and condemned as harmful to the Communist movement in Western Ukraine.[81]

On July 7, the KP(b)U Central Committee passed a resolution "On the KPZU Line on Nationality Policy" that accused the KPZU of being objectively guilty of giving aid and comfort to the enemies of Soviet rule. According to the resolution, the West Ukrainian bourgeoisie had made its peace with Polish "fascism", and this had in turn infected the KPZU, weak in proletarian cadres and traditions, with nationalism.[82] A statement to the Comintern that interpreted the entire history of the

---

[79] Solchanyk, *Communist Party of Western Ukraine*, pp. 250–251; Radziejowski, *Komunistyczna Partia Zachodniej Ukrainy*, pp. 159–164; E. M. Halushko, *Narysy ideolohichnoi ta orhanizatsiinoi diialnosti KPZU v 1919–1928 rr.* (Lviv, 1965), p. 225. See also *Budivnytstvo Radianskoi Ukrainy*, vol. 1, pp. 212–215.

[80] Solchanyk, *Communist Party of Western Ukraine*, pp. 153, 203.

[81] *Budivnytstvo Radianskoi Ukrainy*, vol. 1, pp. 211–212.

[82] "Rezoliutsiia Plenumu TsK KP(b)U pro liniiu natsionalnoi polityky KPZU," *Visty VUTsVK*, July 6, 1927, p. 1.

KP(b)U as a struggle "on two fronts" against Russian and Ukrainian counterrevolution was likewise adopted. It stated that the KP(b)U had established Soviet Ukraine by fighting the Russian counterrevolution of Denikin and the Ukrainian counterrevolution of Petliura. Due to the revival of bourgeois elements under the NEP, both types of nationalism had again appeared: Russian chauvinism in opposition to Ukrainization, and its Ukrainian counterpart in those segments of the Ukrainian intelligentsia that opposed Ukrainian interests to those of other Soviet republics. Both sorts of nationalism had infected certain quarters in the KP(b)U, but the leadership had defeated them. The KPZU majority, however, had sided with the Ukrainian national deviation of Shumskyi, who had found little support in the KP(b)U; thus, the errors of Khvylovyi, Shumskyi, and the KPZU majority were lumped together as a single national deviation, whose efforts to discredit the USSR and its nationality policy provided material for national chauvinists everywhere, encouraging mistrust of the All-Union Communist Party and the Comintern.[83] The KPZU majority was, in short, treasonous. Both documents were forwarded to the Comintern.[84]

Soon thereafter, the KPZU majority recanted in the interests of communist unity, recognizing the errors of both Shumskyi and Maksymovych, while affirming the correctness of the criticisms of the KP(b)U and KPP Central Committees.[85] This retraction did not, however, prevent them from being sharply criticized at the KPP congress being held at the same time.[86] In August, the Executive Committee of the Comintern also formed a Ukrainian commission that endorsed the KP(b)U and condemned Shumskyi, along with his erstwhile supporters in the KPZU.[87]

For a time it appeared that the problem had been solved, but the members of the KPZU minority, which had already tried to oust the majority and take control of the Party, continued their efforts, leading to a full-scale Party split. Late in November, the KP(b)U Politburo endorsed the minority's charges and called for the removal of three leaders of the KPZU majority from its Central Committee. The majority, however, refused to acknowledge this decision, and transferred the matter to the Comintern. Shortly thereafter, the KPP leadership pro-

[83] *Budivnytstvo Radianskoi Ukrainy*, vol. 1, pp. 215–221.
[84] Halushko, *Narysy ideolohichnoi ta orhanizatsiinoi diialnosti KPZU*, p. 226.
[85] *Ibid.*, p. 227.
[86] *Ibid.*, pp. 227–228; Radziejowski, *Komunistyczna partia*, pp. 169–170.
[87] *Budivnytstvo Radianskoi Ukrainy*, vol. 1, pp. 221–228.

claimed the KPZU Central Committee dissolved and replaced by a three-member executive. Meanwhile, the Comintern commission met in Lviv and heard the minority's case without so much as inviting members of the majority faction. On December 24, the Comintern removed Maksymovych from the KPZU Central Committee. In early January, the KPP refused to allow the KPZU Central Committee to meet, and on January 13, the majority convened an "illegal" Party conference, while the minority held what it termed a "general council" of the Party. On January 14, the KPP Politburo condemned the majority-sponsored conference as "factional" and suspended the KPZU from the Central Committee. On February 18, 1928, the Executive Committee of the Comintern expelled the KPZU majority.

The KPZU majority responded in May, 1928, with a pamphlet defending its position. Written by Turianskyi and called *Through the Prism of a Marxist Critique,* this pamphlet is the most thorough and systematic exposition of the views held by Shumskyi's supporters in the KPZU and of "Shumskyism" in general.

After a brief defense of the KPZU's history, in response to the charge that the lack of a strong Galician proletariat had produced a "permanent deviation" toward nationalism, Turianskyi seized on the arguments presented earlier by Mykhailo Volobuiev in order to provide an economic basis for his criticism of KP(b)U policies.[88] As was the case with Khvylovyi, Turianskyi repudiated some of Volobuiev's more extreme views, but he did use Volobuiev's work to strengthen his own case. As he saw it, the nationality question had outgrown its old limitation of being basically a peasant problem and had been transformed into

> the problem of the development of the productive forces of the national republics of the Union and their industrialization. Because building socialism means first of all combatting the economic backwardness of the Union as a whole and primarily of its national components which, thanks to the colonial policy of Tsarism, were more economically and culturally underdeveloped (*uposlidzhenymy*) and because of this the weakest links in socialist construction overall.

And, he added, building socialism also meant strengthening the influence of the proletariat over the peasantry, a task that could be accomplished only if backward areas were industrialized and non-Russian peasants became workers in sufficient numbers to be able to lead the peasant

---

[88] *Cherez pryzmu marksivskoi krytyky* (Lviv, 1928), pp. 3–13.

masses of their nations.[89] This, in turn, meant consolidating the economic life of the non-Russian republics, but what had been happening in fact was that Russian chauvinism had been undermining such consolidation. Shumskyism, far from undermining the unity of the Soviet Union, meant following the only path truly capable of cementing the various nations of the union together:

> The basic content of the so-called 'Shumskyism' in the sphere of economic policy consists in the position that during the present period of socialist construction it is necessary to adopt a resolute course toward the *socialist consolidation* of the national republics as *Republics,* the development of their *productive forces, their industrialization,* because this is the only way to succeed in defeating the great power chauvinism which leads to the restoration of the old 'Russia one and indivisible' as well as the schemes of Ukrainian nationalism to tear Ukraine away from 'Moscow' and restore the bourgeois Ukraine of the UNR, in one word, *the way to cement together the national republics* which have an overwhelmingly peasant character.[90]

Turianskyi then turned to the issue of Ukrainization, arguing that, just as industrialization was the only way to overcome the economic backwardness of the non-Russian republics, indigenization was the only way to overcome their cultural backwardness, by bringing the non-Russian masses into the process of building socialism. Industrialization made Ukrainization all the more urgent as more and more Ukrainian former peasants became urban proletarians, for if the entire working class were to take part in building socialism, proletarians Russified in the past had to be de-Russified as rapidly as possible. Only such de-Russification could maintain the proletariat's hegemony over the Ukrainian cultural revival. Understood this way, Shumskyism became only the insistence that the Party carry through its own announced policy. Ukrainization had to be rapid because of the rapid tempo of the Ukrainian national cultural revival; failure to keep up with the latter held the danger of abdicating leadership of the cultural revival to the bourgeois nationalist intelligentsia. After all, one could not have Ukrainian proletarian literature without a Ukrainian proletariat. This was what Shumskyi said, Turianskyi maintained, and he was right. Actually, the latter conceded, the Ukrainization of the proletariat was progressing; it was leaders like Kaganovich who lagged behind. Charges that Shumskyi

---

[89] *Ibid.,* p. 8. Emphasis in the original.
[90] *Ibid.,* pp. 12–13. Emphasis in the original.

represented forced or "ultra" Ukrainization were false; he represented
only the Party's own officially enunciated policy of Ukrainization against
the foot-dragging of the leadership.[91]

Turianskyi portrayed Shumskyi as a paragon of communist orthodoxy
who sought only to warn the Party of the danger of both Russian and
Ukrainian bourgeois nationalism. In his view, prolonging the campaign
against Shumskyism served only to strengthen the deviation toward Russian chauvinism, for Kaganovich, in opposing "Ukrainian separatism,"
was taking the same position as the Russian nationalist White Guards.
At the same time, the campaign served to strengthen Ukrainian
nationalism, particularly in Western Ukraine, by lessening communism's
appeal to the Ukrainian masses. Thus, Kaganovich was the real "national
deviationist"; Shumskyi supported the policies adopted at the Twelfth
Congress of the Russian Communist Party.[92]

Little response was ever made to Turianskyi's pamphlet, and that,
little more than the empty and hysterical polemics by then typical of
the official communist movement: those who disagreed were simply
portrayed as traitors.[93]

Meanwhile, thanks largely to the fact that it was recognized by the
Comintern as the official Communist Party, the KPZU minority con-
solidated its position. After the failure of repeated requests that the Comintern reopen the matter, and of attempts to gain readmission to the Party,
many of those who had followed the majority faction gradually returned
to the official KPZU or gave up communism altogether. The KPZU's
influence on Western Ukraine's political life declined, but unity was
achieved. In 1929, Maksymovych, who had been transferred to Moscow
at the end of 1927, publicly recanted his past errors. In 1930, Shumskyi followed suit.[94]

As to Shumskyi's subsequent fate, he was arrested in 1933 during
the purge of Ukrainian communists conducted by Pavel Postyshev. He
was last reported seen in June 1934, in the Solovetskii Islands, an inmate
in a forced labor camp. Rumor had it that he was later shot while trying
to cross the Finnish border. Sooner or later, other former Borotbisty

[91] *Ibid.*, pp. 13–26.

[92] *Ibid.*, pp. 26–55.

[93] See Hnat Bryl, "Do likvidatsii zrady v KPZU," *Bilshovyk Ukrainy,* 1929, no. 4,
pp. 88–101; no. 5, pp. 80–101.

[94] Solchanyk, *The Communist Party of Western Ukraine,* pp. 254–289, 296. For the
text of Shumskyi's recantation, see E. M. Hirchak, *Na dva fronta v borbe s natsionalizmom,* p. 219.

suffered similar fates. Not one of them was known to be at liberty in the USSR following the Great Purge of the late 1930s.[95]

*   *   *

The Shumskyi controversy went to the heart of the dilemma inherent in Ukrainization: how to give the regime a measure of national legitimacy without threatening the unity of the USSR; how to foster Ukrainian national development without fostering nationalism. The "national deviations" of which Shumskyism was but one were the concomitant of the regime's own rhetoric. If Ukrainians achieved national liberation, as the authorities proclaimed constantly, then Ukrainians would try to act like it. They would be all the more aware of the strings attached to this Soviet version of "liberation," and they would try to get rid of them, as Shumskyi did in politics, Khvylovyi in culture, and Volobuiev in economics. National liberation means little if it does not include the right to follow a national destiny different from that of the nation from whose empire a colonial nation had been liberated. But following that separate destiny was precisely what Moscow would not permit. It threatened to lead the "liberated" colony in a direction different from the one marked out by the "liberated" empire.

The goal of Ukrainization was to bring the regime closer to the people, so as to lead them toward "the international unity of the proletariat," and this unity was identified with the consolidation of the Soviet Union. The late twenties would be characterized by an attempt to get Ukrainization back on the track, as it were. It would be linked with a struggle against nationalism in general, a struggle "on two fronts" against both Russian and Ukrainian nationalism. This renewed commitment to Ukrainization, its promise and its failure, is indissolubly linked with the name of Mykola Skrypnyk.

---

[95] Majstrenko, *Borot'bism*, pp. 221–261; Dmytryshyn, *Moscow and the Ukraine*, p. 116; S. O. Pidhainy, "Portraits of Solowky Exiles," in *The Black Deeds of the Kremlin: A White Book* (Toronto-Detroit, 1953–1955), vol. 1, pp. 333–334.

CHAPTER FOUR

Mykola Khvylovyi and the Dilemmas of Ukrainian Cultural Development

WHILE THE KP(b)U was engaged in efforts to Ukrainize itself, Ukrainian literary life went through an unprecedented flowering. Party spokesmen spoke of it as "the Ukrainian cultural process" and perceived the need to participate in and ultimately guide it. Eventually, both goals would be accomplished to the point that the "process" itself was virtually destroyed, but this process began as something outside of and parallel to the Party and its policies. At the outbreak of the revolution, the Ukrainian movement was still just emerging from culturalism, and it is as though Ukrainians sought refuge from their failure to create a fully independent state in a return to national cultural activity. The return of the émigrés like Tiutiunyk and Hrushevskyi was but a surface reflection of the process that beckoned them because it seemed somehow more real and lasting than the state which would come to dominate and devour it. To thousands of people, literature and art seemed the highest of callings. According to one account, ten thousand of Kiev's inhabitants described themselves as writers in 1922.[1] The nation was developing its culture, and the writers who did the developing could aspire to a degree of popular adulation which is in the West reserved for popular singers and matinee idols.[2]

There was a sense of newness in the air, a sense that the old world and all its limitations had been swept away. There was, to be sure, a

---

[1] Myroslav Shkandrij points out that according to the memoirs of the writer Antonenko-Davidovych, ten thousand persons in Kiev alone gave "writer" as their occupation in the 1922 census. Myroslav Shkandrij, *The "Literary Discussion" in Soviet Ukraine, 1925-1928* (Ph.D. dissertation, University of Toronto, 1980), p. 90.

[2] Tatiana Kardynalowska, the widow of Serhii Pylypenko, told me that in the 1920s, one popular writer, Volodymyr Sosiura, was treated "like Elvis Presley" and that women

dark side to this newness and sweeping away: the species later classified as "ideological watchdog" was already evolving, albeit as yet with limited authority.[3] And there were already writers who published abroad because they could not be published in Soviet Ukraine.[4] The super-orthodox, the "new men" who would occupy center stage after the Shakhty trial in 1928, were already waiting in the wings, sometimes attacking even pro-communist writers whom they considered insufficiently orthodox. But in the mid-twenties, the stage belonged to a new generation of talented artists, either Party members or people strongly committed to the revolution's goals, who had been unknown before the revolution. Mykola Khvylovyi was the most prominent among them. Other outstanding new talents included the poet Tychyna, the playwright Kulish, the director Kurbas, and the film maker Dovzhenko. Such men as these asked and tried to answer questions as broad as some God might when pondering what kind of world to create, for they felt themselves engaged in creating a whole new cultural universe. How ought Ukrainian culture to develop? In what direction? With what models to guide it? What kind of culture should it be? The very fact that such questions were asked can only begin to indicate the enthusiasm of those who felt themselves to be creators of a new world.

---

would sometimes swoon in his presence. An interesting portrayal of two wide-eyed young lovelies at a Pluh meeting is found in a story by Ostap Vyshnia:

> "Oh, oh, oh. There's Panch!"
> "And there?! And I thought...So that's what he looks like...But I thought...And there's Tychyna...See, there he is hiding behind the table?!"
> "Where?"
> "That's him! Look, you can see his pince-nez behind his leg...that's Tychyna..."
> "So that's what he's like?! And the poems he writes...Is he married?...Pass me the sunflower seeds..."

Ostap Vyshnia, *Tvory v semy tomakh,* (Kiev, 1963), vol. 1, pp. 227–278. The story, "Ponedilok (Monumentalna fotohrafiiasharzh)," was first published in *Literatura, Nauka, Mystetstvo,* October 28, 1923, and again in *Pluh,* 1924, no. 1, pp. 150–54.

[3] When, for example, Volodymyr Koriak, the leading Ukrainian Party critic, attacked the work of Mykola Kulish, the latter was able to rely on a more powerful protector, Skrypnyk. Had this not been the case, he might have been in deep trouble. As early as 1922, Khvylovyi declared that Koriak was always able to run to the GPU and arrange the arrest of writers he did not like. Vasyl Chaplenko, *Propashchi syly: Ukrainske pysmenstvo pid komunistychnym rezhymom, 1920–1933* (Winnipeg, 1960), pp. 26, 27.

[4] L. Biletskyi, "Umovy literaturnoi pratsi na Ukraini (1919–1926)," *Nova Ukraina,* 1927, no. 10–11, p. 68.

Mykola Khvylovyi provided the clearest and most uncompromising answers. To those who wanted to create a proletarian culture by trying to stimulate half-literate workers and peasants to write, Khvylovyi opposed the "Olympian" view that literary quality had to take precedence over the quantity of literary output, that Ukrainian literature had to be worthy of comparison with the great European literatures. To do so, he insisted that Ukrainian literature model itself on the achievements and standards of Europe. He argued for Ukrainian literature to emancipate itself from Russian influences as rapidly as possible. Ukrainians, he pointed out, were both Europeans and victims of colonial oppression. This position, he believed, made Ukraine uniquely qualified to adapt the cultural achievements of a declining and ideologically bankrupt West and pass them on to the rising colonial peoples of the East. Ukraine, in his vision, would thus lead an Asiatic Renaissance of peoples that were liberating themselves from imperialism and thereby inheriting the Earth. Doubtless a contradiction exists in Khvylovyi's own rejection of Russian culture as the culture of Ukraine's former oppressor, and his hope that other colonial peoples would want to embrace the values of their European oppressors. Still there was a Promethean quality in such a grandiose aspiration, a quality which was not at all inconsistent with the times, for they too had something Promethean about them.

The Struggle for Proletarian Culture

The various literary groups which issued their various manifestoes, squabbled, and vied for the Party's favor during the 1920s, have been described elsewhere in greater depth than need be attempted here.[5] Virtually all shared the assumption that in order to complete and fulfill the political and social revolution, a cultural revolution must also occur, that "bourgeois" literature and art had to be supplanted by its proletarian antithesis. Where they differed was in their definitions of what proletarian art was supposed to be and how it was to be created.

The first and most famous attempt to create a "proletarian culture" was the Proletkult movement, led by Bogdanov. It came to Ukraine as early as 1919, and once there it "displayed all the features which it displayed in Russia."[6] Originally a series of workshops for training

---

[5] See George S. N. Luckyj's pioneering study, *Literary Politics in the Soviet Ukraine, 1917–1934* (New York, 1956).

[6] *Ibid.*, p. 36.

workers to be writers, it angered the authorities when it tried to claim a monopoly of literary expression and consequently disintegrated by 1924. Its affinity for Lebedesque ideas of cultural struggle, and its preference for the Russian culture of the cities over its rural Ukrainian counterpart, prevented Proletkult from exerting much influence on Ukrainian writers in its undiluted form.[7] But its indirect influence was great, if unacknowledged. For it brought in its wake two ideas that would have long-lasting impact: that proletarian culture would be created *de novo* without regard to the traditions and standards of the past and that the masses themselves would be the creators of this new culture. The first notion was perhaps best stated by Volodymyr Koriak when in 1921 he wrote:

> ...a new page of history has been turned. No new "school," no new "tendency," no new "current" within the bounds of the old literature, but a complete break with all that has come before. The dawn of a new era.[8]

Later one finds this same idea expressed in different ways. One writer juxtaposed the new and industrial capital of Kharkiv against the old and traditional Kiev.[9] The Futurists, led by Mykhail Semenko, called for the destruction of all that came before and the creation of something totally new.[10] The idea of art as the creation of the masses went further in Ukraine than it did anywhere else in the Soviet Union and was embodied in the so-called mass literary organizations, *Hart* (Tempering) and *Pluh* (Plow), which had no counterpart in Soviet Russia, at least after the demise of Proletkult's writers' workshops. Their closest counterpart on the All-Union level was perhaps Robselkor, the worker and peasant correspondent movement, which encouraged workers at the

---

[7] Ol. Vedmitskyi, "Literaturnyi front (1919–1931): Materiialy do skhemy rozvytku literaturnykh orhanizatsii na Radianskii Ukraini," *Literaturnyi arkhiv*, 1931, no. 4–5, pp. 111–112. For a fuller treatment of the Proletkult movement, see Sheila Fitzpatrick, *The Commissariat of Enlightenment: Soviet Organization of Education and the Arts Under Lunacharsky, October 1917–1921* (Cambridge, 1970), pp. 89–109, 238 *et passim*.

[8] Volodymyr Koriak, "Etapy," *Zhovten*, 1921, no. 10, p. 162, as quoted in B. Iakubskyi, "Ukrainska literatura za desiat rokiv revoliutsii," *Hart*, 1927, no. 6–7, p. 125.

[9] M. Dolengo, "Kyiv ta Kharkiv—literaturni vzaiemovidnoshennia," *Chervonyi shliakh*, 1923, no 6–7, p. 151.

[10] Mykh. Semenko, "Mystetstvo iak kult," *Chervonyi shliakh*, 1924, no. 3, pp. 224–226, 228–229; Semenko, "Die Kunst ist Tot," in A. Leites and M. Iashek, eds., *Desiat rokiv ukrainskoi literatury (1917–1927)* (Kharkiv, 1928), vol. 2, p. 117.

bench and peasants at the plow to write articles for newspapers. Hart
and Pluh grew out of this movement but went much farther; they tried
to make such people poets and writers.[11]

Ukrainian Soviet literature, like virtually everything that was distinctively Ukrainian about the country's brand of communism, began with
the Borotbisty. The "first bold ones" (*pershi khorobri*) of revolutionary
literature in the Ukrainian language were the four Borotbist bards of
the civil war: Hnat Mykhailychenko, Vasyl Chumak, Andrii Zalyvchyi,
and Vasyl Ellan-Blakytnyi.[12] Of the four, only Ellan-Blakytnyi survived the civil war, and he died in 1925, just as the Ukrainian literary discussion was beginning. Before the radical reversal of Bolshevik nationality
policy at the Twelfth Congress, the Borotbisty had argued against the
Bolshevik tendency to be "imperialists by default." During the Piatakovshchyna, Mykhailychenko had declared that "proletarian art can attain
the fulfillment of its international unity only by national paths, not only
in form but in content," and that proletarian art, both in general and
in Ukraine in particular, "is possible only in the concrete conditions
of a nation's life."[13] After the Twelfth Congress, Blakytnyi did more
than any other individual to translate the new directives into practice.
He edited *Visty,* the Ukrainian language daily state organ. He saw to
it that Ukrainian books were published. And he founded Hart.[14]

Founded in 1923, Hart sought to unite both established and aspiring
writers.[15] Along with Pluh, it played a role in Ukrainian literature akin
to that which the old Revolutionary Ukrainian Party played in the
development of the national movement: virtually all Ukrainian writers

---

[11] On *robselkor,* see Andreas Guski, "Zur Entwicklung der Sowjetischen Arbeiter-
und Bauernkorrespondentenbewegung 1917-1932," in Eberhard Knödler-Bunte and Gernot Erler, eds., *Kultur und Kulturrevolution in der Sowjetunion* (West Berlin, 1978),
pp. 94-104. V. Shalnin, "Vid robkorstva do 'Hartu' (Kramatorska, Donbas)," *Kultura
i pobut,* April 16, 1925, p. 3, provides an example of how Hart organizations often
grew out of *robkor* movement, providing guidance and an organizational framework
for worker correspondents. There was undoubtedly a similar relationship between many
Pluh local organizations and peasant correspondents.

[12] Mykh. Ialovyi, "Pershi khorobri," *Chervonyi shliakh,* 1923, no. 9, pp. 111-119.
The phrase is from a poem by Ellan-Blakytnyi: "We are the first bold ones/A million
more shall follow."

[13] Leites and Iashek, *Desiat rokiv ukrainskoi literatury (1917-1927)* (Kharkiv, 1928),
vol. 2, pp. 27-28. There also exists an expanded second edition of this work published
in 1930. Unless otherwise noted, all references are to the first edition.

[14] Jurij Lawrynenko, *Rozstriliane vidrodzhennia: Antolohiia 1917-1933* (Paris, 1953),
p. 138.

[15] Vedmitskii, "Literaturnyi front," p. 114. Luckyj, *Literary Politics,* p. 47.

of communist persuasion belonged to one or both of the two mass literary organizations. Their true importance lay more in what they were than in anything they stood for, because they were actually informal writing schools that taught any and all as long as they accepted the official goals of the Communist Party and wanted to learn how to write.[16]

At a time when various literary organizations seemed more adept in producing manifestoes than readable literature, Blakytnyi showed his impatience by writing a non-manifesto for his organization. This document, entitled "Without a Manifesto," showed that Hart was more certain of what it opposed than what it supported. It was for the Party and its policies, for "collectivism" and against "individualism." It was against those artistic "professionals" who created their own artistic psychology, characterized by individualism, self-love, oppression of the weak, and lack of principle masked by a talent for spinning theories. The organization was above all opposed to the back-biting intrigues in which artists are sometimes wont to engage. At the same time, it opposed all tendencies toward a "primitivization" of art by those who assumed that the proletariat could produce something worthwhile without bothering to master the achievements of the past. Proletarian culture would not be imitative of bourgeois art, but proletarian writers had to master the technical achievements of the past before they could hope to create anything worthwhile of their own. Hart sought simply to unite those Ukrainian writers who wanted to help create an international proletarian culture in Ukraine. It had no advance blueprint for what that culture was supposed to be and poked quite a lot of fun at those who claimed they did. The manifesto could be left vague; the important thing, Blakytnyi wrote, was "practice, concrete constructive work."[17]

While Hart disintegrated in 1925, Pluh endured longer and went farther in the direction of involving the masses in the process of artistic creation. In fact, the founding of Pluh predated that of Hart by some months. Its leader and guiding spirit was another former Borotbist, Serhii Pylypenko.[18] Given that Ukrainian peasants greatly outnumbered workers, it is hardly surprising that Pluh was two or three times the

---

[16] V. I. Pivtoradni, *Ukrainska literatura pershykh rokiv revoliutsii (1917–1923 rr.): Posibnyk dlia studentiv-zaochnykiv filolohichnykh fakultetiv pedahohichnykh institutiv i universytetiv* (Kiev, 1968), pp. 135–143.

[17] V. Blakytnyi, "Bez manifestu," in Leites and Iashek, *Desiat rokiv*, vol. 2, pp. 82–95. Quotation from page 95.

[18] Luckyj, *Literary Politics*, p. 46. Pylypenko was a Borotbist before the party officially merged with the KP(b)U. See Majstrenko, *Borot'bism*, p. 124.

size of Hart and had about two hundred members and another thousand
aspiring writers who studied in its various branches.[19] A satirical account
of a Pluh "evening," written by a member of the organization, shows
how Pluh worked. To start things off, someone would read a poem or
sketch, and the audience would be asked for comments. If nobody had
anything to say, the discussion leader would call someone and ask, for
instance, "Well, Bozhko, what did you think?" Others would then share
their thoughts, and the discussion would get underway.[20]

Pluh had its high-sounding "ideological and artistic platform" full
of Marxian analysis about class differentiation in the countryside and
the need to bring the toiling peasantry into the proletariat's camp.[21] Its
ideology, however, is far better presented in a manner tailored to a peasant audience by the humorist Ostap Vyshnia, whose fictional account
of how Pluh got started begins with an imaginary conversation between
two peasants:

> "What are we peasants going to do?"
> "Who knows! We'll do something!"
> "Something has got to be done..."
> "But just what will we do?"
> "We'll write."
> "Oh, fine! Everything has gone every which way like dust, and we
> have to gather the dust! Maybe we will! But then, brother, the bourgeois
> proprietary element is upon us."
> "It is."
> "Write...Pluh has the goal of uniting the hitherto dispersed peasant
> writers who, basing themselves on the idea..."
> "And what's this 'idea'?"
> "Later! You'll find out at the evening meetings. Write."
> "I am writing."
> "...on the idea of the union of the revolutionary peasantry with the
> proletariat, creating together with the latter a new socialist culture and
> propagating these ideas among Ukraine's peasant masses regardless of
> nationality...Yes?"
> "Who knows! Yes."
> "There has to be an initiative group."

---

[19] The estimate is from Mykola Khvylovyi, *Dumky proty techii* (Kharkiv, 1926), p.
22. According to accounts in *Kultura i pobut* at the time of the literary discussion, Pluh
had a little over two hundred members.

[20] Ostap Vyshnia, *Tvory*, vol. 1, pp. 277–283.

[21] "Platforma ideolohychna i khudozhna spilka selianskykh pysmennykiv 'Pluh' ,"
Chervonyi shliakh, 1923, no. 2, pp. 211–215.

"Who knows..."

"And what sort of people write? What's so special about them? Well, what sort of person are you?"

"Me? I'm Semen Liubystok!"

"Are you a writer?"

"Oh, no!"

"But maybe you are a writer. Do you ever write anything?"

"Well, yes. I wrote a letter to my father to send money for stamps."

"Well then! And you say you don't write!"

"But what sort of people write? Not peasants?"

"Shevchenko was a peasant...A peasant can write."

"Tell me who does."

"Kolliard is one. Krashchenko is one. Senchenko said that anybody who ever wanted to can be a writer."

"Then I will too! Sign me up for the initiative group. Peasants unite! Read."

"There isn't anything to read."

"Write and read..."

And that's how Pluh was born.[22]

It was, of course, an exaggeration to say there was nothing to read, but what there was fell far short of the demand, at least if the frequent *Visty* editorials demanding more books in Ukrainian are any indication.[23] Pluh seemed ready to provide those books by sheer force of enthusiasm. The aspiring writer had no worry about getting published. The need for Ukrainian language reading matter was perceived to be so great that the most clueless of poetasters were published at state expense, and even the most indigestible literary tidbits sold out, Khvylovyi later charged, thanks to "certain beneficent organizations" which stored them in their cellars "to be nibbled and read by ordinary mice."[24]

Still, something amazing shines through the seemingly most commonplace. One reads, for example, that a lecture was given in the Kharkiv public library on Einstein's theory of relativity.[25] What could seem less worthy of note? Then the reader recalls that the lecture was given in

---

[22] Ostap Vyshnia, *Tvory*, vol. 1, pp. 266–267.

[23] "Give us Ukrainian literature! Give us Ukrainian books! Give us Ukrainian songs! We have read such cries from workers, peasants, and Red Army men daily in the pages of *Visty, Bilshovyk*, and other papers." K. Dubniak, "Daite ukrainskoi literatury," *Visty VUTsVK*, March 12, 1924, p. 1 (editorial).

[24] Mykola Khvylovyi, *Kamo hriadeshy: Pamflety* (Kharkiv, 1925), p. 17.

[25] D-k, "Pro teoriiu vidnosnosty Einshteina," *Literatura, Nauka, Mystetstvo*, March 2, 1924, p. 2.

a language which only half a decade earlier was all too easily dismissed as a peasant tongue, and the seemingly mundane occurrence becomes a thing of wonder. A whole new idiom had to be created, and an Institute of Ukrainian Scientific Language was doing just that.[26] The contrasts were enormous. As late as 1926, Soviet Ukraine could afford schools for only 60% of its children, and many of those schools offered only one or two years' instruction.[27] At one point the Soviet Ukrainian government offered jobs to any and all of the country's unemployed intellectuals, if they would teach people to read.[28]

Only the pen of the caricaturist Sashko, who would later win international renown as the filmmaker Oleksander Dovzhenko, could make the contrasts intelligible by making them humorous. Two of his cartoons, published a week apart in the literary supplement of *Visty,* captured it perfectly. One of them is a "friendly fun-poking" at a Comrade Ozerskyi, who lectured to a Pluh evening on cinematic technique. He faces a sea of bored peasants, here and there broken by the point of a Red Army hat, and even his compatriots on the stage have been put to sleep. In the back of the auditorium peasants flirt, munch bits of cheese, and generally carry on while one of their number sneaks on stage and dances a *hopak* behind the hapless lecturer.[29] Another cartoon portrays the eternal conflict between the hard-headed father and his artistically-inclined son. The father, a worker whose tools protrude from his pocket, suggests that in view of the fact that he is getting older, his grown son ought to think about getting a job. The latter, however, sits oblivious with pen in hand and eyes skyward. Scribbled pages flow in a seemingly endless stream from the table where he sits while butterflies hover round his head. He will have nothing to do with work, he tells his father: "Don't interfere with art. You'll see when I write a decade and another *Kobzar* sees the light."[30] It is easy to smile at sons of illiterates, barely tutored in artistic conventions, yet fancying themselves the creators of epics to rival Shevchenko's best. But who could deny them the possibility? After all, Shevchenko *was* a peasant, and who could say that, at any given moment, another potential genius is not waiting to be given his chance?

---

[26] Tadei Sekund, "Deshcho pro ukrainsku terminolohiiu ta Institut Ukrainskoi Naukovoi Movy pry V.U.A.N.," *Literatura, Nauka, Mystetstvo,* March 2, 1924, p. 2.

[27] "Zahalne navchannia na Ukraini ta ioho perspektyvy. Doklad Narodnoho Komisara Osvity tov. Shumskoho," *Visty VUTsVK,* November 20, 1926, p. 2.

[28] "Vykhid dlia bezrobitnoi intelihentsii," *Visty VUTsVK,* April 19, 1924, p. 1.

[29] *Literatura, Nauka, Mystetstvo,* March 2, 1924, p. 1.

[30] *Literatura, Nauka, Mystetstvo,* March 9, 1924, p. 5.

The outburst of literary creativity which made the twenties a remarkable decade in the annals of Ukrainian literature was the child of this even more remarkable outburst of the aspiration to create, an aspiration that most would have found unthinkable under the old regime. Pluh was ready to give this aspiration a name and an ideology. Pylypenko called it massism (*masovyzm*) which he opposed to Khvylovyi's "academicism." Massism, as Pylypenko defined it, meant three things: Art, he argued, should be aimed at the masses, using simple language without debasing, vulgarizing, or primitivizing itself. Pluh had to be a mass organization, maintaining close contact with its "literary youth" by organizing its readers and helping them to become writers themselves. And thirdly, Pluh would devote itself to the principle of mass influence on the mass audience by being responsive to what the masses wanted.[31] It was a doctrine of the highest idealism; it demanded that the masses be given an art they could call their own as something that they had themselves created. Pylypenko was able to cite Lenin in defense of his principles:

> Art belongs to the people. It extends its deepest roots into the most obscure recesses of the broad toiling masses. It must be intelligible to these masses and liked by them. It must be the perception of the thought and the will of these masses; it must uplift them. It must reveal artists among the masses and develop them.[32]

And Pylypenko did it. Volodymyr Sosiura, one of the most popular poets of the 1920s, who continued to be influential into the postwar period, was a product of Pylypenko and Pluh.[33] So were Petro Panch, Ivan Senchenko, Andrii Holovko, Oleksander Kopylenko, Leonyd Pervomaiskyi, Natalia Zabila, Vasyl Chaplenko, Volodymyr Gzhytskyi, Kost Gordiienko, Oles Donchenko, Hryhorii Epik, Vasyl Mysyk, and Dokiia Humenna.[34] The Ukrainian literary revival of the twenties would have been unthinkable without Pylypenko's efforts. He was mentor to virtually a whole generation of writers.[35]

---

[31] Leites and Iashek, eds., *Desiat rokiv...* (2 ed., Kharkiv, 1930), vol. 2, p. 711.

[32] S. Pylypenko, "Pro 'chytabelnu' knyzhku," *Kultura i pobut,* August 30, 1925, p. 1.

[33] According to Tatiana Kardynalowska, Sosiura walked into the editorial offices of *Visty* one day clad in dirty peasant garb, took some poems out of his kerchief, and asked Pylypenko to publish them. Not only did Pylypenko do so, he also got Sosiura a job as a typesetter and took him under his wing as his favorite student.

[34] Anatol Hak, "Ne tak Khvylovyi, iak ti Khvylovyniatka," *Ukrainski visti,* May 23, 1971, p. 5.

[35] On Pylypenko's contribution to Ukrainian literature, see Assya Humesky, "Pamiati Serhiia Volodymyrovycha Pylypenka," *Novi dni,* January 1976, pp. 18–29, February

The problem lay in whether or not this mass art implied a lowering of standards. Some Pluh spokesmen were quite willing to lower them. One of them, B. Iakubskyi, was quite enthusiastic about the idea:

> What is now taking place in the literature of the Soviet countries is an extraordinary thing which deserves the widest possible attention. Literary work, which was hitherto one of the most complicated arts, a "language of the gods"—or at least a language of the upper strata of the ruling class, has been disseminated to an unusually wide degree and inspired the broadest circles of young people—worker and peasant youth—and has been extended into the farthest reaches. New books are awaited, pursued through every step of contemporary art, and are waiting to be written by such broad circles that not long ago could never have been dreamt of. The task of our time in the realm of art is to lower it, to bring it down to earth from its pedestal, to make it necessary and intelligible to all.[36]

All very laudable, but could the product of this lowering be called art? Does art not have to be on a higher level than the masses if it is to uplift them? Plenty of writers would take issue with Pylypenko and Pluh on just these questions.

Red Academicism

Khvylovyi was the most forceful defender of artistic standards, but he was not the first. It was Ellan-Blakytnyi who first proposed the idea of founding a Ukrainian literary academy in 1924, and he even wrote a draft statute and platform for it. According to Blakytnyi's manifesto, "The Ukrainian literature of October must be led out into the broad, all-Union and European arena." Blakytnyi's projected academy was to foster contacts with other national proletarian literatures and to help initiate similar organizations in other Soviet republics. It hoped to draw the masses into literary life but simultaneously keep standards high:

> The Literary Academy intends to awaken the activity of the Ukrainian masses in the field of literature and organize this activity in the proletarian communist spirit and in the highest contemporary style.[37]

1976, pp. 11–14; Dokiia Humenna, "Mii borh Serhiievi Pylypenkovi," *Ukrainski visti,* February 20, 1972, pp. 2–7.

[36] B. Iakubskyi, "Zhyttia molode: Sproba literaturnoi kharakterystyky 'kyivskykh pluzhan' ," *Chervonyi shliakh,* 1925, no. 9, p. 159.

[37] Luckyj, *Literary Politics,* pp. 59–60. Quotations from his translation of the text are taken from pp. 251–252.

When the project was announced in the press, it was dubbed "Red Academicism."[38] It was to be modeled on the "Immortals" of the French Academy and recognize outstanding writers abroad—Upton Sinclair was mentioned—as honorary members. An organizing group was named, and it included Pylypenko as well as Blakytnyi and Khvylovyi.[39]

Blakytnyi's dream of an official and universally recognized literary academy was frustrated by the split between Hart and Pluh over the issue of what attitude they should take regarding VUAPP, the counterpart of the All-Union Association of Proletarian writers (VAPP) in Ukraine. VUAPP, founded in 1924, claimed to be the linear descendant of Proletkult. Pylypenko accepted its offer to federate Pluh with it. Blakytnyi, on the other hand, opposed it as a violation of the principle of separate national literary organizations, and, in consequence, VUAPP began a campaign to win writers away from Hart. The KP(b)U Central Committee intervened in May 1925 with a resolution on Ukrainian literary groupings. Following the same general lines as the Russian Communist Party's 1924 resolution on literature, it condemned attempts by any organization to claim a monopoly in literature, announced that those who accused Hart of nationalism were propagating "harmful agitation," and forbade Pluh to form local organizations if there were no available Party organizations to direct their work. While it praised the work of both Hart and Pluh, it was clearly a vindication of Blakytnyi's position.[40]

The controversy with Pluh and VUAPP had left Hart so seriously weakened that it could not survive the death of its leader. Ellan-Blakytnyi died of a heart attack in December 1925; early the following year, Hart formally dissolved itself. VUAPP ceased to exist about the same time.[41] These events did not leave the field to Pylypenko alone, however. By the time Hart ceased to exist, Pluh faced a far more formidable challenger, the Free Academy of Proletarian Literature (Vaplite). Its guiding spirit was Mykola Khvylovyi.

Vaplite grew out of a meeting held in October 1925. Such Ukrainian cultural lights as Khvylovyi, Dovzhenko, and Tychyna decided to form an organization that would unite writers skilled at their art (*kvalifikovanykh pysmennykiv*) who had belonged to Hart, Pluh, or other

---

[38] "Chervonyi akademyzm", *Literatura, Nauka, Mystetstvo,* May 11, 1924, p. 1.

[39] H-ts, "Ukrainska Literaturna akademiia," *Literatura, Nauka, Mystetstvo,* May 11, 1924, p. 4.

[40] Luckyj, *Literary Politics,* pp. 52–58.

[41] *Ibid.,* p. 59.

organizations.[42] Vaplite was formally organized during the following month, and adopted a statute which coincided in many particulars with the draft statute that Blakytnyi had written.[43] It did not advocate any particular aesthetic but emphasized latitude for individual initiative.[44] According to its statute, Vaplite was open to those who wrote well, regardless of the language in which they wrote. Despite its relative exclusiveness—and it was a good deal less exclusive than the nine-member academy which Blakytnyi had envisioned—it also intended to devote itself to "mass" work, such as opening libraries and kiosks, organizing lectures, debates, and other literary formats for public appearances, as well as to helping its members improve their own literary skills.[45]

Khvylovyi and Khvylovyism

In the Spring of 1925, some militant young writers published an attack on Khvylovyi and the editors of the leading journals as "grey-haired old men" and "Olympians" who arbitrarily rejected the new literature about tractors, communes, and "the negative behavior of monks." On April 30, the literary supplement to *Visty* published Khvylovyi's response with a title borrowed from an old vaudeville farce, "On Satan in a Barrel, or On Graphomaniacs, Speculators, and Other 'Prosvitans'."[46] The first of Khvylovyi's broadsides against massism, it raised issues that dominated the Ukrainian cultural scene. It might be helpful to consider who Khvylovyi was and why he said what he did before studying his actual words.

Pluh's work in teaching peasants to write was often likened to the pre-revolutionary Prosvita movement, a network of village educational societies. Many contemporaries were not at all displeased that the regime should have its own counterpart to a national institution with a long and distinguished record of service to its credit.[47] For others, however, *pro-*

---

[42] The minutes of this meeting are published in George Luckyj, ed., *Vaplitianskyi zbirnyk* (Toronto, 1977), pp. 231–232.

[43] Luckyj points out the similarity in his introduction to *ibid.*, p. 10.

[44] "Khronika zovnishnia i vnutrishnia robota 'Vaplite'," *Vaplite: Zoshyt pershyi*, 1926, p. 98.

[45] "Statut Vilnoi Akademii Proletarskoi Literatury 'Vaplite'," *Vaplite: Zoshyt pershyi*, 1926, pp. 94–95.

[46] Myroslav Shkandrij, *The "Literary Discussion" in Soviet Ukraine, 1925-1928*, pp. 84–85.

[47] V. Koriak, "Vid prosvitianstva do pluzhanstva," *Literatura, Nauka, Mystetstvo*, May 18, 1924, p. 1.

svitianstvo (Prosvitaism) was synonymous with provincialism and thus should be escaped as quickly as possible. Only in the context of this equation can one understand the vehemence of Khvylovyi's philippics against Pylypenko, for there was nothing inherently inconsistent between "massism" and "academicism." If Pluh was a virtual school for beginning writers, Vaplite was really a higher school and saw itself as such.[48] Indeed, one can speak of many writers who graduated from Pluh or Hart to Vaplite. Even Khvylovyi was one.

Khvylovyi was born Nikolai Fitilëv, the son of a Russian village schoolteacher in Ukraine, in 1893. His most reliable biographer notes that there was nothing European or cosmopolitan in his early background and very little to acquaint him with the wider world beyond his own Ukraine. He was drafted into the tsarist army during the First World War, was radicalized as were so many other young men of his generation, and after demobilization, joined the UPSR. During the civil war he worked for a period of time among the peasantry, set up Prosvita societies, and even headed one in his native village. His political evolution seems to have been similar to that of the Borotbisty, although he was never a member of that party. After the war, he became a writer, joined Hart, and in 1922 established his reputation as a literary lion with the publication of a collection called *Blue Études*.[49]

If Khvylovyi cannot be credited with originating the idea of establishing a literary academy for the best writers in Ukraine, neither can he be credited with originating the idea that Ukrainian culture should throw off Russian influence and orient itself toward the West. The old Brotherhood of Taras had corresponded with Ukrainian writers in the 1890s and "tried to steer Ukrainian literature away from its populist bias in order to make it more Western and more European."[50] Kovalevskyi recalled in his memoirs how the intelligentsia had been electrified by this same idea when Dmytro Dontsov suggested it in 1910.[51] George Luckyj traced it to 1917, when Les Kurbas published the manifesto of his Young Theater, calling on Ukrainian culture to orient itself to Europe

---

[48] This point is made by M. Dolengo in his review of *Vaplite: Almanakh pershyi, Kultura i pobut*, January 9, 1927, p. 4.

[49] O. Han, *Trahediia Mykoly Khvylovho* (n.p., n.d.), pp. 8, 12, 16–21, 32. See also Hryhory Kostiuk, "Mykola Khvylovyi: Zhyttia, doba, tvorchist," in Mykola Khvylovyi, *Tvory v piatokh tomakh* (New York, Baltimore, Toronto, 1978–   ), vol. 1, pp. 15–106.

[50] George Y. Boshyk, *The Rise of Ukrainian Political Parties in Russia*, p. 34.

[51] Mykola Kovalevskyi, *Pry dzherelakh borotby*, p. 146.

"without intermediaries or models."[52] In 1918, Mykola Zerov became the founder of a group of writers who sought inspiration in the models of ancient and French classicism, and Khvylovyi's defense of the "Neoclassicist" fellow travelers became the basis of charges that he subordinated political orthodoxy to the aesthetics of art for art's sake.[53] Pylypenko himself had been author of perhaps the most radical of all proposals for the "Europeanization" of Ukrainian culture, the adoption of the Latin alphabet.[54] Even the most original of Khvylovyi's basic ideas, the notion of Ukraine leading an Asiatic Renaissance, is based on Oswald Spengler's idea of the decline of the West.[55] But the fact that Khvylovyi drew on existing ideas does nothing to diminish the force of his argument, for it was he who put these ideas together, made them coherent, and imbued them with the zeal of a convert repudiating the elements of provincialism in his own heritage.

Khvylovyi's first series of articles were later grouped together in a pamphlet that borrowed the name of Sienkiewicz's novel, *Quo Vadis?* (*Kamo hriadeshy?*). His opponents had charged him with having "Satan in a barrel," that is, borrowing ideas from the class enemies who threatened to jump out of the barrel like Satan in the old vaudeville farce. Khvylovyi showed his defiance by quoting Spengler in order to show that he was quite willing to quote even a fascist, as he called the German historian, if what he had to say made sense. His first diatribe was

---

[52] Luckyj, *Literary Politics*, p. 26. The original document is Les Kurbas, "Molodyi teatr," *Robitnycha hazeta*, September 23, 1917, p. 3. The crucial passage reads as follows: "In our literature, which has hitherto reflected the social consciousness of society, after the long epoch of Ukrainophilism, cossackophilism, and ethnographism, after 'modernism' patterned purely on Russian models, we see what is great, what is alone correct and profound. This points directly to Europe and directly to ourselves. Without intermediaries and without models. In art there is but one way." Luckyj cites this passage, but his translation is a bit different.

[53] Mykola Zerov, *Do dzherel: Istorychno-literaturni ta krytychni statti* (reprint: State College, Pennsylvania, 1967), p. 8.

[54] S. Pylypenko, "Odvertyj lyst do vsix, xto cikavyt'sja cijeju spravoju," *Chervonyi shliakh*, 1924, no. 6–7, pp. 267–268 (He wrote it in his own version of Latin script); Mexajlo Johansen, "Prystosuvannia latynytsi do potreb ukrainskoi movy," *Chervonyi shliakh*, 1923, no. 9, pp. 167–169 (an improvement on Pylypenko's version); I. Tkachuk, "Nevidkladne zavdannia (Do spravy zavedennia latynskoho alfabitu v ukrainskim pysmi)," *Chervonyi shliakh*, 1924, no. 4–5, pp. 245–247; Iu. Zh., "De-iaki uvahy z pryvodu prystosuvannia latynytsi do potreb ukrainskoi movy," *Literatura, Nauka, Mystetstvo*, March 16, 1927, p. 1.

[55] For an interesting discussion of Spengler's influence on Khvylovyi, see Petro Holubenko, "Khvylovyi i Shpengler," *Suchasnist*, vol. 3, 1963, no. 5, pp. 53–70.

directed against the self-proclaimed second generation, the representatives of which were often older than those they were ready to toss
into the ashcan of history. To talk about a new literary generation in
the brief span since the civil war was, to Khvylovyi's mind, absurd.
"There is not and never will be an example in the history of literature
where a generation is able to express itself in five or six years: a writer
is not an American typewriter and his work is not a Poltava dumpling."[56]
    What there was, he claimed, was the spark of something new, some
of the representatives of which were mature and some of which were
not. The way to develop Ukrainian literature was not by artificially
dividing it into generations, but by choosing between the eternal cultural
values of Europe and the provincialism of Prosvita. Universals, plat-
forms, and manifestoes might make those who signed them feel important, but they could not solve the problem of qualifications, of learning
how to write well. To solve this problem, Khvylovyi felt that one Zerov,
the fellow traveler of the Neoclassicist school, was worth more than
a hundred Prosvitans who bandied about all sorts of "Red" phrases
and tried to make themselves feel more revolutionary than Lenin himself.
With the speed-up of Ukrainization, Khvylovyi saw the danger of former
kulak ideologists—he mentioned the poet Pavlo Tychyna as the leading
example—switching to an ultra-left peasantism for reasons of pure
opportunism and encouraging a "villagization" of proletarian culture,
albeit under Red phrases. Khvylovyi championed neither Hart nor Pluh;
he proclaimed himself ready to accept talent wherever he could find
it, and portrayed himself as a defender of quality from those who wanted
to debase art to the level of the *komnezamy* and trade unions.[57]
    These young writers, Khvylovyi charged, kept trying to "Octoberize"
their betters and set young against old, while they themselves turned
their backs on the past and had not even bothered to consider the works
of such proletarian thinkers as Belinskii, Dobroliubov, and Chernyshev-
skii. Such illiterate writers were charged with "graphomania" and
literary hooliganism. The only way they could avoid the real Satan jum-
ping out at them was to choose Europe over Prosvita and turn their
energies to the task of becoming good writers. They had to study their
craft and master the achievements of the past. It was necessary to

> deflate or, at least, put in their place various scribblers who, being able
> to write on the level of a so-so journalist, stick their noses in art and

---

[56] Mykola Khvylovyi, *Kamo hriadeshy? Pamflety* (Kharkiv, 1925), p. 7.
[57] *Ibid.*, pp. 5–12.

try to dominate it. It will then become clear that the so-called art for the masses is the product of the dedicated work of many generations but certainly not the "Red" hack. The simplicity and clarity of Tolstoy—that is art of the highest quality. Even if it appeared in the "setting" of the declining possibilities of the Russian bourgeoisie and nobility, it is better for the masses than (Upton) Sinclair in millions of copies.[58]

There was no reason that workers and peasants could not create such art, but to do so they would have to be "intellectually developed, talented, and creative people." Young writers must try to themselves become "Olympians," because only such people could create worthwhile proletarian art. The job called for ethical purity and devoted effort, but young writers had the opportunity of creating a real Renaissance if only they could follow the path that history had marked for them.[59]

Soon after the appearance of his first article, Khvylovyi developed his idea of the Asiatic Renaissance by defending the idea of art as something incapable of being understood by the superficial "class analysis" employed by Russian writers grouped around the journals *Na postu* and *Oktiabr* and their Ukrainian followers.[60] Art, he explained, was not the "meaningless abstraction" some would have it, but "an arch-specific sphere of human activity." Those who thought otherwise were dismissed as troglodytes and were accused of arguing from such nonsensical positions as: "Taking into consideration the fact that Copernicus was of proletarian origin along with the phenomenon of centrifugal force, it is stated that the earth, in fact, circles the sun."[61] To condemn prerevolutionary art because it was not revolutionary, he argued, was absurd. Besides, the avant-garde was itself far from revolutionary. Khvylovyi argued that it in fact reflected the values of that nemesis of socialist construction, the nepman, who liked to believe that the mixed economy of the day was permanent, and who was perfectly willing to let the glittering carnival of the avant-garde supplant social concerns in art and serve as a surrogate for the real social change that might threaten his position. The whole phenomenon had nothing to do with Marxist aesthetics, he pointed out. To realize what a contrast existed

---

[58] *Ibid.*, p. 18.

[59] *Ibid.*, pp. 12–18.

[60] *Na postu* and *Oktiabr* were the organs of the Proletkultists of VAPP. Later *Na postu* became *Na Literaturnom postu*. For a study of "On guardism" in its later phase, see Edward J. Brown, *The Proletarian Episode in Russian Literature, 1928–1933* (New York, 1953).

[61] Khvylovyi, *Kamo hriadeshy*, p. 21.

between Leninism and the avant-garde, one had only to compare the literary platform of the Octobrists with Lenin's speech to the third Komsomol congress.[62]

As for the Ukrainian followers of massism, whom Khvylovyi contemptuously dubbed "enko," they had yet to produce anything worthy of the name of art. Their very definition of the artist seemed to preclude their being able to do so; the artist had to be more than merely able to "give society a valuable work in step with the victorious class" because "a real artist, as an artist, is always ahead of his class." An artist who "is in step with the development of a class ceases to be an artist."[63]

How, then, ought writers to go about creating proletarian art? Khvylovyi drew an analogy between the Renaissance masters and those who faced a similar task of leading the creative rebirth of nations oppressed by imperialism. Where once Europe had produced its Renaissance, Asia was awaiting its own:

> Just as Petrarch, Michaelangelo, Rafael, and others of the Italian school ignited Europe with the fire of rebirth, new artists, among whom are those from the oppressed lands of Asia, new artists-Communards shall go forth with our help, ascend the peak of Hellikon, place there the lamp of renascence, and from under the faroff din of the battles on the barricades it will blaze forth as an azure pentagram over the dark European night.[64]

Borrowing from Spengler's prognosis for the West's eclipse, Khvylovyi placed his hope in Asia for a marriage of communism and anti-imperialism, a hope that seems prophetic in the wake of the Chinese and Indochinese revolutions:

> by talking about the Asiatic Renaissance, we have in mind an extraordinary artistic blossoming of nations like China, India, and so forth. We understand it as a great spiritual rebirth of backward Asiatic countries. It must come, this Asiatic Renaissance, because the idea of communism is a specter that haunts Europe not so much as it does Asia, because Asia, realizing that only communism will free it from economic slavery, will use art as an agent of militancy.[65]

Khvylovyi could not see that by the time communism reached Asia, it would have reached the atrophied stage of Stalinism and would be

---

[62] *Ibid.*, pp. 23–29.
[63] *Ibid.*, p. 30.
[64] *Ibid.*, pp. 31–32.
[65] *Ibid.*, p. 33.

ill-prepared to awaken any new form of artistic creation. Perhaps he sought in Asia the heroic quality which he believed Russian communism had already lost under NEP.[66] At any rate, Khvylovyi saw his Asiatic Renaissance as a return to the vigorous revolutionary romanticism which seemed to have been lost at home.

He had a name for this vision: romantic vitaism, from *vita,* the Latin word for life. Romantic vitaism would create a new heroic myth for revolutionaries:

> The proletarian art of our day is a *Marseillais* which summons the avant-garde of the world proletariat to victory on the barricades. Romantic vitaism creates, not "enko" but Communards.... This is the art of the first phase of the Asiatic Renaissance. It must spread from Ukraine to all the world and play not a provincial role but one common to all mankind.[67]

This was to be the art of the war between capitalism and socialism, the aspiration of a young revolutionary class to liberate all humanity. Those who wanted to forsake the subjective "I", in the name of a faceless collectivism, could never express the militant idealism appropriate to the new age. A hero without individual identity, Khvylovyi declared, could only be a Gogolian pseudo-hero, not a hero ready to die on the barricades. Pylypenko was, Khvylovyi conceded, "a revolutionary to the core," but wrong.[68] The debasement of art which his massism implied could not create an art worthy of the tasks the age had marked out for it. Both Pluh and Hart had, to their detriment, flirted with *prosvitianstvo.* Pluh could best serve art by dropping its artistic pretensions and admitting that it was no more and no less than a voluntary organization of people interested in their own cultural enlightenment. The new art had to look to Europe with its experience of many centuries, not Spengler's

---

[66] Khvylovyi's pessimistic outlook regarding the Soviet Union of his day is perhaps best expressed in a much-quoted and attacked passage from the introduction he wrote for a volume of Blakytnyi's poetry: "the civil war has ended. The Communard (more precisely, the lyric writer) did not move 'the world's concrete foundations'. Instead of 'red stars' 'above a patchwork of clouds' has come the hopeless NEP with its rampant bureaucratism and slippery nepmen. With his mind, his 'pure intellect', the Communard makes mathematical explanations, collects the statistical data for certain real prognoses, and convinces himself that 'everything's alright—don't cry', that in spite of everything we have 'firm, bright hopes', but his heart sings a different tune..." Vas. Ellan, *Poezii* (Kharkiv, 1927), pp. 18-19. Parentheses in the original.

[67] Khvylovyi, *Kamo hriadeshy,* pp. 36–37.

[68] *Ibid.,* p. 41.

declining Europe, but "the Europe of Goethe, Darwin, Byron, Newton, and Marx. This is the Europe without which the first phalanxes of the Asiatic Renaissance cannot rise up."[69]

Khvylovyi's third letter dealt with what he called "the unnatural union" between the revolutionary, Serhii Pylypenko, and "the reactionary and impoverished Prosvita." He explained this union in terms of the lack of perspective that untutored youth carried with them in their attempt to fill the void that opened up when the hitherto oppressed Ukrainian nation entered upon the stage of world history and its artists had to face the *terra incognita* of Marxist aesthetics:

> Even since '18 the young youth came from the wilds of village and town with a confident gait. They were the first detachments of a young art, and they had to fill an empty space. They were brave lads, and they behaved like it with the limits and the blood of that class which was undergoing the first trials in its role as historical dictator. They went forth with burning eyes and deep faith in their victory . . . But when they arrived they saw that they were unarmed. They lacked broad erudition because they were people either wholly without education or with a certificate from a "church school." It was thus apparent to them that they either flee from the front or join an unequal struggle. It was at that very moment when to their aid came the immortal Prosvita—all those lowbrow ideologues of On Guardism, Octoberism, and so forth.[70]

Such people were philistines, hacks who wanted to play a role in art and could mouth the requisite phrases, demagogues and dilettantes who were incapable of playing a positive role in art. Some, like Zerov, had for one reason or another attached themselves to the old intelligentsia and learned from it. Neither the one nor the other could serve as a model for Ukraine's young revolutionary art. But the Zerovs, for all their ideological foreignness to the goals of communism, had mastered the technique of literature far better than had writers devoted to the revolution. The way to deal with the Zerovs was not to suppress them but to learn from them and surpass them. They would have to accept the ideology of communism, but communists who wanted to create something worthwhile would have to recognize the technical mastery of the Zerovs. Only then could Ukraine take part in the Asiatic Renaissance. Only then could it give birth to an art of the quality that Europe expected.[71]

---

[69] *Ibid.*, p. 42.
[70] *Ibid.*, p. 50.
[71] *Ibid.*, pp. 50–64.

Khvylovyi's three letters to young Ukrainian writers were like Luther's theses nailed to the door of the church. One could accept or reject his ideas, but no one who pretended to any role in the Ukrainian literary scene could afford to ignore them. On May 24, 1925, a public debate of representatives of various literary groups was sponsored by the Ukrainian Academy of Sciences in Kiev. Entitled "Paths for the Development of Contemporary Literature," it was in fact a debate over the path marked out by Khvylovyi.

The first speaker, Mezhenko, set the tone by asking just which Europe Khvylovyi wanted to follow. Europe, he pointed out, had its share of Philistinism, and Soviet Russia, its share of achievements. Should one prefer the Tarzan novels of Edgar Rice Burroughs to the poetry of Maiakovskii? Europe, he claimed, was a greater danger to Ukrainian communism than the old Prosvita tradition, because for all its prestige, Europe was bourgeois, philistine, and hostile to the goals of communism:

> Is everything in European cultural life really better than our own *prosvitianstvo?* It is worse, because it is easy to fight *prosvitianstvo.* It has a tradition which is already to a significant degree discredited, but European culture has authority, and this is at the present time a more dangerous thing.[72]

The Europe which Mezhenko described was full of commercial publishing houses which speculated on books by publishing hackwork done for money; at the same time, this Europe was a great unknown, a place heard about on the radio and seen in the products it exported. Ukrainians were unprepared to borrow from Europe and, perhaps, incapable even of understanding it. Hart had sent three writers there; when they returned, two were silent, and the third had nothing good to say about it. Did it mean Ukrainians could not understand Europe, or that they needed something specific rather than to borrow from it indiscriminately? Mezhenko suggested that what was needed was not European culture itself, but the technique for building such a culture. Europe's culture, he argued, was foreign and hostile because it was created under social conditions that Ukraine had not only failed to reproduce, but also had rejected. Its verbal mastery, its musical and theatrical techniques, were nonetheless vital to building a culture for Soviet Ukraine. Pluh's tendency to vulgarize and primitivize were also a threat to cultural achievement. *Prosvitianstvo* and blind Europeanism

---

[72] *Shliakhy rozvytku suchasnoi literatury: Dysput 24 travnia 1925 r.* (Kiev, 1925), p. 8.

were "the Scylla and Charybdis of Ukrainian culture." Mezhenko concluded that Europe could not be wholly embraced or repudiated; its ideology had to be rejected, its technique—which had to be got and could only be got from Europe—adapted.[73]

Not surprisingly, Khvylovyi found his ablest defender in the Neoclassicist, Mykola Zerov, who himself represented the European culture for which Khvylovyi yearned in the name of communist literature. Zerov tried to refocus the discussion by returning to the central issue of literary quality. The *prosvitianstvo* which Khvylovyi had decried was literary philistinism that had manifested itself in proletarian literature. In Europe, he explained, Khvylovyi had seen a weapon that could be used against this philistinism. As Zerov understood it, Khvylovyi looked to Europe as the representative of a strong cultural tradition. The issue thus could be restated, not as Europe vs. Prosvita, but as *kultura* vs. *khaltura*, culture of lasting value vs. hackwork. Europe had to be used as a textbook and a technical guide. Three things had to be opposed: the brazen ignorance of certain critics, the habit of forming small cult-like groups (*hurtkivstvo*), and the reluctance of certain young writers to study their craft. Zerov also had his ideas about what needed to be done. Writers had to be taught to write well. They had to make the classics of European literature their own. They had to create a healthy literary atmosphere, such as Moscow already possessed, instead of the gossip mongering of those who sought the orthodoxy of their own monopolization of literary expression at the expense of literature worth reading. What was needed above all was more literature and fewer manifestoes, more serious literary studies and fewer empty ideological formulas.[74]

Khvylovyi's opponents and defenders largely talked past each other, his opponents discussing ideological purity, and his defenders, the need for readable literature. Representatives of militant groups such as Hart, Pluh, and Zhovten (October), without exception took issue with the idea that the Party in the village represented a return to Prosvita.[75] Those they dismissed as *petit-bourgeois,* accused them of attempting to stifle artistic initiative, and emphasized that the business of literature was to produce books that were worth reading.[76] This dialogue of the deaf aroused wider interest than any other issue of the day. The Kiev debate

---

[73] *Ibid.,* pp. 7–14.
[74] *Ibid.,* pp. 23–29.
[75] *Ibid.,* pp. 22–23, 35, 40–42.
[76] *Ibid.,* pp. 35–38, 43–54.

drew an audience of 800.[77] Those who were not present wanted to know what had happened. *Visty* published an outline version of the debate over two months after it was held.[78]

Khvylovyi's opponents and defenders published their polemical broadsides during the following months. *Zhyttia i revoliutsiia (Life and Revolution)*, journal of the "fellow-traveler" Lanka group, published a two-part survey of the state of Ukrainian *belles-lettres,* quoted long extracts of the barely literate prose all too often found, and ended with the rhetorical question: "Is this not an all-Ukrainian scandal?"[79] A sarcastic attack on Pylypenko was published in the *Visty* literary supplement, accusing the mass organizations of emphasizing the quantity of writers over the quality of literature. To the claim that Pluh had 214 writers, the reply was made that one could doubt whether there were 214 writers in all Ukraine.[80] Beside this attack was Pylypenko's response, which began with the facetious caveat that it was difficult for someone judged guilty of speculating on literature, graphomania, and vulgar Marxism to answer opponents. He wondered what sort of discussion it was, where an opponent was as indiscriminately accused as Khvylovyi had accused him. Coldly addressing Khvylovyi as "academician" rather than "comrade," he explained that his opponents were wrong in thinking that he was hostile to culture in general. He and his followers did not call themselves an academy of proletarian writers, as did Khvylovyi's adherents, but they were actively trying to teach toilers how to write. They were creating a proletarian culture in what seemed to Pylypenko the only way possible, by helping it to grow organically out of the masses themselves.[81] To his credit, Pylypenko faced the issue of what sort of literature ought to be created and how it ought to be fostered. He did not, like so many others, mouth simple phrases about Marxist orthodoxy, although he did note that certain nationalistic elements were using Khvylovyi's arguments to their own purpose. Khvylovyi's reply was

---

[77] Luckyj, *Literary Politics...*, p. 93.

[78] "Shliakhy rozvytku ukr. literatury," *Kultura i pobut,* August 9, 1925, p. 3.

[79] Vas. Desniak, "Krytychni uvahy pro nashi zhurnaly," *Zhyttia i revoliutsiia,* 1925, no. 6–7, pp. 117–123; continued as Desniak, "Ohliad zhurnaliv," *Zhyttia i revoliutsiia,* 1925, no. 8, pp. 77–81.

[80] M. Ialovyi, "Khai zhyve 'Hart' i 'Pluh'," *Kultura i pobut,* January 31, 1926, pp. 2–4.

[81] S. Pylypenko, "Iak na pravdyvomi spotykaiutsia (Pershyi shmat dyskusiinoi vidpovidy akademykam M. Ialovomu i M. Khvylovomu)," *Kultura i pobut,* January 31, 1926, pp. 2–4.

that both sides of the controversy had its "Petliurists"; it was a job for the censor and the GPU to root them out.[82]

Khvylovyi returned to the offensive in a second cycle of articles titled *Thoughts Against the Current*. The basic question, as he put it, was how to develop a proletarian culture in a backward country:

> We Communards take upon ourselves a great responsibility: it depends solely on us the kind of art the proletariat will create during the age of its dictatorship. But this responsibility becomes the more complex when we realize that this art must be created by a nation which is culturally backward.[83]

Khvylovyi saw the main danger to Ukrainian cultural development as being the countryside, not the intelligentsia. He had great respect for Pylypenko as a dedicated revolutionary, but believed that his adversary had objectively fallen under the influence of the kulaks. He emphasized the word "objectively" to show that he considered Pylypenko's alleged errors to have been honest ones, and to avoid even a hint that the founder of Pluh had ever intentionally sided with the "class enemy."[84] Khvylovyi considered the fact that prominent non-communist intellectuals had sided with him to be irrelevant. He declared that even if Zerov, Fylypovych, and Mohylianskyi were unreconstructed right-wingers, Maksym Rylskyi a Polish noble, and the whole *petit-bourgeois* intelligentsia on the side of the "Olympians," the issues at hand would remain unchanged.[85] The problem to be faced originated in the lack of a Ukrainian proletariat. With the working class in Ukraine essentially estranged from Ukrainian culture, the only "masses" available to the so-called mass literary organizations were peasants, and among the peasantry, the mentality of the kulak was far stronger than that of the toiler. If the mass organizations confined themselves to the functions of cultural education, ideological guidance would be comparatively simple to maintain. Instead, they claimed to be leading an artistic movement, and art is the most complex of things. Hence, Khvylovyi saw the situation as one in which people, only semi-literate in art and in Marxist ideology, were surrounded by agents of the rural bourgeoisie and were faced with the inevitability of giving up position after position to the kulaks. Thus Khvylovyi tried to present the choice between

---

[82] Mykola Khvylovyi, *Kamo hriadeshy*, p. 59.
[83] Mykola Khvylovyi, *Dumky proty techii: Pamflety* (Kharkiv, 1926), p. 47.
[84] *Ibid.*, pp. 37–38.
[85] *Ibid.*, pp. 9–10.

Europe and Prosvita as a choice of whether or not to surrender to the kulaks:

> Europe or Prosvita. *This is the single most cardinal question of our age.* In Europe, as a psychological category, is the sum of all those possibilities which we can oppose in art to Prosvita, which is also a psychological category from which the kulaks take sustenance. Although they are abstract things, they exist in a definite time in a definite society and play a no less definite role. Hence there is nothing strange in the fact that *in today's literature two forces are locked* in struggle: the first is that which orients itself toward Europe; the second is that which is used by Prosvita, in other words, by the kulaks. The first continues the old Marxist traditions; the other adheres to vulgar Marxism.

Khvylovyi could see no possibility of compromise between them.[86] And what was this Europe to which Khvylovyi turned?

> You ask which Europe? Take whichever you like: past or present, bourgeois or proletarian, eternal or changing. Because the fact is that there were Hamlets, Don Juans, and Tartuffes in the past, but they are also in the present; consider them eternal, but they are also changing. The dialectic takes such a coquettish path when it wanders into the labyrinth of the superstructure.[87]

It was, in short, the sum of Western culture, that which to him seemed cosmopolitan and eternal.

In order to refute his opponents, Khvylovyi had to do more than argue from the standpoint of aesthetic imperatives. The centerpiece of Marxism is the class struggle and its culmination in the proletarian revolution. That which helps the proletariat and furthers the march of history is progressive; that which does not is reactionary and is automatically lumped with the discredited class enemy. A communist cannot uphold art for art's sake, but must condemn those who take such a position as agents of bourgeois ideology whether or not that be their subjective intent. Right and wrong do not exist outside the dichotomy of the class struggle. And for this reason, Khvylovyi had to do more than refute his opponents; he had to show that they were objectively on the side of the class enemy, the rural *petite-bourgeoisie,* the kulak. Moreover, one could not compromise with the class enemy; he must be destroyed. This is not to say that Khvylovyi and Pylypenko wanted to destroy each

---

[86] *Ibid.,* pp. 23–24. Emphasis in original.
[87] *Ibid.,* p. 44.

other: they most certainly did not. But as Marxists, they had to resort to such polemical devices because their ideology allowed them no others. Khvylovyi had himself been criticized because his line of argumentation was congenial to non-Marxist intellectuals, the *petit-bourgeois* intelligentsia, in the jargon of the day. He attempted to dismiss the issue by saying that any agreement the bourgeois nationalists might express with him did no more to discredit his views than the fact that Ustrialov and the Smena Vekh group supported the Russian Communist Party had discredited Leninism.[88] To those who accused him of idealism by adopting the aesthetic of romantic vitaism, he stated that it had nothing whatever to do with biological vitalism, a point that had evidently confused his critics. He declared that there was nothing contrary to historical materialism in opting for romanticism over realism, because proletarian art would have both: "Proletarian art will go through all the stages of romanticism, realism, and so forth."[89] Nor, he maintained, should he be condemned for formalism. Formalism, he conceded, was a bourgeois approach to art, but the formalists knew more about art than did their Marxist rivals. Marxists would have to learn from them, but as for Khvylovyi, he described himself as a formalist only in the sense that he demanded artistic rigor.[90] Ukrainian culture would have to escape the tradition of "epigonism," the slavish habit of aping Russian developments that went back to Kotliarevskyi. It would do so not by producing "narrowly utilitarian saccharine" or the "semi-barbarous" writing of massism, but by finding its own way by turning to the eternal cultural values of Europe.[91]

Khvylovyi's eagerness to escape Russian cultural influence was more radically expressed in a third series of articles called "The Apologists of Scribblism" (*Apolohety pysaryzmu*). First and foremost among them was Pylypenko. Positions had hardened, tempers flared, and each side was intent in painting its opponent in the blackest terms of class enmity while vehemently proclaiming its own loyalty to the proletariat and the Communist Party.

Khvylovyi described Vaplite as not unlike Don Quixote in its quest for the communist cultural ideal. It was not only a factor in the historical process but also faced overwhelming odds and universal vilification. "In a word," he wrote, "Vaplite is not only an imposing agent on the

---

[88] *Ibid.*, p. 47.
[89] *Ibid.*, pp. 66–67.
[90] *Ibid.*, pp. 69–79.
[91] *Ibid.*, pp. 47–59.

uncharted course of literature (*literaturnomu bezdorizhzhia*) but is
something of a bugbear and a devil.'' He felt it necessary to recall that
what Vaplite had demanded was adherence to the highest criteria of art;
in so doing, it had no choice but to assume a historic role in the development of proletarian art. It had to challenge the pretensions of Pluh to
a hegemony which would have meant the domination of art by ''the
ideologues of *petit-bourgeois* groupings.'' The sole hegemon of the process of artistic development was, according to Khvylovyi, neither
Russia's VAPP nor Ukraine's Pluh but the Communist Party and its
leadership. It was of dubious wisdom at best to divide literature into
self-described militant class organizations that were perpetually at one
another's throats. Vaplite, he wrote, did not consider itself a ''proletarian
academy'' or proletarian in any sense; it was a free academy of proletarian literature, something altogether different. As such, it was an
institute of Marxist aesthetics that tried to produce worthwhile art for
the proletariat, at present all that any literary organization could attempt.[92]

Khvylovyi maintained that Pylypenko's fundamental error consisted
in mixing massism with Prosvita. As a method of upbringing directed
at the mass psyche, massism was laudable policy. He even declared that,
''As a slogan outside of time and place, we accept massism. . . But in
accepting it, we make the slogan concrete in the way that the given socio-
economic situation has made it.''[93] That situation had forced massism
toward provincialism, peasantism, and artistic illiteracy, Khvylovyi
charged. The reason he gave hearkened back to a fear as old as Lenin's
question, *Kto kogo*? (Who beats whom?), the fear that the communist
vanguard of the proletariat would be swallowed by the rural *petite
bourgeoisie* that surrounded it like an atoll surrounded by the South
Pacific. Khvylovyi phrased his fear differently but his meaning was the
same. He wrote:

> When we say that the broad masses cannot be drawn into art, then we
> have first of all in mind the peasantry—that mass which is brought up
> in its own *petit-bourgeois* atmosphere. This does not at all mean that these
> masses must not have an outlet in art, but it means that they cannot direct
> it as an ideological center. One cannot have children (in the best of cases)
> bring up children.[94]

---

[92] Mykola Khvylovyi, ''Apolohety pysaryzmu (Do problem kulturnoi revoliutsii),''
Kultura i pobut, March 21, 1926, p. 8.
[93] *Ibid.,* p. 9.
[94] *Ibid.,* p. 10.

In his view, that was precisely what Russian's VAPP and Ukraine's Pluh were attempting to do, to raise children with children. Such an attempt was less absurd than dangerous, because in a setting where even factory wrokers still bore the marks of rural origin, such an attempt would ultimately come to rest on the peasantry. When it came to the peasantry, it would ultimately come to the "strong" on which the tsarist minister Stolypin had once wagered, the so-called "Stolypin peasant," the kulak who outdid all others in acting the part of a rural capitalist. Unconsciously and unwillingly, the adherents of massism, whether Russian or Ukrainian, came ultimately and inevitably to the Stolypin peasant. It was this progression that brought Soviet Ukrainian literature to a crisis, and even those who could not discern its cause admitted that the crisis was real. Khvylovyi charged that his opponents' attacks had been only a mask for their own deviation. Pylypenko had likened Khvylovyi's views to Trotskyism, and Khvylovyi replied that Pylypenko had taken a position analogous to that of the Leningrad opposition of Zinoviev and Kamenev, by trying to establish an independent ideological center with its own orthodoxy when the only legitimate guardian of orthodoxy was the Party itself.[95] "There is only one ideological center," Khvylovyi wrote, "and its name is the Communist Party."[96]

Had the level of the discussion remained on this rather unsavory plane, Moscow would probably have found no cause to intervene. Party authorities in Ukraine might ultimately have felt obliged to issue a reproof designed to pull the disputants apart and to ensure their coexistence. Such a statement would likely have followed the general principles of the RKP's 1924 resolution on literature and its Ukrainian counterpart of the following year, words of caution to the effect that no group had a monopoly on truth, and that those who thought differently but were generally loyal to the regime ought to be left in peace.

It was the last article in Khvylovyi's cycle that changed the situation by giving full vent to his previously hinted at conviction that cultural orientation to Europe meant conscious opposition to all cultural influences emanating from Russia. He published it at a time when the leading Russian opponents to Stalin were moving toward alliance. Khvylovyi could not have known the machinations taking place in Moscow. Had he known, he would perhaps have discovered that he had chosen the worst possible time to make his conviction explicit.

---

[95] *Ibid.,* pp. 10–14.
[96] *Ibid.,* p. 14.

Thus far, Khvylovyi had said nothing particularly offensive to Moscow. Even his references to Europe were relatively innocuous, that "Europe" was for him a synonym for cultural renaissance. His opponents might dispute such an equating of Europe with culture, and might suggest that there was something to be gained from post-revolutionary Russian literature, but they understood that Khvylovyi equated Europe with cultural development and could find nothing overtly disloyal to Moscow in it.[97]

Khvylovyi began the last installment of his "Apologists of Scribblism" by returning to the problem of cultural development. The basic problem that Ukrainian communism faced, as he saw it, was how to foster the ideological development of the Ukrainian nation, how to carry forth a Ukrainian cultural revolution. No lasting effects could be anticipated if communists satisfied themselves with creating a "hothouse art" that had no foundation in the nation's life. It meant organizing the ideology of the nation's press and literary forces so as to guarantee the ideological hegemony of the proletariat. The problem was that the proletariat could never be the ideological hegemon of the Ukrainian nation so long as it failed to master Ukrainian culture. A Ukrainian cultural revolution could produce no certain results unless the proletariat were Ukrainized. Hence, Khvylovyi wrote, "We demand that the necessity of the Ukrainization of the proletariat be taken seriously."[98] Ukrainization was not only the result of the desires of a nation of thirty million, but also the sole way for the proletariat to take charge of Ukrainian culture without a social basis for that culture, i.e., a Ukrainian proletariat.[99]

Khvylovyi also met the charges of those of his critics who accused him of opposing an "art of the intelligentsia" to proletarian art. Marxism, he pointed out, does not consider the intelligentsia a class, but a dependent social stratum which serves the interests of one class or another. The proletariat needed its intelligentsia, especially in the realm of culture. After all, he argued, the masses as such cannot create a cultural revival; only their intelligentsia can do that.

---

[97] See, for example, S. Shchupak, "Psevdomarksyzm Khvylovoho," *Zhyttia i revoliutsiia,* 1925, no. 12, pp. 61–69. Shchupak pointed out that Khvylovyi equated Europe with culture, accused him of seeking culture and art for their own sake, and tried to find some evidence of nationalism in this, without much success, for his *en passant* accusation of nationalism simply did not follow from anything else in his article, the main tenor of which was that Khvylovyi had gone over to the *petit bourgeois* intelligentsia.

[98] Mykola Khvylovyi, "Apolohety pysaryzmu," *Kultura i pobut,* March 28, 1926, p. 1.

[99] *Ibid.,* pp. 1–3.

We ideologically organize the forces of literature only through *our own* intelligentsia. And this means that *we must devote all our attention not to the amorphous mass but to the cadres of the young intelligentsia*...[100]

Devoting attention meant teaching them. It meant heeding the "fellow-travelers" like Zerov who were ready to place their knowledge at the disposal of this new intelligentsia. It meant the repudiation of the massism that would ignore such learning.[101]

What got Khvylovyi into trouble was the last section of his article, written as an afterthought in response to a brochure by one Kost Burevii. This final section was entitled "Moscow's Dusty Backwaters" (*Moskovski zadripanky*) and began with a quotation from Vissarion Belinskii, the radical nineteenth century Russian literary critic, noting how Russia's poets were caught between their own history and Europe's, and predicting that "Little Russia" would produce poetry only when the best sections of its people exchanged its indigenous trepaks and hopaks for the French quadrille. Khvylovyi argued that those who wanted to follow the Russian pattern of literary life sought to adopt what Belinskii had rejected long ago. It was not a question of whether Russia had produced talented writers; Khvylovyi conceded that it had. But Ukrainian realities produced other tasks for its writers than what Russia demanded of its art. Ukraine was a young nation with a young literature, and as a nation it was as independent as Russia. This independence did not mean questioning the political ties of Ukraine with Russia, but allowing Ukrainian literature to follow its own path of development. In an oft-quoted passage, Khvylovyi declared:

> Hence, insofar as our literature at last follows its own path of development, the question before us is: toward which of the world's literatures must it chart its course?
>
> *In no case toward the Russian.* This is absolute and unconditional. Our political union must not be confused with literature. From Russian literature and its styles Ukrainian poetry must run away as fast as it can. The Poles could never have produced a Mickiewicz had they not repudiated any orientation toward Russian art. The essence of the matter is that Russian literature has weighted us down for centuries, as the master of the situation who accustomed our psyche to slavish imitation. For our young art to nourish itself on [Russian literature] would thus mean stunting its growth. We know the ideas of the proletariat without Muscovite art; on the contrary, as representatives of a young nation, we

---

[100] *Ibid.*, p. 4. Emphasis in the original.
[101] *Ibid.*, pp. 3–6.

will feel these ideas faster and pour them out sooner in a responsible way. Our orientation is toward the art of Western Europe, toward its style, toward its reception...[102]

Khvylovyi argued that what Belinskii had known more than half a century earlier was true: culture had to be got from Europe. For Ukraine to try to attain such European culture through Russian art would mean eternal cultural subordination.

Within a month after the publication of the above passage, Stalin himself intervened with his letter to Kaganovich and the KP(b)U Central Committee.[103] "Khvylovyism" was condemned along with "Shumskyism" as a manifestation of "bourgeois nationalism," that is, as threats to the unity of the Soviet state. The June 1926 plenum of the KP(b)U Central Committee convicted Khvylovyi of eight separate deviations ranging from "reviving the theory of the struggle of two cultures" to disseminating the ideas of Ukrainian fascism.[104] Khvylovyi wrote a fourth pamphlet that was not published, except for snippets designed to "convict" him of impermissible deviation. In this last work, known only in fragments, Khvylovyi developed his opposition to Russian cultural influence. In it, he described Moscow as the all-Union center of *mishchanstvo* (a particularly Russian sort of philistinism) in which communism existed only as an oasis. This was so, he wrote, because of Moscow's history and its tradition of backwardness. For Ukraine to have its own Soviet culture did not mean that culture would cease to be communist and proletarian, he added: it would merely be different, just as Ukraine was different from Russia.[105] It was alleged that a threat

---

[102] *Ibid.*, p. 8. Original emphasis.

[103] See chapter three above.

[104] E. F. Hirchak, *Na dva fronta v borbe s natsionalizmom*, p. 50, drew up the following shopping list of deviations on the basis of the resolution of the June plenum: 1) orienting Ukrainian literature away from Red Moscow to bourgeois Europe, 2) reviving the theory of the struggle of two cultures in a Ukrainian national modification, 3) adhering to the theory of a capitalist rebirth of the nation, 4) forming a bloc with "bourgeois nationalist" elements (i.e., the Neoclassicists) and in that respect adopting the idea of a united national front, 5) misunderstanding the proletariat's role as an "active factor, active leader, and creative participant in cultural construction in Ukraine," 6) promulgating a Spenglerian cyclical theory of history in his messianic idea of a Ukrainian-led Asiatic Renaissance, 7) adopting a view of life in the Soviet Union like that of Trotsky's, and 8) disseminating the ideas of Ukrainian fascism. These ideas, according to Hirchak, were developed "under the influence of class forces hostile to us" and contaminated communism with the Ukrainian chauvinism of the Neoclassicist poets.

[105] In Lawrynenko, *Rozstriliane vidrodzhennia*, pp. 830–831.

of "bourgeois counterrevolution" existed in such arguments. It is difficult to see in what manner, but they were certainly incompatible with the type of unitary state that Stalin would build, and perhaps to some ears that meant the same thing.

The Vaplitans and Their Work

It is impossible in so brief a space as this to describe adequately the movement of which Khvylovyi was the guiding spirit. It can only be hinted at.

Khvylovyi himself is often a joy to read. A literary critic, far more qualified to judge than I, wrote that Khvylovyi infused his work with the smell of words.[106] He used that smell of words to expose the ludicrous and the pathetic. His writing was above all political. He could be funny, as in his satire on a local Proletkult group headed by a former waiter who had left his job in a Tula inn to mouth misunderstood phrases about Marxist aesthetics, to berate his assistant for not knowing that "existence precedes consciousness," and to create a society devoted mainly to his own admiration. That society had members so militant that one of them could almost imagine the train whistles tooting "ka-pay-bay-oo," the Party's initials. Instead of literature, they produced travesties.[107] Khvylovyi could be tragic, as he explored the tensions of his own ambivalence toward the revolution that had promised so much and produced so little. One of his best stories is about a Chekist and the contrast between his job as an executioner and his visions of the beautiful, unattainable commune that sustained him until at last he was led to the ultimate crime, matricide.[108] In the *Woodsnipes,* a novel of which only

[106] "Khvylovyi loved the smell of words...He wove words into arabesques and vignettes, ordered them in melancholy processions, and arrayed them in dancing groups." Iurii Sherekh, *Ne dlia ditei: Literaturno krytychni statti i esei* (New York, 1964), p. 55.

[107] Mykola Khvylovyi, "Liliuli," *Chervonyi shliakh,* 1923, no. 6–7, pp. 3–24; republished in Khvylovyi, *Tvory v piatokh tomakh,* vol. 1, pp. 365–391.

[108] Mykola Khvylovyi, "Ia (Romantyka)," in George S. N. Luckyj, ed., *Modern Ukrainian Short Stories* (Littleton, Colorado, 1973), pp. 114–115. Written in the first person, it led to claims that Khvylovyi was himself a Chekist, and Professor Luckyj has been assured by a person he feels to be trustworthy that he was personally interrogated by "Comrade Fitilëv" (Khvylovyi's real name) during the civil war. Hryhory Kostiuk, who knew Khvylovyi and has made probably the most extensive study of the writer's life and work, hotly denies this, calling those who make such claims vulgar "attention grabbers and sausage makers." It should be noted that the standard biography of Khvylovyi asserts that the story came from Khvylovyi's experience during the Civil War when he served as a military commissar and that he based the story on personal

the first half was published—the journal that carried it was closed for having done so—Khvylovyi gave his protagonist the name of Dmitrii Karamazov and charted for him a Dostoevskian dilemma of accepting the easy life of a bureaucrat or rediscovering his ideals.[109] In the words of a contemporary, Khvylovyi was "the eldest writer and recognized literary authority," eldest not in years but in his craft.[110]

Vaplite attracted the most ambitious writers of the day because it represented quality rather than for any nationalistic reasons. Iurii Smolych, a Soviet writer who carefully explained how he could have associated with the "deviationists" of Vaplite, declared that he joined simply because Vaplite was the only alternative to the Ukrainian provincialism of Prosvita and the avant-garde posturing of the Russian *Na postu* group.[111] What the members of Vaplite shared was less a common aesthetic than a common commitment to creating something of aesthetic value. They were not, as their opponents charged, committed to art for art's sake. They were committed to Marxism, and artistic purity as a self-sufficient ideal smacked too much of "bourgeois idealism" for them to accept. They hoped to make their art "relevant" in the sense that word has been used in this country, but they realized that before art could hope to be politically functional, it had to be worthwhile as art.

Mykola Kulish, the talented playwright who served as president of Vaplite in its last year, wrote a dramatic trilogy which explored the dilemmas of Soviet nationality policy. The first and best known play in the cycle, *Narodnii Malakhii* (People's Malakhii), revived the traditional character of the holy fool, the prophetic madman whose apparent insanity gives him the freedom to enunciate painful truths that "sane" people would never dare speak. The protagonist is Malakhii Stakanchyk, a former postman who sought to escape the revolution by having himself walled up in a closet. After spending two years there and reading his fill of Bolshevik literature, he emerged during the NEP imagining himself a reformer, and sent a project off to the government. This project was aimed at solving the basic problem of Ukrainian communism: "the immediate reform of man, of the Ukrainian nationality in par-

---

conflicts felt by Chekists he was acquainted with. See O. Han, *Trahediia Mykoly Khvylovoho*, p. 31.

[109] Mykola Khvylovyi, "Valdshnepy," *Vaplite: Literaturno-Khudozhnii zhurnal*, 1927, no. 5, pp. 5–69.

[110] Iurii Smolych, *Rozpovid pro nespokii* (Kiev, 1968–1972), vol. 1, p. 34.

[111] *Ibid.*, vol. 1, 89.

ticular... and reform of the Ukrainian language from the viewpoint of perfect socialism..."[112] He receives a bureaucratic reply to the effect that his project has been taken under advisement. He sets out to see the head of the government, but ends up in an insane asylum where he preaches reform to the inmates. He proclaims himself "People's Commissar Malakhii", People's Malakhii, for short. He escapes to preach his reforms to workers in a factory and ultimately to whores in a brothel. His adventures become a vehicle for the satire of Soviet Ukrainian life as he wanders through the country like a Don Quixote of the revolution.[113] A later play in the trilogy, *Sonata Pathétique,* could not be performed in Ukraine because of the opposition of official critics. Kulish arranged for a Russian translation to be performed in Moscow where it enjoyed such success during its three-month run that it was difficult to obtain tickets to see it.[114] As leader of Vaplite, Kulish was no less forceful than Khvylovyi in trying to defend literature from obscurantism. Once, in a reply to Volodymyr Koriak, the official critic and guiding spirit behind the All-Ukrainian Union of Proletarian Writers which had been formed to limit Vaplite's influence, Kulish reviewed the charges and wondered whether Koriak's criticism might better have come from a prosecutor than from someone claiming to be a literary critic.[115]

Kulish worked intimately with Les Kurbas, whose 1917 manifesto of the Young Theater proclaimed the need for Ukraine to orient its culture to the West long before Khvylovyi did so. Kurbas was leader of the Berezil theater group in Kharkiv in the 1920s, and his relationship with Kulish can in some ways be compared to that of Chekhov and Stanislavskii. Together they were the main innovators in Ukrainian dramatic life, creating a Ukrainian version of Europe's expressionism.[116] Kurbas, outlining his ideas in Vaplite's journal, demanded clarity and originality, a high level of culture and "the most active relationship to present concerns," the rearing of a new generation to be placed at the proletariat's

---

[112] Mykola Kulish, *Tvory* (New York, 1955), p. 40.

[113] For a critical study of this play, see Valerian Revutsky, "The Prophetic Madman: *The People's Malakhiy*—A Play by Mykola Kulish," *Canadian Slavonic Papers,* vol. 1, 1956, pp. 45–48.

[114] For the text of the two plays mentioned as well as Hryhory Kostiuk's reminiscences on the production of Sonata Pathétique, see Kulish, *Tvory,* pp. 9–104, 205–292, 412–414.

[115] Mykola Kulish, "Krytyka chy prokurorskyi dopyt?" *Vaplite,* 1927, no. 5, pp. 146–157.

[116] See Romana Bahrij Pikulyk, "The Expressionist Experiment in Berezil': Kurbas and Kulish," *Canadian Slavonic Papers,* vol. 14, 1972, no. 2, pp. 224–244.

disposal; at the same time, he rejected cardboard heroes mouthing revolutionary cant and demanded that characters have psychological depth.[117]

Vaplite also made its influence felt in the cinema through Oleksander Dovzhenko. With the possible exception of Pavlo Tychyna's poetry, Dovzhenko's work remains the best known of all that Vaplite produced. Giving a subjective ranking in the triumvirate of Soviet cinematic pioneers, he might be placed between Eisenshtein and Pudovkin. His early films, as he frankly admitted in his autobiography, portrayed class categories, not individuals.[118] But he was able to breathe dramatic impact into the conflict of those categories, as when the non-entity of a Ukrainian schoolteacher-turned-cossack is unable to shoot the heroic worker looking him in the eye; the worker steps up to him, takes the gun, and looking him straight in the eye, kills him. The scene is in his epic of the proletarian revolution, *Arsenal.* In his earlier treatment of the revolution in the countryside, *Zvenyhora,* the action surrounds the two sons of an old peasant, one communist and one nationalist, who struggle for Ukraine's secret treasures. The nationalist, a lout nourished on old legends and cossack symbols, is led by his search for these treasures to absurdity, moral bankruptcy, and suicide, while the communist realizes that Ukraine's real secret treasures can only be unlocked by socialism, progress, and technology. The father is finally won over to the new age, symbolizing the winning over of the Ukrainian nation. For all the didactic cant of the film's plot line and characterization, its complex structure and unusual use of lighting make it a universally acknowledged classic of the silent cinema. Perhaps of all the Vaplitans, Dovzhenko was the most forceful in equating "pure" art with "bourgeois" art.[119]

The twenty-seven Vaplitans could each be the subject of a monograph. Only the briefest hint of what they were and what they represented can be indicated in so short a space, but one phrase sums it up: aesthetically worthwhile revolutionary art.

The End of Vaplite

After the June Plenum of the KP(b)U Central Committee, Khvylovyi stood condemned by the highest Ukrainian Party authority. Mykola

[117] Les Kurbas, "Shliakhy Berezolia," *Vaplite,* 1927, no. 3, pp. 141–165, esp. 142–143.

[118] Translated by Marco Carynnyk in Alexander Dovzhenko, *The Poet as Filmmaker: Selected Writings* (Cambridge, Mass. and London, 1973), p. 15.

[119] See, for example, Oleksander Dovzhenko, "Do problemy obrazotvorchoho mystetstva," in Luckyj, ed., *Vaplitianskyi zbirnyk,* pp. 163–173.

Skrypnyk, then emerging as the Party's foremost spokesman on the nationality problem, declared the Ukrainian literary discussion to be at an end. Nationalism, he explained, was bourgeois, and the Party opposed its proletarian solution to all bourgeois influences. It was bourgeois to set Ukrainian culture against Russian culture. Neither was superior to the other; neither would tutor the other. They would live together side by side in an atmosphere of "fraternal cooperation."[120]

Khvylovyi could either openly defy the Party or recant. To defy it would have meant placing himself outside it; even in 1926, such a course meant political death in the Soviet Union. He chose to recant. In December 1926, he and two associates, O. Dosvitnyi and M. Ialovyi, published a long self-critical letter in *Visty*, admitting their errors. In hopes of parrying mounting Party attacks, Vaplite expelled the three writers on January 28, 1927. It did so without Party approval and found the Party's displeasure with it intensified.[121]

As it turned out, Skrypnyk's proclamation of the end of the literary discussion was premature. Vaplite continued to uphold quality in literature.[122] It provided Khvylovyi with a forum from which to respond to critics.[123] And it published his novel, *The Woodsnipes*.

Only the first half of *The Woodsnipes* could be published before Vaplite's journal was closed down for this so-called crime. It is difficult to judge half a novel, but it was a remarkable work to come from the pen of a communist. Its hero, Karamazov, is a disillusioned communist who at one point confesses that he had killed in the name of the revolution, and cynically declares, "I put the word 'crime' in quotation marks, because killing in the name of social ideals is never considered a crime." He rejects Shevchenko, Ukraine, and "this idiotic Ukrainization" until his cynicism is challenged by Ahlaia with whom he falls in love. He tells her of his past, including the murders he committed as a Chekist during the civil war. She sees him as a type, as one of thousands of Karamazovs whose romantic revolutionary ideals led them to kill for a dream that did not come true. They felt guilt;

---

[120] Mykola Skrypnyk, *Statti i promovy z natsionalnoho pytannia* (Munich, 1974), pp. 57–81.

[121] Luckyj, *Literary Politics in the Soviet Ukraine*, pp. 70–74; Luckyj, *Vaplitianskyi zbirnyk*, pp. 15–18, 235–238.

[122] See, for example, Observator, "Dumky pro molodu beletrystyku," *Vaplite*, 1927, no. 4, pp. 194–201.

[123] Mykola Khvylovyi, "Otvertyi lyst do Volodymyra Koriaka," *Vaplite*, 1927, no. 5, pp. 158–173.

however, they could not leave the Party for all its shortcomings, because to do so would be a betrayal of their ideals and of themselves. They were caught in an absurd rage from which they could see no escape.[124]

The Party considered nothing more offensive than to portray publicly the disillusionment felt by Ukrainian communists, because the very existence of types like Khvylovyi's Karamazov implied that the revolution had taken a wrong turn. Andrii Khvylia led the attack on behalf of Party orthodoxy, dredging up all Khvylovyi's old sins, quoting extensively from the unpublished ''Ukraine or Little Russia,'' and denouncing the novel as an attack on the revolution itself.[125] Khvylovyi, abroad at the time, could have stuck to his guns in emigration. The dissident majority wing of the KPZU leadership asked him to do so and to contribute to its journals.[126] But Khvylovyi, like his character Karamazov, was unable to break with the Party; he chose to recant.

Khvylovyi revealed himself to be a master of the art of ostensible surrender, that is, confessing whatever was necessary and then continuing to do what his convictions dictated in a more subtle manner. In February 1928, Khvylovyi published a letter to the editor in *Komunist,* in which he admitted that he had ''revived the theory of the struggle of two cultures,'' but managed to condemn his ideas in such a way as to preserve their gist. He admitted that he had been wrong in calling Moscow the center of philistinism, not because it was not so, but because one could also say the same thing with equal justice about Kiev. He regretted having advocated the adoption of the ''psychology of Europe,'' but portrayed his error more as a matter of phrasing than content. He explained that what he had really meant was a cosmopolitan outlook opposed to provincialism, an outlook which was not uniquely European but one which was shared by the Communist Party. He confessed to every single error his critics had attributed to him and even announced that he had destroyed the second part of *The Woodsnipes,* but he did so in such a way that he left open the possibility of fighting another day for his beliefs.[127]

---

[124] Mykola Khvylovyi, ''Valdshnepy,'' *Vaplite,* 1927, no. 5, pp. 5–69.

[125] A. Khvylia, *Vid ukhylu v prirvu* (Kharkiv, 1928), reprinted as *Vid natsionalnoho komunizmu do ukrainskoho antykomunistychnoho natsionalizmu* (New York, 1954).

[126] Shkandrij, *The ''Literary Discussion'' in Soviet Ukraine,* pp. 272–273.

[127] Khvylovyi's letter, first published in *Komunist* on February 22, 1928, was reprinted in *Budivnytstvo Radianskoi Ukrainy,* vol. 1, pp. 199–201 and also in Leites and Iashek, eds., *Desiat rokiv ukrainskoi literatury* (2nd ed.), vol. 2, pp. 318–320.

The suppression of Vaplite did not end Soviet Ukraine's literary renaissance; it merely served to mark the limits of what the Party would allow. The straightjacket of Stalinist socialist realism was still not dreamt of. Khvylovyi still wrote stories, Kulish and Kurbas produced plays, Tychyna published lyric poetry, and Dovzhenko made films. Even the journal *Vaplite* was replaced by *Literaturnyi iarmarok* (Literary Bazaar), in which the former Vaplitans continued to write pieces that were both worthwhile and a pleasure to read.

Founded soon after the suppression of Vaplite, *Literaturnyi iarmarok* was affiliated with no group and, as George Luckyj put it, "was the last unrestrained and spontaneous reflection of the literary undercurrents" still able to exist in Soviet Ukraine.[128] Each issue was organized by a different writer, contained a running commentary on its offerings called intermediums, and often contained Aesopian criticism of the political scene of the day. Sometimes the Aesopian criticism gave way to blatant sarcasm, as when Khvylovyi reacted to the growing proletarianization and regimentation of Soviet literature in the following passage published in *Literaturnyi iarmarok* in 1930:

> I know that you are now in a distant corner of our "Ukrainized" Ukraine, sitting on the bank of a river, catching perch and gathering material for a beautiful new short story. True, this is a deviation on your part. Other proletarian writers are now sitting high up on the chimneys of factories, observing the worker's life in order to write a saccharine epic called *The Father*, or *The Uncle*, or *Welcome, We Are Your Relatives*. And for this they will receive from the same sort of scribblers the title of honorary, proletarian, revolutionary, Soviet, people's, international, universal scribbler.[129]

Such an attack on what by then passed for proletarian literature could not go unnoticed; some people accused Khvylovyi of repeating his old sins.[130] However, he also had defenders such as Skrypnyk, who opposed trying to force all writers into a single organization and subordinating them to the type of scribbler Khvylovyi was discussing.[131] One of Skrypnyk's closest associates, and head of the philosophy section of the Ukrainian Institute of Marxism-Leninism, Volodymyr Iurynets, was a con-

[128] Luckyj, *Literary Politics*, p. 151.
[129] Quoted in *ibid.*, p. 153.
[130] See, for example, S. Antoniuk, "Proty khvylovyzmu," *Literatura i mystetstvo* (*Visti VUTsVK* supplement), February 23, 1930, pp. 1–2.
[131] M. O. Skrypnyk, "Proty zaboboniv," *Krytyka*, 1929, no. 6, pp. 16–23.

tributor to *Literaturnyi iarmarok* and edited one of its issues.[132] Still, this sort of thing was no longer permissible in 1930; *Literaturnyi iarmarok* had to give way to *Prolitfront*, Khvylovyi's last independent literary enterprise.

Prolitfront was an outwardly orthodox journal which was the organ of a group which called itself the Union for the Study of a Proletarian Literary Front and contained many of the old Vaplitans. *Prolitfront* issued a "notification" which expressed the group's loyalty to the Party's program and proletarian ideology while dedicating itself to "the struggle against bourgeois art, against ideology hostile to us whether in obvious or hidden forms, the struggle against nationalistic phenomena."[133] The journal itself contained a number of attacks on nationalism, particularly that of the New Generation group which included the historian-turned-critic Sukhyno-Khomenko.[134] Once again Khvylovyi seemed to have mended his ways, published an article condemning his past errors, and joined a writers' brigade visiting collective farms. Party lights such as Kosior and Khvylia expressed their conviction that Khvylovyi had at last joined the fold of Soviet writers. By late 1930, however, *Prolitfront* came under fire from critics associated with the Party-sponsored All-Ukrainian Union of Proletarian Writers (VUSPP); early the following year, *Prolitfront* passed a resolution of self-criticism, dissolved itself, and gave the names of thirty-five members ready to join VUSPP. Eighteen of them, including Khvylovyi, were accepted.[135] Although he con-

---

[132] Iurynets, a critic and philosopher, has been compared to Benedetto Croce (Lawrynenko, *Rozstriliane vidrodzhennia*, p. 837) in the sense that he concentrated on the philosophy of literature in the European sense. In 1928 he was made a member of VUAN as part of the party's attempt to pack that body with its own. A student of Pokrovskii and Deborin, Iurynets fell into disrepute during the campaign against Deborinist philosophy in the Soviet Union, and Skrypnyk was forced to condemn him in 1930. He was expelled from the Party in 1933 and later arrested for alleged participation in a Nationalist-Trotskyite Bloc. He is believed to have been executed. Kostiuk, *Stalinist Rule in the Ukraine*, pp. 54–56; M. Boiko, "Prof. V. O. Iurinets," *Nauka i osvita* (*Visti* supplement), June 2, 1928, p. 1; Shkandrij, *The "Literary Discussion"*, pp. 141–146; Mykola Skrypnyk, "Za leninsku filosofiiu," *Bilshovyk Ukrainy*, 1931, no. 6, pp. 18–35, and also his remarks in *Vestnik Kommunisticheskoi akademii*, no. 40–41, 1930, pp. 85ff.
[133] Leites and Iashek, eds., *Desiat rokiv* (2 ed.), vol. 2, p. 624.
[134] M. Khvylovyi, "Krychushche bozhestvo," *Prolitfront*, 1930, no. 1, pp. 247–252; Khvylovyi, "Chym prycharuvala 'Nova Generatsiia' tov. Sukhyno-Khomenka," *Prolitfront*, 1930, no. 3, pp. 229–269; N. Kyrychenko, "Apolohety kurkulstva," *Prolitfront*, 1930, no. 7–8, pp. 269–290.
[135] Luckyj, *Literary Politics*, pp. 157, 159, 164–165.

tinued to publish stories, Khvylovyi's career as an independent literary force was at an end.

Khvylovyi's surrender is only one manifestation of the lasting and debilitating changes taking place in Soviet literature during the late twenties and early thirties. There was always a tendency on the part of the Party leadership to choose political orthodoxy over readable literature. Zatonskyi probably expressed this tendency best when he declared that the main reason all was not well in literature was "because our writers are weak on Leninism."[136] Literary hacks, ready to pander to a political leadership who wanted nothing more than professions of loyalty, abounded. First came the "proletarian" literature of the On Guardist movement.[137] Then came the narrowly utilitarian literature of socialist realism. That the writers of such works gained a monopoly of literary expression can only be described as the triumph of *khaltura* over *kultura,* of hackwork over literature. Soviet Ukrainian literature lost whatever distinctive quality it had possessed during the cultural revival of the twenties.[138]

Producing literature in response to social demand became a euphemism for the regimentation of literary production. In fact, what occurred was a blatant disregard of readers' preferences. Evidence of the type of literature people wanted to read was provided by a survey conducted in Soviet Ukraine in 1928, based on questionnaires sent to libraries, workers' clubs, and similar institutions, asking which works were most requested by readers. This survey found that by far the most requested Ukrainian writer was Volodymyr Vynnychenko. After him came the classics of Ukrainian literature written by writers such as Franko, Kotsiubynskyi, and Shevchenko. Khvylovyi, the most popular Soviet writer, ranked far behind the classical authors, and the "proletarian" writers were little read, even by the proletarians. The study concluded that, "Ukrainian classical literature obviously still remains in the center of the interests and sympathy of the mass reader."[139] The regimentation of literature in response to "social demand" obviously meant the end of the kind of literature which the members of society preferred to read.

---

[136] V. Zatonskyi, *Natsionalna problema na Ukraini,* p. 13.

[137] The standard work on On Guardism in literature is still Edward J. Brown, *The Proletarian Episode in Russian Literature, 1928–1933* (New York, 1953).

[138] See Luckyj, *Literary Politics,* pp. 231–243 on the subsequent fate of Ukrainian writers.

[139] Kost Dovhan, "Ukrainska literatura i masovyi chytach," *Krytyka,* 1928, no. 8, p. 39.

As for Khvylovyi, he remained an active member of Ukraine's literary community until 1933. In the spring of that year, when his country suffered a devastating and deliberately created famine, he went into the villages, saw what was happening, and tried to get various officials to do something, anything, about the situation. At last, he came to realize that the famine was the result of a deliberate policy. He bade his friends farewell, and committed suicide.[140]

*   *   *

Khvylovyi's arguments were far too complex to be placed under such a simple rubric as "nationalism." What emerged from his polemics was a whole theory of national cultural liberation that sought the development of a Soviet Ukrainian culture that would be socialist but emancipated from the national culture of Ukraine's former colonial oppressor. He made no secret of his belief that the revolution had taken a wrong turn, but he never repudiated the revolution; he wanted to set its course aright in Ukraine.

Khvylovyi's main argument was that Ukrainian culture ought to develop in its own way, rejecting its own provincialism and the cultural legacy of Russian colonialism. He reasoned that if his country had really been liberated from imperialism, then it ought to be able to develop independently of Russia. This seemed to him no more than a corollary of the Party's own nationality policy.

It is a great distance from the modest beginnings of Soviet Ukrainian literature in the early twenties to the flowering which took place in just a few short years. Similarly, it was a great distance from the Party's decision to foster Ukrainian cultural development to Khvylovyi's rejection of Russian influence on his nation's culture. The Party, when it adopted Ukrainization as official policy, could have little idea of where its path would lead. When it found spokesmen for the "liberated" Ukrainian nation actually acting independently, it could not comprehend it. And men of little understanding have always regarded what they could not understand as a threat.

---

[140] Arkadii Liubchenko, "Ioho taiemnytsia," *Novi dni,* vol. 2, 1943, no. 5, pp. 4–5, 10–12.

CHAPTER FIVE

Mykhailo Volobuiev and the Problem of the Ukrainian Economy

MYKHAILO VOLOBUIEV WAS was a communist of Russian origin and a high functionary in the Ukrainian Commissariat of Education. He was thus a representative of the new "Ukrainized" Party created by the Ukrainization policy. Borrowing on Soviet Ukrainian scholarship, he constructed an impressive argument designed to show that Soviet Ukraine was being exploited by the Soviet Union no less than it had been by its imperial predecessor, and called for a fundamental reappraisal of Russo-Ukrainian economic relations in order to overcome the legacy of colonialism. When his work was published in 1928 in *Bilshovyk Ukrainy,* the organ of the KP(b)U, it became a *cause célèbre.*

Marxism holds that the economic relationships in a society provide the key to understanding the essential nature of that society. For anyone who adheres to that doctrine, the charge of economic injustice becomes the most potent indictment possible to level against a given state of affairs. If the largest former colony of the Russian Empire was being exploited, then the USSR was no less guilty of the sins of imperialism than its predecessor had been. Volobuiev's argument thus implicitly discredited the communist claim that Soviet power offered a viable alternative to imperialism, for it showed that a Soviet regime was quite as able to adopt imperialistic policies as those European imperialists it so vehemently denounced.

The Problem of the Ukrainian Economy

The most remarkable aspect of the problem of the Ukrainian economy is the belated recognition given it by the Soviet theorists. Before the adoption of the New Economic Policy, the Bolsheviks simply did not think of separate national economies under socialism. They saw the problem of nationality as a transitory side effect of capitalism, and applied the label of "bourgeois nationalism" to all hopes by non-Russians that

161

they might act differently from the Russians. It was assumed that once the bourgeoisie were cast out, the problem of nationality would cease to exist. The complete economic unity of different nations under socialism was taken as axiomatic.

The change that took place in the Bolsheviks' perception after 1921 was illustrated by Lenin's greater tolerance of national distinctiveness and greater sensitivity to national aspirations. However, the reversal of Bolshevik nationality policy symbolized by the adoption of the Ukrainization policy in 1923 did not extend to economics. The economic unity of socialist nations was still taken for granted and was seen as the basis for the eventual breakdown of national distinctions under socialism. The complete economic unity of socialist states appeared to be a logical consequence of the international unity of the proletariat, unquestioned and unquestionable. Yet this too came in time to be questioned.

The Ukrainian Borotbisty questioned this seemingly unquestionable axiom as early as 1919. They were ready to join the Bolsheviks, but only on condition that the Bolsheviks would recognize Ukraine's separate identity. While representing the Borotbisty in the talks which preceded the 1920 Party merger, Hryhorii Hrynko insisted that Soviet Ukraine not be swallowed up by Russian economic bodies. He warned that the wholesale extension of Russian organs to Ukraine would lead to bad results, and advocated the institution of some sort of federally regulated *sovnarkhoz*.[1] This would seem a moderate enough demand, but it was ahead of its time. Before the Twelfth Congress, views such as those of Dmitrii Lebed were common in the KP(b)U leadership; in economics, Lebed's most outspoken counterpart was Iurii Larin, the economist who was later to become the most outspoken critic of the Ukrainization policy. In 1921, Larin expressed his unalloyed enthusiasm for the complete economic unity of the reconstituted Russian Empire:

> The real economic history of Soviet Russia begins only in 1921 because it was only in the second half of 1920 that Russia was reconstituted as a single economic organism. Before that, during the first years of the proletarian revolution, there was only the prerequisite, only a step toward such a history, a struggle to create the initial prerequisites for making normal economic development possible by gathering resources into a single unit from all parts torn to pieces by the bourgeois-gentry counter-revolution and by the Entente powers—Ukraine, Great Russia, Siberia, Turkestan, the Caucassus, and the Don region.

---

[1] See chapter two above.

> Now, when the Russian proletariat, when militant Bolshevism has gathered the land like a new Ivan Kalita, only now will proletarian Russia have the ability to demonstrate its energy and organizational prowess on the necessary scale. . . Now with the reunification of Russia, the capitalist countries of the Entente will finally have to give up their hope that Bolshevism will be destroyed by internal economic disintegration.[2]

One would be hard put to find a more perfect expression of the Great Russian chauvinism which Lenin denounced in his later days. Larin portrayed the Bolsheviks as successors to the medieval Muscovite princes and the saviors of Russia. The reunification of the Russian Empire was portrayed as the saving of the proletarian revolution. Aspirations for national liberation became simple machinations of the world bourgeoisie. Larin was more extreme than the official line, but not a great deal. The official KP(b)U position was that there had to be "complete economic unity of all parts of the federation."[3] A 1921 resolution of an All-Ukrainian Congress of Soviets called such unity an absolute necessity if the economy was to recover from the tremendous devastation wrought by war and revolution.[4] In truth, the amount of destruction can hardly be exaggerated. By 1921, Soviet Ukraine's heavy industrial output had declined to a mere 12% of what it had been in 1913. The working class had largely disintegrated, many proletarians having returned to the countryside and lost their skills. Of the 25,000 Donbas miners who had produced two-thirds of Russia's iron ore in 1913, only about 1200 remained. The regime had to rebuild not only its industries but also the entire class of industrial workers.[5] Available resources were meager, and it seemed to make sense that what there was had to be pooled on an all-Union scale.

---

[2] Iu. Larin and L. Kritsman, *Narys hospodarskoho zhyttia i organizatsiia narodnoho hospodarstva radianskoi Rosii* (Kiev, 1921), p. 65 as quoted by I. Mazepa, *Bolshevyzm i okupatsiia Ukrainy,* pp. 82–83.

[3] Resolution "On Economic Construction" adopted by Fifth KP(b)U Congress in November 1920. *Komunistychna Partiia Ukrainy v rezoliutsiiakh i reshenniakh zizdiv, konferentsii i plenumiv TsK,* vol. 1, p. 102.

[4] Resolution "On Economic Construction" adopted by the Fifth All-Ukrainian Congress of Soviets in 1921 as cited by B. M. Babii, *Ukrainska radianska derzhava v period vidbudovy narodnoho hospodarstva (1921-1925 rr.)* (Kiev, 1961), pp. 91–92. Chubar, then head of the industrial bureau of Ukrainian Vesenkha, said much the same thing at an August 1920 conference of *sovnarkhozy* of Ukraine's guberniias. See V. A. Chirko, *Kommunisticheskaia Partiia—organizator bratskogo sotrudnichestva narodov Ukrainy i Rossii v 1917-1922 gg.* (Moscow, 1967), pp. 221–222.

[5] V. E. Loburets, *Formuvannia kadriv radianskoho robitnychoho klasu Ukrainy (1921-1932 rr.)* (Kharkiv, 1974), pp. 6–12.

The economic provisions of the Constitution of the USSR expressed this tendency to think in terms of a single economic entity rather than smaller national ones. The economic powers of the Union government were specified in great detail, while the framers clearly gave little thought to the problem of national economies. The Union was empowered to conclude internal and external loans as well as to authorize such loans for the republics. It had the power to direct foreign trade and to determine the system of internal trade. It was to establish the bases and general plan of economic development for the entire USSR, to define which industries were of all-Union interest, and to grant foreign concessions in both its own name and in the name of the individual republics. The budgets of the republics were included in the Union budget and approved by the Union government. The Union was given the power to tax, to alter taxes in order to balance republic budgets, and to authorize or reduce taxes on the republic level. General principles of land use and the exploitation of natural resources were the province of the Union, as were labor legislation, the monetary system, statistics, weights and measures. The Union's exceedingly broad economic powers were mitigated somewhat by the fact that the administration of economic affairs fell largely to the so-called joint commissariats, departments which were jointly responsible to Union and republic authorities, but the principle of the economic unity of the USSR was clear.[6]

As in politics and culture, national aspirations began to reemerge in the economic sphere before much time had passed. Despite the constitutional principle of budgetary unity, Skrypnyk in 1924 opposed a draft budget statute on the grounds that the proposal would make the republics too dependent on the Union's generosity, and would permanently relegate them to the position of poor relations, unless a fixed proportion of Union tax receipts were returned to the government of the republic from which they were collected. Skrypnyk was unsuccessful in getting his revenue sharing proposal adopted, but Soviet Ukraine was nevertheless able to keep its deficits small and manageable. This ability no doubt helped place Soviet Ukraine in a position where it could maintain its economic autonomy far more effectively than could other national

---

[6] Article one of the 1923 Constitution spells out the powers of the Union government, including its economic powers. English translation in James H. Meisel and Edward S. Kozera, eds., *Materials for the Study of the Soviet System: State and Party Constitutions, Laws, Decrees, Decisions and Official Statements of the Leaders in Translation* (2 ed., Ann Arbor, 1953), pp. 155–156.

republics, the growing deficits of which made them more dependent on Union coffers with the passage of each year.[7]

National economic priorities also made themselves felt in other ways. For example, Ukraine's *Vesenkha* (Supreme Council of People's Economy) grew to be far stronger than its counterparts in other republics, claiming the right to run the day-to-day operations of even Union-owned industries in Ukraine. Soviet Ukrainian officials were unable to make that claim stick, but they were often successful in making certain that Ukraine received its share of new development projects.[8] Whenever possible, Soviet Ukrainian authorities seemed to operate on the principle that if Russia had something, Ukraine should get one too, be it a hydroelectric complex or a society of Marxist historians. For example, after an All-Russian Conference to Study the Natural Productive Forces was held in 1923, Soviet Ukraine organized an All-Ukrainian Congress to Study the Productive Forces. When it opened at the end of 1924, not only did it have the more prestigious designation of congress, but it also dealt with additional issues which the Russian conference had not, such as the human and technological aspects of economic development.[9]

Immersed as it was in the effort to Ukrainize itself and take part in the flourishing revival of Ukrainian culture, even in the economic sphere the KP(b)U could not remain immune to Ukrainian aspirations. Struggles to enlarge the bureaucratic turf of Soviet Ukrainian officialdom tended imperceptibly to become mixed with elements of national pride. A measure of Ukrainianness had become legitimate, even obligatory, for Ukrainian communists, so Ukrainian aspirations were bound to make themselves felt in economic affairs. Communists who had once been oblivious to the problem of the Ukrainian economy became aware of it and began to think in terms of Ukrainian interests.

Taking the lead in legitimizing the idea of Ukraine as an economic entity was Hryhorii Hrynko, the former Borotbist who became deputy head of Gosplan (the all-Union economic planning agency). Hrynko iden-

---

[7] E. H. Carr, *Socialism in One Country, 1924–1926* (Baltimore, 1970), vol. 1, pp. 564–568.

[8] E. H. Carr and R. W. Davies, *Foundations of a Planned Economy, 1926–1929* (Baltimore, 1974), vol. 1, pp. 388, 467–470, 479, 481.

[9] A. Artemevskyi, "Organizatsiia ta naukova rabota zizdiv," *Zhyttia i revoliutsiia*, 1925, no. 1–2, p. 31. This was the first of a series of articles in this issue included under the heading "Pershyi vseukrainskyi zizd po vyvchenniu vyrobnychykh syl ta narodnoho hospodarstva Ukrainy."

tified the economic interests of the USSR with those of its constituent republics, and with those of Ukraine in particular. In his writings, he was fond of referring to Soviet Ukraine as "the Western stay (upor) of the USSR." He insisted—successfully as it turned out—that the practice of dividing the Union into economic regions (*raionirovanie*) should lead "not to the division of Ukraine by regions, but to the further consolidation of the Ukrainian Socialist Republic." Dividing Ukraine into such regions, he argued, could only lead to the assumption by the regions of broad administrative authority at the expense of the republic. "In Ukraine," he wrote, "this could lead only to the disintegration of Ukraine as a republic."[10] He also maintained that economic development had to be planned so that it would reflect the interests of the individual Soviet republics and regions. Economic development could not simply reflect the old economic geography of tsarist Russia but had to build on the new national units. As he put it, "The task for which the directing organs of the Soviet Union are responsible consists in serving and urging on to the maximum the economic creativity of the individual republics and regions so that they will contribute to the economic development of the Union as a whole." This would serve "not the narrow economic interests of this or that republic or region and not even those of the USSR as such, *but the overall interests of the proletarian revolution.*"[11] It would do this, he argued, by showing that nations formerly oppressed by imperialism could achieve economic development without relying on Western capital, thereby advancing the revolutionary process among the backward peoples of the East. This advancement, he added, was particularly important at a time when Western capitalism appeared to have stabilized itself for the foreseeable future.[12]

For all the growing willingness to think in Ukrainian terms and to assert Ukraine's economic interests, strong reasons still existed for concluding that Soviet Ukraine was being exploited. There was the matter of "subventions", the subsidies without which local budgets could not be balanced. These subventions were higher on a *per capita* basis in the RSFSR, than in Soviet Ukraine. Since these subsidies came out of Union tax revenues, and Ukrainians paid the same taxes to the Union as anyone else, Ukrainian taxpayers were indirectly subsidizing local

---

[10] H. Hrynko, "Narys ukrainskoi ekonomiky," *Chervonyi shliakh,* 1926, no. 5-6, pp. 120–123. Quotations from p. 122.

[11] Hrynko, "Zapadnyi upor SSSR (Ukraina)," *Khoziaistvo Ukrainy,* 1925, no. 10, p. 3. Emphasis in the original.

[12] *Ibid.,* p. 8.

government expenditures in Great Russia. Even more galling, the subventions went mainly to finance education, culture, and social services, at a time when Ukrainian *per capita* expenditure on these items had dropped substantially below the level spent in tsarist times, both in comparison to what was spent in Russia and in absolute terms.[13]

As early as 1925, O. Popov demonstrated that Soviet Ukraine contributed substantially more to the Union than it received back in the form of Union expenditures, and that it contributed a greater proportion of its wealth to the Union than it did to tsarist Russia.[14] While Popov

---

[13] In 1924–25, 5.7% of the local budgeted expenditures in the RSFSR were paid from subventions, while only 3.8% of local budgeted expenditures in Soviet Ukraine were covered from this source. Figures for per capita expenditures in areas largely financed from subventions were as follows:

Per capita expenditure in 1913	RSFSR	Soviet Ukraine
Public education	81k.	1 R 12k.
Other cultural and social needs	1 R 2k.	1 R 19k.
Per capita expenditure in 1924–25		
Public education	1 R 77k.	1 R 30k.
Other cultural and social needs	1 R 12k.	82k.

It should be noted that the rubric "cultural and social needs" was broadly defined so as to include items like veterenarians', doctors', agronomists', and militiamen's pay. Kyianyn, "Na Ukraini," *Nova Ukraina,* 1926, no. 1–2, p. 122. The original source is Rzhevusskii, "Rol subventsii v mestnom biudzhete Ukrainy," *Ukrainskii ekonomist,* no. 211 for September 16, 1926, which this author has been unable to locate.

[14] Percentage figures on Ukraine's contribution to Union coffers and receipt of Union expenditures were demonstrated by two different sets of figures. The first were from the economist Raievskyi:

	1923/24	1924/25 budget
Ukraine contributes	16.5%	19.7%
Ukraine receives	13.9%	18.4%

Different figures from the Budget-Finance Commission of Gosplan led to the same conclusion:

Ukraine contributes	21.7%	22.0%
Ukraine receives	18.95%	18.4%

Figures on the gross budgetary return to Ukraine on its contribution in comparison with tsarist times were presented as follows:

	1913	1924–25 budget
Ukraine	88.5%	84.9%
USSR as a whole	94.5%	100.0%

stated that Ukraine should indeed contribute more to the Union than Russia because of its greater economic wealth, others disagreed. The most serious evidence of economic exploitation of Ukraine by Russia, was the transfer of a substantial part of Ukraine's investment capital to Russia. According to a study made by Viktor Dobrohaiiev, a young teacher and economist who published on budgetary affairs in the journal *Khoziaistvo Ukrainy* (The Economy of Ukraine), fully 20% of Soviet Ukraine's investment capital was diverted to other parts of the Union between 1924 and 1927.[15] In spite of all Soviet communism's rhetoric of anti-imperialism, this seemed like a particularly blatant case of imperialist exploitation. Indeed, the Prague-based *Nova Ukraina* charged that Dobrohaiiev's figures showed that Soviet Ukraine was really a Muscovite colony that was being exploited in the most blatant fashion.[16]

Volobuiev and Volobuievism

Little is known about Volobuiev's life. He is usually assumed to have been an obscure teacher or economist.[17] Actually, he was head of *Holovpolitosvita*, a large branch of the Ukrainian Commissariat of Education responsible for all adult education, literacy schools, etc.[18] One article he published in 1923 shows that he was an economist as well as a pedagogue.[19] In any case, he was a high official, and his views must have reflected those of a significant part of the political leadership.

Volobuiev's work "On the Problem of the Ukrainian Economy" was published in the January 30 and February 15, 1928, issues of *Bilshovyk Ukrainy*. The work provided an analysis of Ukraine's economic situation that complemented the arguments earlier made by Shumskyi and Khvylovyi. It attempted to explain cases other than the simple stereotype of a relatively backward colony to which the metropolis exported capital, and to consider cases where the colony was relatively more advanced than the metropolis, such as with Poland and Finland under the Rus-

---

O. Popov, "Narodne hospodarstvo Ukrainy ta Radianskyi Soiuz," *Zhyttia i revoliutsiia*, 1925, no. 8, pp. 65–66.

[15] V. Holubnychy, "The Views of M. Volobuyev and V. Dobrohaiyev and Party Criticism," *Ukrainian Review*, no. 3, 1956, p. 6.

[16] E. Vlasenko, "Finansy Ukrainy," *Nova Ukraina*, 1927, no. 12, p. 20.

[17] Holubnychy, "The Views of M. Volobuyev...," p. 5.

[18] Bohdan Krawchenko, "The National Renaissance and the Working Class in Ukraine During the 1920s" (unpublished paper, Canadian Institute of Ukrainian Studies, 1982), p. 30n.

[19] M. Volobuiev, "Orhanizatsiia pratsi," *Radianska osvita*, 1923, no. 1, pp. 20–24, as cited in *ibid.*

sian Empire. The article provided one of the few serious Marxist economic analyses of the question of what ought to follow imperialism in a case where the empire had been taken over by those who considered themselves anti-imperialists. As such it ought to hold an important place in the intellectual history of Marxism.

Volobuiev posed the question of how the former subject nations of the Russian Empire ought to develop economically within the USSR. As with other national communists, he was not a nationalist in any conventional sense. But he warned that "It cannot be forgot that our economy is a composite whole (*skladna iednist*), and the individual parts of this composite whole must be approached as social and economic complexes."[20] Thus he saw the Soviet Union as a complex of separate nations that had banded together in the interests of socialism without renouncing their distinct economic identities. This view was no more than a corollary of what the Soviet Union claimed to be: a voluntary union of nations that happened to coincide territorially with the Russian Empire but that repudiated any notion of Russia's imperial domination over other nations. The question was whether the Soviet Union was living up to this claim and, if not, how it could do so.

Volobuiev took as his starting point the idea of Ukraine as an economic entity. The idea was Hrynko's; Volobuiev merely reiterated it and criticized those Russian economists who used euphemisms such as "the South," "the Southern region," "the Southwest," "Southern European Russia," or "the South Russian economy," instead of saying simply "Ukraine." This, he argued, was not a simple quibble over terminology, but rather, the consequence of a fundamental error of methodology which stemmed from their failure to understand the history of pre-revolutionary Russo-Ukrainian economic relations.[21]

In order to understand the nature of the Ukrainian economy and its relationship to Russia, Volobuiev felt obliged to consider the nature of colonialism and whether one could speak of a single kind of colony. Russia, he noted, had been an empire that was itself a semi-colony of Western capitalism, but this fact made it no less a colonial power in relation to its own colonies. Usually, one thought in terms of a more advanced "metropolis" ruling over relatively backward colonial nations to which it exported capital. Finland, however, had been more advanced

---

[20] *Idem.*, "Do problemy ukrainskoi ekonomiky," in *Dokumenty ukrainskoho komunizmu* (New York, 1962), p. 132.

[21] *Ibid.*, pp. 133–137.

than Great Russia and, despite its colonial dependence, had also been an exporter of capital. From this example it became apparent that a distinction had to be made between colonies to which the metropolis exported capital and from which it imported raw materials, and colonies that had their own manufacturing industries, exported capital, and actually imported raw materials from the metropolis. The seeming reversal of economic roles in the case of economically advanced colonies like Poland and Finland did not mean that these countries ceased to be colonies, but that they were clearly a different sort of colony. This circumstance led Volobuiev to draw a fundamental distinction between types of colonies based on their level of development. He called the more advanced, capital exporting ones, colonies of the European type, and the more backward, raw materials producing ones, colonies of the Asiatic type. Imperial Russia had ruled both types of colonies. Turkestan and Transcaucasia were examples of colonies of the Asiatic type; Finland, Poland, and Ukraine, had been colonies of the European type.[22]

After setting up this general framework, Volobuiev then turned his attention to Russian colonial policy in Ukraine during the age of industrial capitalism. He first reminded his readers that the degree of political dependence and the degree of economic dependence of a given colony did not necessarily coincide. For example, the Egypt of his day had more legal independence than did Ukraine under the tsars, although it was economically more dependent than tsarist Ukraine had been. By the same token, Ukraine had not always had the same colonial status. Drawing upon the works of Oleksander Ohloblyn and Mykhailo Slabchenko, the two leading Ukrainian economic historians of the 1920s, Volobuiev traced Ukraine's evolution from a colony of the Asiatic type to one of the European type. Throughout this process, the Ukrainian economy had never been completely merged with Russia; it had remained a discrete entity, albeit a dependent one. He argued that this pattern of evolution from Asiatic to European type colonial status was a universal tendency. The very terms ''European'' and ''Asiatic'' were primarily a convenience, because Asian colonies such as India were beginning to develop industrially to the point where they could export capital. Even in tsarist times, Azerbaijan, with his highly developed oil industry, had showed signs of being transformed into a colony of the European type.[23]

Having dealt with the stage of industrial capitalism, Volobuiev tackled

---

[22] *Ibid.*, pp. 137–141.
[23] *Ibid.*, pp. 141–157.

the general problem of world imperialism in the era of finance capitalism. Like Lenin, he saw an inherent antagonism between imperialism's expansion of commercial relations and consequent tendency toward national homogeneity, on the one hand, and its tendency to spawn national movements, on the other. With copious citations from Lenin, Hilferding, Hobson, and a host of lesser known scholars, Volobuiev constructed an argument designed to show that imperialism broke down national barriers within the colonies in such a way that it actually served to consolidate the national distinctiveness of the colony itself. The higher the level of economic development, the stronger this tendency toward national consolidation would become. In both types of colonies, he wrote, "National unity is the consequence of all economic development." In colonies of the Asiatic type, the quest of the indigenous bourgeoisie for mastery of the internal market provided the basis for anti-imperialist national movements. In colonies of the European type, such movements grew in strength to the point where they tended to strive for national independence and autarky, although even complete political independence within the capitalist framework left former colonies at the mercy of the world market. However, in European-type colonies, economic development was distorted in the interests of foreign investors, and it was this distorted development of the productive forces, its deviation from what would have been the most rational path of development, that constituted the essence of the legacy of colonialism.[24]

Volobuiev then turned his attention to Ukraine's position during the last years of the Russian Empire in an attempt to show how colonialism had distorted Ukrainian economic development. While he analyzed several industries in detail, one example will serve to demonstrate his point. The Ukrainian black soil region was (and still is) one of the world's major flax growing areas, but Ukraine's textile industry was inadequate for the country's needs. Ukrainian linen had to be shipped to Russia or Poland, then shipped back and sold in Ukraine in the form of a shirt. Obviously, it would have made better economic sense to have built a textile factory in Ukraine because such a factory would have been closer to its sources of raw materials, and this would have lowered the cost of manufacture. By examining several sectors of the Ukrainian economy, Volobuiev attempted to show a pattern of such irrationality that left Ukraine's internal market firmly in Russian hands. This distorted pattern of economic development had occurred, he explained, because the

---

[24] *Ibid.*, pp. 157–168. Quotation from p. 165.

extraordinarily rapid industrialization of Ukraine during the late nineteenth century had been fueled by Western European capitalism more interested in profit than in promoting the balanced development of Ukraine's economy. Even this distorted capitalist development had promoted the national consolidation of Ukraine as an economic organism, however, with the result that "the Ukrainian economy was not a true province of tsarist Russia but a country which was held in a colonial position."[25]

This discussion led Volobuiev to his main concern: how to overcome the legacy of colonialism in Ukraine after the revolution. Of Russia's former colonies of the European type, Poland and Finland had become juridically independent capitalist states—and he was careful to point out the relative nature of such independence—while Ukraine had entered the Soviet Union not as a colony, but as an independent republic with full rights. Ukraine, as the sole former colony of the European type, had needs different from those of other Soviet republics that had been Asiatic type colonies, but official pronouncements on nationality policy had been made with the concerns of colonies of the Asiatic type in mind. Such pronouncements addressed the problem of overcoming economic backwardness, of catching up with the rate and level of Russian economic development. Volobuiev argued that the policy adopted by the Twelfth Party Congress was not really applicable to Soviet Ukraine, with its different set of concerns. The Ukrainian economy did not have to catch up with Russia; it had done so even before the revolution. Volobuiev believed that something altogether different was needed by Ukraine: "Our task must become the liquidation of that distortion (*vidkhylennia*) of the development of the productive forces from what would have been objectively the most rational, a distortion which resulted from a definite colonial policy."[26]

In other words, Ukraine was different from other Soviet republics because it had been a colony of the European type. Consequently, the problem of overcoming the legacy of colonialism had to be approached differently. With the arrival of the proletarian revolution, he explained, the relatively backward colonies of the Asiatic type could achieve liberation only under the guidance of the more advanced socialist countries, and could enter the world socialist economy only through a developed socialist economy. This economic tutelage would gradually come to an

---

[25] *Ibid.*, pp. 168–186. Quotation from p. 186.
[26] *Ibid.*, pp. 186–190. Quotation from p. 190.

end, as the level of the former Asiatic-type colonies' economic development was raised. Former European-type colonies that had already attained independence, as Ukraine had, could enter the socialist economic complex only on the basis of full equality with all other participants. The fact that the proletarian revolution had thus far been victorious only on the territory of the former Russian Empire had created what Volobuiev considered a mistaken impression that the Soviet economy was a single Russian economic organism, and this error was reflected in the controversy over whether it was possible to build socialism in one country. Volobuiev maintained that, while it might be proper to refer to the Soviet Union as one country when juxtaposing it, as an entity, against the rest of the world, the very manner of posing the question was wrong when considering the internal economy of the Union, because what had actually happened was the division of the world economy into two parts, one capitalist and one socialist. The USSR was, in its internal economic life, more than one country: it was a socialist economic system consisting of equal national economic organisms. Within this international socialist commonwealth, economic development faced the task of fostering the *relative* (and Volobuiev emphasized this word) autarky of its parts. Such relative autarky under socialism would not be based on the antagonism characteristic of capitalist relationships, but on economic cooperation among equals. Volobuiev considered this as an absolutely vital principle. He called for recognition of the fact that the USSR was not one nation with relatively fixed borders, but the kernel of the future world socialist system.[27]

In those days, it was the official doctrine that the Soviet Union was a voluntary union of all socialist states. Until the end of the Second World War, the extension of socialism was identified with the territorial expansion of the USSR. If one believed that the triumph of socialism throughout the world was inevitable, then the Soviet Union *was* a future socialist world government in embryo. Volobuiev argued only that it should act accordingly. If one looked forward to the day when there would be, say, a Soviet France, it would make little sense to carry out economic policy in it the same way policy regarding Turkestan was carried out.

Volobuiev insisted that economic relationships within the USSR be conducted in such a way as to be consistent with the Soviet Union's future as a world state. The economic division of labor among nations implied the cooperation of relatively autarchic national economic units.

---

[27] *Ibid.*, pp. 190–193.

Inside the USSR, national economies had to be treated as separate units—potential, in the case of former colonies of the Asiatic type; actual, in the cases of Russia and Ukraine.[28]

All this enabled Volobuiev to draw practical consequences from his excursion into history and theory. The Five Year Plan, he noted, had already assigned Ukraine a faster tempo of economic growth than it had to the Union as a whole. Dniprelstan, the giant hydroelectric complex, stood as a monument to the determination to effect the socialist transformation of the economy. The rate of economic development was not the problem. What was needed, Volobuiev insisted, was a reappraisal of economic policy, so that it would take into account the fact that Ukraine was a national economic unit that faced the task of preparing for participation in the world socialist economy by overcoming the legacy of irrationality in its past economic development. Often, economic planners actually increased the irrational element in the Soviet economy by building new factories in the Urals when the same products could be produced more cheaply close to their sources of raw materials in Ukraine.[29]

What was to draw most attention in Volobuiev's work was his popularization of Dobrohaiiev's budgetary analysis showing a massive transfer of investment capital out of Ukraine. Volobuiev cited figures from Dobrohaiiev showing that from 1893 to 1910, tsarist Russia had taken 3.29 billion rubles out of Ukraine, and had returned only 2.6 billion.[30] Dobrohaiiev's figures showed that in the mid-1920s, the Soviet Union was still collecting about 20% more in taxes than it spent in Ukraine. Volobuiev cited these statistics along with long quotations to the effect that such a massive drain on Ukraine's resources could not help but retard Ukraine's own economic and cultural development.[31] He did not draw comparisons. He did not have to. The implication was that Ukraine was being exploited by Russia as a part of the Soviet Union, no less than it had been by the tsars. In terms of the economic relationship between Russia and Ukraine, the revolution had changed nothing.

Volobuiev did not begrudge less developed regions some kind of economic assistance, but he considered Ukraine's burden disproportionately large, and asked that Russia share a greater part of the expense. He also objected to spending Ukrainian resources to build factories in

---

[28] *Ibid.*, pp. 193–194.
[29] *Ibid.*, pp. 194–214.
[30] *Ibid.*, p. 183.
[31] *Ibid.*, p. 223.

the Urals when it made more economic sense to build them in Ukraine. That, he argued, merely intensified the economic distortions and irrationalities originally wrought by imperialism.[32]

Volobuiev concluded that when economic questions were broached in the future, Ukraine ought to be viewed neither as a province, nor as the Southern USSR, but as a national economic organism created by history. He made several concrete proposals to help overcome the legacy of colonialism in Ukraine: 1) that the regionalization program be effected in a way that recognized the territorial and economic integrity of Ukraine; 2) that Ukrainian authorities have full control of Ukraine's public economy; 3) that the ways of supervising industries be changed so as to give greater authority to officials on the republic level; 4) that the role of Gosplan and other Union organs be limited to general guidance of economic policy; 5) that the Soviet Ukrainian government be given full budgetary authority; 6) that industrialization plans be reviewed in order to purge them of Russocentric biases; 7) that the location of new industry be based solely on considerations of economic rationality; 8) that there be a Ukrainian body in charge of manpower management; and 9) that the republics be given real power in shaping the decisions of Union bodies. For Volobuiev, this last point meant, above all, challenging the "great power tendencies" of the academic economists who tended to shape the decisions of such bodies.[33]

Volobuiev added that economic policy was the central factor in solving the nationality problem. The legacy of colonialism in the Ukrainian language, literature, and culture could be overcome only in tandem with an economic policy that took into account the national economic organism, and that realized that the Soviet Union was more than the sum of its regions. As things stood, national hostilities threatened to revive on an economic basis. Volobuiev ended with the following prescription: "It must not be forgot that Ukraine is not only the 'Southern USSR'; it cannot be, it would be unforgiveable to forget that it is also *Ukraine!*"[34]

Volobuievism, then, was a declaration of the economic independence of Ukraine, a demand that Soviet Ukraine be treated the same way one might expect a Soviet France to be treated after the anticipated victory of socialism throughout the world. Volobuiev did not intend to be iden-

---

[32] *Ibid.*, pp. 220–226.
[33] *Ibid.*, pp. 228–229.
[34] *Ibid.*, p. 230. Emphasis in original.

tified with Shumskyi and Khvylovyi. He sincerely believed that his position was the logical conclusion of the fundamental assumptions of the Soviet system, assumptions that he believed had been obscured by the circumstance that the Soviet Union happened to correspond to the territory of the Russian Empire. Perhaps he hoped that his ideas would lead to a fundamental reexamination of Soviet economic policy. Certainly, he succeeded in stirring controversy. In the personal archive of the writer Arkadii Liubchenko were found slips of paper on which workers wrote their questions during a visit of prominent Ukrainian writers to the Donbas, over a year after Volobuiev's work was published. One question was written in the semi-literate *patois* of a Donbas Russian proletarian:

> Comrade lecturer, please explain this. Volobuiev's theory about building (socialism) is being spread in *Ukr. Bolshevik* (actually, *Bilshovyk Ukrainy*). If you try to build and spread theories like this, you won't get very far.[35]

Volobuiev's Critics

When *Bilshovyk Ukrainy* carried Volobuiev's work as a discussion article, it was accompanied by a response authored by Andrii Richytskyi entitled "On the Problem of Liquidating the Vestiges of Colonialism and Nationalism." Richytskyi had headed the Ukrainian Communist Party, and joined the KP(b)U in 1925 when the Ukapisty were dissolved as a separate group. Like the Borotbisty, Richytskyi and his former followers were burdened with the political liability of a "non-Leninist" heritage and needed to demonstrate that they were now good Party men. On the other hand, his record of criticizing the Soviet Ukrainian regime from a Ukrainian radical standpoint—he was the author of the Ukapist memorandum to the Comintern—probably convinced the Party that he was the best possible figure to write a refutation of Volobuiev. Richytskyi probably had little choice about whether to write a critique of Volobuiev's work, yet his arguments differed substantially from later official criticisms of Volobuievism. His refutation, cogently argued and in its way as interesting as Volobuiev's, can be considered representative of the official Party viewpoint.

Richytskyi argued that Volobuiev had misunderstood the nature of the Soviet Union. He stated:

---

[35] Luckyj, ed., *Vaplitianskyi zbirnyk,* p. 64. Parenthetical explanations added.

Voluntary entry into the USSR and the right of secession from it are une-
quivocably guaranteed by the Soviet Constitution. The USSR is not a
closed country but a union open to all peoples who adopt the Soviet
socialist system.

This did not mean that the system was without shortcomings. It was
"a workers' state with a bureaucratic *apparat*," but one which had
largely succeeded in purging itself of "the spirit of bureaucratism, red
tape (*kazenshchyna*), and chauvinism." Volobuiev had rightly seen that
the use of euphemisms, such as South Russia, the southern region, the
southern USSR, the southernmost part of the USSR, represented more
than verbal lapses; they were indicative of the chauvinistic mind of those
who used them, and they were often found in Russian economic journals. Richytskyi charged Volobuiev with confusing these indications
of chauvinism in the works of a few Ukrainophobic Russian economists
with a problem of structure and policy. Such chauvinism came with
bureaucracy. Volobuiev had overemphasized its strength and had implied
that it represented official policy, but the Party had never supported
such views. "On the contrary," Richytskyi wrote, "from the time the
USSR began to be organized the Party has been aware of these tendencies and waged total war on them." According to Richytskyi, Volobuiev
had mistaken the chauvinism of economists and *apparatchiki* as an inherent feature of the system, and this had led him to attack Soviet
nationality policy without really understanding what that policy was.[36]

Volobuiev's excursion into Marxist theory and economic history had
left Richytskyi unconvinced. He dismissed the idea of Ukraine's
economic self-sufficiency as a straw man argument. Volobuiev, he
charged, had neither proven the idea nor shown how it might be relevant to the issue at hand. In any case, it was superfluous to demonstrate
the legitimacy of Ukrainian aspirations for national liberation, because
Leninism had always favored national liberation, as proved by Lenin's
polemics with Rosa Luxemburg—at least as Richytskyi interpreted them.
He also attacked Volobuiev's claim that Lenin made a clear distinction
between European and Asiatic types of colonialism. What, he asked,
was the point of such a distinction? Did it mean Ukraine was not
exploited? The most serious problem, however, with Volobuiev's distinction between the two types of colonial dependence, Richytskyi believed,

---

[36] And. Richytskyi, "Do problemy likvidatsii perezhytkiv koloniialnosty ta natsionalizmu (Vidpovid M. Volobuievu)," *Bilshovyk Ukrainy*, 1928, no. 2, pp. 73–79. Quotations from pp. 73, 74, and 77.

was his failure to relate it to various social classes, the *sine qua non* of Marxist methodology. Richytskyi was thus able to claim—with some justice—that the distinction was nothing more than a form of special pleading, designed to show that Ukraine deserved to be treated differently from other parts of the Soviet Union. As he interpreted it, Volobuiev had argued that the Soviet Union was not a free union of socialist states, but a socialist system consisting of a former metropolis and its Asiatic-type colonies. The clear implication of such a view of the Soviet Union was that Ukraine ought to leave it. Richytskyi wrote:

> The USSR is either the sole possible form of the dictatorship of the pro-letariat, of building socialism, and of fraternal coexistence among nations liberated from the yoke of imperialism, a form of organization of the proletarian state during the transition period leading to the amalgama-tion of nations, a state which has certain practical shortcomings caused by bureaucratic distortions; or the USSR is a kind of political system which does not solve the nationality question and the distortions arise from it inevitably, that is to say that it is fundamentally neither socialist nor internationalist. M. Volobuiev takes the latter view of the system of the USSR as far as economic construction is concerned.

Richytskyi was saying that Volobuiev had gone over to the other side of the barricades, that he had given up on the Soviet Union as capable of overcoming the legacy of colonialism, while in fact this attempt was the main thrust of its economic policy.[37]

Richytskyi developed his critique of Volobuiev in the second install-ment of his work. He began by replying to Volobuiev's claim that the opposition had been wrong because the USSR was more than one coun-try. The USSR was, Richytskyi replied, one country in the sense of constituting a single socio-political camp with a single planned economy. To deny this reality was to find oneself in a "naive theoretical bloc with Trotskyism." He further noted that the regionalization proposals which Volobuiev attacked had already been defeated and relegated to the archives. His main fire was directed at Volobuiev's implicit claim that the USSR was executing a colonial policy relative to Ukraine. Richyt-skyi denounced this claim as untrue, anticommunist, grist for the mill of Dontsov and the Ukrainian fascists, and a bourgeois nationalist devia-tion. Then he turned to Volobuiev's statistics. Taking his figures from sources other than those Volobuiev had used, Richytskyi claimed that tsarist Russia's fiscal exploitation of Ukraine had been roughly twice

---

[37] *Ibid.*, pp. 79–86. Quotation from p. 85.

what Volobuiev had claimed, and the difference between Union revenues and expenditures in Ukraine perhaps only half of what Dobrohaiiev and Volobuiev had indicated. Furthermore, Richytskyi announced—obviously with official sanction—that Gosplan expected to close the gap between revenues and expenditures during the Five Year Plan. He tried to show that, far from retarding Ukraine's development, as Volobuiev had claimed, the Soviet Union had actually bestowed a number of economic benefits on Ukraine. He concluded that Volobuiev's argument was greatly similar to the national deviation of Shumskyism and Khvylovyism, although he certainly did not stoop to the hysterical tone of outrage so often encountered in communist polemics.[38]

Richytskyi's work was the only real attempt to refute Volobuiev on a rational and factual basis. He was not altogether unsuccessful. He was right in pointing out the lack of clear distinction between Asiatic and European colonies to be found in Lenin. If one credits this rather scholastic form of reasoning from authority, as did both Volobuiev and Richytskyi, then Richytskyi carried the point. Without this, Volobuiev's case did become a form of special pleading for Ukraine. The problem with Richytskyi's case was that if the USSR were really the voluntary union he claimed, then arguing that a given nation was different and ought to be treated differently was valid. He did not respond to the central point that colonialism had led to a distortion of Ukraine's economic development, and that the USSR was increasing the irrationality of the system by making investments which made little economic sense. Lastly, the promise to end the imbalance between Ukrainian revenues and receipts was simply not kept. Recent studies have shown that the rate of capital transfer out of Ukraine actually increased during the following decade.[39]

What followed was more abuse than criticism. The following issue of *Bilshovyk Ukrainy* (No. 4 for February 29), condemned Volobuievism in a lead editorial entitled "In the Swamp of Nationalism." Volobuiev's

---

[38] Richytskyi, "Do problemy likvidatsii perezhytkiv," *Bilshovyk Ukrainy,* 1928, no. 3, pp. 64–84.

[39] According to Z. L. Melnyk, over 27% of Union revenues collected in Ukraine during the First Five Year Plan were withdrawn from Ukraine and spent elsewhere in the USSR. Iwan Koropeckyj, who studied the first two Five Year Plans found that during the second period Ukraine's share of investment declined from what it had been during the first. See Zinowij Lew Melnyk, *Soviet Capital Formation: Ukraine 1928/29-1932* (Munich: 1965), pp. 106–108; Iwan Swiatoslaw Koropeckyj, *The Economics of Investment in Ukrainian Industry, 1928–1937* (Ph.D. dissertation, Columbia University, 1964), p. 78ff.

views were listed as the latest edition to the national deviations of Shumskyi, Khvylovyi, and Maksymovych, who were lumped together as
representatives of "the national chauvinist aspirations of the Ukrainian
kulaks and bourgeoisie." Criticism of Soviet nationality policy was identified as serving the interests of the "nationalist counterrevolution."
Volobuiev, it was charged,

> provides an economic foundation for Khvylovyism and Shumskyism, a
> foundation for thir theory of the struggle of two cultures which Lebed
> in his time voiced in Russian chauvinist tracts, a *de facto* foundation for
> Ukraine's need to leave the Union, criticizes the Party's economic policy
> on national grounds, and predicts a struggle of two economies.
> Volobuiev's views are no less hostile and foreign to the Leninist Party
> of the proletariat than were the views of Shumskyi and Khvylovyi.
> Volobuiev's views lend complete and abundant support to the views of
> the nationalist counterrevolution, are grist for the mill of the bourgeoisie
> (*lliut vodu na mlyn burzhuazii*), and aid them in their struggle against
> Soviet Ukraine and the USSR.[40]

The author of this statement was unwilling to be distracted from such
name calling to actually consider the issues Volobuiev had raised.

At the March KP(b)U plenum, called to denounce the KPZU majority for its support of Shumskyi, Kaganovich himself denounced Volobuiev
for what the First Secretary called "deeply false, incorrect, harmful,
and shameful answers" to the questions he had raised about the nature
of the USSR and for creating a "kulak ideology" aimed at "the
liquidation of the monopoly of trade and, hence, the liquidation of the
dictatorship of the proletariat."[41] Any correspondence between the views
Volobuiev had actually presented and Kaganovich's characterization of
them would seem to be purely coincidental.

Bilshovyk Ukrainy devoted the bulk of an entire issue to abuse of
Volobuiev. L. Perchyk declared, "The basis of Comrade Volobuiev's
theory of the Soviet economy is economic nationalism which under-
mines the economic unity of the USSR's economy." Aside from some
superficial attacks on Volobuiev's methodology, Perchyk's attempt at
refutation consisted of merely reiterating Richytskyi's observation that

---

[40] "V bahni natsionalizmu," *Bilshovyk Ukrainy*, 1928, no. 4, pp.3–11. Quotation
from p. 10.

[41] L. Kaganovich, "Rozlam v KPZU i natsionalna polityka KP(b)U," *Bilshovyk
Ukrainy*, 1928, no. 6, p. 20.

Volobuiev found himself in a "naive theoretical bloc with Trotskyism" and misrepresented Lenin's views on the economic unity of the USSR.[42]

Ievhen Hirchak, never at a loss when cataloging the ideological errors of others, listed no less than eleven heresies in Volobuiev's work. They may be summarized as follows:

1) Comparing Soviet Ukraine with prerevolutionary Ukraine in a way that favored the latter.

2) Denying that the October Revolution provided the key to the national liberation of oppressed peoples, especially in Ukraine.

3) Providing a basis for those seeking Soviet Ukraine's secession from the USSR.

4) Opposing Soviet Ukraine to other Soviet Republics, especially the RSFSR.

5) Providing a foundation for a theory of the struggle of two economies, the Ukrainian and the Russian.

6) Misunderstanding the nature and content of the USSR.

7) Denying the existence of Ukrainian statehood and Soviet Ukraine's economic, political and cultural consolidation.

8) Accusing the VKP's constituent parties and the KP(b)U of Russian chauvinism.

9) Stirring up hostility between the workers of Russia and Ukraine.

10) Committing a Trotskyite deviation on the question of socialism in one country.

11) Committing a Trotskyite deviation on the question concerning the threat of "national limitation."[43]

It is worthwhile considering these charges because they are extremely revealing as to what passed for argument in the Soviet Union. In the first place, Volobuiev did not argue that Ukraine was better off under the old regime than at the time of his writing; he drew no direct comparisons, and his figures showed Ukraine to be slightly less exploited than in the past, although the change was insignificant. In any case, Volobuiev had made a claim of fact, reducible to hard data; declaring the argument unacceptable did nothing to refute it. Whether the revolution had provided a key to national liberation was again not disputed by Volobuiev. Rather, he claimed that distinctions between different types of colonialism had to be made, and found fault with Soviet economic

---

[42] L. Perchyk, "Nainovisha 'teoriia' radianskoi ekonomiky," *Bilshovyk Ukrainy*, 1928, no. 6, pp. 51–59. Quotation from p. 52.

[43] Ie. Hirchak, "Platforma ukrainskoho natsionalizmu," *Bilshovyk Ukrainy*, 1928, no. 6, p. 29.

policy regarding Ukraine. How to overcome the legacy of colonialism was a policy question that had led to the resolutions of the Twelfth Party Congress, a change in policy which implicitly admitted that previous policy had been inadequate. He did not question the value of the Twelfth Congress decisions, but merely argued that they had failed to recognize the fact that Ukraine was different from, say, Turkestan, and that a corresponding distinction should be made in policy. It was in any case no more "un-Bolshevik" to question the universal applicability of the Twelfth Congress policy than it had been for Bolsheviks to point out the inadequacies of prior policy at the Twelfth Congress.

Soviet Ukraine's right of secession from the USSR was a right guaranteed by the Constitution of the USSR, and a right implies considering whether it ought to be exercized. A right that no one can so much as consider exercising ceases, by definition, to exist. In any case, Volobuiev did not advocate secession, merely a change in policy which would give Soviet Ukraine control over its economic resources. Condemning Volobuiev for providing a basis for others who might want to exercise a constitutionally guaranteed right, not only demonstrated that the much touted "right of secession" was a farce, but also provided evidence more conclusive than any Volobuiev had given, showing that the terms of Ukraine's "national liberation" were rather questionable. What sort of national liberation is it, when it is impermissible even to suggest that a nation ought to control its own economic resources?

Volobuiev did not oppose Soviet Ukraine to other republics; he merely charged that Ukraine was not getting a fair deal in economic questions and called for Ukraine to have greater control over its economy. He protested against Ukraine being required to subsidize economic projects elsewhere in the Soviet Union when those projects made no economic sense. Nor did he create a "theory of the struggle of two economies"; he merely sought that they be more independent from each other and that they should cooperate as equals. Was this a misunderstanding of what the USSR was? As late as 1931, Richytskyi provided the following as the official Marxist prescription for the evils of colonialism:

> Communism realizes that the unification of peoples into a single world economy is possible only on the principles of mutual trust and voluntary consent, that the way to create a voluntary union of peoples is through the separation of the colonies from the "unified" imperialist "whole," through their transformation into independent states.[44]

---

[44] And. Richytskyi, *Natsionalne pytannia doby nastupu sotsiializmu v svitli XVI zizdu VKP(b)* (Kharkiv, 1931), pp. 4–5.

This official formulation goes considerably further than anything Volobuiev demanded. Why, then, was Volobuiev condemned for viewing the USSR as a complex of various nations which ought to develop freely and in cooperation with one another? Condemning him implied that the Soviet Union could only be understood as an empire in which all important decisions were made centrally and national resources were distributed without the consent of the nation to which they belonged. The content of Hirchak's attack on Volobuiev was thus implicitly far more damaging to Soviet claims to provide a framework for national liberation than anything Volobuiev had written.

Hirchak's remaining charges were even more farcical. Volobuiev simply did not deny the existence of Soviet Ukraine's economic, political, and cultural progress; rather he said that they had been somewhat retarded by the drain on Ukrainian resources by the Union. If resources were being drained from Soviet Ukraine—and no one denied that they were—this statement was merely logical. If what he had said stirred up hostility between Russian and Ukrainian workers, this was hardly Volobuiev's fault. The fact that such hostility already existed was evidenced by communist policies designed to mitigate it, policies such as Ukrainization and efforts to foster the development of national cultures. Indeed, one of Volobuiev's major points was that a change in economic policy was needed to prevent a revival of ethnic animosity. To call Volobuiev a Trotskyite was absurd. Trotskyism had nothing to do with national aspirations, and there is no evidence that Trotsky was ever particularly sensitive to Ukrainian rights until perhaps the last year of his life. Besides, the whole point of Volobuiev's argument on the issue of "socialism in one country" was to show how wrong the opposition had been. If the USSR was more than one country, as Volobuiev maintained, then the Trotskyite argument on the impossibility of building socialism in one country became irrelevant.

One must wonder whether Hirchak could have seriously believed such absurdities. Probably not. As an editor of *Bilshovyk Ukrainy,* he undoubtedly bore some responsibility for the publication of Volobuiev's work, and he was probably trying to defend his own reputation for ideological orthodoxy. He certainly felt obliged to explain why Volobuiev's article had been published in the first place:

> It may be asked how it is that this counterrevolutionary literature from the pen of a communist was published in the pages of *Bilshovyk Ukrainy.* We published it wholly conscious (of its content—JM) in order to show, to audaciously, resolutely, and firmly reveal all the cankers (*boliachky*) which impede our work. We published so as not to be afraid to show

these cankers, to lance them, and remove them. The nationality policy of our Party is politically correct, Leninist, and proletarian. This policy is supported by millions of workers in Ukraine, Russia, and the whole world. No slanders and sudden attacks—not even those of the Volobuievs—can frighten us away from the correct and certain road we have taken. We have published it in order to completely eradicate the Ukrainian and Russian chauvinism which is reflected from the bourgeois throng onto some of the members of our Party. And we have published it in order to bear clear witness, among other things, to the fact that we understand "the particular nature of nationality policy in Ukraine."[45]

Did *Bilshovyk Ukrainy* publish Volobuiev merely in order to refute him? This lame explanation might actually be closer to the truth than it initially appears; perhaps the hope was to strengthen Skrypnyk's hand in bargaining for greater investment in Ukraine before the public split in the KPZU upset this rather subtle maneuver. Perhaps Ukrainian Party figures then secured Stalin's promise that they would repair the damage done. The very fact that not a word about Volobuiev was published outside Ukraine tends to suggest as much. The somewhat hysterical attacks on Khvylovyi which occasionally appeared in Russian literary journals, and the campaign against the Ukrainian communist historian Matvii Iavorskyi only a few months later, are sufficient indication that Russian communists did not feel obliged to be reticent when they believed that their Ukrainian comrades had erred.

Mykola Skrypnyk addressed the section on the nationality question of the Ukrainian Institute of Marxism, expressing his disappointment that the Institute's graduate students had not been more creative in exposing Volobuiev's errors. Volobuiev was himself an example of how the Party rewarded independent thinking, so perhaps Skrypnyk should have expected that debates in the Institute would produce little that Richytskyi had not already said. One poor student, Krykun by name, was singled out for abuse because he had dared to criticize Richytskyi's method of refuting Volobuiev and was therefore accused of being on Volobuiev's side. In any event, Skrypnyk assured the aspiring adepts of dialectical materialism not only that Volobuiev was completely wrong from a scientific viewpoint, but also that his views were cut from the same cloth those of Shumskyi and Khvylovyi, views which he claimed led to fascism as well as the splitters in the KPZU. Skrypnyk denounc-

---

[45] Ie. Hirchak, "Platforma ukrainskoho natsionalizmu," p. 43.

ed such views as those of the Ukrainian *petite bourgeoisie* and said of those who held them:

> They believe that our cultural work, our line, our Party's line are great power chauvinism (*velykoderzhavnist*), that we are somehow controlled by Kaganovich's group and so on. The next step will be a fight against the entire line we are pursuing. However, this *petite bourgeoisie*, ideologically fascist, says that we have a Ukrainian colony in the Union, that Moscow is exploiting the Ukrainians and so forth. And these treasonous Shumskyite groups provided the slogans regarding Party, cultural, and practical matters.
>
> *Volobuiev provides a theory of the KP(b)U's line from an economic viewpoint. He provides an anti-Leninist theory which can be used to fight against the KP(b)U, the VKP, the Comintern, and later for venomous work among the workers and peasants of Western Ukraine.*[46]

In short, Volobuiev was a traitor. His views were beyond the pale of legitimate discussion. He would either have to identify himself with the Party or against it. The Party would permit no third alternative, no hope of changing Party policy through criticism.

Volobuiev's Renunciation of Volobuievism

Volobuiev could have continued to uphold his views. In 1928, it was still possible to go abroad. The enthusiasm with which the Ukrainian emigration greeted his arguments guaranteed that he would not have lacked an audience for his views.[47] He did not go abroad. The very boldness of his criticism was indicative of a certain naive faith in the revolution and the Party. He had probably written his work believing that he could convince the Party to change its policies simply by force of argument. The calumnies heaped upon him must have convinced him that the Party was clearly unwilling to permit any rational discussion of the arguments he had presented. He had but two alternatives: he could either support his beliefs and break with the Party, or he could remain loyal to the Party by repudiating his views. He chose the latter course, and published a somewhat limited confession of error in a letter to the editors of *Komunist*, the daily organ of the KP(b)U, in 1928. He declared that his facts had been correct, but that he had failed to realize that they represented the exception and not the rule. The overall situation of Soviet Ukraine in the USSR, he declared, was quite good. This confession

---

[46] M. Skrypnyk, "Z pryvodu ekonomichnoi platformy natsionalizmu," *Bilshovyk Ukrainy,* 1928, no. 6, pp. 44–50. Quotation from p. 46. Emphasis in the original.

[47] This point was made by Holubnychy, "The Views of M. Volobuyev," p. 11.

represented an acceptance of Richytskyi's criticisms but not of those of his more vociferous Party critics.[48]

Volobuiev published a complete and detailed repudiation of his earlier views in a two-part article carried by *Bilshovyk Ukrainy* in the Spring of 1930. Entitled "Against the Economic Platform of Nationalism (Toward a Critique of Volobuievism)," it was a measure of the complete self-abasement which the Party came to demand in rituals of self-criticism.

Volobuiev began with an expression of gratitude to Party criticism for helping him to recognize his "deep errors of principle" as well as the fact that his arguments had become weapons in the hands of the Ukrainian bourgeoisie, the KPZU splitters, and the fascists. He had, he declared, objectively served the cause of Polish and Ukrainian fascism by expressing views that were an economic counterpart to Shumskyism and Khvylovyism. Even when he had published his letter in *Komunist*, he added, he had erred in failing to go far enough in discrediting Volobuievism. His doctrine had become "objectified"; it had assumed an existence independent of its author, and had become a weapon in the hands of the class enemy. This existence, he wrote, had convinced him of the need to refute Volobuievism, which contained five fundamental errors of methodology:

1) An incorrect conception of colonial development in the period of imperialism, especially the theory of two types of colonies.

2) Consequently, an incorrect approach to the analysis of the colonial position of Ukraine under tsarism.

3) An incorrect understanding of the Communist Party's task regarding formerly oppressed peoples in the realm of nationality relationships and, connected with the two aforementioned groups of errors, a harmful and erroneous intepretation of our whole economic construction.

4) Against the background of this objectively and inevitability arose the allegation that the USSR was pursuing a colonial policy relative to Ukraine, which—

5) Led to the so-called "practical propositions," the objective content of which can be briefly formulated as "orientation toward Europe," in other words, detaching Ukraine from the USSR.[49]

Thus Volobuiev confessed his "objective guilt" in helping the bourgeois counterrevolution without having intended to do so. Every one of his

---

[48] *Ibid.* Text in Ie. F. Hirchak, *Na dva fronta v borbe s natsionalizmom,* pp. 215–216.
[49] M. Volobuiev, "Proty ekonomichnoi pliatformy natsionalizmu (Do krytyky volobuivshchyny)," *Bilshovyk Ukrainy,* 1930, no. 5–6, pp. 54–55. Quotation from p. 55.

propositions, and much of the evidence he had used to support them, were repudiated.

He first of all repudiated his earlier concept of types of colonial dependence which, he declared, had led him to portray prerevolutionary Ukraine's situation in far too favorable a light. The idea that there was a European type of colonial dependence characterized by a process of national consolidation and the weakening of the economic basis of colonialism, was now rejected. Such a view, he maintained, looked at the economic development of the colonies only from the standpoint of the colonies themselves. There had been, to be sure, a distortion in the pattern of the economic development of the colonies, but he had erred in seeing this distortion as the essential hallmark of the exploitation of colonies of the European type. Most of all, he had erred in viewing the export of capital from the colonies as an agent of decolonization. However valid the theory of decolonization might seem from the standpoint of the later twentieth century after the dissolution of all the old empires except the Russian, Volobuiev followed the Comintern in rejecting this theory. The export of capital from the colonies, he now declared, not only failed to signify the disintegration of imperialism's economic basis, but actually added a powerful new dimension to colonial exploitation. He had seen only that the influx of foreign capital into Ukraine had led it to attain a level and tempo of economic development which surpassed Russia's. What he had earlier failed to see, he now added, was that the process merely added a new layer of direct exploitation by European capitalism to Ukraine's age-old exploitation by Russia. It had led him to believe that Ukraine's economic development heralded a process of decolonization, while whatever industrial development that took place, had the distinct mark of monoculture economy that served not Ukrainian, but imperialist interests. The real state of affairs under tsarism, he now affirmed, was that the colonial oppression of Ukraine, far from being weakened, was actually being intensified.[50]

Volobuiev then confessed his errors in understanding the postrevolutionary tasks facing the Communist Party in finding a solution to the nationality problem. He attributed these errors not only to his "mistaken" idea that imperialism created a path of economic development that favored eventual decolonization, but also to his having viewed economics in isolation from the class struggle. Evidently, the idea of distinct national economic organisms somehow contradicted this latter

---

[50] *Ibid.*, pp. 56–60.

fundamental of Marxist methodology. He indicated that this was the case without being at all clear as to why this should have been so. He added that the tendency of "concurrence" between the pre-revolutionary Russian and Ukrainian economies had influenced the very nature of their economic relationship such that the Soviet Union's economic development was possible only as a single economic organism. How this view was any more compatible with Marxist notions of the class struggle than were his earlier ideas, was essentially left to the reader's imagination. Quoting Lenin, he noted that since capitalism had created large economic organisms, it was somehow reactionary to break them up. It thus became "petit-bourgeois" to argue that socialism could be built on the basis of economically independent nations. Also, the unity of the postrevolutionary economy was completely different from the antagonist unity of prerevolutionary imperialism:

> The socialist economy is a totality of socialist and not antagonist productive relations. The socialist camp does not recognize the exploitation of man by man. It also does not recognize the exploitation of colonies by a metropolis or the oppression of one nation by another. The socialist economy is based upon the broadest possible and most complete all round development of all individual economic regions. It maintains the equality of their development which, however, in the stage of transformation means speeding up the tempo of the development of former colonies. The unity of the socialist economy is the unity of the friendly and voluntary cooperation of the toilers of all nations on the basis of the most rational division of labor. In this the interests of the whole completely safeguard the requisite development of its various parts, in contrast with imperialism, where the excessive development of one part is paid for by impeding the development of the others.[51]

This profession of Leninist faith did little to refute Volobuiev's earlier arguments. Whether or not socialism recognized colonial exploitation had very little to do with the argument that Ukraine was being exploited by Russia. Nor did the assertion that socialism guaranteed the greatest possible rationality of development do much to refute concrete examples of how Soviet planners were perpetuating the economic irrationalities of the prerevolutionary pattern of economic development. It was, in short, a retreat into scholasticism: something cannot be so, because the dogma does not recognize it.

Volobuiev then confessed his specific sins. The idea that the Soviet Union was more than one country became "Trotskyite" (Trotsky would

---

[51] *Ibid.*, pp. 60–63. Quotation from pp. 62–63.

no doubt have been amazed at this). His economic separatism had echoed the ideas of the Ukapisty; this meant that the ideas were counterrevolutionary because Skrypnyk had somewhere said so. He had misunderstood Lenin. He had found himself in the same camp with Khvylovyism and the "traitors" of the KPZU majority. He had been guilty of Ukrainian chauvinism.[52]

In the second installment of his recantation, Volobuiev attempted to refute his earlier factual material. He had gotten his figures wrong, he now maintained. He attempted to show with facts and figures "how triumphant socialist construction corrects and destroys Volobuievism."[53]

The Party could hardly have asked for more, and Volobuiev seems to have bought a brief extension of life. The only certainty is that he perished sometime in the 1930s. One account says that he was sent to a concentration camp and never returned. Another claims that he was shot in 1938. Whether executed or worked to death, it is certain that he paid for his ideological sins with his life.[54]

*   *   *

Volobuiev's voice was the last in the KP(b)U to argue openly for fundamental alteration of the terms of Ukraine's union with Russia in the direction of greater Ukrainian independence. His case for a fundamental reappraisal of Ukraine's economic relationship with Russia was forcefully made in the name of communism's own slogan of national liberation. After all, could a nation be said to have achieved national liberation if it was being exploited, if it did not control its own economic resources, if its real economic needs were being ignored? The question itself was far too embarrassing ever to be answered directly. Only Andrii Richytskyi attempted to do so, and his arguments quickly gave way to empty denunciation.

The Volobuiev affair, like the earlier controversies surrounding Shumskyi and Khvylovyi, served to emphasize the fundamental dilemma the Soviet Union faced in its attempt to maintain the restored unity of the old Russian Empire, and simultaneously to give some concessions to the aspirations of non-Russian nations through indigenization and official sponsorship of national cultures: how to keep the process within bounds that did not threaten the old empire's unity. Ukrainization pro-

---

[52] *Ibid.*, pp. 63–69.
[53] Volobuiev, "Proty ekonomichnoi pliatformy natsionalizmu," *Bilshovyk Ukrainy*, 1930, no. 7, pp. 28–40.
[54] See Holubnychy, "The Views of M. Volobuyev," p. 12.

vided a measure of legitimacy to Ukrainian aspirations; even the Party could not remain immune to these aspirations. The very phenomenon of Volobuiev, a Russian communist accusing the regime of failing to do enough to overcome the economic legacy of colonialism in Ukraine, is indicative of just how deeply Ukrainian aspirations had affected the Party. The relatively free discussion of which Volobuiev was the last example became impossible in the wake of the Shakhty affair in the Spring of 1928, but the final chapter in the history of Ukrainian self-assertion within the Soviet communist framework was only just beginning. Associated with the name of Mykola Skrypnyk, it was the most powerful attempt of all.

PART THREE

Soviet Ukraine Under Skrypnyk

CHAPTER SIX

Mykola Skrypnyk and Ukrainian Communism

AFTER 1925, MYKOLA Skrypnyk emerged as the Party's leading authority on nationality policy in Ukraine. When in 1927 he succeeded Oleksander Shumskyi as Soviet Ukraine's Commissar of Education, he assumed broad responsibility for all aspects of Soviet Ukrainian culture. He was thus in a position to define the official goals in the sphere that dominated the politics of the day and to carry out policies to attain those goals. Although he headed neither Party nor state, he became his country's dominant political figure. A crucial period in his nation's history bears the stamp of his personality, his thought, and his policies; the temporary victory and final defeat of the Ukrainian quest for its own road to socialism are inseparable from his career.

Skrypnyk was not a nationalist in any conventional sense of the term; rather, he was a national communist, an Old Bolshevik and astute politician who portrayed himself as a true proletarian internationalist dedicated to policies which alone could mitigate national hostility. Unlike those whom he denounced as national deviationists, he rejected any hint of hostility toward Russia, tried to calm Moscow's apprehensions, and achieved almost everything figures like Shumskyi and Khvylovyi had demanded. An able defender of Ukraine's national interests and constitutional prerogatives, he seems to have sincerely believed that the Soviet Union could be something more than a successor to the old Russia; he saw it as a socialist world state in embryo, and the relations between Soviet Ukraine and Soviet Russia as the model for the future relations between a socialist Germany and France. As his biographer Iwan Koszeliwec said, "He believed on the one hand in the world proletarian revolution and on the other hand that it was possible in the process of its realization to achieve Ukrainian national sovereignty without separating from Russia."[1]

---

[1] Iwan Koszeliwec, *Mykola Skrypnyk* (Munich, 1972), p. 67.

Skrypnyk has been described as a sort of commissar of the nationality question with everything but the title.[2] He was the leading authority on Ukrainization, Ukrainian culture, and the nationality question in Ukraine; these, taken together, were the central questions of the day. Ukrainian communism became so intimately bound up with his person, that his disgrace and suicide in 1933 can be taken as the point at which the search for national roads to socialism within the USSR came to its definitive end.

The Making of a Ukrainian Bolshevik

An ethnic Ukrainian, Skrypnyk was born in 1872 in Katerynoslav Province. His father was a railroad employee and his mother, a midwife. He later recalled that he first came into contact with illegal Marxist literature through Ukrainian translations of the Marxist classics published by the Radical Party in Galicia. He became a Marxist in 1897, although he later confessed that at the time his Marxism was still tainted with revisionism. Noting that the date of one's entry into the RSDRP depended on how one defined membership, he was vague on the precise date when he joined the Party but stated that in any case he had become a Party member no later than the end of 1900.[3] While he himself was silent about any active involvement in the Ukrainian movement, certain Ukrainian sources indicate that he was a member of the Ukrainian Student Hromada in St. Petersburg during his stay there at the turn of the century.[4] Whatever involvement he may have had with this organiza-

---

[2] *Ibid.*, p. 115.

[3] His most detailed autobiography, written for the Party verification campaign of 1921, appears in *ibid.*, pp. 261–272. What is essentially a shortened version of this appears in *Entsiklopedicheskii slovar russkogo bibliograficheskogo instituta Granat: Deiateli SSSR i Oktiabrskoi revoliutsii* (Moscow, n.d.), vol. 3, pp. 47–59. See also "Biohrafiia Mykoly Oleksiiovycha Skrypnyka," *Visti VUTsVK*, January 26, 1932, p. 3; M. A. Rubach, "Profesiinyi revoliutsioner," in Rubach, ed., *Shliakhamy zaslan ta borotby (Dokumenty do zhyttiepysu t. Skrypnyka)* (Kharkiv, 1932), pp. 9–10, which also contains documents relating to his early career.

[4] Koszeliwec, *Mykola Skrypnyk*, pp. 33–34, discusses the testimony of Lototskyi, who claimed to have met Skrypnyk among the members of the Ukrainian Student Hromada in St. Petersburg but gives a date too early for Skrypnyk to have been in the capital. Another prominent Ukrainian claimed to have met him in the same capacity in 1902, which is too late because of Skrypnyk's arrest in 1901. See Dmytro Doroshenko, *Moi spomyny pro davnie-mynule (1901–1914 roky)* (Winnipeg, 1949), p. 27. While dates can be mistaken, especially after the passage of decades, the fact that two memoirs mention Skrypnyk as a member of the same organization in the same place should not be discredited simply because he did not mention it in his autobiography.

tion was over by 1901, when he was arrested and exiled from the city for trying to organize workers.[5]

What is certain is that Skrypnyk abandoned Ukrainian radical politics and joined the RSDRP before its split into Bolshevik and Menshevik factions in 1903. Skrypnyk sided with the Bolsheviks and seems never to have wavered in his allegiance to Lenin's faction. His career during the decade and a half preceding the October Revolution was that of a typical professional revolutionary: missions on behalf of the Bolsheviks to various parts of the Russian Empire, arrests, administrative exile, escapes, a taste of emigre life in Paris. In 1913 he was assigned to serve on the editorial board of the Bolshevik *Pravda,* but he was arrested the following year along with the entire editorial staff. He was exiled first to Siberia and then to Morshansk in Tambov province, where he remained until 1917.[6]

Shortly after the February Revolution, Skrypnyk helped to organize a Soviet of Workers' Deputies in Morshansk. He attended the Moscow Regional Congress of Soviets and the First All-Russian Congress of Soviets as a delegate of the Morshansk Soviet. He also participated in the Bolsheviks' April Conference and the Sixth Congress, being elevated at the latter to the Central Committee. He then helped edit *Proletarii,* a Petrograd Bolshevik organ, and took part in the October Revolution as a member of the Military-Revolutionary Committee of the Petrograd Soviet, the body that actually took power from the Provisional Government.[7]

In December 1917, Lenin sent Skrypnyk to Ukraine as his personal representative. His certification, dated December 22 and signed by Sverdlov, identified him as an agent of the Bolshevik Central Committee and directed all Party organizations to cooperate with him in every way possible.[8] Even before he left Moscow, the Bolshevik-dominated rump session of the First All-Ukrainian Congress of Soviets named him

---

[5] See note 3 above.

[6] Iu. Babko and I. Bilokobylskyi, *Mykola Oleksiiovych Skrypnyk* (Kiev, 1967), pp. 13–95; Koszeliwec, *Mykola Skrypnyk,* pp. 30–37; Rubach, *Shliakhamy zaslan ta borotby,* pp. 10–18; "Biohrafiia Mykoly Oleksiiovycha Skrypnyka," *Visti VUTsVK,* January 26, 1932, p. 3.

[7] Babko and Bilokobylskyi, *Mykola Oleksiiovych Skrypnyk,* pp. 100–112.

[8] "Udostoverenie, vydannoe na imia N. A. Skrypnika, v tom, chto on komandiruetsia po Ukraine v kachestve agenta TsK RSDRP(b)," *Bolshevistskie organizatsii Ukrainy v period ustanovleniia i ukrepleniia Sovetskoi vlasti (noiabr 1917 - aprel 1918 gg.) (Sbornik dokumentov i materialov)* (Kiev, 1962), p. 29.

Secretary of Labor in the first Soviet Ukrainian government.[9] He thus arrived in Ukraine both as an agent of the Russian Bolshevik Central Committee and a member of the government of a country he had not seen in years. He was clearly Lenin's man in Ukraine, sent there to moderate the divisive rivalry between the Kievan and Katerynoslavan Bolshevik factions, as well as to carry out whatever other orders Lenin might have given him.

After the Germans had driven the Bolshevik regime out of Kiev in February 1918, Skrypnyk became head of the Ukrainian Soviet government. His government made a number of attempts to appear to be independent from Russia. On February 25, 1918, for example, an "Extraordinary Plenipotentiary Embassy," headed by Skrypnyk, was sent to Moscow to proclaim the independence of the "Ukrainian Soviet Federative Socialist Republic" from the RSFSR and to establish diplomatic relations.[10] This did not amount to much, since the newly-proclaimed "Ukrainian Soviet Federation" would cease to exist within a couple of months.

The most important legacy of Skrypnyk's mission to Ukraine in 1917–1918 came out of the Taganrog Party Conference, held simultaneously with the Third All-Ukrainian Congress of Soviets. By that time Soviet Ukraine consisted of only a tiny corner of Ukraine, and it was a foregone conclusion that even this would be lost very shortly. The Congress of Soviets thus had little to do beyond liquidating what was left of the Soviet government, while the Party conference faced the task of laying the basis for future revolutionary struggle in Ukraine.[11] With the Kievans and Katerynoslavans at loggerheads over the question of founding a Communist Party for Ukraine, Skrypnyk personally drafted the resolutions adopted. They called for a territorial Communist Party (bolshevik) of Ukraine, with its own Central Committee and representation in the Comintern, and defined the Party's main tasks.[12] Skrypnyk may thus be considered the founder of the KP(b)U.

All this could lead one to believe that Skrypnyk had already adopted the views he would later champion. Skrypnyk did try to maintain

---

[9] Babko and Bilokobylskyi, *Mykola Oleksiiovych Skrypnyk,* p. 120.
[10] The full text of this document was first published in *ibid.,* pp. 131–132.
[11] "At the Taganrog Conference we moved...along two separate moments: on the one hand, the task of reconstructing the Party, and on the other, the task of liquidating the People's Secretariat." Epshtein, *Vtoroi sezd KP(b)U* (Kharkiv, 1927), p. 48.
[12] See chapter one above and Evgeniia Bosh, *God borby,* pp. 218–220.

Ukraine's territorial integrity by attempting to prevent the creation of
the Donets - Krivoi Rog Republic at the end of 1918, and he occasionally
surpassed what Lenin was willing to support on the question of Ukrainian home rule.[13] Still, it would be misleading to credit him at this juncture with the views he would later uphold, since in July 1918, at the
First KP(b)U Congress, he stated that the KP(b)U had always opposed
separation from Russia because independence was a smokescreen for
"the counter-revolutionary struggle against Soviet power."[14]

This position was neither a capitulation nor an abandonment of any
principles that Skrypnyk might earlier have held. It can be fully
explained by the changed situation. Before May 1918, Ukraine's
Bolsheviks were engaged in a civil war against the Ukrainian Central Rada and its German allies. The Rada, in its Fourth Universal,
proclaimed Ukraine independent on January 22, and the Bolsheviks, having earlier proclaimed the Rada overthrown, could not possibly recognize the Rada's authority to make such a declaration. Consequently, a declaration of Soviet Ukrainian independence became a
political necessity. With Soviet Russia's acceptance of the Treaty of
Brest-Litovsk, it became all the more vital to avoid embroiling Russia
in a conflict with the Germans, and this made it necessary to establish
a formally independent Communist Party of Ukraine. After the Germans halted their advance, such considerations became less pressing.
The Bolsheviks were now expecting a new revolutionary upsurge to
sweep Europe, and the revolutionaries were again preoccupied with the
prospect of expanding the territory under the revolution's sway. Preparations for an armed uprising were begun amid reports of peasant upris-
ings in Ukraine. The political necessities of April seemed no longer to
exist, and talk of Ukrainian independence, never taken seriously by most
Bolsheviks, could be dropped altogether.[15]

Skrypnyk was in no way connected with such national communist
oppositions as those of Shakhrai and Lapchinskii. After the First KP(b)U
Congress, Skrypnyk seems to have ceased to have any ties with Ukraine
at all; he was assigned to serve on the directing board of the Cheka.

---

[13] See Yaroslav Bilinsky, "Mykola Skrypnyk and Petro Shelest: An Essay on the Persistence and Limits of Ukrainian National Communism," in Jeremy R. Azrael, ed.,
Soviet Nationality Policies and Practices (New York, 1978), pp. 108–111.

[14] *Protokoly pervogo sezda Kommunisticheskoi Partii (bolshevikov) Ukrainy* (Kharkiv,
1923), p. 138, as cited by E. S. Osilovskaia and A. V. Snegov, "Za pravdivoe
osveshchenie istorii proletarskoi revoliutsii," *Voprosy istorii,* 1956, no. 3, p. 140.

[15] Koszeliwec, *Mykola Skrypnyk,* pp. 49–56, argues in a somewhat similar vein.

He returned to Ukraine at the beginning of 1919 to serve as Commissar of State Control, a position with economic rather than political importance.[16] He also represented the KP(b)U at the First Comintern Congress.[17] After the fall of the Piatakov-Rakovskii regime, he was assigned to the guerrilla war against Otaman Zelenyi. This assignment was less of a change than it might seem, since Skrypnyk took part in military operations even while a member of Rakovskii's government.[18]

Skrypnyk returned to Ukraine in April 1920, this time to stay; from this period, a substantial alteration in his views can be discerned. After brief stints as Ukrainian Commissar of Worker-Peasant Inspection and Foreign Affairs, he was appointed Commissar of Justice and Procurator General in 1922. These were not exactly posts of first-rate importance.[19]

In the summer of 1920, Skrypnyk published an article entitled "Donbas and Ukraine." Framed as a critique of the Katerynoslavan wing of the KP(b)U, the article is actually a thoroughgoing reappraisal of the regime's whole policy toward the rural Ukrainian-speaking majority of Ukraine's inhabitants. Skrypnyk's main argument was that the national hostility between the Russian or Russified urban proletariat and the Ukrainian peasantry had been the basic stumbling-block in the way of establishing a firm Soviet regime in Ukraine. What he concluded ought to be done clearly foreshadowed the policy with which he would later be associated:

> Ukraine and Russia are united in a single military federation against world imperialism. Fostering the development of Ukrainian culture is the task now confronting the proletarian state of Soviet Ukraine. Ukraine is at last established as a political whole uniting the proletarian forces of both the Dnipro valley and the Donbas. And there is but one way to unite these toiling masses in building communism: the proletariat of the Donbas must strive to win over the Ukrainian peasantry for the joint effort of building a proletarian Ukraine as part of the Soviet federation.[20]

This is essentially what Ukrainization would be all about.

Skrypnyk then became an outspoken advocate of fundamental change. At the Fifth KP(b)U Congress in November 1920, he complained that the KP(b)U was not even a political party in its own right, because a

---

[16] Babko and Bilokobylskyi, *Mykola Oleksiiovych Skrypnyk*, pp. 141–145.

[17] "Mykola Oleksiiovych Skrypnyk," *Visti VUTsVK*, July 8, 1933, p. 4.

[18] *Ibid.*, "Biohrafiia M. O. Skrypnyka," *Visti VUTsVK*, January 26, 1932, p. 3.

[19] Babko and Bilokobylskyi, *Mykola Oleksiiovych Skrypnyk*, pp. 152–157; Koszeliwec, *Mykola Skrypnyk*, p. 97.

[20] "Donbas i Ukraina" in Mykola Skrypnyk, *Statti i promovy z natsionalnoho pytannia*, Iwan Koszeliwec, ed. (Munich, 1974), p. 18.

party decides what its policy will be, whereas the KP(b)U submitted all important questions to Moscow. This, he argued, was bad politics, because "we have special conditions in Ukraine which call for a Party line different from what it is in Russia."[21] At the Eleventh RKP Congress, he warned against the subtle infiltration of Russian nationalism (*smenovekhovstvo*) into the Bolshevik consciousness, and professed to see it manifest in the tendency to drain the statehood of the non-Russian republics of all real content. He argued that the nationality question was far more than just an internal problem of what used to be the Russian Empire: it was crucial to the fate of the world revolution as a whole, because the ultimate success of the revolution on a world scale required that communists be able to lead the national liberation struggles of oppressed peoples against imperialism. In order to lead national liberation struggles elsewhere, communism had first to provide a desirable model of national liberation in the areas already under the sway of Soviet power.[22]

In the negotiations preceding the formation of the Soviet Union, Skrypnyk was a leading advocate of reserving broad rights to the national republics. In this attempt, one of his chief opponents was Stalin, who envisioned a much stronger federal structure. Skrypnyk did not by any means get everything he wanted. He tried, for example, to keep foreign trade and foreign affairs under the partial control of the republics by relegating these areas to joint commissariats. Largely because of Lenin's intervention, however, Skrypnyk did get substantial concessions, notably a bicameral legislature in which one house functioned as the common voice of the sovereign Union republics.[23]

Skrypnyk also came into conflict with Stalin twice in 1923: at the Twelfth Party Congress and at the conference of workers in the nationality republics called to discuss the Sultan-Galiev affair. At the Twelfth Congress, he saw Stalin's view that the Party should simultaneously combat the evils of Russian chauvinism and local nationalism as a kind of double bookkeeping. He argued that the nationalism of non-Russians was simply a reaction to the Russian chauvinism all too common among officials in the outlying areas of the former empire. Therefore, fighting Russian chauvinism had to be given top priority, the sovereignty of the non-Russian republics respected, and the development of non-Russian

---

[21] M. Ravich-Cherkasskii, *Istoriia Kommunisticheskoi Partii (b-ov) Ukrainy*, p. 175
[22] Mykola Skrypnyk, *Statti i promovy z natsionalnoho pytannia*, pp. 19–22. Koszeliwec *Mykola Skrypnyk*, p. 73.
[23] *Ibid.*, pp. 86–87.

cultures actively fostered—even in the RSFSR. In addition, he insisted that the Russification of Ukrainians in the Red Army be stopped by providing separate units in which Ukrainian would replace Russian as the language of command.[24]

At the conference of workers in the nationality republics, Skrypnyk made basically the same points and attempted to show that Sultan-Galiev's anti-Russian statements were purely a reaction to Russian chauvinism in Party ranks. He also suggested the possibility that the Muslim communist might have been victim of a provocation arranged by his Russian opponents. He pointedly noted that such provocations had happened in the past: for example, in Berdiansk, Ukraine, the former Borotbist Stepovyi was on a mission for the KP(b)U Central Committee to investigate allegations that certain officials were abusing their power over the local Ukrainian peasants, when he was arrested for supposedly being connected with the Petliurist underground. Skrypnyk charged that the arrest had in all likelihood been engineered by those Stepovyi had been sent to investigate, in particular a Chekist named Bronskii. This suspicion led him to wonder whether Sultan-Galiev had been victim of a similar provocation.[25]

The Twelfth Congress resolution on the nationality question did not give Skrypnyk everything he wanted: local nationalism was still recognized as a danger to be combated, albeit a lesser danger than Russian chauvinism. Still, Skrypnyk succeeded enough to consider the resolution a personal victory. After returning from the Congress, he let his jubilation show through the facade of Bolshevik modesty, saying that when the final draft of the resolution was read,

> some of the comrades at he session then turned to me and said, ''You must feel like it's your birthday, because the view you have long upheld in Kharkiv has now been generally accepted.'' I have worked hard for a long time to get this across, so why shouldn't I feel like it's my birthday? But I don't feel anything of the sort, comrades, because we aren't concerned with such little things. What we recognize is that we must take what has now been accepted and carry it to fruition.[26]

Skrypnyk had good reason to liken the decisions of the Twelfth Congress to a birthday present, one that he would fight to the death to keep.

---

[24] Skrypnyk, *Statti i promovy z natsionalnoho pytannia,* pp. 23–28; Koszeliwec, *Mykola Skrypnyk,* pp. 73–77.

[25] Skrypnyk, *Statti i promovy z natsionalnoho pytannia,* pp. 29–38; Koszeliwec, *Mykola Skrypnyk,* pp. 77–79; Iwan Majstrenko, *Storinky z istorii Komunistychnoi Partii Ukrainy* (Munich, 1969), vol. 2, pp. 23–27.

[26] Mykola Skrypnyk, *Statti i promovy* (Kharkiv, 1929–1931), vol. 2, part 1, p. 32.

From Apparatchik to Theoretician

During the so-called Cultural Revolution which began in 1928, virtually every field of endeavor produced its "little Stalin" whose every word was considered authoritative. To be sure, the actual power wielded by these seemingly omnipotent and infallible figures was often more apparent than real. Still, they dominated their respective spheres for however long they enjoyed their positions.

Skrypnyk became, to all intents and purposes, the Ukrainian Stalin; his statements were considered authoritative in all matters of Ukrainian culture, scholarship, and the nationality question. As with many other authoritative figures of the day, he may not have felt altogether comfortable or secure in his role. The point is that he assumed it, and it is of more than passing interest to examine how he got into a position where he could do so.

Just as many non-Party people in the twenties aspired to become writers and scholars, Party leaders often aspired to recognition as members of the Party intelligentsia, that is, as theoreticians. Before the revolution, and even during the civil war, one can discern an almost mystical attachment to theory, an assumption that if one finds the proper theory concerning a problem, that problem would be virtually solved. As the Bolsheviks became more and more occupied with the technicalities of wielding power, the theoretician was more and more eclipsed by the *apparatchik*. One can see the process in the *apparatchik* Stalin defeating his theoretician opponents: Trotsky, Zinoviev, and Bukharin. Yet, as the *apparatchik* supplanted the theoretician, he became less and less satisfied with his role and aspired to become a theoretician, too. Thus did Stalin make his own less than happy contributions to the store of Marxist doctrine. If the *apparatchiks* were the Party's hands, successful *apparatchiks* aspired to recognition as its brains as well.

After the Twelfth Congress, Skrypnyk remained an *apparatchik*. His posts as Soviet Ukraine's Commissar of Justice and Procurator General, involved him deeply in the nuts and bolts of power, including such unsavory aspects as the 1925 assassination of Kotovskyi, a former pro-Bolshevik otaman whose murderer was tried by an extraordinary tribunal, found guilty, sentenced, and shortly thereafter set at liberty. Skrypnyk's deep involvement is evidenced in that extraordinary tribunals were secret tribunals dealing with matters affecting internal security and were directly responsible to the Commissar of Justice. The assassin's relatively speedy release after trial by such a court led some to suspect that he was a Chekist carrying out an assignment.[27]

---

[27] Oleksander Semenenko, *Kharkiv, Kharkiv...* (Munich, 1977), pp. 118–120;

Skrypnyk was in a good position to defend the legal prerogatives of Soviet Ukraine, both in his Ukrainian posts and as a member of the All-Union Council of Nationalities. Throughout his tenure as Commissar of Justice, he upheld the view that all questions relating to private property and land fell under the exclusive jurisdiction of the republics. He opposed moves toward greater legal standardization of republic practices, most notably at the December 1923, conference of republic Justice Commissars, when he opposed the proposals presented by Kurskii, his RSFSR counterpart.[28]

Skrypnyk also consistently defended the rights of the Union republics in the Council of Nationalities. In 1925, for example, he opposed the election of a joint presidium of both legislative houses on the grounds that such an action violated the constitutional principle of separate and independent Central Executive Committees.[29] He was among those who, in 1927, answered Iurii Larin's charge that Ukrainization violated the rights of non-Ukrainians in Soviet Ukraine.[30] The number of such instances could be multiplied *ad infinitum*. The point is that Skrypnyk became the leading defender of the rights of the republics in all-Union bodies.

Skrypnyk's aspiration to be recognized as a theoretician is most clearly seen in his association with the Ukrainian Institute of Marxism-Leninism (UIML) and its consequent evolution from relative insignificance to a body which aspired to be a Ukrainian counterpart to Russia's Communist Academy. Throughout the Institute's eight-year history, Skrypnyk was its main patron in the hierarchy. In fact, he was the prime mover behind the organization of what was originally known as the Ukrainian Marxist Institute at the beginning of 1923.[31] Originally founded to train lecturers in Marxist theory for the higher schools and Party schools, its status was enhanced almost immediately after Kaganovich replaced Kvir-

---

Oleksander Semenenko, "Narkomiust Skrypnyk," *Suchasnist*, vol. 1, 1961, no. 6, pp. 96–97.

[28] Koszeliwec, *Mykola Skrypnyk*, pp. 90–93.

[29] *Soiuz Sovetskikh Sotsialisticheskikh Respublik. Tsentralnyi ispolnitelnyi komitet, 3 sozyva, I sessiia. Stenograficheskii otchet* (Moscow, 1925), pp. 12–13.

[30] See chapter three above; Koszeliwec, *Mykola Skrypnyk*, pp. 112–113.

[31] *Ibid.*, p. 115. There is some controversy over just when UIML was founded. While recent Soviet sources give the date as late 1922, Koszeliwec says 1923. Skrypnyk himself was rather vague, once stating that the Institute was founded in 1923/24. See "Pervaia vsesoiuznaia konferentsiia marksistsko-leninskikh nauchno-issledovatelskikh uchrezhdenii (Iz stenograficheskogo otcheta)," *Vestnik Kommunisticheskoi akademii*, no. 27, p. 304. By this, Skrypnyk in all likelihood meant the 1923–24 academic year. Some additional light is shed on the problem by the fact that one Soviet scholar has mentioned that, while some archival documents indicate that the Institute was founded

ing as First Secretary of the KP(b)U. A Central Committee resolution announced on April 25, 1925, directed the Institute to become a center of Marxist thought "concentrating around itself all the forces of Ukrainian Marxist scholarship."[32]

In 1926, what had by then become known as the Ukrainian Institute of Marxism-Leninism added a chair on the nationality question, occupied by Skrypnyk himself. Skrypnyk requested, albeit without success, that the Communist Academy in Moscow recognize his chair as the all-Union center for the study of the nationality question. His claim was based on Ukraine's being the best laboratory for studying the problem, inasmuch as it had suffered national and colonial oppression under the autocracy, then became a national republic with its own minorities whose rights had to be protected.[33] Behind Skrypnyk's argument was obviously a personal bid for acceptance as the leading theoretical interpreter of Marx, Lenin, and Stalin on the nationality question.

Later, when Skrypnyk served as director of UIML, he described it as the type of institution that the Communist Academy had set out to be, combining the bid for recognition with an implicit rebuke to the institution which harbored theoreticians of the nationality question whose views he considered downright chauvinist.[34] By mid-1929, UIML

---

late in 1922, another group of documents states that it began to function on January 1, 1923, N. V. Komarenko, *Ustanovy istorychnoi nauky v Ukrainskii RSR* (Kiev, 1973), p. 43.

[32] "Pro Ukrainskyi Institut Marksyzmu," *Visty VUTsVK*, April 25, 1925, p. 2. A newspaper account published several months earlier at the beginning of the 1924–25 academic year, the Institute's second, tells how many students were studying what but makes no mention of any original scholarly work being carried on under its auspices. Stepovyi, "Ukrainskyi Marksivskyi Institut," *Literatura, Nauka, Mystetstvo*, September 21, 1924, p. 3. It should be noted that while the report of the April 1925 resolution does not definitely indicate that scholarship (*nauka*) was a completely new function for the UIML, earlier reports on the organization of science and scholarship do not mention the Institute. See, for example, Prof. O. Ianata, "Do organizovanoho rozvytku nauky na Ukraini," *Chervonyi shliakh*, 1923, no. 2, pp. 173–182; S. Posternak, "Stan i perspektyva naukovoi pratsi na Ukraini ta pokhodzhennia ii z pratseiu naukovykh ustanov S.R.S.R.," *Zhyttia i revoliutsiia*, 1925, no. 1–2, pp. 37–38. The latter account is especially significant in that it is a report of speeches by Professors M. I. Iavorskyi and S. Iu. Semkovskyi, who are identified in the article as representatives of Ukrholovnauka but who were also in charge respectively of the UIML history and sociology sections. One may be sure that if the Institute was expected to play a significant role in scholarship at the time they spoke, they would have mentioned it.

[33] Koszeliwec, *Mykola Skrypnyk*, pp. 115–116.

[34] "Pervaia vsesoiuznaia konferentsiia marksistsko-leninskikh nauchno-issledovatelskikh uchrezhdenii," *Vestnik Kommunisticheskoi adademii*, no. 27, p. 304.

was described in the Soviet Ukrainian press as the center of Marxist-Leninist thought in Ukraine.[35] In June 1931, by which time indications that Skrypnyk's position was becoming insecure abounded, the KP(b)U Central Committee passed a resolution announcing that UIML had been guilty of harboring national deviationists and was to be broken up into a loose association of autonomous institutions rechristened the All-Ukrainian Association of Marxist-Leninist Scholarly-Research Institutes (VUAMLIN).[36]

The fate of UIML thus paralleled Skrypnyk's, being something of a barometer of his fortunes. That its upgrading began shortly after Kaganovich's arrival is far from coincidental. With Kaganovich's arrival, Skrypnyk was made the Party's leading authority on all questions relating to the Ukrainization of the Party, the *apparat,* and the press. The various resolutions on Ukrainization adopted by the KP(b)U Central Committee during Kaganovich's tenure from 1925 to 1928 were all basically his work, as were the major Comintern pronouncements on the nationality question, the resolution of the Fifth Comintern Congress on the nationality question in Central Europe and the Balkans, as well as those sections of the 1928 Comintern Program which dealt with the national and colonial problem.[37] It was precisely because of Skrypnyk's known commitment to Ukrainian interests that he was chosen to be the leadership's main theoretical spokesman against Shumskyi, Khvylovyi, and Volobuiev. When in 1927 he replaced Shumskyi as Commissar of Education, he was able to bring to the post a degree of prestige and authority that his predecessor could never command. Bukharin is said to have stated that Stalin made a deal with the Ukrainians to withdraw Kaganovich. Certainly, Stalin's opponent had reason to think so. Once Kaganovich was gone, Skrypnyk, in spite of his official subordination to the new First Secretary, Stanislav Kosior, was Ukraine's undisputed political strongman, as well as its most authoritative spokesman on the most vital questions.

Regarding the adoption of the name UIML, Komarenko, *Ustanovy,* p. 46, states that it occurred with the addition of an institute of Lenin in January 1924.

[35] Dm. Bovanenko, "Naukovyi tsentr marksystskoi dumky na Ukraini," *Chervonyi shliakh,* 1929, no. 5–6, pp. 184–196; Feldman, "Tsentr marksystsko-leninskoi dumky na Ukraini," *Nauka i Osvita (Visti* supplement), May 19, 1929, p. 1.

[36] *Kulturne budivnytstvo v Ukrainskii RSR,* vol. 1, pp. 540–544.

[37] Koszelwec, *Mykola Skrypnyk,* pp. 105–109. On Skrypnyk's role in drafting Comintern statements on the nationality question, see his 1929 report in UIML, "Natsionalne pytannia v prohrami Kominternu," Skrypnyk, *Statti i promovy,* vol. 2, part 2, pp. 158–228.

Skrypnyk's Theory of the Nationality Question

Skrypnyk's work as an official theoretician of the nationality question frequently took the form of refutations of those who criticized the Party line. His work therefore helped to define precisely what the official position was and attempted to explain the reasoning behind it.

The starting point of Skrypnyk's theory was Lenin's juxtaposition of bourgeois nationalism and proletarian internationalism. This juxtaposition implied a basic identity common to all manifestations of nationalism, even those hostile to one another. In Soviet Ukraine the problem was to oppose both Russian and Ukrainian nationalism or, as Skrypnyk was fond of saying, to fight nationalism on two fronts.

The major theoretical problem that Skrypnyk faced was thus one of how to demonstrate that Russian and Ukrainian nationalism shared an essential sameness in spite of their mutual hostility. His major theoretical innovation was in finding this sameness in the very hostility they shared. He revived Dmitrii Lebed's theory of the struggle of two cultures, and called any idea in which an element of national antagonism might be found to be either a Russian or Ukrainian modification of Lebed's theory. This gave Skrypnyk a convenient label for any deviation from the Party line in the nationality question, because he argued that only the official policy based upon proletarian internationalism could avoid national hostility.

Thanks to Skrypnyk, denunciations of the theory of the struggle of two cultures became so routine that Lebed himself, having renounced the notion long before, expressed the hope that it be mercifully buried in the archives. But Skrypnyk refused to allow it, claiming that the theory had taken on a life independent of its original author.[38] The truth was more prosaic: Skrypnyk had hung so many of his own ideas on the theory of the struggle of two cultures that he simply could not afford to let the matter drop.

Skrypnyk developed his idea of the essential sameness of mutually antagonistic nationalisms in an article entitled "Concerning the Theory of the Struggle of Two Cultures." While the phrase had been coined by Lebed, Skrypnyk argued that the idea it designated had been in existence for a long time. He traced it to the pre-revolutionary Ukrainophobe S. Shchegolev, who had argued that Ukrainian aspirations were anti-cultural because the Ukrainian tongue was allegedly incapable of serving as a medium of cultural expression. The revolution had

---

[38] Skrypnyk's 1928 letter to Lebed. *Budivnytstvo Radianskoi Ukrainy*, vol. 1, p. 166.

brought freedom for every people to develop its cultural potential in
a fraternal socialist union capable of ending national oppression and of
supporting the "internal spiritual and material forces of every people,"
but it had also left a number of countervailing forces intact. In good
Marxist fashion, Skrypnyk asserted that cultural controversies mirrored
social contradictions, and forces striving for socialism were locked in
a struggle against other essentially bourgeois elements. The bourgeoisie
in Ukraine was internally divided by national antagonisms, the most
visible of which was that between the Russian or Russified urban
bourgeoisie and a new Ukrainian kulak bourgeoisie which had urban
as well as rural supporters. The national struggle between these two
bourgeoisies was simultaneously a joint struggle against the proletariat,
for Ukrainian and Russian nationalism, both by their nature opposed
to the internationalism of the Communist Party, were so similar that
they often seemed to mimic each other. Their influence had crept into
Soviet institutions on every level, and their hostile ideology had even
infiltrated the Party, brought there by alien elements disguising
themselves as communists and influencing even subjectively loyal
comrades.[39]

Skrypnyk then attempted to examine the Russian version of the theory.
The Russification of the cities under the autocracy had produced a national
antagonism that during the Revolution and Civil War had divided the
Russian or Russified urban proletariat from the Ukrainian peasantry.
That the workers were of the same nationality as the landlords, had made
the peasants naturally suspicious of appeals made to them by the urban
proletariat. This suspicion had severely retarded the development of the
revolution, and had provided the Petliurists with the basis of their rural
support. Many communists reacted to this suspicion by also falling into
the trap of becoming even more hostile to Ukrainian aspirations. Lebed
was the classic example. Fortunately, the Party had eventually recognized
the legitimacy of Ukrainian demands for national aspirations, and had
taken their side. Skrypnyk recalled that he had called for this in 1920,
and that the Party, with Lenin's approval, had adopted the same position at the Twelfth Party Congress.[40]

Skrypnyk then considered what the alternative would have been by
noting how socialists had erred in the past. Under capitalism the question of national hostility could only be one of oppressed and oppressor

---

[39] Mykola Skrypnyk, *Do teorii borotby dvokh kultur* (2nd ed., Kharkiv, 1928), pp.
9–13.
[40] *Ibid.*, pp. 13–15.

nations, but the higher level of the oppressor nation's cultural development had often tempted socialists to choose policies that isolated them
from oppressed peoples. He illustrated this point with the example of
the Czech-German conflict in pre-war Bohemia. While the migration
of Czechs into Bohemia's cities had gradually Czechized them and the
working class, the culture of virtually the entire urban bourgeoisie
remained German into the 1880s. This enabled Germans to claim that
theirs was a higher culture, while the Czech-German national struggle
came to reflect increasingly the struggle between workers and capitalists.
Because of the dynamics of economic development in Bohemia, the future
belonged to the Czechs, but German Social Democrats—subjectively
far more revolutionary than their Czech counterparts—pursued
disastrously a pseudo-internationalist policy that isolated them from the
Czechs, and this ultimately spelled their doom. Their main argument
had been similar to Lebed's: that internationalism required alignment
with the more highly developed German culture. According to Skrypnyk, this view might well have been subjectively internationalist, but
it was objectively a German chauvinist position. After all, the higher
level of German cultural and artistic attainment merely reflected the
greater wealth at the disposal of the German ruling classes, a wealth
made possible by class oppression.[41]

Skrypnyk believed that communists in Ukraine faced essentially the
same problem that had been the downfall of the German Social Democrats
in Bohemia. Communists, however, had found the correct solution in
promoting Ukrainization and fostering the development of Ukrainian
national culture, two sides of the same process, inseparable from each
other. To attempt to divide them would be like trying to "remove the
hammer from the sickle" on the Soviet banner. Following Stalin's
prescription, Skrypnyk declared that the main problem was one of tempo:
going either too slowly or too quickly would threaten to break the tie
(*smychka*) that bound workers and peasants together. Going too slowly
would threaten to destroy the proletariat's influence on the Ukrainian
peasantry, and too rapid a pace would violate the rights of Russian
workers and alienate them from the Soviet state. Not surprisingly, Skrypnyk found the tempo then being observed to be just about right.[42]

Only then did Skrypnyk consider the Ukrainian national deviation as
it had been expressed by Khvylovyi. He began with the rather questionable assertion that the class basis of Khvylovyism was the new

---

[41] *Ibid.*, pp. 13–15.
[42] *Ibid.*, pp. 20–22.

Ukrainian bourgeoisie of town and country. The mistake Khvylovyi and his followers had made was in demanding the rejection of everything Russian simply because it was Russian. Skrypnyk called this a Ukrainian version of the theory of the struggle of two cultures. Even Khvylovyi's insistence on artistic excellence had transformed itself into chauvinism by demanding that Ukrainian culture be the best on earth. Skrypnyk maintained that Khvylovyi's advocacy of the psychology of Europe was objectively nationalistic, in that it took meaning only in its rejection of things Russian, and anti-Marxist, in that it established Europe as a psychological category above classes. This concept, according to Skrypnyk, reflected the ideological imperatives of the new Ukrainian urban bourgeois intelligentsia. Khvylovyi had thus become the Ukrainian Lebed.[43]

Skrypnyk concluded by emphasizing the Party's rejection of the theory of the struggle of two cultures in all its manifestations. What the Party represented was not a struggle of two cultures, but a struggle on two fronts against both Russian and Ukrainian bourgeois nationalism. This struggle was the only way to cement the union of Russian workers and Ukrainian peasants, the sole course compatible with proletarian internationalism.[44]

Skrypnyk's argument was quite sophisticated and persuasive. It was also impeccably Marxist and Leninist. However, this type of dialectical reasoning can be used to prove practically anything, depending on how one defines the contradiction to be superseded. After all, a follower of Rosa Luxemburg could argue that the only way to avoid the Scylla and Charybdis of two mutually antagonistic nationalisms was by a purely internationalist policy of favoring neither and concentrating on fighting capitalism, which Marxism considers the root of all national oppression and hostility. Shumskyi's supporters in the KPZU turned against Kaganovich the very same arguments Skrypnyk used against them. By the same token, a defender of Khvylovyi could argue that the only way to avoid the twin evils of Ukrainian peasantism (*prosvitianstvo*) and Russian philistinism (*mishchanstvo*) was to embrace the highest cultural achievements in world history, those of European civilization. Since each could find a class basis for each of the undesirable alternatives—a simple matter since Marxism considers all nationalism fundamentally bourgeois—their arguments would be as impeccably Marxist as Skrypnyk's.

---

[43] *Ibid.*, pp. 23–29.
[44] *Ibid.*, p. 29.

Skrypnyk defended the Party line in the nationality question against virtually everyone who questioned it. The most interesting of his works of this type was directed against Khvylovyi, as well as against some of the writer's more vociferous critics. Titled "Results of the Literary Discussion," it was published almost immediately after the June 1926 plenum of the KP(b)U Central Committee, and was largely an explanation of its resolution "On the Results of Ukrainization." In this article, Skrypnyk referred to the resolution repeatedly, emphasizing the need to study it closely and in depth. Well he might: Skrypnyk himself had largely drafted it as the fundamental expression of the official KP(b)U line in the nationality policy.[45] What is common to the resolution and to Skrypnyk's elaboration, however, is the condemnation of unacceptable "bourgeois" nationalism and the rejection of the idea that Ukrainian culture needed any sort of tutelage. Ukrainian culture, Skrypnyk made clear, had to be recognized as a full participant in international cultural life. It sought to cooperate with other national cultures, but rejected subordination to any of them.

Skrypnyk began by proclaiming that the literary discussion had ended with the Party's firm rejection of "both modifications of the theory of the struggle of two cultures" as manifestations of bourgeois ideology that were anti-Marxist, anti-Leninist, and anti-proletarian. At the June plenum, the Party had reaffirmed its devotion to proletarian internationalism and its repudiation of all nationalism. Khvylovyi's rejection of everything Russian had been unmasked as bourgeois nationalism, but at the same time, the Party had upheld the separate development of Ukrainian culture:

> The Party has underscored this path for the development of Ukrainian culture. The Party has recognized this path as the sole proletarian path, the only one which leads to socialism, to the construction of a socialist culture: *this path is the path of the independent development of the Ukrainian people.*[46]

Skrypnyk then examined the relationship between Ukrainian and Russian literature. He first of all felt obliged to deny the old dilemma of quality vs. quantity in art, the point from which the discussion began. The dilemma of whether art is to be by or for the toilers, i.e., semiliterate scribbling or high-quality work of professional writers, simply

---

[45] For a discussion of this resolution, see chapter three above.

[46] Mykola Skrypnyk, *Statti i promovy z natsionalnoho pytannia*, pp. 57–63; quotation from p. 63. Emphasis in the original.

did not exist. The dilemma could not exist, he explained, because if it did, it would of necessity lead to *Proletkult* on the one hand and to bourgeois literature on the other. The only answer was that art must be of high quality *and* come from the masses. In so doing, Ukrainian art had to reject the temptation to look for some other national art to serve as a model. Ukrainian art and literature, he explained, had to step into the arena of world proletarian art as a full participant, not as the pupil of some other nation. After all, a Ukrainian proletarian writer was in the same position as his Russian counterpart in building the new proletarian culture. The notion that one should lead the other, that one nation should exercise hegemony over another, was alien to the very essence of socialism. In education, for example, Russia and Ukraine had different systems; they had both accomplished a great deal by cooperating, not by one leading and the other copying the other. The idea that one national culture should lead, and another, follow, implied that one was a full participant in world culture, and the other, a participant of the second order, dependent upon its "tutor" and able to take part only through its sponsorship. Of course, some nations did require such tutelage: Russians aided the cultural development of the Kirgiz, Tartars, Yakuts, and so forth, while Ukrainians did the same for the Moldavians. But Ukrainian culture did not need to orient itself toward Russian culture, to set it up as an infallible model and guide. What was required was that they cooperate as equals.[47]

Skrypnyk then addressed the problem of the relationship of the new Ukrainian proletarian literature, to the literature of the past. Certainly, the new literature could not be created except on the basis of what preceded it:

> Every literature in every country, of every people at every moment is the heir to all who ever worked in that realm. The proletariat does not simply "break away" from all preceding development—this primitive and simplistic view of the proletkultists has nothing in common with Leninism.

The new literature faced new tasks. It took the October Revolution as its point of departure, but could not simply reject the past *in toto*. The question of the relationship of the new literature to the old was thus one of the central questions writers had to face.[48]

Skrypnyk pointed out that the Central Committee theses on Ukrainiza-

---

[47] *Ibid.*, pp. 63–69.
[48] *Ibid.*, pp. 69–71; quotation from p. 70.

tion had declared that Ukrainian literature had to master all the attainments of world literature, and to make a final break with the provincialism and colonial legacy of the past. Ukrainian writers therefore had to take everything of value in world culture and their own national past, and then had reshape it to fit the requirements of the proletariat and of building socialism. Ukrainian literature had its own history, including periods when Ukrainian literature had been deeply influenced by its Russian counterpart. The main thing, however, was to master the attainments of world culture, without giving any special priority to Russian cultural achievements.[49]

Skrypnyk concluded by noting that there had been errors as well as achievements in the past. The Central Committee theses had rejected the theory of the struggle of two cultures, and writers had to do likewise. The new culture would be built on the achievements of the past, rejecting what was superfluous in it. The new Ukrainian culture would follow its own course of development, while cooperating as an equal with all other proletarian cultures. To do so, Ukrainian culture had to "separate the Party line from all bourgeois influences, from everything superfluous in the past, from the hoary, musty, closed past."[50]

Skrypnyk's excursions into Marxist theory provide the key to understanding his politics. While rejecting any hint of hostility toward Russia and things Russian, he emphasized that Ukraine did not feel the need to model itself on Russia. As he saw it, Ukraine and Russia were partners in building socialism; they were equal, distinct and independent entities. "The equality of Ukraine with all other Soviet republics and the equality of all peoples is the basis of the Union of Soviet Socialist Republics which we have organized."[51] For Skrypnyk, this was more than rhetoric; from 1920 he based his entire career on it.

Skrypnyk's Pursuit of Ukrainian National Interests

Once Kosior replaced Kaganovich as Party head, Skrypnyk was given a relatively free hand to pursue a policy that went considerably beyond what is usually associated with Soviet nationality policy, that is, a policy to neutralize separatist aspirations. Rather, he pursued policies more typical of conventional nation-states, policies designed to serve his state's interests as a national entity. We have seen how he lobbied to obtain for Soviet Ukraine a greater share of Union investments and

---

[49] *Ibid.*, pp. 72–77.
[50] *Ibid.*, pp. 78–81; quotation from p. 81.
[51] "Pro ukapizm," Mykola Skrypnyk, *Statti i promovy*, vol. 2, part 2, p. 65.

expenditures. Indeed, the whole Volobuiev affair might well have been a part of that lobbying, since Richytskyi's "orthodox" rebuttal contained the assurance that the imbalance between what Ukraine contributed to and received from the Union could be corrected in the immediate future.

Throughout his career, Skrypnyk missed few chances to argue that serving the interests of Ukraine served those of the world revolution. As early as 1924, Skrypnyk argued in the Union Central Executive Committee that the nationality question was vital to the Soviet Union's prospects for expanding into neighboring regions of Eastern Europe, and chided Foreign Minister Chicherin for not making better use of the issue.[52] At the beginning of 1927, he argued in the Presidium of the All-Union Council of Nationalities for using linguistic policy to expand Soviet influence along the Western border by bringing the cultures of peoples inside the USSR closer to those of their counterparts across the border. In this instance he maintained that favoring Finnish elements in the Karelian language and culture would help introduce Soviet values to the Finns through their Karelian neighbors, while creating a national division in Finland. Karelia, he maintained, could become a springboard for extending Soviet influence in Finland through radio broadcasts and the press. As an example of what could be achieved, he pointed to the policy of linguistic "Galicianization" in Soviet Ukraine and the subsequent rise of Sovietophilism in Western Ukraine.[53] Skrypnyk was trying to justify a policy designed to build a Ukrainian nation-state within the Soviet framework, a state to which Western Ukrainians would be drawn as if by a magnet. In 1929, he was able to announce that he had in fact succeeded in making Soviet Ukraine "the real cultural Piedmont of the Ukrainian people."[54] For the moment, it looked as though he had, although the achievement was destined to be short-lived.

Skrypnyk's primary goal was to draw Ukraine into the ranks of the nations of Europe. One sees this in the pride with which he presided over the transformation of Kharkiv from what he called "a backward provincial town" to "the new capital of a new socialist Soviet

---

[52] Skrypnyk's argument, made in the All-Union TsIK on November 31, 1924, concentrated on the fact that the existence of a Moldavian Autonomous Republic in Soviet Ukraine gave the "oppressed Moldavians of Bessarabia" a political entity and alternative in Soviet Ukraine. *Ibid.*, vol. 2, part 2, p. 31.

[53] "Natsionalne pytannia u Karelii," *ibid.*, vol. 2, part 2, pp. 60–63.

[54] Mykola Skrypnyk, *Statti i promovy z natsionalnoho pytannia*, p. 180.

Republic."[55] In 1930 Kharkiv hosted the Second World Congress of Proletarian Literatures, and Ukrainian cultural luminaries addressed the leading "militant" authors from the West. Skrypnyk himself gave the main speech on Soviet culture, ticking off the achievements of the "cultural revolution" in the Soviet Union.[56] The Congress was a major event in Kharkiv's bid for a place alongside Paris, Vienna, and Berlin.

Ukrainization, especially the replacement of Russian language newspapers by Ukrainian-language counterparts in the largest cities, was for Skrypnyk a tool for transforming those cities into Ukrainian urban centers. The high point of this policy was the Ukrainization of Odessa's *Izvestiia;* it became *Chornomorska komuna,* a Ukrainian-language daily, on August 31, 1929. At the time, Skrypnyk took special pride in the fact that a city which a little more than a decade earlier even the Central Rada admitted did "not belong to Ukraine," was being transformed into a Ukrainian city.[57] While the Ukrainization of the main Odessa daily was certainly a notable event, it nonetheless represented only the visible tip of the iceberg. The overall figures on the Ukrainization of the press in the first year after Kaganovich's removal gave Skrypnyk a free hand, are quite impressive:

Press in Ukraine	1928	1929	
General Political Newspapers	48	84	
Daily Circulation	2,635,246	4,220,363	
Ukrainian Language Newspapers	45	58	
Circulation of Main Ukrainian Language Dailies:			
Komunist	28,000	122,000	(Jan. 1930)
Visti VUTsVK	46,000	90,000	
Proletar	11,000	79,000	
Radianske selo	172,000	600,000	
Factory Newspapers	110	224	(Jan. 1930)
Percent of Factory Newspapers Published in Ukrainian	43.6%	63.4%	(Jan. 1930)[58]

---

[55] Mykola Skrypnyk, "Za sotsiialistychne misto," *Visti VUTsVK,* November 25, 1931, p. 2.

[56] Mykola Skrypnyk, "Kulturna revoliutsiia v SRSR," *Visti VUTsVK,* November 13, 1930, p. 7.

[57] Mykola Skrypnyk, *Statti i promovy z natsionalnoho pytannia,* pp. 142–145.

[58] Mykola Skrypnyk, *Statti i promovy,* vol. 2, part 2, p. 357.

The figures on factory newspapers are particularly significant, since Ukrainians had traditionally been most poorly represented in large cities and factories. The Ukrainization of factory newpapers both reflected the large influx of Ukrainians into the industrial work force and served as a powerful lever to prevent their denationalization. The conventional wisdom among Ukrainian communists was that, as industrialization brought more Ukrainians into the industrial work place, the cities would be Ukrainized. As Zatonskyi succinctly put it, "as industry develops, so will Ukrainization."[59] And until the end of Ukrainization in 1933, this seemed to be holding true: from 1926 to 1932, Ukrainians in the industrial work force increased from 41% to 53% of the total.[60] Preventing the assimilation of these new workers was basic to the whole strategy of Ukrainization, and Skrypnyk made strong efforts to Ukrainize even the country's strongest bastion of Russian culture, the industrial Donbas, by providing Ukrainian books, theaters, newpapers, and libraries in an effort to encourage the workers there to give up their "neither Ukrainian nor Russian" *patois* for the Ukrainian language.[61] He believed he was succeeding. At the end of 1929, he could proudly declare:

> Ukrainian culture, the new Soviet proletarian culture, is not just the culture of a few individual members of the intelligentsia—teachers, workers in cooperatives, and so forth. Ukrainian culture is *the culture of new hundreds, thousands, millions of new Ukrainian workers in our country's new factories and plants.*[62]

Skrypnyk believed that not only would industrialization foster Ukrainization but also that collectivization would do likewise.[63] Indeed, up to the abandonment of Ukrainization in 1933, he seemed to be right: by early 1933, fully 88% of all factory newspapers in Ukraine were published in Ukrainian; in traditionally Russian Kharkiv, over half of "proletarian youth" were enrolled in Ukrainian language schools as early as 1928.[64] Ukrainization was undeniably succeeding and it was ultimately abolished, as one Canadian scholar has put it, "perhaps because, finally, the party realized that it could succeed."[65]

[59] V. Zatonskyi, *Natsionalna problema na Ukraini,* p. 84.
[60] Bohdan Krawchenko, "The Impact of Industrialization on the Social Structure of Ukraine," *Canadian Slavonic Papers,* 1980, no. 3, p. 354.
[61] Mykola Skrypnyk, *Statti i promovy z natsionalnoho pytannia,* pp. 151–152.
[62] Mykola Skrypnyk, *Statti i promovy,* vol. 2, part 2, p. 270. Skrypnyk's emphasis.
[63] *Ibid.,* vol. 2, part 2, p. 345.
[64] Bohdan Krawchenko, "The Impact of Industrialization...," p. 354.
[65] *Ibid.,* p. 357.

In addition to his vigorous pursuit of Ukrainization in Soviet Ukraine, Skrypnyk also established himself as defender of the rights of Ukrainian communities in Russia. While denying the charge that he sought to assume responsibility for all Ukrainians throughout the Soviet Union, he emphasized that Soviet Ukraine was helping, and would continue to help, Russia's Ukrainians, whether in the Kuban or Kazakhstan:

> Wherever teachers are needed, then we must send teachers there. Of course, much is given for the cultural assistance of the entire Ukrainian population of the USSR as a whole by Soviet Ukraine, where the forces of the proletariat's state is building and developing a Ukrainian culture national in form and socialist in content.[66]

The issue was not solely whether the national cultural needs of Ukrainians outside the Ukraine would be met. After all, there were areas outside Ukraine, such as the North Caucasus, where Ukrainization was carried out. The issue probably most disturbing to Moscow was whether such policies would be guided from Moscow or Kharkiv, for Stalin was not a man to relish the prospect of a rival ruler attempting to create a protectorate over his subjects.

Skrypnyk even made territorial demands on the Russian republic, arguing for the inclusion in Soviet Ukraine of adjacent areas containing Ukrainian majorities. Skrypnyk was on solid ground in reminding Moscow that the Comintern Executive Committee and the VKP(b) Central Committee had both called for their inclusion in 1924, but had neglected to do it. Stalin must have been quite perturbed at Skrypnyk's complaints about the Russian republic's failure to raise literacy among its Ukrainian citizens, to provide them with books and textbooks, and that it had dragged its feet so much that it was giving political ammunition to the anti-Soviet Ukrainian National Democratic Union in Poland.[67] Perhaps it is less than surprising that Skrypnyk failed to achieve this particular goal.

For a policy such as Skrypnyk's, two sticking-points have to be considered: whether Ukrainization violated the rights of non-Ukrainians living in Ukraine, and whether it was at all consistent with the Marxian doctrine that under socialism national distinctions would ultimately fade away.

Certainly, there were complaints—usually from Russians—that Ukrainization violated their rights and constituted a form of national

---

[66] Mykola Skrypnyk, *Statti i promovy,* vol. 2, part 2, p. 247.

[67] Mykola Skrypnyk, *Statti i promovy z natsionalnoho pytannia,* pp. 101–117.

oppression. Actually, the rights enjoyed by national minorities in Soviet Ukraine were rather broad. In fact, if we place them within the context of their historical period and compare the treatment of, say, Ukrainians in Poland with Poles in Ukraine, the latter situation would seem almost utopian by comparison. Non-Ukrainians in Soviet Ukraine were guaranteed the right to separate cultural development, the right to primary education in their native tongue, the right to appear in court and to deal with all administrative offices using their native tongue, and the right to their own political institutions in regions where they formed a majority of the total population. In accordance with this last guarantee there were, as of June 1928, 388 Russian village Soviets in Soviet Ukraine, 251 German Soviets, 143 Polish, 77 Jewish, 57 Moldavian (not counting those in the Autonomous Moldavian Socialist Soviet Republic), 43 Bulgarian, 30 Greek, 13 Czech, 3 Belorussian, and 1 Swedish.[68] While Skrypnyk had at one point mentioned Ukrainian aid to the development of Moldavian culture, he also specifically repudiated the idea of Ukrainian tutelage of Jewish culture in Ukraine, maintaining that the two cultures should coexist in full cooperation and equality.[69]

A certain amount of friction between Russians and Ukrainians was inevitable to the extent that Ukrainization was seen as a process of de-Russification, yet Soviet spokesmen maintained that there was absolutely no contradiction between Ukrainization and the right of national minorities to carry on their own national revivals. The reason this was so, asserted N. Cherliunchakevych, was that the Russifying policies of tsarism had placed the minorities on an even lower cultural level than the Ukrainians, and that their cultural advancement actually helped advance the development of Ukrainian culture.[70] Nor were Ukraine's Russians neglected. Skrypnyk was able to demonstrate convincingly that the cultural needs of Russians living in Ukraine were far better served than those of Ukrainians living the RSFSR. At the same time that Soviet Ukraine provided 1771 Russian language schools for its Russian minority of two million, the RSFSR provided only 240 Ukrainian language schools in the North Caucasus, where three million Ukrainians lived.[71]

---

[68] For a discussion of national minorities in connection with the adoption of the Ukrainian Constitution of 1929, see *Visti VUTsVK*, May 16, 1929, p. 5. The rights of minorities are fully discussed there. The figures on non-Ukrainian Soviets are from A. Butsenko, "Den Konstitutsii i natsmenshosty," *Visty VUTsVK*, July 1, 1928, p. 1.

[69] Mykola Skrypnyk, *Statti i promovy z natsionalnoho pytannia*, pp. 118–122.

[70] N. Cherliunchakevych, "Natsionalni menshosty na Ukrainy," *Bilshovyk Ukrainy*, 1926, no. 4–5, p. 107.

[71] Koszeliwec, *Mykola Skrypnyk*, p. 161.

The problem with Skrypnyk's policy, from the standpoint of Marxist theory, was in its seeming contradiction with the Leninist postulate of the convergence and merging (*sblizhenie i sliianie*) of nations. A number of writers, most in Soviet Russia but also some in Soviet Ukraine, either looked to convergence and merging as something to be welcomed in the near future, or identified local nationalism with the "rightist danger" and Russian nationalism with the left at a time when the rights were officially considered the main danger.[72] Skrypnyk was on relatively weak ground here, which probably explains why he postponed considering the question in a systematic fashion until 1931. His position was strengthened in 1930, when Stalin at the Sixteenth All-Union Party Congress rebuked those who looked for an early end to national differences and who advocated a retreat from the Party's sponsorship of national cultural development. Stalin denounced such views as national deviations, and announced that national differences would remain important until the final victory of socialism on a world scale. Only then, he asserted, would the convergence and merging of nations take place.[73]

In February 1931 Skrypnyk addressed the All-Ukrainian Academy of Sciences commission on the national question on the convergence and merging of nations under socialism. Widely circulated and considered authoritative, it was Skrypnyk's last major pronouncement on the theory of the nationality question.

Skrypnyk began his lecture, "The Convergence and Merging of Nations in the Period of Socialism," by recalling the discussion that took place in 1927, when V. Vaganian, a relatively minor figure associated with the Communist Academy, published a book, *On National Culture.* Vaganian had argued that the Russian language as the language of the October Revolution was an "international" language and that it was therefore wrong to isolate linguistically the "Russo-Ukrainian" workers and peasants by imposing upon them "the language of the Galician Ukrainian intelligentsia." Instead of such "linguistic separatism," Vaganian frankly advocated the hegemony of Russian culture over its Ukrainian counterpart and a policy of bringing the Ukrainian culture and language closer to the Russian. This, Skrypnyk pointed out, was reminiscent of positions held by Kautsky, Bauer, and Luxemburg. It was exactly the sort of thing Stalin had denounced at the Sixteenth Party

---

[72] V. Vaganian of the Communist Academy in Moscow may be considered representative of the former viewpoint; L. Perchyk of UIML may be considered representative of the latter.

[73] I. Stalin, *Stati i rechi ob Ukraine: Sbornik* (Kiev, 1936), pp. 211–218.

Congress.[74] (And it was exactly what Stalin would do after 1933.)

Skrypnyk argued that precisely the opposite imperatives were in fact operative in the "reconstruction period," when the "electric tempo of our work demands, without question, the further strengthening of our national work." The task of building a national culture became all the more urgent because the cadres who would carry out the policies of industrialization and agricultural collectivization had to be national cadres, and because the future workers and collective farmers had to be taught to read and write—a task which could only be accomplished in their native tongue. It was also necessary to overcome the heritage of colonial oppression, both culturally and politically, through the consolidation of the statehood of the peoples liberated by the October Revolution. Any talk about national distinctions diminishing before the final achievement of national equality—and such equality in the cultural and material spheres was not yet achieved—was pointless. Great strides had been made: in Tadzhikistan, for example, there had been only one percent literacy at the time of the revolution; it had risen to 30% But that improvement was still considerably short of what had to be done.[75]

Skrypnyk repudiated the positions of those who refused to recognize the importance of national liberation, as well as of those who rejected the ultimate disappearance of national identities as utopian. He based himself on the position Stalin had taken at the Sixteenth Congress: national differentiation would come to an end, but only in some future stage of the development of socialism. For the present, he declared, the task was to effect the complete elimination of every remnant of national inequality left over from the prerevolutionary era. So long as nations had not attained complete cultural and economic equality, the convergence and merging of nations would mean their subordination to the more highly developed Russian culture, in other words, forced assimilation.[76]

Following Stalin, Skrypnyk stated that the immediate prospect was one of a flowering of different national cultures. As it was, even the shape of the new "international" language was beyond anyone's ken, and those who, like Karl Kautsky, assumed it would be a European language, were merely falling prey to the ideology of the imperialism of the white race. The same was true of the advocates of Esperanto, which after all, was an artificial tongue based on European languages.

---

[74] Mykola Skrypnyk, *Statti i promovy z natsionalnoho pytannia*, pp. 229-232.

[75] *Ibid.*, pp. 232-236; quotation from p. 233.

[76] *Ibid.*, pp. 237-243.

About the only trend toward national convergence then discernible was the growth of multilingualism as seen, for example, in the growing number of Russians in the RSFSR who had studied Ukrainian in order to read Ukrainian literature and scholarly works.[77]

The convergence and merging of nations, inevitable though it might be, was something to be faced only after the victory of socialism and the attainment of *de facto* equality throughout the world, for only then could the billions of participants in the process take part in it on a footing of complete equality. For the present, the basis for the ultimate disappearance of national differences was being built in the form of a unified economic system; while it was still being built, the growth of linguistic differentiation was to be considered a natural outgrowth of the flowering of national cultures, each of which would strive for equality on a higher plane than any one culture had yet attained. The process was thus dialectical: each national culture would flourish until all achieved equality under communism, then divisions of nationality would begin to melt away. Further effort in building a Ukrainian culture, national in form and socialist in content, thereby became an integral part of the process of creating a new, unified, and classless humankind.[78]

While Skrypnyk's lecture had the character of an elaboration of Stalin's statements on the nationality question, it is still pure Skrypnyk. Besides, Stalin's remarks at the Sixteenth Congress were probably largely shaped so as to correspond to what Skrypnyk and his counterparts in the other national republics wanted to hear. Some of Skrypnyk's arguments seem compelling. Unfortunately, he was to find that the "basis for the future convergence and merging of nations," the growing administrative and economic unity of the USSR, would be combined with an attack on his own constituencies. Skrypnyk would find that he, and what he stood for, had become expendable.

Skrypnyk's Commissariat of Education

Under Skrypnyk, Soviet Ukraine's Commissariat of Education (Narkomos) became the central political institution in the nation's cultural life. Even under his predecessors, Narkomos was the first state institution to be Ukrainized and was in charge of overseeing Ukrainization in all areas.[79] It was also broadly responsible for cultural affairs. Since

---

[77] *Ibid.*, pp. 243–251.

[78] *Ibid.*, pp. 251–254.

[79] A Ukrainian government decree of September 21, 1920 directed Narkomos to work

most scholarship takes place in institutions of higher education, its responsibility and power over scholars is obvious. It also dominated literature through its Council of Political Education, which could subsidize publications, encourage or discourage a given writer's plans, or hold competition for the best literary and musical productions in praise of the revolution.[80] In the May 1927 KP(b)U Central Committee resolution on Party policy in literature, Narkomos was entrusted with its implementation.[81] When Shumskyi's work as head of Narkomos was officially condemned, his single alleged failing was the countenancing of national deviations in literature and art.[82] When Skrypnyk was attacked by Postyshev in 1933, the same basic accusation was the same, albeit in the surreal style characteristic of the new era: Skrypnyk was accused of having shielded and abetted Ukrainian nationalists and foreign spies in the cultural and educational institutions for which he was responsible.[83]

Yet Skrypnyk's supercommissariat came from extremely humble beginnings. In the early years, when Narkomos was headed by Volodymyr Zatonskyi, the commissariat basically followed the lead of whatever was done by its counterpart in Great Russia. In January 1919, Zatonskyi said in the collegium of Narkomos that his ministry had two tasks: "apply the entire educational experience of Soviet Russia to Ukraine and work out those problems which have not arisen in Russia."[84]

Narkomos, like all other institutions, devoted itself mainly to political tasks during the civil war. One major problem was the open hostility

---

out a plan for introducing Ukrainian as a language for instruction in all educational institutions as well as organize night schools in each province and *povit* town to teach the Ukrainian language to state employees. "Pro vvedennia Ukrainskoi movy v shkolakh i radianskykh ustanovakh," *Kulturne budivnytstvo v Ukrainskii RSR*, vol. 1, pp. 71–72. Very little was done regarding the establishment of language instruction for state employees. A newspaper report from mid-1924 notes that such courses had been established in Kharkiv but nowhere else. An account published three years later declares that most state employees did not take seriously the task of learning Ukrainian until 1926. P. Kobyliatskyi, "Do ukrainizatsii," *Visty VUTsVK*, July 24, 1924, p. 1; "U Kharkovi. Stan ukrainizatsii ustanov mista i okruhy," *Visty VUTsVK*, June 10, 1927, p. 5.

[80] George Luckyj, *Literary Politics in the Soviet Ukraine*, p. 81.

[81] *Kulturne budivnytstvo v Ukrainskii RSR*, vol. 1, p. 355.

[82] *Ibid.*, vol. 1, pp. 342–343.

[83] Luckyj, *Literary Politics*, p. 192.

[84] As quoted by V. Iu. Nikolaienko, "Zhovtneva revoliutsiia i dokorinna perebudova narodnoi osvity na Ukraini," *Naukovi pratsi z istorii KPRS*, no. 5, 1965, p. 18. For a frank acknowledgement that Narkomos in this period basically followed the practices of Russian Narkompros, see S. K. Hutianskyi, *V. I. Lenin i kulturne budivnytstvo na Ukraini* (Kiev, 1965), p. 47.

of Ukrainian schoolteachers, even in Kharkiv province where the Ukrainian movement was far weaker than elsewhere.[85] During the Polish-Soviet War, Narkomos was charged with organizing anti-Petliurist "political education" for adults, and Education Commissar Hrynko ordered provincial Narkomos sections to direct all their energies to propaganda against the Poles, Petliura, and Ukrainian nationalism. Even at this juncture, education was seen as a tool to bring up a new type of person who would be "a member of communist society, a communist person for whom the communist way of life would be easy and necessary."[86] At the same time, Narkomos was instructed to "Sovietize" the educational system, hitherto considered a hotbed of nationalism.[87] While the system was being "Sovietized," the student body was "proletarianized" by an ongoing purge in higher education. Fully 20% of the students in higher education were expelled in 1921 alone, and by 1924, the purge of "alien class elements" had become continuous and routine.[88]

The fact that Narkomos was entrusted to the former Borotbist Hrynko and later, to Oleksander Shumskyi, demonstrates that it was not considered to be one of the more important posts. For a time it seems even to have been subordinate to the Komsomol.[89] In the administrative chaos of the early Soviet period, lines of authority were often vague and sometimes shifted radically. Hrynko's tenure in Narkomos is a particularly good example of this chaos because he not only asserted the independence of his ministry, but also successfully challenged the educational practices of Russian Narkompros and established an educational system radically different from that which prevailed in Russia. The so-called Hrynko system was in no way related to national differences between Ukraine and Russia.[90] It attempted to integrate "social upbringing" with professional education and led to much earlier specializa-

[85] M. I. Kulichenko, *Bolsheviki Kharkovshchiny v borbe za vlast Sovetov (1918–1920 gg.)* (Kharkiv, 1966), pp. 229–230.

[86] I. Krylov, *Systema osvity v Ukraini (1917–1930)* (Munich, 1956), pp. 37–39. The quotation cited (p. 39) was taken from the 1920 All-Ukrainian Conference on Public Education.

[87] *Kulturne budivnytstvo v Ukrainskii RSR,* vol. 1, p. 152.

[88] Narodnyi komissariat prosveshcheniia USSR, *Narodnoe prosveshchenie na Ukraine* (Kharkiv, 1924), pp. 77–78.

[89] A directive of May 25, 1920 signed by Hrynko as "Commissar of Education of the Central Committee of the Komsomol" and one from the following month attempting to sort out which organization was responsible for what are quoted by Krylov, *Systema osvity,* pp. 39–41.

[90] Skrypnyk said as much in 1930. See the quotation in Krylov, *Systema osvity,* p. 80.

tion than did Lunacharskii's educational system in Russia. Worked out in 1920 and lasting a decade, the Hrynko system was a radically different system and philosophy of education that had as much claim to universality as the Russian system that replaced it.[91]

Until the mid-twenties, the grand ambitions of the Ukrainian education system went unfulfilled because of the country's poverty, which was in turn the legacy of the devastation of the civil war. Despite the goal of providing universal primary and secondary education, insufficient resources forced a cutback in education such that as late as 1924, no schools of any kind were available to over half Ukraine's children.[92] The number of teachers dropped from 85,000 in 1921, to 40,000 in 1924, while the number of students simultaneously dropped from 1.9 to 1.4 million.[93] A 1924 newspaper account frankly admitted that even those teachers who kept their jobs were poorly qualified, with very few ever having attended a teaching course and most never having gone beyond the Gymnasium. Two-month courses designed to provide some exposure to teaching methods, science, Ukrainian studies, and anti-religious education were offered too sporadically to have much effect.[94] A report of a provincial teachers conference in January 1924 described the situation well. The conference passed a resolution saying that educational work would be greatly stimulated "if there were but a minimum of moral support," and that there were schoolbooks in the stores, but 80% of the students could not afford them, since it cost fifty poods (about 1800 pounds) of grain to buy schoolbooks for one student.[95]

Conditions began to improve rapidly thereafter, and the number of students and teachers grew from year to year. Perhaps the most remarkable achievements were made in the campaign to wipe out adult illiteracy, a goal to which the regime committed itself as early as 1921.[96]

---

[91] On the disagreements between Hrynko and Lunacharskii, see Sheila Fitzpatrick, *The People's Commissariat of Enlightenment: Soviet Organization of Education and the Arts under Lunacharskii, October 1917-1921* (Cambridge, 1970), pp. 67, 191, 199. The main difference between the systems are described in Krylov, *Systema osvity,* pp. 77–78, and Ia. Riappo, "V chim osnovni roskhodzhennia mizh systemamy narodnoi osvity USRR i RSFRR," *Nauka i Osvita* (supplement to *Visti VUTsVK*), March 17, 1929, p. 2, and March 24, 1929, p. 1.

[92] Ia. Riappo, "Shkilnytstvo na seli," *Visty VUTsVK,* February 6, 1924, p. 2.

[93] "Vseukrainskyi uchytelskyi zizd," *Visty VUTsVK,* January 10, 1925, p. 3.

[94] D. Ortenberh, "Pro pidvyshchennia kvalifikatsii narodnikh uchyteliv (Na uvahu Hubnarosvity)," *Visty VUTsVK,* May 7, 1924, p. 1.

[95] Ia. Svashchenko, "Kultura zamerzaie," *Visty VUTsVK,* February 9, 1924, p. 1.

[96] *Kulturne budivnytstvo v Ukrainskii RSR,* vol. 1, pp. 120–121.

It was only in 1923, however, that Narkomos began a systematic campaign to eradicate illiteracy in the 18-to-35 age bracket by 1927.[97] In 1924, Butsenko, a secretary of the Ukrainian Central Executive Committee, announced that the full force of the state was behind the campaign.[98] The trade unions and the *komnezamy* were pressed into service.[99] *Visty* announced in a lead editorial that any intellectual needing a job could have one teaching people to read.[100] The result of such efforts was the literacy among adults rose from its pre-revolutionary level of 42% to 70% in the cities, and from 15.5% to 50% in the villages by 1927. Despite the failure to achieve universal literacy by the tenth anniversary of the revolution—the goal was pushed back several times—the results were impressive. Equally noteworthy were the results of the campaign to provide universal primary education, at least for children aged eight through eleven. While Ukraine's primary schools served a million children before the revolution, 2.2 million were enrolled in 1927 and 2.5 million in 1929.[101] This enrollment fell short of the goal: in 1927 75-80% of urban and 55% of rural eight-through-eleven-year-olds were in school, and only 10.1% in the twelve-through-fifteen age group were in school.[102] Still, for a poor country without outside aid, this was impressive progress.

Especially under Skrypnyk, Narkomos vigorously carried out the Ukrainization policy. In 1927, for example, all students in higher education were required to learn Ukrainian by the end of the 1928–1929 academic year, and it was forbidden to appoint professors who could not lecture in Ukrainian or to admit students who did not know Ukrainian to institutions of higher education in Soviet Ukraine. At the high point of Ukrainization in 1929, 80% of general education schools, 55%

---

[97] "Perspektyvy likvidatsii nepysmennosty na Ukraini," *Visty VUTsVK*, September 16, 1926, p. 2.

[98] A. Butsenko, "Radianske suspilstvo do roboty," *Visty VUTsVK*, February 14, 1924, p. 1.

[99] See M. I. Horlach, "Uchast profspilok Ukrainy v borotbi za rozvytok narodnoi osvity v period dovoiennykh piatyrichok," *Naukovi pratsi z istorii KPRS*, no. 5, 1965, pp. 113–124; Horlach, "Rol profspilok Ukrainy v zdiisnenni kulturnykh peretvoren u period pobudovy sotsializmu (1925–1937 rr.)," *Naukovi pratsi z istorii KPRS*, no. 10, 1966, pp. 57–72; M. D. Berezovchuk, "Borotba komnezamiv za rozvytok narodnoi osvity na seli v 1921–1925 rr," *Naukovi pratsi z istorii KPRS*, no. 5, 1965, pp. 61–71.

[100] "Vykhid dlia bezrobitnoi intelihentsii," *Visty VUTsVK*, April 19, 1924, p. 1.

[101] *Kulturne budivnytstvo v Ukrainskii RSR*, vol. 1, p. 440.

[102] "X-i zizd Komunistychnoi Partii (bilshovykiv) Ukrainy. Doklad tov. Skrypnyka pro kulturne budivnytstvo Ukrainy," *Visty VUTsVK*, December 3, 1927, pp. 3–4.

of vocational schools, 54% of technicums, and 30% of institutes offered instruction only in Ukrainian, with the rest either offering some courses in Ukrainian or holding all instruction in other languages.[103]

By 1929, the first indications of a major policy reversal began to appear, not least among them the criticism and gradual limitation of the authority of Skrypnyk's commissariat. What made criticism of Narkomos so ominous is that it was the administrative centerpiece of all that made Soviet Ukraine a distinct national polity, and the power base of the figure most committed to it.

As early as the adoption of the Five Year Plan in 1928, certain economists noted that Soviet Ukraine did not have enough educated people to carry out the tasks envisioned, and rather than admitting that the goals were unrealistic, they blamed the educational system, charging that the campaign to eradicate illiteracy had run out of steam.[104] It is true that between 1927 and 1929 the impressive strides of the mid-twenties were not equalled. In these years urban adult literacy rose from 70% to 74%, rural literacy from 50% to 53%[105] However, it may well have been that the strategy of offering access to education had reached a point of diminishing returns, and that only compulsory adult education could increase the percentage figures more rapidly. This possibility was suggested when the Soviet Ukrainian government issued regulations ordering adult illiterates to register with their local Soviet in order that they could be taught to read.[106] It should be noted also that Soviet Ukraine's literacy (71% in 1929) was considerably ahead of the USSR as a whole (50.1% in 1929).[107] At the same time, the goal of universal primary education for children aged eight through eleven remained a top priority.[108] Despite this evidence, Narkomos work in "cultural construction" and in extending general education received official criticism

[103] John Kolasky, *Education in Soviet Ukraine: A Study in Discrimination and Russification* (Toronto, 1968), pp. 14–17.

[104] *Puti narodno-khoziaistvennogo razvitiia USSR. Materialy k postroeniiu piatiletnego plana* (Kharkiv, 1928), pp. 441–443.

[105] *Kulturne budivnytstvo v Ukrainiskii RSR,* vol. 1, p. 440.

[106] Illiterates between the ages of 14 and 35 were ordered by a Soviet Ukrainian regulation of July 3, 1929 to register with their local Soviets by January 1, 1930; a similar regulation affecting the 35 to 50 age bracket was adopted on September 11, 1931. *Kulturne budivnytstvo v Ukrainskii RSR,* vol. 1, 461–467, 568.

[107] "Stan i perspektyvy kulturnoho budivnytstva na Ukraini. Doklad Narkomosvity USRR tov. Skrypnyka M. O.," *Visti VUTsVK,* May 15, 1929, p. 6.

[108] *Kulturne budivnytstvo v Ukrainskii RSR,* vol. 1, pp. 488, 512, 568, 590–593.

on several occasions by the KP(b)U Central Committee and the Union authorities in 1930–1932.

By 1930, the education system was more or less standardized throughout the Soviet Union, a move Skrypnyk had favored since 1927 on the grounds that the Russian (Lunacharskii) system was better suited to Ukrainian needs than the one Hrynko had established.[109] At the same time, however, he opposed all talk of placing the administration of education in Union hands.[110] Nevertheless, the early 1930s were marked by a process of creeping administrative centralization in education that Skrypnyk was unable to halt. A September 5, 1931 VKP(b) Central Committee decree described in detail how the education system ought to be run, and a USSR government decree of September 19, 1932, placed higher education under direct Union supervision.[111] Although the complete centralization of Soviet education was proclaimed only in May 1934, ten months after Skrypnyk's death, the process was well-advanced during his lifetime. With education being centralized, it was only a matter of time before other realms would follow.

What was the new system supposed to do? As early as 1928, the KP(b)U ordered that students in higher education be educated in a "militantly materialist" spirit, with Party members taking a large role in the institutions where they worked and studied.[112] With collectivization and industrialization, emphasis was placed on "raising the consciousness" of the new workers and "liberating" them from their "*petit bourgeois* peasant" psyches.[113] As Skrypnyk put it, education must be a tool to "reconquer" from the kulak class its younger generation.[114] On another occasion, Andrii Khvylia warned that the kulaks were trying to maintain their influence in the schools and had to be combated.[115] Such warnings of class enemies in the educational system would be given further credence by the 1930 show trial of the so-called Union for the

---

[109] "X-i zizd Komunistychnoi Partii (bilshovykiv) Ukrainy. Doklad tov. Skrypnyka," *Visty VUTsVK*, December 3, 1927, pp. 3–4.

[110] "Za iedynu systemu narodnoi osvity: Narkomos—shtab tsilnoho kultosvitnoho protsesu (Vseukrainska narada okrinspektora Narosvity)," *Visti VUTsVK*, May 10, 1930, p. 3.

[111] *Kulturne budivnytstvo v Ukrainskii RSR*, vol. 1, pp. 559–567, 593, 604.

[112] *Ibid.*, p. 411.

[113] M. Skrypnyk, "Na perelomi," *Visti VUTsVK*, January 11, 1930, pp. 2–3.

[114] M. Skrypnyk, "Rekonstruktsiia krainy i perebudova shkoly," *Visti VUTsVK*, February 28, 1932, p. 2.

[115] "Vseukrainska partiina narada v spravi narosvity," *Visti VUTsVK*, April 22, 1930, p. 6.

Liberation of Ukraine, when a group of prominent scholars was accused of running an underground terrorist organization, carrying on "wrecking" in various spheres of culture and plotting to establish an independent fascist state. Many teachers as well as scholars would be removed— or worse.

Bringing Narkomos to heel in the educational sphere was the first encroachment upon Skrypnyk's bureaucratic power base. Since abolition of the Hrynko system was a question of structure rather than national culture, this first step could be accomplished with Skrypnyk's consent. From this, however, it was a much smaller step toward all-Union organs interfering in, and ultimately taking over, various parts of the educational administration. Because Narkomos was the main outpost of the Soviet Ukrainian state in cultural affairs, Union involvement in it opened the door to Russian interference in the cultural sphere. The defeat of Narkomos should therefore be seen as one of the steps toward what later became a general offensive against Ukrainian cultural distinctiveness and cultural elites, everything that in the 1920s made Soviet Ukraine different from Russia. This step was, in short, the beginning of the end of the Ukrainian road to socialism.

Skrypnyk and the Problem of "Linguistic Separatism"

One of the most intriguing accusations leveled against Skrypnyk after his fall from power, was that he had fostered the separation of the Ukrainian language from Russian. This was equated with high treason to the Soviet state. If only for this reason, it is worthwhile to consider what was accomplished in the field of linguistic standardization as well as what Skrypnyk actually contributed to it.

The revolution of 1917 came long after Ivan Kotliarevskyi, whose travesty on the *Aeneid* was published in 1798, and Taras Shevchenko, whose *Kobzar* was published in 1840, laid the basis for modern Ukrainian literature, but the Ukrainian language still did not possess any set of universally recognized standards. This lack was felt bitterly at a time when the nation was embarking on a period of unprecedented literary and cultural creativity. As late as 1925, the Ukrainian linguist Vsevolod Hantsov could lament the fact that each Ukrainian writer tended to rely on his own native dialect and that variant spellings existed for even the most common words.[116] This was a time, when Ukrainian writers

---

[116] Vsevolod Hantsov, "Problemy rozvytku literaturnoi movy," *Zhyttia i revoliutsiia*, 1925, no. 10, pp. 61–62.

aspired to create a literary culture of European caliber. How could they, if they could not even agree on how to spell?

Linguistic standardization requires the making of fundamental value judgments regarding purism, foreign models, and the possible inclusion of archaisms and colloquialisms. When Ukrainian writers needed words which did not exist in Ukrainian, they were often tempted to borrow from Russian or Polish. Such words often became part of the common Ukrainian speech. Should they be accepted, or be purged from the language and some indigenous equivalent be coined? What about "international" words common to several European languages and taken from Greek or Latin roots? How should such words be adapted to the Ukrainian language? What dialect should be taken as the basis of the literary language? Should other dialects also contribute? Behind virtually every entry in the dictionary were assumptions based on the answers to such questions. It was unavoidable; and it affected the very shape of the language.

The Party did not try to impose any linguistic orthodoxy on scholars during the 1920s, although it did sponsor the years of effort leading to the adoption of a standard orthography in 1928. This system, the so-called *Skrypnykivka,* was adopted by Ukrainians outside Soviet Ukraine almost immediately. It was suppressed in Soviet Ukraine in 1933 as a manifestation of "linguistic separatism," but it remained in use in Western Ukraine until its inclusion in the Soviet Union, and is still used by Ukrainians outside the Soviet bloc.

Ukrainian linguists in the 1920s did share certain assumptions, although they also disagreed on a large number of issues. Both in Soviet Ukraine and Western Ukraine, linguists generally agreed that the Kiev-Poltava dialect should serve as the basis for a common literary language, with other Ukrainian dialects contributing to some degree. Soviet Ukrainian authorities tended to agree that the literary language should be brought as closely as possible to the spoken language and often condemned Galician writers, rightly or wrongly, for their highflown verbiage divorced from the common speech. A number of linguists argued that some Galician terminology be accepted into the literary language, but only after critical scrutiny. Nearly all condemned foreign influence on the language, although many believed that purging Ukrainian of all borrowings from Russian and Polish would lead to the impoverishment of the language. Where foreign terms were adopted, the linguists clearly preferred classical and German models over borrowings from Russian and Polish, hardly surprising, since these languages had long been seen as threatening the existence of Ukrainian. Paul Wexler has divided the linguists of the 1920s into two groups: those who favored a purely ethnographic approach of relying on native sources, even if it meant turning to archaic and purely colloquial terms; and those who favored a modified ethnographic approach more open to foreign models. According to Wexler, Western Ukrainians were usually more devoted to ethnographic purism than were their Soviet counterparts.[117]

The most important contribution to the development of the Ukrainian language made in the 1920s was the standardized orthography adopted in 1928. In 1921, the Ukrainian Academy of Sciences published a spelling system which was basically a reiteration of one approved in 1918 under the Hetmanate. The Ukrainian Commissariat of Education officially recognized the Academy's system as authoritative, while directing VUAN to carry on further work in this area and to submit its findings to the Commissariat for confirmation.[118]

The problem of linguistic standardization fell within the province of the Academy's Institute of Ukrainian Scientific Language, established in June 1921 when the merger of the Ukrainian Academy of Sciences and the Ukrainian Scientific Society led also to the merger of their respective terminological institutes. A. Iu. Krymskyi, permanent secretary of the Academy, also served as director of the institute. Unfortunately, the almost total neglect of VUAN by the Soviet regime in the early years placed the Academy in such financial straits that scholars associated with the language institute were dispersed, and the institute was unable to add anything to the technical dictionaries already published by the Ukrainian Scientific Society. According to a report published at the beginning of 1923, the Institute of Ukrainian Scientific Language could afford to employ only one research associate, the philologist O. Kurylo.[119] However, the condition of the Academy improved markedly thereafter, and by 1926, the Institute included a number of separate sections.[120] Also in 1926, the Institute published its most important work, a Russo-Ukrainian dictionary of legal terms edited by Krymskyi.[121]

Not only academicians were concerned with the Ukrainian language

[117] Paul N. Wexler, *Purism and Language: A Study in Modern Ukrainian and Belorussian Nationalism (1849–1967)*. Language Science Monographs, Vol. 11 (Bloomington, 1974), pp. 113–133.

[118] *Kurs istorii ukrainskoi literaturnoi movy* (Kiev, 1958, 1961), vol. 2, p. 16; Mykola Skrypnyk, "Pidsumky pravopysnoi dyskusii," *Visty VUTsVK*, June 19, 1927, p. 2.

[119] "Institut Naukovoi Movy Vseukrainskoi Akademii Nauk," *Chervonyi shliakh*, 1923, no. 1, pp. 245–246.

[120] Fedir Savchenko, "Institut Ukrainskoi Naukovoi Movy Ukrainskoi Akademii Nauk," *Ukraina*, 1926, no. 5, pp. 179–186.

[121] For a critical review of this work see Oleksa Baikar, "Krymsko-ukrainska pravnycha mova," *Chervonyi shliakh*, 1930, no. 1, pp. 134–156.

in the 1920s. Questions of terminology and spelling were often discussed in the popular press. Perhaps the most noteworthy incident in this discussion—one which certainly demonstrates its breadth—occurred in 1923, when Serhii Pylypenko, who had been trained in philology at Kiev University before the revolution, proposed that the Cyrillic alphabet be abandoned, and that Ukrainians adopt the Latin alphabet of the West.[122] While nothing happened, his suggestion continued to be discussed at least until 1927.

The state began to take an active interest in the problem of linguistic standardization in the mid-twenties. In June 1924 a Society to Aid the Development and Diffusion of the Urainian Scientific Language was organized in Kharkiv, headed by no less a luminary than the head of the Soviet Ukrainian government, Vlas Chubar.[123] In July 1925 a State Orthography Commission was established.[124] Relying heavily on VUAN for expertise, this commission was able to release a proposed spelling system in 1926.[125]

In May and June 1927, an all-Ukrainian orthography conference was sponsored by Narkomos. In retrospect, it seems quite remarkable. Its seventy-five participants included linguists, philologists, writers, teachers, and other interested parties, drawn from Soviet Ukraine, Ukrainian areas of the RSFSR, and abroad. The account published in *Ukraina,* the VUAN organ, described it as having "the character of a great national cultural manifestation."[126] A core group of fifteen worked eight to nine hours a day on the orthography, with representatives of such non-Soviet institutions as the Shevchenko Scientific Society in Lviv and the Ukrainian Pedagogical Institute in Prague playing particularly influential roles. While the 1926 orthography proposal was given as the basis for discussion, Pylypenko and his supporters raised the question of adopting the Latin alphabet, thereby provoking a particularly heated discussion during the course of which even Skrypnyk suggested that Cyrillic be supplemented by using the Latin letters S and Z.[127]

---

[122] S. Pylypenko, "Odvertyj lyst do vsix, xto cikavyt'sja cijeju spravoju," *Chervonyi shliakh,* 1923, no. 6–7, pp. 267–268.

[123] "T-vo Dopomohy Rozvytku ta Poshyrenniu Ukrainskoi Naukovoi Movy," *Chervonyi shliakh,* 1924, no. 6, pp. 248–249.

[124] E. Tymchenko, "Ustaleniia ukrainskoho pravopysu," *Ukraina,* 1925, no. 4, p. 187.

[125] M. Hrushevskyi, "V pravopysnii spravi." *Ukraina,* 1926, no. 5, p. 191.

[126] Fedir Savchenko, "Vseukrainska konferentsiia v spravi uporiadkuvannia ukrainskoho pravopysu," *Ukraina,* 1927, no. 3, p. 203.

[127] On the orthography conference and its aftermath, see especially Mykola Skryp-

The whole way the problem was approached is revealing. The Soviet Ukrainian government did not simply settle the issue by fiat, but called together the best experts it could find, regardless of their place of residence or political convictions, added other interested parties, and had them thrash out the issues. As a result, a real sense of national participation evolved, and when Narkomos officially adopted the new orthography in 1928, it was immediately accepted by Ukrainians outside the USSR as well as in it. Such a way of proceeding would have been totally unthinkable only half a decade later. It was not just a different world, but a completely different moral universe.

While the orthography was established and the tendency was in favor of linguistic purism, one cannot speak of a genuine Party line on the development of the language before 1930. This was demonstrated in mid-1928, when the most important Soviet Ukrainian cultural monthly, *Chervonyi shliakh,* published back-to-back two articles advocating sharply different views on how the language ought to develop. One was written in a strongly purist vein, making the argument that the predicate nominative grammatical construction made Ukrainian unique among Slavic languages and bemoaning the infiltration of the predicate instrumental from Polish and Russian into Ukrainian speech as "unorganic." The other took a more dynamic view of the development of the Ukrainian language and welcomed its evolution toward other languages. The argument was made that excessive linguistic purism was a barrier to progress and that, in any case, it was inevitable from the very proximity of the four languages used in Ukraine's cities—Ukrainian, Yiddish, Polish, and Russian—that they would assimilate certain features from one another.[128] Who was right is less important than the fact that such a clash of ideas and values could take place.

Thus, questions relating to the development of the Ukrainian language were basically left to the national intelligentsia, including that part of it which lived outside the borders of the Soviet Union. The role played by Skrypnyk, his commissariat, and the Soviet state was supportive; the Party did not dictate to linguists. This linguistic self-determination,

---

nyk, "Pidsumky pravopysnoi dyskusii," *Visty VUTsVK,* June 19, 1927, pp. 2–3; A. Khvylia, "Vykorinyty, znyshchyty natsionalistychne korinnia na movnomu fronti," *Bilshovyk Ukrainy,* 1933, no. 7–8, pp. 49–51.

[128] S. Smerechynskyi, "Kudy ide ukrainska mova (Do pytannia pro predykatyvnyi nominatyv ta 'predykat' instrumental v ukrainskii movi)," *Chervonyi shliakh,* 1928, no. 5–6, pp. 172–189; Prof. B. Larin, "Movny pobut mista," *Chervonyi shliakh,* 1928, no. 5–6, pp. 190–198.

as we shall see, was to change radically in 1930 with the show trial of the Union for the Liberation of Ukraine, having ominous implications for Skrypnyk and the policies he stood for.

*   *   *

In 1927, Volodymyr Zatonskyi listed four goals the regime sought to achieve through Ukrainization:

> a) Strengthening the Ukrainian Socialist Soviet Republic as a state organism which is a constituent part of the Union of Soviet Socialist Republics.
> b) Mastering the language and learning the local conditions.
> c) Party leadership of Ukrainian culture. Leading is possible only through a process of intimately participating in work. Leading is impossible if this culture is built exclusively by non-Bolshevik hands.
> d) The selection, Bolshevik rearing, and attraction of Ukrainians to our work (above all from the workers and peasants).[129]

To a substantial degree, Skrypnyk can be said to have achieved all these goals. Soviet Ukraine was strengthened politically to the extent that the crucial decisions affecting it were, by and large, made in Ukraine by Ukrainians. The proportion of Ukrainians in the KP(b)U increased from 13.4% at the beginning of 1924 to 60% in the Fall of 1933.[130] The Party exercised leadership over culture not only by fiat but also by fostering situations where Ukrainians outside the Party could work questions out for themselves, as in linguistics. In short, Skrypnyk temporarily achieved what Ukrainian communists had advocated since Mazlakh and Shakhrai, recognition that Ukraine was a country in its own right, ruled by a regime which was clearly Ukrainian in its policies and goals.

Skrypnyk's Ukraine can in some ways be seen as the fulfillment of the demand the Ukrainian Central Rada put forth in 1917: the national territorial autonomy of Ukraine with safeguards for the rights of national minorities. Although the fundamental questioning of the political state of affairs by such figures as Shumskyi, Khvylovyi, and Volobuiev, was condemned, Soviet Ukraine was becoming more and more a nation-state within the Soviet Union. The national intelligentsia was given relatively free rein in the cultural sphere, and the communist regime actively supported in it whatever was in the interest of the nation's cultural pro-

---

[129] V. Zatonskyi, *Natsionalna problema na Ukraini*, p. 23.
[130] Basil Dmytryshyn, *Moscow and the Ukraine, 1918–1953*, pp. 241, 245.

gress. The Party spared no reasonable effort in Ukrainizing the administration, the cities, and the KP(b)U itself. Skrypnyk's policies were directed at fostering the consolidation of the nation while simultaneously attempting to avoid anything which threatened to revive the old hostility between Ukrainians and Russians. His work on the theory of the nationality question was but an attempt to justify this course. What Skrypnyk attempted to do was reconcile socialist internationalism with the legitimate national aspirations of the Ukrainian people. And in some measure, he succeeded.

CHAPTER SEVEN

Matvii Iavorskyi and the
Vicissitudes of Interpreting the Past

AT THE END of 1928, Matvii Iavorskyi, head of historical studies
in the Ukrainian Institute of Marxism-Leninism and hitherto considered
a sort of court historian of Ukrainian communism, was attacked for
allegedly committing "nationalistic deviations" in interpreting Ukrainian history. Iavorskyi was in no sense a "dissident" like Shumskyi or
Khvylovyi; he never, so far as is known, questioned the official Party
line. Rather, he was a close associate of Mykola Skrypnyk, and the hue
and cry raised against "Iavorskyism" in historical scholarship was actually an indirect attack upon Skrypnyk. It had the distinction of being
the first such attack; it would not be the last.

For yet another reason, Ukrainian historiography ought to be considered. Except for literature, it was the main point of contact between
the non-Party national intelligentsia and the new communist intellectuals reared by the Party. The regime could not just confine itself to
organizing conferences on history, then leaving the field to the national
intelligentsia, as it had done with such fields as linguistics. History is
central to a nation's sense of its own identity—Ukraine's great historians
had also often been its most revered leaders. The undisputed *doyen* of
non-communist historians working in Soviet Ukraine was Mykhailo
Hrushevskyi, former president of the Central Rada and, to many, still
the symbol of Ukrainian aspirations. An additional consideration was
that Marxism claims to provide the key to understanding history: this,
in fact, is one of the doctrine's central claims. Thus the Party could
not have abdicated the field of historical scholarship even had it wished
to do so. The Party needed to field its own experts; chief among them
in Ukraine was Matvii Iavorskyi.

The specific charge leveled against Iavorskyi was that he had fallen
under the influence of the school of Hrushevskyi. The reality was that
no historian of Ukraine could have avoided his influence to some degree,
but Iavorskyi attempted to recast the findings of traditional scholarship

232

in the Marxist mold. Besides, the official policy of cooperating with the national intelligentsia created a milieu in which some degree of mutual influence between Party-sanctioned and non-Party scholarship was inevitable. Dmytro Bahalii, one of the most talented of traditional Ukrainian historians, announced his conversion to Marxism and began to write history from a Marxist viewpoint. Osyp Hermaize, also a non-Party historian, was concerned with the origins of the modern Ukrainian revolutionary movement, and thus inevitably with the prehistory of Soviet Ukraine. The 1920s were a time of intellectual ferment among historians, amid which Iavorskyi's role was to be the voice of Party orthodoxy. Later generations have given the position he occupied an unofficial but descriptive name: ideological watchdog.

Significantly, the campaign against "Iavorskyism" began in Russia rather than Ukraine. With the exception of Stalin's intervention in the Shumskyi controversy—and we have seen that he wrote his 1926 letter to the KP(b)U Central Committee only after Shumskyi had appealed to him—this was Moscow's first blatant interference in Soviet Ukrainian cultural affairs. The whole Iavorskyi affair was created by Moscow, with only one possible reason why: A decision had been made to renege on the tacit agreement upon which Soviet rule in Ukraine had hitherto been based.

M. S. Hrushevskyi's Interpretation of History

As in so many other spheres of the nation's cultural life, Ukrainian historiography enjoyed a period of creativity in the twenties which gave way to complete regimentation in the thirties.[1] Soviet Ukraine's historians

---

[1] There is a rich body of secondary material on Soviet Ukrainian historiography in the 1920s. See, for example, Myron Korduba, *La littérature historique soviétique-ukrainienne: compte-rendu 1917-1931* (Munich, 1972); Olexander Ohloblyn, "Ukrainian Historiography, 1917-1956," *Annals of the Ukrainian Academy of Arts and Sciences in the U.S.*, vol. 5-6, 1957, pp. 307-455; Borys Krupnytskyi, *Ukrainska istorychna nauka pid Sovietamy (1920-1950)* (Munich, 1957); Borys Krupnytskyi, "Die ukrainische Geschichtswissenschaft in der Sowjetunion, 1921-1941," *Jahrbücher für Geschichte Osteuropas*, vol. 6, 1941, no. 2-4, pp. 125-151; D. Doroshenko, "Die Entwicklung der Geschichtsforschung in der Sowjetukraine in den letzten Jahren," *Mitteilungen des ukrainischen wissenschaftlichen Instituts in Berlin*, Heft 2, 1928, pp. 35-56; O. M. "Ukrainska istorychna nauka v 1920-kh rokakh," *Suchasnyk*, vol. 1, 1948, no. 1, pp. 76-84; Viach. Zaikin, "Ukrainskaia istoricheskaia literatura poslednikh let," *Na chuzhoi storone*, vol. 10, 1925, pp. 236-251. Among the Soviet Ukrainian works, the following are especially valuable: the journal *Istoriohrafichni doslidzheniia v Ukrainskii RSR* (Kiev, 1968-1972); V. A. Diadchenko, F. E. Los, V. G. Sarbei, "Razvitie istoricheskoi nauki na Ukraine (1917-1963 gg.)," *Voprosy istorii*, 1964, no. 1, pp. 3-26; N. V.

were able to draw on a considerable body of prerevolutionary scholarship, and the non-Party historiography of the 1920s can be seen largely as a continuation of what had already been accomplished.[2] As in Russia, the privations of the civil war had cost Ukraine many of its best scholars.[3] Within a few short years, however, the life of the mind recovered. Compared to the restrictive policies of the autocracy and the far more restrictive intellectual straightjacket of Stalinism, the twenties appear in retrospect to have been almost a golden age, a time when different schools of thought could coexist, disagree, and learn from each other.

The most important event in early Soviet Ukrainian historiography was Mykhailo Hrushevskyi's return from exile in 1924. The *doyen* of Ukrainian scholars, leading prerevolutionary spokesman for Ukrainian aspirations, and first president of the Ukrainian Peoples Republic, his role in Ukrainian history invites comparison with that of the Czech scholars and political leaders Palacký and Masaryk.[4] He has been called "not merely the child but the personified symbol of the Ukrainian people."[5] His return was a major political event in the history of Soviet Ukraine, bestowing on the regime a much-needed aura of national legitimacy at a crucial juncture in its history. Yet the regime was ambivalent about having so prominent a national figure so close at hand. Communists who argued for the Party's participation in the Ukrainian cultural revival often did so on the grounds that failure to take part would

---

Komarenko, *Ustanovy istorychnoi nauky v Ukrainskii RSR (1917–1937 rr.)* (Kiev, 1973); N. V. Komarenko, *Zhurnal "Litopys revoliutsii": Istoriohrafichnyi narys* (Kiev, 1970). It should be noted that Soviet works often suffer from politically mandated gaps which extend even to the level of journal bibliographies printed in very small editions. Except for the purpose of condemnation, those who were purged in the thirties and not rehabilitated are never mentioned, even in bibliographies, and the only way to locate the works of Marxist historians such as Matvii Iavorskyi and Osyp Hermaize is by searching the tables of contents of journals or the year-end lists of contents in the journals themselves. This circumstance is an indication of the current state of Ukrainian historiographic research in the USSR.

[2] The standard work on pre-revolutionary Ukrainian historiography is Dmytro Doroshenko, "A Survey of Ukrainian Historiography," *Annals of the Ukrainian Academy of Arts and Sciences in the U.S.*, vol. 5–6, 1957, pp. 3–304.

[3] See the collective obituary of the fifty Ukrainian scholars who perished in the years 1918–1923: "Zasluzheni dlia ukrainskoi nauky i ukrainoznavstva diiachi, shcho pomerly v rr. 1918–1923," *Ukraina*, 1924, no. 3, pp. 180–191.

[4] The comparison is rightly drawn by Stephen M. Horak, "Michael Hrushevsky: Portrait of a Historian," *Canadian Slavonic Papers*, vol. 10, 1968, no. 3, pp. 345–346.

[5] Hans Koch, "Mychajlo Hruševśkyj (1866–1966): Zum 100 jährigen Geburtstag," *Ukraine in Vergangenheit und Gegenwart*, vol. 13, 1966, no. 37, p. 151.

mean leaving the field to Hrushevskyi. The degree of the regime's distrust, even fear, of Hrushevskyi is perhaps best evidenced by a secret internal GPU memorandum dated August 1925, and found among local Party archival documents taken out of Ukraine during the Second World War:

To all raion/representatives, Lubnyi okruh   *Top Secret*
To Comrade L--yi, Chornuskyi raion   August 1925

The *History of Ukraine-Rus,* by the ideologue of Ukrainian nationalism Hrushevskyi, is recognized as a pseudo-scholarly history, hostile and harmful to the Soviet regime. The question of banning this book is now being considered by the government of the USSR and the OGPU in Moscow. Meanwhile, we propose that raion residents concentrate on all who show interest in the above-mentioned book and disseminate it among the population. You are to inform our secret agents of this and order them to intensify their surveillance of such individuals.

Dvianinov,   Kazantsev,
Chief of Lubnyi Okruh OGPU Section   OGPU Representative[6]

Although the book was not banned at this time, there can hardly be better evidence than this of just how uncomfortable the regime was in dealing with Ukraine's most prominent scholar.

Hrushevskyi returned on the understanding that he would eschew politics and devote himself to scholarship. Upon returning, he immediately threw himself into the work of VUAN and reorganized its historical section.[7] At times he acted almost like a lobbyist for the Academy: soon after the Russian Academy of Sciences was renamed Academy of Sciences of the USSR, he publicly deplored the tendency to treat Russian institutions as Union ones. Union scholarly institutions could only be federations of republic institutions, he insisted, and VUAN had been treated like a poor relation. If the Russian Academy was to be considered a Union institution, VUAN should also; if the Russian Academy received Union funds, so should VUAN.[8]

Hrushevskyi's major influence, however, stemmed from his historical scholarship, particularly his ten-volume *History of Ukraine-Rus,* the first volume of which was published in the 1890s and the last in the 1930s.

---

[6] P. Lykho, " 'Sovetskaia vlast na mestakh': Robota komunistychnoi partii Chornuskoho raionu na Poltavshchyni (1921–1941)," *Ukrainskyi zbirnyk,* no. 8, 1957, p. 147.

[7] Doroshenko, "Die Entwicklung der Geschichtsforschung...," 41–42.

[8] M. Hrushevskyi, "Perspektyvy i vymohy ukrainskoi nauky," *Ukraina,* 1926, no. 1, pp. 7, 10–12.

Even his critics could not help but be influenced by this centerpiece of Ukrainian historical writing.[9]

Hrushevskyi was certainly no Marxist. In exile he even published a critique of the theorists of primitive society revered by Marxists and offered his own genetic (developmental) sociology.[10] He was, as a colleague of his put it, a pluralist in his rejection of single causes in history.[11]

Hrushevskyi's most important idea was the integrity and continuity of Ukrainian national history, and he insisted upon marking Ukrainian history off from that of neighboring peoples. He expressed this idea most clearly and concisely in a 1904 lecture, "The Traditional Schema of 'Russian' History and the Problem of the Rational Organization of the History of the Eastern Slavs." In this lecture, as in his other work, he challenged the traditional presentation of Russian history for shifting its geographical focus from Kiev to Vladimir-Suzdal to Moscow, arguing that this made little sense, because the descendants of the medieval Kievans were Ukrainians, not Russians. What would later become Muscovy had been colonized by Kievan Rus, but was not really an integral part of it. Kievan laws and culture were transplanted there much like Roman laws and customs had been in ancient Gaul. The traditional schema ignored the process of this transplantation, and thereby left Russian history without a beginning and rendered the histories of the other East Slavs unintelligible. He maintained that the Galician principalities of Halych and Volodymyr, as well as Lithuania, were the real heirs of Kievan political and cultural traditions. He concluded that the best way to straighten out the confusion inherent in the old schema was to look for the beginnings of Great Russian history on Great Russian soil and rigorously distinguish among the histories of the three East Slavic nations.[12]

---

[9] For a good brief discussion of Hrushevskyi's *Istoriia Ukrainy-Rusy,* see D. I. Bahalii, *Narys istorii Ukrainy na sotsiialno-ekonomichnomu grunti* (Kiev, 1928), vol. 1, pp. 73–88.

[10] Mykh. Hrushevskyi, *Pochatky hromadianstva (Genetychna sotsiologiia)* (Vienna, 1921), especially p. 8, where he wrote: "But the formulae of the development of society which Engels took from Morgan were, in fact, wholly lacking in rigor and validity." For a Soviet Marxist response, see: A. Richytskyi, "Iak Hrushevskyi 'vypravliaie' Engelsa," *Chervonyi shliakh,* 1924, no. 3, pp. 183–190.

[11] Osyp Hermaize, "Iuvilei ukrainskoi nauki: Sorok rokiv diialnosty akad. M. S. Hrushevskoho," *Zhyttia i revoliutsiia,* 1926, no. 10, p. 98.

[12] Mychaylo Hrushevsky, "The Traditional Scheme of 'Russian' History and the Problem of a Rational Organization of the History of the Eastern Slavs," *Annals of the Ukrainian Academy of Arts and Sciences in the U.S.,* vol. 2, 1952, no. 4 (6), pp. 355–364. See also: Lubomyr Wynar, "Ukrainian-Russian Confrontation in Historiography: Michael

Hrushevskyi won for his idea of separating Russian and Ukrainian history some notable supporters among Russian historians. Presniakov, for example, took Hrushevskyi's thesis as the starting point for his own attempt to trace the origins of the Great Russian state.[13] Even the Bolshevik historian M. N. Pokrovskii, who was usually less than generous in his appraisal of "bourgeois" historians, held Hrushevskyi's work in high esteem for its refutation of the traditional schema. In his lectures on historiography, Pokrovskii called him "one of the freshest and most European of historians," recommending the first volume of *The History of Ukraine-Rus* as the best possible source for the history of Kievan Rus.[14]

In later years, Hrushevskyi would come under attack by Marxist historians for allegedly manufacturing the notion that the Ukrainian people had never produced a national bourgeoisie. Although on some occasions Hrushevskyi did make statements to this effect,[15] it would be misleading to credit him with the creation of a theory of "Ukrainian bourgeoislessness." Rather, it was a matter of simple observation. In any case, those who professed to see a Ukrainian bourgeoisie usually referred to the "kulaks" rather than to any traditional commercial or industrial class.

Hrushevskyi's historical work was not without political as well as scholarly importance. He himself was well aware of the intimate connection between Ukrainian historiography and political consciousness. As he once wrote, "It must not be forgot that our historiography is at the same time the history of Ukrainian political thought; Ukraine's great historians were its great ideologues and gave direction and tone not only to the historical but also to the social and political consciousness of our society."[16] By placing Ukrainian history on a firm scholarly basis,

---

Hrushevsky versus the Traditional Scheme of 'Russian' History," *Ukrainian Quarterly*, vol. 30, 1974, no. 1, pp. 13–25.

[13] A. E. Presniakov, *The Formation of the Great Russian State* (Chicago, 1970), pp. 6–8ff. See also: Natalia Polonska-Vasylenko, *Two Conceptions of the History of Ukraine and Russia* (London, 1968).

[14] M. N. Pokrovskii, *Izbrannye proizvedeniia* (Moscow, 1965–1967), vol. 1, p. 345.

[15] An admirable collection of such statements may be found in M. A. Rubach, "Burzhuazno-kurkulska natsionalistychna ideolohiia pid mashkaroiu demokratii 'trudovoho narodu' (Sotsiialno-politychni pohliady M. S. Hrushevskoho)," *Chervonyi shliakh*, 1932, no. 5–6, pp. 122–128.

[16] M. Hrushevskyi, "V dvadtsat piati rokovyny smerty O. M. Lazarevskoho: Kilka sliv pro ioho naukovu spadshchynu ta ii doslidzhennia," *Ukraina*, 1927, no. 4, p. 17.

Hrushevskyi asserted the national distinctiveness and aspirations of his people.

The Fellow Travellers

Before the creation of a regimented "historical front," the lines between Marxists and non-Marxists were not so sharply drawn that they could not influence each other and even win converts without coercion. Perhaps the most striking example of the situation is provided by the case of D. I. Bahalii. Like Hrushevskyi, Bahalii came from a humble background, studied history at Kiev University with V. B. Antonovych, and became one of the old empire's most respected scholars. Before the revolution, he twice served as rector of Kharkiv University and its representative in the Council of State. When the Ukrainian Academy of Sciences was established in 1918, he was named head of its historical section. In the early twenties, he became one of the first scholars to announce his allegiance to the Soviet state and his conversion to Marxism; he wrote his later works from a Marxist standpoint.[17]

One of the most revealing moments in early Soviet Ukrainian historiography occurred in 1923, when Iavorskyi published his *Outline History of Ukraine,* which attempted to interpret the whole of Ukrainian history in the Marxist framework.[18] Bahalii published a critique in *Chervonyi shliakh,* pointing out that Iavorskyi's dogmatic attempt to force the nation's past into Marxist categories did violence to the facts of history, and that Iavorskyi really did not understand what Ukrainian historians of the past had tried to do. For example, Iavorskyi's charge that past historians had concentrated primarily on princes, hetmans, and the upper classes, simply was not true of Ukrainian populist historians like Hrushevskyi or of much of Bahalii's work. Bahalii also pointed out that Iavorskyi, unlike such Russian Marxist historians as M. N. Pokrovskii and N. A. Rozhkov, showed little familiarity with primary sources and almost completely ignored such vital aspects of the historical process as culture and ideology. It also seemed rather strange that a Marxist historian would divide Ukrainian history into periods without

---

[17] "Akademik D. I. Bahalii," *Visti VUTsVK,* February 11, 1932, p. 5; D. D(oroshenko), "D. I. Bahalii," *Zeitschrift für osteuropäische Geschichte,* vol. 6 (2), 1932, no. 2, p. 312; Doroshenko, "Ukrainische Akademia der Wissenschaften in Kyjiv," *Mitteilungen des ukrainischen wissenschaftlichen Institutes in Berlin,* no. 1 (April 1927), p. 11; I. D. Boiko, "Do storichchia z dnia narodzhennia vydatnoho ukrainskoho istoryka D. I. Bahaliia," *Ukrainskyi istorychnyi zhurnal,* 1957, no. 2, p. 105.

[18] M. Iavorskyi, *Narys istorii Ukrainy* (Kiev, 1923).

ever mentioning feudalism. In short, Professor Iavorskyi had a few things to learn about history.[19]

Iavorskyi published a reply, full of phrases like "fetishism of science" and citations from Marx and Georg Lukacs. Bahalii, in turn, published a rebuttal.[20] The elder of the two polemicists got the better of the exchange, although Iavorskyi seemed to learn from it. When several years later he published his major work, *Sketches in the History of the Revolutionary Struggle in Ukraine*, Iavorskyi clearly had kept his fondness for terms like "hegemony" and "totality" borrowed from Gramsci and Lukacs, but he also made copious references to primary sources.

One of the most interesting of the so-called fellow traveller historians of the 1920s was Osyp Hermaize, a Marxist who was in charge of the section of methodological and sociological fundamentals and led a seminar in Marxism-Leninism in Hrushevskyi's Ukrainian history department (*katedra*) in Kiev.[21] Hermaize's most important work was a monograph on the history of the Revolutionary Ukrainian Party intended to be the first volume in an ambitious survey of the development of revolutionary Marxism in Ukraine. In it Hermaize completely ignored the role of Russian socialist parties, portraying the Ukrainian revolutionary process as something completely distinct from what was happening in the Russified cities.[22] Indeed, this lack is probably the reason no succeeding volumes appeared. Hermaize attempted to show that the Ukrainian revolutionary movement consisted of a peasant constituency and a national intelligentsia of high culture that had overcome its provincialism, that is, to show that the Ukrainian movement was in no way inferior to its Russian counterpart.[23] Iavorskyi criticized Hermaize for a number of errors: for failing to take into account Russian influence on the Ukrainian revolutionary movement, and for excluding from his work all groups which were not exclusively Ukrainian, as well as for

[19] Dm. Bahalii, "Persha sproba nacherku istorii Ukrainy na tli istorychnoho materiializmu," *Chervonyi shliakh*, 1923, no. 9., 145–161.

[20] M. Iavorskyi, "De-shcho pro 'krytychnu' krytyku, pro 'obiektyvnu' istoriiu ta shche i pro babusynu spidnytsiu," *Chervonyi shliakh*, 1924, no. 3, pp. 167–182; Dm. Bahalii, "Z pryvodu antykrytyky prof. M. I. Iavorskoho," *Chervonyi shliakh*, 1924, no. 6, pp. 149–160.

[21] Z. Hurevych, "Psevdomarksyzm na sluzhbi ukrainskoho natsionalizma (Do ostannikh vystupiv O. Hermaize), *Bilshovyk Ukrainy*, 1929, no. 9, p. 55.

[22] O. Hermaize, *Narysy z istorii revoliutsiinoho rukhu na Ukraini. Tom. I. Revoliutsiina Ukrainska Partiia (RUP)* (n. p., 1926).

[23] See especially Osyp Hermaize, "Desiatylittia Zhovtnevoi revoliutsii i ukrainska nauka," *Ukraina*, 1927, no. 6, pp. iii–iv.

portraying the Ukrainian people as an amorphous ethnographic mass. This, Iavorskyi claimed, ignored the class struggle and substituted Hrushevskyi's approach to history for that of Marx.[24] In fact, Hermaize was to become something of a whipping boy for Iavorskyi as the decade ended. Hermaize was last seen in public as one of the defendants in the 1930 show trial of the Union for the Liberation of Ukraine, accused of being one of the principle conspirators in that imaginary conspiracy. According to a Gulag survivor, Hermaize was then placed in an isolation cell in the Solovky Islands, sentenced to an additional ten years after finishing his original sentence in 1937, and was never heard from again.[25]

Two distinguished economic historians of Ukraine, Mykhailo Slabchenko and Oleksander Ohloblyn, should be mentioned at this point. Slabchenko, author of a four-volume history of *The Ukrainian State from Khmelnytskyi to the World War* and of *The Social and Economic Organization of the Zaporozhian Sich,* was recognized for his outstanding work by being awarded the title of Academician. Along with many of his VUAN colleagues, he too was convicted of being a member of the so-called Union for the Liberation of Ukraine and was confined in an isolation cell in the Solovky Islands until the end of 1936 when his prison term ended.[26] Ohloblyn is best known for his three-volume *History of Ukrainian Industry.*[27] Unlike so many of his colleagues, Ohloblyn survived without being arrested, and emigrated to the West during the Second World War.

Party Historiography in Soviet Ukraine

While the traditional scholars were working in VUAN and institutions of higher education, the Party was building its own cadres of historians under the auspices of the Commission for the Study of the History of the October Revolution and the Communist Party (bolshevik) of Ukraine—Istpart, for short. Russian Istpart was founded in 1920, and its Ukrainian counterpart came into existence the following year in accordance with a decision of the Soviet Ukrainian government. Later, Ukrainian Istpart was subordinated to the KP(b)U Central Committee

[24] M. I. Iavorskyi, "Suchasni techii sered ukrainskoi istoriohrafii," in *Kryza suchasnoi burzhaznoi nauky ta marksyzm: Zbirnyk* (Kharkiv, 1929), pp. 33–34.

[25] S. O. Pidhainy, "Portraits of Solowky Exiles," in *The Black Deeds of the Kremlin: A White Book* (Toronto and Detroit, 1953, 1955), vol. 1, pp. 342–343.

[26] *Ibid.,* p. 342.

[27] Reprinted as Oleksander Ohloblyn, *A History of Ukrainian Industry* (Munich, 1971).

in conformance with Russian practice.[28] In 1923, the work of Ukrainian Istpart was criticized at an all-Russian conference of Istpart sections.[29] The reason its work was found wanting stemmed less from any political heterodoxy than from simple neglect; with all the problems the Soviet Ukrainian regime had to face in the first half of the twenties, such neglect of Party history is hardly surprising.[30]

During its first year, Istpart seemed more like a club than a bureaucracy. It published primarily memoirs. The central bureau had difficulty overseeing the work of local organizations; a plan of work was not even drawn up until 1925.[31] While Istpart was dominated by Russians and its organ, *Letopis revoliutsii* (Chronicle of Revolution), was published in Russian until 1929, it allowed a broad range of views. Arnold Rish, for example, considered the Spilka, a Ukrainian group allied with the Mensheviks, to have been an ancestor of the KP(b)U and published a survey history of the Spilka in *Letopis revoliutsii*.[32] When such "liberalism" came under criticism in 1926, the editor of *Letopis revoliutsii* replied that the discontinuities in the history of Bolshevism in Ukraine made it imperative to discuss the important revolutionary

---

[28] A. I. Alatortsova and G. O. Alekseeva, compilers, *50 let Sovetskoi istoricheskoi nauki: khronika nauchnoi zhizni* (Moscow, 1971), pp. 30–31, 39. The decree founding Istpart placed it under Rabkrin (see text in *Kulturne budivnytstvo*, vol. 1, pp. 112–113), but it was placed under the Central Committee in September 1922. "Vokrug raboty Istparta," *Letopis revoliutsii*, no. 2, 1923, p. 283.

[29] "Vokrug raboty Istparta," *Letopis revoliutsii*, no. 4, 1923, pp. 316–317.

[30] At the beginning of 1924 M. Ivanov complained that the conditions under which Istpart worked in both Kharkiv and the provinces was "not entirely favorable" and that many comrades did not realize how important Istpart work was. Shortly thereafter Medvedev, a secretary of the KP(b)U Central Committee, sent out a circular letter to all provincial Party committees stating that the work of *Letopis revoliutsii* was extremely important and should be included in libraries, clubs, Party schools, and read by Party members. In 1925 it was reported that the Poltava Istpart section was assigned only 100 rubles by its Party committee, Chernihiv received only 200 rubles, and the Donbas gubkom decided not to create (i.e., abolish) the provincial Istpart and use those who had worked in it elsewhere. See *Letopis revoliutsii*, 1924, no. 1, p. 278; 1924, no. 3, p. 238; 1925, no. 3, pp. 238–243.

[31] "Plan raboty Istparta TsK KP(b)U i Gub-Istpartov na 1925 god," *Letopis revoliutsii*, 1925, no. 4, p. 233. At the first All-Ukrainian Conference of Istparts, various local delegates sharply criticized the center (i.e., Kharkiv) for trying to stifle local initiative, while the center accused the local organizations of not paying attention to it and trying to go their own way. "Vseukrainskoe Soveshchanie Istpartov," *Letopis revoliutsii*, 1925, no. 3, pp. 225–236; 1925, no. 4, pp. 165–174.

[32] Arnold Rish, "Ocherki po istorii 'Spilki'," *Letopis revoliutsii*, 1925, no. 2, pp. 125–173; 1925, no. 3, pp. 77–107.

movements of the past, even if they opposed the Bolsheviks. As he put it, "There were only two alternatives: either not deal with this or that period because at that time the Bolsheviks were weak or describe the mass revolutionary movements, what these organizations did, how things were...One had to talk about the Mensheviks."[33]

The first systematic treatment of the history of the KP(b)U was published in 1923, by Moisei Ravich-Cherkasskii, a frequent contributor to *Letopis revoliutsii*. Before the revolution he had been an agitator and something of a theoretician in the Jewish Bund in the Cherkasy region under the name Moisei Rabinovich.[34] He joined the Bolsheviks in 1917, and published articles on a number of topics in the twenties, but was best known for his historical work. His *History of the Communist Party (bolshevik) of Ukraine* was for several years the officially sanctioned textbook on the subject.

Ravich-Cherkasskii was later accused of having invented the theory that the KP(b)U had grown up from "dual roots," that is, from non-Bolshevik Ukrainian sources as well as Russian Marxism. The idea was that the KP(b)U was an amalgam of different currents, and that the Ukrainian current arose from the process by which Ukrainian revolutionaries overcame their "chauvinism" and split from the mainstream of the movement to form their own groups more in the spirit of the international socialist movement. This process, as he saw it, began with the withdrawal of the Spilkists from the RUP shortly before the revolution of 1905, and continued with the secession of the Borotbisty and Ukapisty from the UPSR and USDRP.[35] The Russian current of the revolutionary movement in Ukraine meanwhile underwent a somewhat similar process of wandering in the wilderness, since up to 1912, the history of the RSDRP in Ukraine was mainly the history of its "opportunistic" Menshevik wing.[36] These two currents coalesced in the Bolshevik-Borotbist merger of 1920. As he put it,

> Actually, the merger of the Borotbists with the Communist Party is the end of the road along which the two revolutionary currents (*stikhii*) in Ukraine travelled separately for twenty years. One from the RUP to the KPU and the other from the first circles of the RSDRP to the KPU.[37]

---

[33]"Vtoroe vseukrainskoe soveshchanie Istpartov," *Letopis revoliutsii,* 1926, no. 3–4, p. 291.

[34] A. Iuditskii, "Bund v Cherkasskom raione v 1904–5 gg.," *Letopis revoliutsii,* no. 5, 1923, pp. 138, 140, 142.

[35] M. Ravich-Cherkasskii, *Istoriia Kommunisticheskoi Partii (b-ov) Ukrainy,* p. 40.

[36] *Ibid.,* p. 11.

[37] *Ibid.,* p. 165.

By presenting the history of the KP(b)U as a process in which native currents merged with the Bolsheviks, Ravich-Cherkasskii not only gave those non-Bolshevik groups a historical revolutionary legitimacy, he also presented the KP(b)U as a separate party with its own unique historical tradition and mission. Ravich-Cherkasskii's presentation of the Party's history was designed to emphasize its Ukrainian heritage and mission, to show that Soviet Ukraine and the KP(b)U were not "a masquerade, a fiction, or playing at independence."[38] The work was as much a historical justification for Ukrainization as a Party history.

The first real political intervention in historiography occurred when the Shumskyi affair made Ravich-Cherkasskii's emphasis on the Party's indigenous antecedents politically embarrassing. In 1927, his "dual roots" thesis was denounced as the basis of the national deviations committed by Shumskyi and Khvylovyi, and castigated as a theory of "the philistine (*mishchanskoho*) ancestry of the KP(b)U." His ideas were found to contradict the idea of proletarian hegemony as represented by the Bolsheviks, and therefore were a misrepresentation of the Party's very nature.[39]

Little is known of Ravich-Cherkasskii's fate. In 1930, he published an article on literature, and an editorial note identified him as a minor cultural functionary.[40] In 1932, he was purged from the Party and declared a counterrevolutionary.[41]

Ravich-Cherkasskii's history was replaced in 1928 by N. N. Popov's *Outline History of the Communist Party (bolshevik) of Ukraine*. Popov joined the Bolsheviks in 1919, and ultimately held such high posts as KP(b)U Central Committee secretary and candidate membership in the All-Union Party Central Committee. His history of the Russian Communist Party went through sixteen editions before Stalin's *Short Course* replaced it, and Popov was, as the formula goes, "defamed, illegally repressed, and killed."[42]

Popov's Ukrainian Party history began by assailing his predecessor's work not only for "the mistakes and inaccuracies of this history but also for the very spirit in which it was written." Popov argued that the KP(b)U was and always had been a part of Bolshevism and that its only

---

[38] *Ibid.*, pp. 5–6.

[39] D. Frid, "Do pytannia pro korinnia KPU," *Bilshovyk Ukrainy*, 1927, no. 10, pp. 39–50; no. 14, pp. 27–38.

[40] M. Ravich-Cherkasskii, "Ukrainska khudozhna literatura ruskoiu movoiu," *Krytyka*, 1930, no. 3, pp. 27–36.

[41] *Entsyklopediia Ukrainoznavstva*, vol. 2, 23–31.

[42] *Sovetskaia istoricheskaia entsiklopediia*, vol. 11, columns 410–411.

legitimate ancestors were those it shared with the Russian Bolsheviks. He claimed that the "dual roots theory" was refuted by the fact that the RUP and USDRP had produced a number of anti-communists while Bolshevism had produced such Ukrainian leaders as Skrypnyk and Petrovskyi. Could parties which produced anti-communists lead to the KP(b)U?

> Why did Comrade Ravich-Cherkasskii commit such gross errors? It seems to me that he had good intentions. He wanted to somehow project Ukrainization on our Party's past and did so, undoubtedly, in order to provide yet another justification and support for our present nationality policy. I state that our nationality policy does not need such a justification created only by altering the facts of the revolutionary movement and history of our Party.[43]

While Popov was not nearly so generous to his predecessor in later editions as he was in this first version, he nevertheless rather obviously, if implicitly, misconstrued his opponent's argument, which was that the KP(b)U's Ukrainian heritage stemmed from those who repudiated the "chauvinism" of the RUP and USDRP, left those groups, and evolved toward Ukrainian Bolshevism.

Popov's eagerness to provide a unilinear ancestry for the KP(b)U led him to disparage completely any historical contributions made by Ukrainian populists like Drahomanov, the RUP, the USDRP, or the socialists of the Ukrainian national movement in general. He referred to the Old Hromada as "the so-called Hromada" and emphasized Drahomanov's evolution toward liberalism late in life. He portrayed the RUP as a group of confused chauvinists who fomented pogroms. Despite the broad rural support of the Central Rada in 1917, Popov saw the Russified workers as the basic revolutionary force in the country. While the Bolsheviks had been guilty of some errors in the nationality question, Ukrainian groups had done nothing to correct them. Ukrainians who joined the Bolsheviks contributed nothing of value from their own revolutionary heritage; they had become good communists only to the extent that they had overcome their past prejudices and embraced undiluted Bolshevism.[44]

Popov's radical departure from hitherto accepted views was briefly challenged by V. Sukhyno-Khomenko, a Ukrainian Party historian and former student of Iavorskyi's. Sukhyno-Khomenko published a discussion article in *Bilshovyk Ukrainy* combining praise for refuting Ravich-

---

[43] M. M. Popov, *Narys istorii Komunistychnoi Partii (bilshovykiv) Ukrainy*, pp. 3–10; quotations from pp. 3, 9.

[44] *Ibid.*, pp. 15–21, 38–45, 109–112, 218–219.

Cherkasskii with criticism of Popov's neglect of the Ukrainian movement's historical contribution. Sukhyno-Khomenko pointed out a number of inaccuracies and distortions in Popov's work, especially the fact that Popov falsely implied that all of Drahomanov's followers had become liberals, when actually such Drahomanovites as Tuchapskyi joined the RSDRP. The Ukrainian side of the revolutionary process had actually made an extremely important contribution to Russian Social Democracy and the KP(b)U, but Popov had ignored it.[45] Popov did not need to reply, since his critic would soon have his own troubles.

Matvii Iavorskyi and Soviet Ukrainian Historiography

Matvii Iavorskyi was the premier communist historian of Ukraine. As head of Ukrnauka, the Ukrainian counterpart of Glavnauka in charge of supervising all science and scholarship, as well as head of the historical section of UIML, Iavorskyi was as much an *apparatchik* as a historian, a scholar-bureaucrat whose role in Ukraine closely paralleled that of M. N. Pokrovskii in Russia.[46]

Though not primarily known as a Party historian, Iavorskyi's views on the historical nature of the KP(b)U are helpful in attempting to understand his general conception of Ukrainian history. A brief but fact-filled survey of the Party's history, which he published in 1922, contains his basic ideas on the subject, showing him to occupy a position midway between the arguments later made by Popov on the one hand and Ravich-Cherkasskii on the other. As Iavorskyi saw it,

> The Communist Party of Ukraine, although it is a regional organization of the RKP's history, part of the history of the Proletarian Revolution within the borders of the former empire, nevertheless has its own past and distinctive traits of development which reflect so clearly the peculiarities of the revolution in Ukraine from 1917 on. In it the imprint of the particular Ukrainian byways of the general Russian revolutionary road come clearly into view.
>
> The KPU is the child of the Ukrainian revolution and proletariat.[47]

---

[45] V. Sukhyno-Khomenko, "Problemy istorii KP(b)U (M. M. Popov—Narys istorii Komunistychnoi Partii (bilshovykiv) Ukrainy)," *Bilshovyk Ukrainy,* 1928, no. 13, pp. 69–78.

[46] *Bolshaia sovetskaia entsiklopediia* (1st ed., Moscow, 1931), vol. 45, column 328. Although this and other secondary accounts do not mention his work with Ukrnauka, a number of press accounts and interviews cite him in this role. See "Na shliakhakh orhanizatsii ukrainskoi nauky (Rozmova z zav. Ukrholovnaukoiu M. I. Iavorskym)," *Visty VUTsVK,* February 5, 1924, p. 2.

[47] M. Iavorskii, "K istorii KP(b)U," in *Oktiabrskaia revoliutsiia: Pervoe piatiletie* (Kharkiv, 1922), p. 93.

In Iavorskyi's view, the KP(b)U simultaneously fit into the general history of the Russian revolutionary movement and was the product of distinctively Ukrainian conditions and processes. In his later work he concentrated upon delineating the Ukrainian revolutionary movement and process. Although this later research did not deal directly with the KP(b)U, it was, in fact, an attempt to provide a set of historical antecedents for Soviet Ukraine's Party and state.

Iavorskyi's most ambitious work is his *Sketches in the History of the Revolutionary Struggle in Ukraine,* published in two parts in 1927 and 1928. Despite the fact that the campaign against Iavorskyism prevented the publication of its final portion, such that the narrative breaks off in the 1880s, what remains is an attempt to reinterpret Ukraine's whole history as a process culminating in Ukrainian communism. Ukrainian communism was, in turn, the product of a revolutionary movement which was not just a struggle for socialism but also for national liberation. While Iavorskyi rejected the idea that the Ukrainian nation was a homogeneous peasant mass, he was well aware that the long-felt lack of a Ukrainian proletariat presented special difficulties in tracing which class led the evolving movement. Iavorskyi saw this problem in terms of class hegemony, and had little choice but to emphasize the role of the peasantry.[48]

Iavorskyi traced the "revolutionary struggle" back to the very beginnings of class differentiation in Ukraine during the tenth century, and professed to see the laboring masses reacting against class exploitation even in the Kievan period. Drawing heavily upon M. N. Pokrovskii's ideas about the role of commercial capital in Russian history, Iavorskyi pointed to what he saw as a struggle of commercial capitalist interests against feudalism in Kievan Rus and even called the Kiev riots of 1068 "a bourgeois revolution in the primitive sense of the term."[49]

Iavorskyi saw the period of Ukraine's inclusion in the Grand Duchy of Lithuania as one characterized by feudalism not unlike its counterpart in Western Europe, giving way to the hegemony of commercial capital by the beginning of the sixteenth century. The Union of Lublin, which incorporated Ukraine into the Kingdom of Poland in 1569, was connected with bringing Ukraine into the sphere of the German market and the process of dispossessing the agricultural population for the benefit of the Polish *szlachta* who profited from grain sales. This social strug-

---

[48] M. Iavorskyi, *Narysy z istorii revoliutsiinoi borotby na Ukraini (Kharkiv, 1927–1928),* vol. 1, pp. 7–9.

[49] *Ibid.,* vol. 1, pp. 13–18.

gle set the stage for the antagonism between the Polish gentry and Ukrainian cossacks that errupted in the Cossack Wars. While noting that the ideology of the struggle was one of a religious conflict between Catholicism and Orthodoxy, Iavorskyi claimed that religion only "masked the real motives of the struggle which were the economic and social liberation of the masses." The registered cossacks and *starshyna* (officer corps) led the struggle of the Ukrainian masses against the Polish *szlachta,* as a historically progressive war of nascent capitalism against feudal oppression. The distinction between masters and serfs never disappeared, however, and the cossack *starshyna* found a buttress for its class interests in the Muscovite tsar. After the cossacks accepted the tsar as their suzerain, the cossack upper crust gradually merged with the Muscovite gentry into a single serf-owning commercial capitalist class. The ultimate result of the cossack revolution was thus a synthesis of native and Muscovite commercial capitalism.[50]

The next stage of the revolutionary struggle, as Iavorskyi saw it, corresponded to the new forms of exploitation characteristic of rising capitalism. The early nineteenth century was a period of struggle against the decaying economy of serfdom, a struggle carried on under the hegemony of the bourgeoisie. While the development of manufacturing was stimulated during the Napoleonic Wars, the nobles' state faced crisis as the more progressive elements of the aristocracy adapted themselves to the new economic realities and came under the influence of French revolutionary ideals, translated on Russian soil into two hopes: abolition of serfdom and democratization of the administration. Speranskii's reform proposal expressed bourgeois reformist aspirations; the Decembrists gave such aspirations a more revolutionary cast.[51]

The Decembrist revolt of 1825 and the Polish Uprising of 1830 ended one chapter of the revolutionary struggle; the next was dominated by Taras Shevchenko. In this period, as in the one before, Ukrainian aspirations developed under the influence of both Polish and Russian radical thought. The Brotherhood of Saints Cyril and Methodius represented the first Ukrainian *petit-bourgeois* revolutionary group which mixed the romantic ideal of universal Slavic brotherhood with leftist democratism and Ukrainian nationalism. One of its alumni, Shevchenko, evolved toward a utopian socialism influenced by Fourier, while others in the group drifted toward "opportunism."[52]

---

[50] *Ibid.,* vol. 1, pp. 22–81.
[51] *Ibid.,* vol. 1, pp. 82–117.
[52] *Ibid.,* vol. 1, pp. 108–189.

The years between 1848 and 1861 were characterized by the contradiction between the still feudal superstructure and the rising forces of capitalism, the struggle of the peasants for liberation, and the formation of radical conspiratorial circles. It was a period of growing small industry and commercial capital. Only a bourgeois revolution could sweep away the remnants of feudalism; the reforms of the 1860s were but a maneuver of the old superstructure, a response to the crisis made acute by the Crimean War defeat and a part of its death agony. Some of the Russian revolutionaries began to express rudimentary understanding for Ukrainian aspirations: Herzen, for example, in 1859, called for recognition of Ukraine's right to independence as a way to counter Ukrainian suspicion of Polish revolutionary propaganda. Meanwhile, secret student societies were forming in Kiev; police archives mentioned over a hundred "communists" at Kiev University in 1860. Iavorskyi, not quite convincingly, declared that this movement was based on Ukrainian small capital, and he condemned these "*petit-bourgeois* democrats" for their tactics of compromise.[53]

Next came the Narodnik revolutionaries with an ideology which Iavorskyi called "a copy of West European utopian communism." Iavorskyi saw Narodnik socialism as an ideology of bourgeois revolution based on the nascent "farmer" stratum of the peasantry. Ukrainian petty capital, and its spokesmen among the intelligentsia, tied themselves to the forces of bourgeois revolution which protested against both the feudal land-holding classes and large-scale urban capital. Under such circumstances, Ukrainian national democratic thought came more and more under the influence of socialism, while an increasingly restive peasantry found its echo in the growing radicalism of groups that adopted names like the Robespierreists. Kiev in the 1870s was one of the empire's many sites of a revolutionary student movement, while more moderate Ukrainian Narodniks sought refuge in "cultural ethnographism" and "*petit-bourgeois* Ukrainian nationalism." Two opposing Narodnik tendencies arose, revolutionary and liberal, one tending toward bourgeois democracy and the other hoping for a path of evolution similar to that of Germany.[54]

At this point the working class appeared in the arena of history as the first proletarian circles responded to the rural egalitarian socialism of Lavrov. Relying on Lenin's *Development of Capitalism in Russia,* Iavorskyi traced the progress of rural class differentiation and the pro-

---

[53] *Ibid.,* vol. 1, pp. 190–308.
[54] *Ibid.,* vol. 1, pp. 317–414.

letarianization of the peasant masses. Meanwhile, the rapid development of Donbas, Kiev, Odessa, and Katerynoslav signified the transformation of commercial capital into modern industrial capital, and the populism of national capital evolved into a weaker "pseudosocialism."[55]

The formation of the South Russian Workers Union in 1875 marked the start of the proletariat's transformation from a class in itself into a class for itself, that is, into a class conscious of its interests and historical mission.[56] Two Ukrainian associates of Drahomanov, Mykola Ziber (Sieber—his father was Swiss) and Serhii Podolynskyi, were converted to Marxism and introduced the new ideology to Ukraine, although neither, Iavorskyi believed, adequately understood "Marxist science and its dialectical method."[57] Iavorskyi also confronted the touchy question of Drahomanov himself, and found that the father of Ukrainian socialism was, in spite of his evolutionary doctrine, creator of a historically progressive response to national oppression and the economic exploitation of the peasantry.[58]

The campaign against Iavorskyi prevented him from continuing his work; at this point, the narrative breaks off. His views on the nature of the Ukrainian revolution can nonetheless be discerned from a 1927 work published in two issues of *Chervonyi shliakh,* "The Problem of the Ukrainian National-Democratic Revolution in 1917, Its Historical Foundations, and Its Motive Forces."

For Iavorskyi, the central question was that of hegemony. Which class was the hegemon of the Ukrainian revolution? Which class led it? The central Ukrainian demand in 1917 was economic and political autonomy, later independence. Iavorskyi viewed this as a platform of the *petite bourgeoisie* and kulaks, but refused to abstract the movement's class content from its program, and insisted upon "concrete Leninist historical analysis." He believed that the demand for independence was really the outgrowth of a long historical process:

> The tendency of the national movement in Ukraine in the direction of the economic and political liberation of a dismembered nation is as old as capitalism in Ukraine. This tendency made itself manifest as soon as the first elements of this capitalism took shape and along with it the first embryonic beginnings of this nation. We see the first indications of the

---

[55] *Ibid.,* vol. 2, part 1, pp. 8–28.
[56] *Ibid.,* vol. 2, part 1, pp. 38–69.
[57] *Ibid.,* vol. 2, part 1, pp. 125–126.
[58] *Ibid.,* vol. 2, part 1, p. 129.

birth of this idea already in the beginnings of the so-called "rebirth" of Ukrainian culture at the end of the eighteenth century.[59]

Iavorskyi compressed the stages of the revolutionary movement's development such that the first stage extended from the start of the Ukrainian cultural revival with Kotliarevskyi to the language ban of 1876, and attributed this stage to the beginnings of a Ukrainian internal market and capitalist development. The second stage, dominated by Drahomanov, coincided with the beginnings of a kulak stratum in the villages and an urban proletariat, but Drahomanov's ideology was still, in his view, a revolutionary program without revolutionary tactics that was based on the peasantry as a whole. The Poltava *jacquerie* of 1902 demonstrated the revolutionary instincts of the peasantry, but as a class it was by its nature *petit-bourgeois* and incapable of becoming a self-conscious social force or even a class in itself. The peasant class became even more deeply divided against itself with the Stolypin reform, and the more prosperous "farmer" stratum became hegemon of the peasantry as a whole.[60]

Iavorskyi described the Ukrainian movement in 1917 as thoroughly *petit-bourgeois.* As Iavorskyi put it, "only the Ukrainian *petite bourgeoisie* with its program of a national-democratic and bourgeois revolution remained to build Ukrainian nationalism."[61] The party leaders were all members of the Narodnik intelligentsia unable to see beyond the bourgeois democratic revolution. They all called themselves socialists, "but this socialism was only a fashionable little word which covered a program which was bourgeois by nature."[62] The national revolution led by the Central Rada was, in Iavorskyi's words, "a revolution of the farmer bourgeoisie." The main issue dividing the movement was whether or not to follow a more feudal "Prussian" model of agricultural development of the Rada's *petit-bourgeois* utopia of a free agrarian Ukraine. The Rada gave way to the aristocratic Hetmanate because "this Ukrainian nationalism, *petit-bourgeois* by nature and seeing itself standing on its own feet, inevitably had to seek an ally in the absence of a ready bourgeois class of its own." This ally, needless to say, was the army of the German Kaiser.[63]

---

[59] M. Iavorskyi, "Problema ukrainskoi natsionalnoi-demokratychnoi revoliutsii u 1917 r., ii istorychni osnovy ta ii rukhovi syly," *Chervonyi shliakh,* 1927, no. 2, p. 112.

[60] *Ibid.,* pp. 93–116.

[61] Iavorskyi, "Problema ukrainskoi natsionalnoi-demokratychnoi revoliutsii," *Chervonyi shliakh,* 1927, no. 4, p. 100.

[62] *Ibid.,* p. 103.

[63] *Ibid.,* p. 96, 104–110. Quotations from pp. 104, 110.

The Ukrainian declaration of independence, the Rada's Fourth Universal, was an act of counterrevolution, in spite of the fact that so much history had pointed to Ukrainian independence, because it was directed against the Soviet Russian government rather than against the autocracy. The decision to turn to Germany was really a turning against the masses, a betrayal of their agrarian aspirations:

> In this way the leading problem of the national democratic revolution in Ukraine, the self-determination of national capital along the path of bourgeois revolution in the land question, was lost at the very moment of its emancipation. Together with it, the political formula of this self-determination was also lost, lost at the exact time that was the most favorable moment for its temporary realization.[64]

Ukraine went over to imperialism against the proletarian revolution, and after the October Revolution, vestiges of the old ruling classes offered their services and advice on "orientations." By siding against the Bolsheviks, Iavorskyi argued, the Rada had to reconstitute itself as a counterrevolutionary force, and this altered the very content of national self-determination. Ukrainians were split into proletarian and bourgeois camps, and at Brest, the Ukrainian *petite bourgeoisie* decided to lean upon the big bourgeoisie of Germany and Austria. Iavorskyi held the land law of January 1918 to be irrelevant, a maneuver that the Rada was convinced to attempt only by the sound of Bolshevik shrapnel. The Fourth Universal was, by the time of its adoption, only a way of legalizing the German-Austrian occupation, and Ukrainian nationalism "went bankrupt at the very moment of its emancipation." There could be no middle course between revolution and counterrevolution; as a result, the Rada gave way to the Hetmanate. The Hetman was supported by those who had denounced the Rada for having violated the rights of property, and opposed by the Ukrainian workers, peasants, and *petite bourgeoisie.*

The forces formerly associated with the Rada were implacable in their hostility to the Hetman, in spite of the latter's overtures, and launched a war of *revanche* the moment the Armistice reduced the Hetman's allies to impotence. By then, however, it was too late for the *petite bourgeoisie,* and the result was the Red occupation of Kiev rather than the Rada's revival. This was the decisive turning point, the discrediting of the Ukrainian national bourgeoisie:

---

[64] *Ibid.,* p. 112.

To build a bourgeois Ukraine with *petit-bourgeois* hands in a period of
social revolution was already no less *"zu spät"* than it had been to revive
it with the hands of a feudal parasite, even it he were dressed up in the
garb of the old cossackdom which his two-faced Ukrainian nationalism
tied under the flag of the *"*Agrarian Democrats*"* after the *"*socialist*"*
posters of bourgeois democracy had failed. Ukraine could henceforth be
built only by those who were themselves emancipated from their
nationalism and chauvinism and had suppressed not only national oppression but also the class rule of man over man and had liberated labor
from exploitation.[65]

By presenting Soviet rule as a result of the defection of Ukrainian
elements from a bankrupt national movement, Iavorskyi gave one of
the most convincing historical justifications of Ukrainian communism
ever attempted.

Iavorskyi's grand conception of the Ukrainian national historical process was a notable attempt to fit the whole of his nation's history into
the Marxist framework and to present it as a process culminating in
the establishment of Soviet Ukraine. Unlike Ravich-Cherkasskii, Iavorskii did not firmly distinguish between Russian and Ukrainian revolutionary currents, but lumped them together in a single schemata of the
development of the revolutionary movement in Ukraine. This procedure
enabled him to avoid the politically dangerous course of relying too
heavily on purely Ukrainian groups, while still allowing him to present
Soviet Ukraine with its own heritage. Like Hrushevskyi, he treated
Ukrainian history as a separate national historical process, influenced
by the histories of neighboring nations but distinct from them. He treated
Ukrainian history as a whole, regardless of the political boundaries cutting
one part of Ukraine off from the other. A native Galician, he considered
the history of Galician Ukrainians an integral part of Ukrainian history
and gave far more weight to events in Galicia than the above summary
of his major works would indicate. He did not deny outside influence:
he traced the influence of Russian radicalism on Ukrainian social thought
without hesitation, but he counterbalanced it by noting also the influence
of the West.[66] If the history of the peoples of the USSR were to mean
anything other than a single *"*Soviet*"* history, a revival of the old *"*all
Russian*"* schema under a new name and a new set of terms, then Iavor-

---

[65] *Ibid.,* p. 116.

[66] He devoted an article to the problem of Western influence on the Ukrainian revolutionary movement: Iavorskyi, *"*Westeuropäische Einflüsse auf die Ideengestaltung der
sozialen Bewegung in der Ukraine im zweiten und dritten Viertel des XIX. Jahrhunderts,*"*
in Otto Hoetzsch, ed., *Aus dem historischen Wissenschaft in der Sovet-Union: Vorträge*

skyi's work should have remained permissible. The fact that it was repudiated is decisive evidence of the new turn of affairs apparent by the end of the 1920s.

He was, in a sense, the victim of a state of affairs he had himself helped create, for Iavorskyi served as Soviet Ukraine's leading guardian of ideological orthodoxy. When he surveyed the achievements of post-revolutionary Ukrainian historiography for foreigners, he expressed pride in the achievements of non-communist scholars such as Hrushevskyi and Bahalii.[67] When he was in the Soviet Union, his punctiliousness in pointing out the ideological errors of his colleagues was without peer. At the First All-Union conference of Marxist-Leninist Scholarly Research Establishments, sponsored by the Communist Academy in March 1928, he interjected attacks on virtually every leading Ukrainian historian into a discussion on planning scholarly research. That he made such remarks at a time when they were uncalled for, indicates that Iavorskyi rather enjoyed the role of ideological watchdog.[68] At the All-Union Conference of Marxist Historians held over the Christmas holidays in 1928–29, he read a report on the pseudo-Marxism of Ukrainian historians, denouncing Bahalii as a "pseudo-Marxist," Osyp Hermaize for tracing the origins of the KP(b)U to the old Revolutionary Ukrainian Party, and the economic historians Ohloblyn and Slabchenko for smuggling hostile nationalist ideology into their studies of the pre-revolutionary Ukrainian economy.[69] Back home in Soviet Ukraine, he lectured on contemporary trends in Ukrainian historiography, declaring that every single trained scholar who had attempted to become a Marxist had failed.[70] Since he and his students were the only officially sanctioned historians, he seemed to see himself as head of the only ideologically orthodox Ukrainian school of historians.

Unfortunately for Iavorskyi, he was brought low at the very moment of his most vehement attacks on his "pseudo-Marxist" colleagues.

---

ihrer Vertreter während der "Russischer Historikerwoche," veranstaltet in Berlin 1928 von der deutschen Gesellschaft zum Studien Osteuropas (Berlin, 1929), pp. 88–97.

[67] M. Iavorskyi, "Die Ergebnisse der ukrainischen Geschichtsforschung in den Jahren 1917–1927," in Hoetzsch, ed., *Aus dem historischen Wissenschaft in der Sovet-Union,* pp. 98–105.

[68] "Pervaia vsesoiuznaia konferentsiia marksistsko-leninskikh nauchno-issledovatelskikh uchrezhdenii," *Vestnik Kommunisticheskoi Akademii,* 1928, no. 2 (26), pp. 272–273.

[69] *Trudy Pervoi Vsesoiuznoi konferentsii Istorikov-marksistov* (2nd ed., Moscow, 1930), vol. 1, pp. 426–435.

[70] M. I. Iavorskyi, "Suchasni techii sered ukrainskoi istoriohrafii," in *Kryza suchasnoi burzhuaznoi nauky ta marksyzm,* pp. 18–138.

The Campaign Against "Iavorskyism"

In 1928, Iavorskyi's former student Sukhyno-Khomenko published an article in *Litopys revoliutsii,* the newly Ukrainized organ of Ukrainian Istpart, arguing, as Iavorskyi did, that the Ukrainian revolution was not just a part of the Russian revolution, but a distinctive national event, the product of a distinct Ukrainian historical process.[71] This view was soon challenged when the December issue of the journal carried attempts at refutation. M. Harin took issue with a number of facts in Sukhyno-Khomenko's article. More importantly, I. Redkina challenged his basic argument. Redkina maintained that, although Ukraine had been a colony of Russia, it had not entered the Soviet Union as a separate country, but as an integral part of the old empire. In this analysis, a distinct Ukrainian revolutionary process did not exist; the Ukrainian revolution was merely a part of the Russian revolution.[72] This line of argumentation constituted a denial that Ukrainian history had any distinctive characteristics. The question was whether this was an aberration, a "spontaneous" instance of resistance from what had long been a preserve of Russian Old Bolsheviks, or the beginning of a reversal of the whole course of Soviet Ukraine's national political development. Events were soon to demonstrate that the latter was the case.

At the end of 1928, Pavel Gorin, a rising star in the firmament of the communist historical establishment in Moscow, attacked Iavorskyi at the All-Union Conference of Marxist Historians. Iavorskyi had just portrayed himself as valiantly struggling for the purity of Marxism in the midst of anti-Marxists and pseudo-Marxists surrounding Hrushevskyi. Gorin agreed on the generally hostile ideological character of Ukrainian scholarship, but launched a diatribe against a number of heresies in Iavorskyi's work, singling out Iavorskyi's attribution of a positive role to kulaks and other capitalist elements in the Ukrainian revolutionary process. Gorin charged that Iavorskyi had borrowed too freely from pre-revolutionary Ukrainian historiography. The attack on

---

[71] V. Sukhyno-Khomenko, "Z pryvodu osoblyvostei proletarskoi revoliutsii na Ukraini," *Litopys revoliutsii,* 1928, no. 4, pp. 79–119.

[72] M. Harin, "Iak ne treba pysaty istorii," *Litopys revoliutsii,* 1928, no. 6, pp. 321–334; I. Redkina, "Do pytannia pro osoblyvosty proletarskoi revoliutsii na Ukraini," *Litopys revoliutsii,* 1928, no. 6, 333–350. Sukhyno-Khomenko, like many other historians, made occasional forays into literary criticism and was also attacked in 1928 by the critic Koriak for allegedly being a nationalist. See V. Koriak, "Iak marksyst Sukhyno-Khomenko 'vziav' marksysta Lenina," *Krytyka,* 1928, no. 6, pp. 99–110. Khvylovyi also attacked him on the same grounds in *Prolitfront.*

Iavorskyi was far less a frontal assault on Ukrainian historiography than that which Sukhyno-Khomenko faced at the same time—Gorin maintained that he had no intention of denying any distinctive features of Ukrainian historical development—but it was still an attack on the emerging paragon of Ukrainian communist historiography.[73] Gorin's position was given the highest official sanction when *Pravda* published his brutal review of Iavorskyi's *History of Ukraine in Its Briefest Outline* on February 10.[74] Iavorskyi published a reply in *Prapor marksyzmu*, the UIML organ, and even a limited confession of error in the daily *Komunist*, but when *Istorik-marksist* (Marxist Historian, All-Union Society of Marxist Historians organ) published Gorin's rejoinder, it was clear that the campaign against Iavorskyi was backed by the Union historical establishment. Gorin charged that Iavorskyi had denied the hegemony of the proletariat in the Ukrainian revolution, slighted the RSDRP's role and exaggeraged that of Ukrainian nationalists, falsely considered the kulaks the hegemon of the revolution of 1905 in Ukraine, and overemphasized the progressive role of the cossacks in earlier centuries.[75]

To make the hopelessness of Iavorskyi's case even more apparent, the issue of *Istorik-marksist* which carried Gorin's letter also published a review of Iavorskyi's book by T. Skubitskii, who used Gorin's arguments as a starting point for an assault on Ukrainian historical scholarship as such. In what was to become an oft-quoted indictment of Iavorskyi and of Ukrainian historiography, the critic wrote:

> The basic error of Comrade Iavorskyi's book is that it portrays the history of Ukraine as a distinct process. Comrade Iavorskyi sees the nationality question as a factor dominant over the class struggle, eclipsing more genuine considerations.[76]

If portraying Ukrainian history as a distinct process is classified as an error, it also becomes erroneous to consider Ukrainians a distinct na-

---

[73] *Trudy Pervoi Vsesoiuznoi konferentsii Istorikov-marksistov*, vol. 1, pp. 448–452.

[74] P. Gorin, review: M. Iavorskyi, *Istoriia Ukrainy v styslomu narysi*, *Pravda*, February 10, 1929, p. 5.

[75] P. Gorin, "Pismo v redaktsiiu," *Istorik-marksist*, no. 12, 1929, pp. 334–335. Iavorskyi's defense, published in *Prapor marksyzmu*, 1929, no. 2, has not been available to me, but it was cited by Gorin who dismissed it was mere "literary polemics." Iavorskyi's limited confession of error has also been unavailable to me but is cited by Korduba, *La littérature historique soviétique-ukrainienne*, p. 166.

[76] T. Skubitskii, review: M. Iavorskyi, *Istoriia Ukrainy v styslomu narysi*, *Istorik-marksist*, no. 12, 1929, p. 285.

tionality requiring their own brand of socialism. The implications were ominous.

As a result of this frontal assault by their Russian counterparts, Ukrainian Marxist historians were in disarray. A Conference of Ukrainian Marxist Historians scheduled for may 1929 had to be postponed; in its place, a series of meetings were held in UIML to discuss Iavorskyi's errors.[77] Of the participants, only Sukhyno-Khomenko attempted to defend the idea that Ukraine had a history and a revolution that were not simply part of Russia's.[78] In September, even he recanted, by publishing in *Bilshovyk Ukrainy* a long critique of his former mentor's work. Taking Gorin's criticisms as his starting point, Sukhyno-Khomenko expressed complete agreement with Skubitskii and charged that Iavorskyi had actually adopted Hrushevskyi's theory of Ukrainian "bourgeoislessness" while ostensibly criticizing it.[79] After this statement, the erstwhile *doyen* of Ukrainian Marxist historians was left without a single defender.

Among Ukrainian Marxist historians, the attack on "Iavorskyism" was led by M. A. Rubach, originally on Istpart archivist who began his path to prominence by attending Pokrovskii's seminar in the Institute of Red Professors. While there he wrote a long and careful analysis of the "federalist tradition in Russian historiography," i.e., Ukrainian historiography, with Shchapov thrown in for good measure. Moderate in tone and painstakingly researched, Rubach's paper was published only in 1930, but even before then it was mined for quotations from the newly abominated traditional historians that could be placed next to similar statements by Iavorskyi.

Rubach's original paper surveyed the works of the most important Ukrainian historians since Kostomarov, was obviously based on extensive study of them, and praised them for helping to refute the old all-Russian view (*obshcherusskaia skhema*) of a single history for all the East-Slavic nations, although Rubach considered them incapable of creating a coherent system to replace the old one.[80] The research that

---

[77] John Barber, *Soviet Historians in Crisis, 1928–1932* (New York, 1981), p. 44.
[78] "Dyskusiia z pryvodu skhemy istorii Ukrainy M. Iavorskoho," *Litopys revoliutsii*, 1930, no. 2, pp. 264–324. See especially the remarks by Sukhyno-Khomenko, pp. 281–294.
[79] V. Sukhyno-Khomenko, "Na marksystskomu istorychnomu fronti," *Bilshovyk Ukrainy*, 1929, no. 17–18, pp. 42–55; no. 19, pp. 40–56.
[80] M. Rubach, "Federalisticheskie teorii v istorii Rossii," in M. N. Pokrovskii, ed., *Russkaia istoricheskaia literatura v klassovom osveshchenii* (Moscow, 1927, 1930), vol. 2, pp. 3–120, especially p. 107.

went into the paper—Pokrovskii was a product of Vinogradov's seminar and knew how to push a student to work hard—undoubtedly made Rubach the Ukrainian communist with the most extensive working knowledge of traditional Ukrainian historiography, thereby also making him best qualified to convict his colleagues of "borrowing from the arsenal of the class enemies" (as the oft-repeated phrase of the day went) because he knew exactly where to find the proper passages. When the campaign against Iavorskyi began, Rubach was the natural choice to lead it in Ukraine.

Rubach's official refutation of Iavorskyi was published in *Bilshovyk Ukrainy* in September 1929, under a title borrowed from one of his opponent's best known articles: "Revision of the Bolshevik *Skhema* of the Motive Forces and Character of the Revolution of 1905–1917 (Right Platform on the Historical Front)." Considerably more sophisticated than Gorin's blunderbuss approach, Rubach's conclusions were substantially the same. According to Rubach:

> The central erroneous idea of Comrade Iavorskyi's un-Bolshevik views is in putting foreward the Ukrainian bourgeoisie, the Ukrainian kulaks, as the independent and separate motive force of the democratic revolution in Ukraine from the turn of the century right up to 1917. This erroneous idea is connected with the idea that the task of creating an independent Ukrainian bourgeois state was the basic problem of the bourgeois-democratic revolution in Ukraine which, in the first instance, is connected with the interpretation of the nationality question as the basic question determining the character of the revolution, as a question of equal (and not subordinate) importance to the fundamental economic problem of social class, which the revolution faced.[81]

According to Rubach, Iavorskyi's errors began with an erroneous treatment of the transition from Narodnik ideology to Marxism, such that Iavorskyi overemphasized the influence of the Ukrainian movement in Galicia and understated the influence of Russia and Poland, saw Drahomanov and the Old Hromada as precursors of Marxism, and Podolynskyi and Ziber as full-fledged Marxists.[82] After having thus demolished Iavorskyi's laboriously constructed Ukrainian genealogy of Ukrainian communism, Rubach then attacked him for the view that the

---

[81] M. Rubach, "Reviziia bilshovytskoi skhemy rukhomykh syl i kharakhteru revoliutsii 1905–1917 (Prava pliatforma na istorychnomu fronti)," *Bilshovyk Ukrainy,* 1929, no. 17–18, p. 21.

[82] *Ibid.,* pp. 21–24.

old Ukrainian narodnik liberalism had represented the interests of the Ukrainian peasantry as a whole, and not just those of its bourgeois elements. Rubach considered this evidence that his opponent, while appearing to attack Hrushevskyi and the idea of Ukrainian "bourgeoislessness" was actually to a significant degree under Hrushevskyi's influence:

> M. I. Iavorskyi *ostensibly* struggles against Hrushevskyi and against the ideology of the Ukrainian nationalists. But in essence M. I. Iavorskyi in significant measure embraces the positions of Ukrainian nationalism. Comrade Iavorskyi disputes the thesis of the absence of classes in the Ukrainian nation (*bezkliasovist ukrainskoi natsii*), but where does he show the *class struggle* in this nation of classes? How can Iavorskyi claim that the liberal, the narodnik, the village bourgeoisie, the smallholding and landless strata of the peasantry all "had *the same* interest" in "urgently demanding the liquidation of gentry landholding"?
>
> Thus we note *in the fundamental question of the bourgeois-democratic* revolution—the liquidation of *gentry landholding—a discrepancy:* there was no struggle among the above social class groups of the Ukrainian people.
>
> It is not enough to acknowledge the existence of classes; one must still seek the *class struggle* in historical reality, and in Iavorskyi's presentation it is somewhere around the edges.
>
> For Iavorskyi the national cause, national capital, the self-determination of the Ukrainian nation fill the historical landscape. Actually, the class struggle literally drowns in these questions.
>
> Instead of conforming to historical reality by clearly showing the *dependence* of the bourgeois-democratic movement on the workers' movement, on the proletariat, instead of clearly showing and emphasizing the inability of the bourgeoisie, the *petite-bourgeoisie,* and the *petit-bourgeois* parties to lead the masses, instead of this Comrade Iavorskyi has painstakingly and at length, on many pages (this in a brief textbook), under the banner of "national capital" paints the force, revolutionary nature, and organization of the Ukrainian bourgeoisie, portraying the latter as a not altogether hopeless pretender to the hegemony of the revolutionary movement.[83]

At this moment when the final "liquidation of the kulaks as a class" was already drawing near, Iavorskyi was accused of falling prey to "kulak ideology" in distinguishing between the "feudal" moneylending kulaks, who did not derive their primary income from agriculture (this was the proper meaning of the term until Lenin extended—or rather

---

[83] *Ibid.*, pp. 25–26. Emphasis in the original.

abused—its meaning to include all relatively successful peasant farmers), and the farmer-bourgeois kulaks who did. Rubach had a point when he showed that the less prosperous peasants had a higher rate of participation in disturbances than did their more prosperous neighbors; however, rate of participation in revolutionary activity does not really address the question of class hegemony, since even in "bourgeois" revolutions, those with less to lose are more likely to revolt than those with more to lose. Rubach dubbed this a theory of "two kulakdoms" so as to echo the old denunciations of Ravich-Cherkasskii's "dual roots" idea, declared the idea to be anti-Bolshevik, and bolstered his argument with appropriate quotations from Lenin.[84]

What Rubach accomplished with these criticisms had little to do with improving anyone's understanding of the past. The idea that the Ukrainian national revolution depended on the Russian workers was patently absurd to anyone who had the least familiarity with the actual events of 1917. The point was to connect Ukrainian national consciousness, the national revolution, and the idea of a Ukrainian historical process as distinct from Russia's, with the class enemies, the Ukrainian kulaks, at a time when the regime had already begun to expropriate their property. The idea that Ukraine had a history was identified as kulak ideology, and the war against the kulak was a fact of everyday life which no one could ignore.

Soon the Party itself intervened. In December 1929, the Kharkiv *okruh* committee of the KP(b)U officially endorsed the campaign against Iavorskyism and portrayed UIML as a hotbed of nationalistic deviations. The resolution declared that Ukrainian nationalism had to be fought as well as Russian chauvinism, and demanded "consolidation," i.e., uniformity of views in strict conformity with the Party line.[85] At the beginning of 1930, even Skrypnyk, who must have been aware that the implications of the campaign boded ill for the policies he had long championed, published "The Errors and Corrections of Academician M. Iavorskyi" in the form of corrections to a manuscript which Iavorskyi had given him in his capacity as head of UIML. While Skrypnyk found

[84] *Ibid.*, pp. 26–41.
[85] "V oseredku Ukrainskoho Instytutu Marksyzma-Leninizma. Postanova Biura Kharkivskoho Okruzhkomu KP(b)U vid 5-XII-29 roku. Zatverdzhena TsK KP(b)U 7-XII-1929 roku," *Visti VUTsVK*, December 8, 1929, p. 3.

plenty of errors, his article was written less in the tone of a polemic than that of a teacher correcting a student.[86]

The vigor with which the Union historical establishment pursued the campaign against Iavorskyi bordered upon constituting a violation of Soviet Ukrainian sovereignty. On March 1, 1930, the History Institute of the Union Communist Academy passed a resolution declaring that

> M. Iavorskyi over the course of many years cloaked himself with the name of KP(b)U member and Marxist historian of Ukraine so as to carry on ideological wrecking and discredit Marxist historical science in Ukraine.

The resolution stated that this was a ''difficult fact,'' but that the KP(b)U and Ukrainian Marxist historians should spare no effort in fighting this ideological wrecking.[87] The KP(b)U leadership must have bristled at the spectacle of Russian historians telling them how to clean house ideologically. On April 6, Kosior, First KP(b)U Secretary, published a letter to the editor of *Pravda* in response to the Communist Academy's action, informing Iavorskyi's Russian critics that Ukrainian historians were doing quite well in criticizing Iavorskyi, who had meanwhile been purged from the Party.[88]

The campaign against Iavorskyi did not lag in Ukraine. The Eleventh KP(b)U Congress in June 1930 denounced ''the anti-Marxist theory of Iavorskyi'' in a resolution which equated it with the past national deviations of Shumskyi, Khvylovyi, and Volobuiev.[89] Andrii Khvylia, in an authoritative book on solving the nationality question in Ukraine, accused Iavorskyi of having fallen under the pernicious influence of Hrushevskyi and of portraying the Central Rada as a socialist barricade against the Hetman, and declared that fighting Iavorskyism was the main task of the historical front in Ukraine.[90] In June 1931, the KP(b)U denounced UIML for shielding deviations, most notably Iavorskyism, and ordered it broken up into autonomous research institutes.[91] Thus,

---

[86] Mykola Skrypnyk, ''Pomylky ta vypravlennia akademyka M. Iavorskoho,'' *Bilshovyk Ukrainy,* 1930, no. 2, pp. 12–26.

[87] ''Rezoliutsiia, vynesennaia kollegiei Instituta istorii Kommunisticheskoi akademii po delu M. Iavorskogo,'' *Izvestiia,* March 5, 1930, p. 4.

[88] S. Kosior, ''Pismo v redaktsii,'' *Pravda,* April 6, 1930, p. 6.

[89] *Kulturne budivnytstvo v Ukrainiskii RSR,* vol. 1, p. 490.

[90] Andrii Khvylia, *Do rozviazannia natsionalnoho pytannia na Ukraini* (Kharkiv, 1930), pp. 48–50.

[91] *Kulturne budivnytstvo v Ukrainiskii RSR,* vol. 1, pp. 540–544.

a major casualty of the Iavorskyi campaign was the institution that had been one of Skrypnyk's main outposts in the ideological realm. The campaign against Iavorskyi occurred at a time of far-reaching changes in Soviet scholarship, the transformation of the humanities and social sciences into outposts on "the ideological front." The murky world of the so-called Cultural Revolution will be explored more fully below; however, certain characteristics peculiar to history should be noted. It was a time of widespread arrests of scholars and of whole disciplines virtually wiped out. The campaign against Iavorskyism in history was part of a larger effort to replace national histories with a history of the USSR. At the same time as the campaign against Iavorskyi, Russian "bourgeois" historians, as well as non-Russian historians, were attacked.[92] In Soviet Ukraine, however, attacking traditional scholarship was secondary to the campaign against the developing communist cadres around Iavorskyi. One anti-Iavorskyi polemic written by T. Skubitskii and published in *Istorik-marksist* compared the views of Hrushevskyi and SVU defendant Osyp Hermaize with Iavorskyi's in an attempt to relegate the latter to the camp of the class enemy and to charge the Ukrainian cultural establishment with exercising insufficient ideological vigilance:

> Having compared the statements of Hrushevskyi, Hermaize, and Iavorskyi, it is not difficult to become convinced that M. Iavorskyi's works in general never had anything in common with Marxism and remained wholly under the influence of the school of Hrushevskyi. It must be mentioned, however, that despite their pseudo-Marxist character M. Iavorskyi's textbooks were for many years basic reading in our schools, widely published by Narkomos of Ukraine, and met with a sympathetic response from some of our Party organs as well. All this demands the serious attention of communist historians and necessitates the broad unmasking of Iavorskyism, a fact which Ukrainian Marxist historians have still not sufficiently realized. The growth of genuinely Marxist cadres of Ukrainian historians, who struck a serious blow against Iavorskyism in the May 1929 discussion, appears to hold the promise of success in rooting out of the arsenal of Marxist science the many positions defended by Iavor-

---

[92] See S. Piontkovskii, "Velikoderzhavnye tendentsii v istoriografii Rossii," *Istorik-marksist*, No. 17, 1930, pp. 21–26; S. Piontkovskii, "Velikorusskaia burzhuaznaia istoriografiia poslednego desiatiletiia," *Istorik-marksist*, no. 18–19, 1930, 157–176. M. Iugov, "Polozhenie i zadachi istoricheskogo fronta v Belorussii," *Istorik-marksist*, no. 17, 1930, pp. 42–50; L. Mamet, "Otrazheniia marksizma v burzhuaznom vostokovedenii," *Istorik-marksist*, no. 17, 1930, pp. 69–96.

skyi and his students (Sukhyno-Khomenko, Svidzinskyi, and others), positions which never had anything in common with Marxism.[93]

It was only after the anti-Iavorskyi campaign had run its course that
attention was turned to the most prominent of "bourgeois" Ukrainian
historians. In 1931, a nebulous underground organization, the Ukrainian National Center, was "discovered" by the GPU to include virtually
every one of Hrushevskyi's former political associates. Hrushevskyi
himself was transferred to Moscow, where he had to report regularly
to the GPU but was able to continue historical research. At the same
time, vicious attacks on his "bourgeois-kulak nationalist ideology" appeared in Soviet Ukraine. Ukrainian "bourgeois" historians who escaped
earlier purges were arrested by the end of 1933, and Hrushevskyi himself
was removed to Kislovodsk, where he died in 1934. Iavorskyi was
arrested in March 1933, charged with membership in an underground
military organization, and was last seen in the Solovky camps. Other
Ukrainian Marxist historians were branded as counterrevolutionaries
and, for the most part, were arrested within the next few years.[94] Meanwhile, the history of the peoples of the USSR gave way to a schema
indistinguishable from the old Russian nationalist presentation of the
nineteenth century, albeit dressed up with some superficial borrowing
from the vocabulary of Marxism. After the purge of M. N. Pokrovskii's followers in Russia in the mid-thirties, Soviet patriotism became
the watchword of historical scholarship; under this rubric Russian imperial history was rehabilitated, tsars and all.[95] Soviet Ukrainian historical

---

[93] T. Skubitskii, "Klassovaia borba v ukrainskoi istoricheskoi literature," *Istorik-
marksist*, no. 17, 1930, pp. 39–40.

[94] Hryhory Kostiuk, *Stalinist Rule in the Ukraine: A Study in the Decade of Mass
Terror (1929–39)*, pp. 51–53; Lowell Tillett, *The Great Friendship: Soviet Historians
on the Non-Russian Nationalities* (Chapel Hill, 1969), pp. 36–40; Robert S. Sullivant,
Soviet Politics and the Ukraine, 1917–1957, pp. 183–184, 197–198; Hryhory Kostiuk,
"Ostanni roky zhyttia Mykhaila Hrushevskoho (Za sovietskoiu presoiu i spohadamy
suchasnykiv) 1934–1954," *Ukrainskyi zbirnyk*, 1954, no. 1, pp. 83–84; *The Black Deeds
of the Kremlin* vol. 1, pp. 339–340. The most authoritative attack on Hrushevskyi's
historical ideas is A. Khvylia, "Burzhuazno-natsionalistychna trybuna," *Bilshovyk
Ukrainy*, 1931, no. 6, pp. 46–58; and most encyclopedic—M. A. Rubach, "Burzhuazno-
kurkulska natsionalistychna ideolohiia pid mashkaroiu demokratii 'trudovoho narodu',"
Chervonyi shliakh, 1932, no. 5–6, pp. 115–135, no. 7–8, pp. 118–126; no. 11–12, pp.
127–136.

[95] On Russian nationalism in Soviet historiography, see Tillett, *The Great Friendship;* Konstantin Shteppa, *Russian Historians and the Soviet State* (New Brunswick, N.J.,
1962), pp. 146–150, 169–177; Konstantin Shteppa, "The Lesser Evil Formula," in Cyril

studies simply ceased to exist, save for the odd book or article designed to justify some new policy or to declare eternal loyalty for Ukraine's "elder brother," the Russian nation. Only after Stalin's death could even a chastened and tightly controlled Ukrainian historical scholarship reappear. The name of Matvii Iavorskyi, the true father of Ukrainian Soviet scholarship, remains unmentioned and unmentionable in Soviet Ukraine.

*   *   *

The campaign against Iavorskyi was not only the beginning of the end of Ukrainian historical scholarship; by denying the distinctive nature of Ukrainian history, it removed a major part of the ideological justification for Ukraine's distinctive brand of socialism. This campaign was the prelude to an assault upon Skrypnyk, his policies, and his nation.

E. Black, ed., *Rewriting Russian History: Soviet Interpretations of Russia's Past* (New York, 1962), pp. 107–119; Erwin Oberländer, *Sowjetpatriotismus und Geschichte: Dokumentation* (Cologne, 1967).

CHAPTER EIGHT

The Suppression of Ukrainian National Communism

IN JANUARY 1932, when Skrypnyk turned sixty, the jubilee celebration in Kharkiv rivaled the observances of Stalin's fiftieth birthday in 1929. For several days Skrypnyk's picture was displayed everywhere; the official newspapers carried little else besides tributes and biographical sketches of Soviet Ukraine's unofficial but universally recognized leader. Eighteen months later Skrypnyk committed suicide in disgrace, and everything associated with him was in the process of being destroyed—not only a regime but also a nation.

If one may permitted to draw an analogy, Skrypnyk's Ukraine held a position in the Soviet Union rather like that of Gomulka's Poland in the Soviet bloc: it was that part of the whole which was most conscious of its distinctiveness, assertive of its prerogatives, and least willing to follow blindly after Moscow in arranging its internal affairs. While Skrypnyk eschewed all espressions of hostility against things Russian, he always upheld Ukraine's right to be different and to manage its own affairs in its own way. As time passed, it became increasingly evident that Ukraine would always be the main factor preventing the homogenization and centralization essential to the consolidation of a personal despotism like the one that Stalin was to build.

The question of what became of Ukraine's quest for its own national road to socialism is inseparable from the larger question of the nature of the transformation that the Soviet Union underwent in the decade between the Shakhty trial of 1928 and the culmination of the Great Purge in 1938. These were the years of the first two Five Year Plans, and the distinction between them consists primarily in the different targets of these two "socialist offensives." The first Five Year Plan was primarily an offensive by Stalin and his supporters against those forces of Soviet society that can be broadly described as civil society. Moshe Lewin summed it up quite well when he wrote:

This was a unique process of state-guided social transformation, for the state did much more than just 'guiding': it substituted itself for society, to become the sole initiator of action and controller of all important spheres of life. The process was thus transformed into one of 'state building,' with the whole social structure being, so to speak, sucked into the state mechanism, as if entirely assimilated by it.[1]

This process could have taken place on the basis of the "indigenized" national republics of the twenties. However, had this option been chosen, Stalin would have been only the first among equals, presiding over a collection of national totalitarian states to a greater or lesser extent dominated by his Russia, but nevertheless distinct from it. By the mid-1930s, however, he was clearly creating a unitary Russocentric totalitarian state in which all inhabitants would be equally and directly subject to his personal despotism, without the mediating levels of strong and nationally conscious republican governments. To achieve this goal, he had to crush the republics as relatively autonomous entities, usually by purging their elites of "national deviationists" and ending the indigenization programs. Thus, for example, the late 1920s saw campaigns against "Sultan-Galievism" in the Muslim republics. In Soviet Ukraine the Ukrainization policy had gone farther and deeper than elsewhere; consequently, the destruction of society necessary to obliterate what was euphemistically referred to as "bourgeois nationalism," had to go much further, to the point of an undeclared but nevertheless real war against the Ukrainian nation as such. As a result of these transformations, from a heterogeneous assemblage of Soviet republics, the USSR became an administratively centralized entity and adopted a distinctly Russian national character, relegating non-Russian nations to the status of the "little brothers" of the Great Russian "elder brother." In other words, the Soviet Russian Empire was born.[2]

The target of the second Five Year Plan was the elite which had been produced in the preceding period. By the end of the first plan, Stalin had removed his opponents from all positions which could have given them even a remote chance of ever seriously challenging his authority. They were replaced by supporters and clients, but even supporters must be heeded and can limit the action of those they support. Robert Con-

---

[1] M. Lewin, "Society, State, and Ideology During the First Five Year Plan," in Sheila Fitzpatrick, ed., *Cultural Revolution in Russia, 1928-1931* (Bloomington and London, 1978), p. 41.

[2] For a provocative study of the USSR as an imperial system, see Hélène Carrère d'Encausse, *Decline of An Empire: The Soviet Socialist Republics in Revolt* (New York, 1979).

quest has argued convincingly that it was, in fact, Stalin's supporters who delayed his introducing the death penalty for Bolsheviks and temporarily held back the purge.[3] The Great Terror was thus a transformation of the elite itself, the replacement of Stalin's supporters by clients who were dependent upon and terrified of him.

What Stalin wrought was neither a revolution nor a counterrevolution. There were strong elements of things unprecedented alongside equally marked themes of return to the Russian imperial past. These elements of revolution and tradition were molded together into something new and still not fully understood. Stalin created the first truly totalitarian dictatorship and recentralized what has survived as the last empire.

One cannot help but be struck by the extent to which Stalin seemed determined to undo what the revolution had accomplished. The liberal social legislation of the Bolshevik intelligentsia, crowned by easy divorce and abortion on demand, was replaced by laws designed to uphold traditional family-oriented values. The relative freedom of cultural experimentation and intellectual inquiry was subordinated to a censorship far more restrictive than of old. The workers, by and for whom the revolution had supposedly been made, suffered a drastic decline in living standards. The peasants, who had taken the land from the old propertied classes and thereby become the revolution's chief beneficiary, lost their farms and were herded into collective farms on which they were virtual serfs, effectively tied to the land by means of an internal passport system. Marxism-Leninism became an emasculated and ossified collection of phrases which covered a return to Russian nationalism under the official rubric of Soviet patriotism. The imperial Russian past was rehabilitated, tsars and all. All those changes that had given some credence to claims that non-Russians in the Soviet Union had at least to some extent achieved national liberation were completely eliminated.

Equally striking are those changes that were unprecedented. Not even the most repressive tsar ever thought of subordinating the esoterica of linguistics and genetics to politics; now even the most apolitical of artists, writers, scholars, and scientists were regimented into "fronts" in the class war, each with assigned tasks. Enemies, real and imagined, were placed on trial and made to confess to crimes so fantastic, so apocalyptic, that they sound almost like an indictment God might present against Satan. Even filial piety was sacrificed to the state, and young Pavlik Morozov, a child who informed on his parents, was held up as a hero

---

[3] Robert Conquest, *The Great Terror: Stalin's Purge of the Thirties* (New York, 1973).

and an example to the young. Every facet of human endeavor, from what historians should write about events of the preceding millenium, to the supplies and production of factories thousands of miles apart, was decided by Moscow.

Implicit in the very existence of the Five Year Plans was a strong element of centralization. As the late Vsevolod Holubnychy put it:

> The very system of the Five Year Plans, for which the distribution and marshalling of resources and productive programs were carried out from one center, Moscow, was a new and unprecedented integrating factor, organizational superstructure, which transformed the economy of the USSR into a single unified whole.[4]

To be sure, the change from a state of affairs where the Ukrainian economy was in Ukrainian hands, such that Kharkiv would try to take over the day-to-day operations of even Union-owned industries, to one where Moscow made all the important economic decisions, is a major transformation. Nationality was far more a matter of politics and culture than it was of economics, however. Our attention must turn now to the so-called Cultural Revolution, where the offensive against Ukrainian nationhood really began.

The Suppression of Ukrainian National Culture

The so-called Cultural Revolution of 1928–1932 was an integral part of the totalitarianization of the Soviet Union. It contained elements of revolution from below and took the form of "an aggressive movement of the young, proletarian, and communist against the cultural establishment."[5] The fact remains, however, that the unleashing of these self-proclaimed representatives of proletarian thought and culture was an act of policy carried out at the highest levels of political authority, a policy orchestrated by show trials and widespread repression. Even more important from the standpoint of Soviet Ukraine, the self-proclaimed proletarianizers looked to Moscow for leadership and inspiration, whether to Averbach and the "On Guardists" in literature, or to the historians around *Istorik-Marksist*. Some of the most prominent spokesmen of Ukrainian communist thought, the historian Matvii Iavorskyi and the philosopher Volodymyr Iurynets, were victimized by the

---

[4] Vsevolod Holubnychy, *Try lektsii pro ekonomyku Ukrainy* (Munich and New York, 1969), p. 11.

[5] Sheila Fitzpatrick, "Cultural Revolution in Russia, 1928–1932," *Journal of Contemporary History*, vol. 9, 1974, no. 1, p. 34.

Cultural Revolution, along with "bourgeois" thinkers like Mykhailo Hrushevskyi and Serhii Iefremov. In Ukraine, it was not just the "bourgeois" national intelligentsia that suffered, but also the budding "proletarian" intellectuals of Ukrainian nationality. The result of the Cultural Revolution was thus twofold. On the one hand, the intelligentsia was regimented to the extent that it ceased to exist as an autonomous component of civil society. On the other hand, Ukrainian intellectual life was strictly subordinated to Moscow.

The feeling had always existed in the more militant wing of the Party and the security organs that the concessions forced on the regime during the NEP were only a temporary aberration, and that the day would come when the accounts left unsettled would at last be called in. In June 1925, the very height of the regime's "liberalism," the following document was circulated secretly to all raion GPU residents in the Lubnyi okruh of Ukraine:

> It has been established that counterrevolutionary organizations and groupings are well aware of the fact that at the present moment the GPU is forced to a certain, so to speak, passivity, called for by the New Economic Policy and also by governmental considerations of a higher order.
>
> We all know that this situation is temporary. And therefore in connection with this the GPU must not let slip by this favorable moment for unmasking our enemies, in order to deal them a crushing blow when the time comes. It is namely for this reason that we remind raion residents of the need for deep knowledge and correct understanding of the current moment which puts in our hands such unique opportunites to expose counterrevolutionaries among all strata and layers of the population. We particularly emphasize that such a moment may never again be repeated in our history. We are certain that illusions of our enemies, who permit themselves to think the Soviet regime might capitulate, will soon disappear, and the happy smiles on their faces will change to a grimace of horror and wild animal fear in the face of the all-conquering strategy of communism.[6]

The same secret police officials who circulated this memorandum also ordered special vigilance towards followers of the "class enemy" Mykhailo Hrushevskyi and the Ukrainian Autocephalous Orthodox Church.[7] Perhaps Marxist doctrine, with its emphasis on class struggle, encouraged this paranoia about class enemies. During the NEP the

---

[6] P. S. Lykho, "Sovetskaia vlast na mestakh," *Ukrainskyi zbirnyk,* no. 8, p. 146.

[7] *Ibid.,* pp. 142, 147.

paranoia was kept in check; in 1928 the GPU was unleashed with the "exposure" of saboteurs in the Shakhty mines, and with it arose self-proclaimed guardians of class purity who carried out a pogrom of the intelligentsia known at the time as the Cultural Revolution.

The Cultural Revolution began in conjunction with Stalin's offensive against Bukharin and the "Right deviation." It was closely connected with Stalin's decision to collectivize agriculture, and his immediate political purpose seems to have been to discredit his rivals, who were on record as favoring both the peasants and the non-communist specialists.[8] Accusing those associated with one's opponents of treason and sabotage has always been a convenient way to discredit them, and Bukharin was known as a defender and associate of "bourgeois" intellectuals and specialists. Therefore, the cultural revolution began with an attempt to discredit the "bourgeois specialists."

The announcement in March 1928 that a conspiracy of fifty-five mining engineers had been uncovered in the Shakhty region of the Donbas was used to throw suspicion on all "bourgeois specialists."[9] Before the end of March, well over a month before the trial began, Emeliian Iaroslavskii, one of Stalin's closest associates, was in the Donbas whipping up the workers' resentment against "spetsy" by warning that such specialists might well be serving foreign enemies, and by calling on the workers to verify all they did. According to Iaroslavskii,

> The Shakhty affair is the inevitable continuation of that struggle which the workers carried on for decades against the capitalists and landlords and which ended in victory in October of 'seventeen. But this struggle is still not over. After the Civil War, when it finally became clear that we would not be defeated by armed force, the capitalists began organizing conspiracies from below.[10]

Later, Stalin declared that Shakhtyites were ensconced in every branch of industry and that their "wrecking" was one of the most dangerous

---

[8] Sheila Fitzpatrick, "Cultural Revolution," pp. 40–41. See also Sheila Fitzpatrick, "Culture and Politics Under Stalin: A Reappraisal," *Slavic Review*, vol. 35, 1976, no. 2, pp. 211–231.

[9] Good treatments of the Shakhty trial, the later Industrial Party trial, and their effect on the specialists may be found in Kendall E. Bailes, *Technology and Society under Lenin and Stalin: Origins of the Soviet Technical Intelligentsia, 1917–1941* (Princeton, 1978), 69–140; E. H. Carr and R. W. Davies, *Foundations of a Planned Economy, 1926–1929*, vol. 1, pp. 621–627.

[10] "Tov. Iaroslavskyi pro ekonomichnu kontr-revoliutsiiu v Shakhtynskomu raioni," *Visty VUTsVK*, March 23, 1928, p. 2.

manifestations of the counterrevolution. The charges against the alleged conspirators included organizing mine accidents, wrecking, maintaining contact with former mineowners, receiving money and instructions from foreign enterprises and governments, and importing unnecessary equipment.[11] As political theater, the Shakhty trial was not nearly as successful as the regime had hoped. According to Louis Fischer, who witnessed the proceedings as a foreign journalist, Defendant Rabinovich, a man past seventy, all but worsted the prosecutor. At one point, one of the defendants confessed to having bribed the old man, who replied by going over to him, looking him in the eye and saying, "Why do you lie, eh? Who told you to lie?" The prosecutor looked crestfallen.[12] Yet, despite such awkward moments, the Shakhty trial served the regime adequately as the first of the great show-trials which orchestrated the transformation of Soviet society from 1928 to 1938.

The most important single event in the Party's offensive against the intelligentsia was undoubtedly the subordination of the Academy of Sciences of the USSR, the very pinnacle of the non-Party intellectual establishment. The Party tried to seize control of the Academy by issuing new regulations that doubled its membership, and by lobbying hard for the inclusion of its own candidates. When the Academy refused to elect a number of the Party's nominees, a purge of academicians was begun in 1929, and many of its most prestigious members were arrested. Those who remained gave in.[13]

In Ukraine, the All-Ukrainian Academy of Sciences (VUAN) suffered a similar assault, culminating in the show-trial of the Union for the Liberation of Ukraine, an imaginary conspiracy designed to brand some of the country's most respected scholars as terrorists. If anything, VUAN was more prestigious among Ukrainians than the Soviet Academy of Sciences among Russians, because VUAN contained a number of figures who were as prominent for their participation in the national liberation struggle as for their scholarship. The regime even tried to claim credit for establishing the Academy by falsifying the date on which it was founded, and the academicians seem to have accepted this manipulation since they acquired a certain official legitimacy when considered

[11] Roy A. Medvedev, *Let History Judge: The Origins and Consequences of Stalinism* (New York, 1972), pp. 111–113.

[12] Louis Fischer in Richard Crossman, ed., *The God That Failed* (New York, Toronto, and London, 1965), pp. 189–190.

[13] Loren R. Graham, *The Soviet Academy of Sciences and the Communist Party, 1927–1932* (Princeton, 1967), pp. 89–130.

a "Soviet" institution.[14] Contemporary press reports give ample testimony to VUAN's prestige among the people. For example, the official Soviet Ukrainian state organ reported that when VUAN president D. K. Zabolotnyi died in December 1929, "tens of thousands of workers passed by the coffin."[15]

The first step toward "Sovietizing" VUAN was taken in 1927, when the Academy was required to submit its membership to Narkomos for confirmation.[16] An election campaign much like that which took place in Russia resulted in VUAN electing thirty-four new members in June 1929, including such Party luminaries as Skrypnyk and Zatonskyi as well as Party intellectuals like Iavorskyi and Iurynets.[17] The campaign preceding the VUAN election involved immense outside pressure. After the election, this pressure was admitted even by the official press.[18]

Serhii Iefremov, an academician in the history of literature and former Ukrainian Socialist Federalist Party leader, criticized VUAN's leadership for its tendency to do what the regime required of it. At the end of 1928 the presidium of VUAN condemned him and removed him from

---

[14] Despite the fact that the Ukrainian Academy of Sciences was founded in 1918 under the Hetmanate, all Soviet sources given the date 1919 and have done so with only a few exceptions since the mid-1920s. As early as 1924, a five year jubilee was celebrated according to the false date. "Piat rokiv VUAN," *Literature, Nauka, Mystetstvo,* March 16, 1924, p. 1. At the time of the SVU trial, however, one of the ways the regime tried to discredit VUAN was by recalling that it had in fact been founded under the Hetmanate in 1918 and was therefore a product of the "class enemies." See "Spilka Vyzvolennia Ukrainy (Z vynuvalnoho vysnovku v spravi 'SVU')," *Visti VUTsVK,* March 8, 1930, p. 2. It is interesting to note that as late as 1923, accounts in the Soviet press freely acknowledged that VUAN had been founded in 1918. See, for example, Prof. O. Ianata, "Do orhanizovanoho rozvytku nauky na Ukraini," *Chervonyi shliakh,* 1923, no. 2, p. 177.

[15] "Perevezennia ostankiv prezydenta VUAN, akad. D. K. Zabolotnoho do mistsia pokhoronu," *Visti VUTsVK,* December 19, 1929, p. 2.

[16] N. Polonska-Vasylenko, *Ukrainska Akademiia Nauk (Narys istorii)* (Munich, 1955, 1958), vol. 1, p. 53.

[17] "Vybory do Vseukrainskoi Akademii Nauk," *Nauka i Osvita (Visti* supplement), June 30, 1929, p. 1.

[18] Two weeks after the election a newspaper article was published which portrayed the basic problem of VUAN as one of how to involve the "cadres of highly qualified scholars who are rooted in byegone social formations liquidated by the revolution" in socialist construction. VUAN was pictured as a den of hostility to the proletariat during the Civil War which had been transformed by the proletariat's having mastered it, a task accomplished by "creating an atmosphere" in which the influence of "social opinion" would be felt. Iu. Ozerskyi, "Iak prokhodyly vybory do VUAN," *Visti VUTsVK,* July 14, 1929, p. 3; July 17, 1929, p. 3. Quotations are from the first installment.

the organization and administration of the Academy.[19] He was also censured by the Kharkiv section of scientific workers.[20] As late as mid-February 1929, however, Iefremov was dismissed as a representative of "a certain insubstantial portion of scientific workers" who were hostile to the proletariat.[21]

In November 1929 the GPU "discovered" a conspiracy called the Union for the Liberation of Ukraine and the Kuban and arrested a number of scholars.[22] On December 22, the Ukrainian Autocephalous Orthodox Church, which had split off from Russian Orthodoxy during the revolution, was tied in with the alleged conspiracy, and was forced to proclaim its own liquidation in January 1930. The resolutions forced upon the so-called liquidation Sobor were particularly noteworthy in that they repudiated not only the principles which had guided the church but also implicitly repudiated the principles of Ukraine's national and political distinctiveness: autocephaly was denounced as "a symbol of Petliurite independence," clerical Ukrainization as "a means of inciting national animosity," and conciliarism as a "demigogical means of political influence."[23] To extend the condemnation of such ecclesiastical ideas to the secular sphere required little imagination.

Early in 1930 the name of the conspiracy was shortened to the Union for the Liberation of Ukraine (SVU) which had been "uncovered and liquidated by the GPU in the latter half of 1929." Supposedly led by Iefremov, former head of the VUAN Pedagogical Section Volodymyr Durdukivskyi, and former Autocephalous Church leader Volodymyr Chekhivskyi, the SVU was accused of plotting to overthrow Soviet power and to restore capitalism in Ukraine by means of an armed uprising supported by foreign capitalist states. The SVU was also accused of trying

---

[19] "Postanova prezydii VUAN u spravi akad. S. O. Iefremova," *Visti VUTsVK,* January 1, 1929, p. 1.

[20] "Kharkivski naukovi robitnyky skhvaliuiut postanova VUAN v spravi Iefremova," *Visti VUTsVK,* January 31, 1929, p. 2.

[21] "Vseukrainskyi zizd naukovykh robitnykiv, *Visti VUTsVK,* February 15, 1929, p. 1 (lead editorial).

[22] Hryhory Kostiuk, "M. Zerov, P. Fylypovych, M. Drai-Khmara," *Ukrainska literaturna hazeta,* vol. 6, 1960, no. 1, p. 8.

[23] Bohdan R. Bociurkiw, "Ukrainization Movements Within the Russian Orthodox Church and the Ukrainian Autocephalous Orthodox Church," *Harvard Ukrainian Studies,* vol. 3–4, 1979–1980, part 1, p. 111. On the formation and early history of the Autocephalous Church, see Bohdan R. Bociurkiw, "The Church and the Ukrainian Revolution," in Taras Hunczak, ed., *The Ukraine, 1917–1921: A Study in Revolution,* pp. 220–246.

to organize the kulaks and bourgeoisie for the continuation of the Ukrainian nationalist counterrevolution of the Civil War period. According to the published indictment, Iefremov and his associates were directed by the emigre Chykalenko, who had ordered Iefremov to organize the SVU in 1926. The conspiracy had originally hoped to reestablish the Ukrainian Peoples Republic as a bourgeois democracy, but later opted for a fascist dictatorship. It also planned to undo the agrarian reforms instituted during the revolution and to restore the property rights of the former landlords. The seven principal conspirators held their meetings in Iefremov's VUAN offices and organized at least fifteen cells of five members each (*piatyrky*). After the alleged conspirator Cherniakhivskyi met with émigré leaders abroad, attempts were made to organize a united front of non-Russian nationalities against the Soviet state. Cells were organized in several VUAN institutes and in the hierarchy of the Ukrainian Autocephalous Church. Iefremov even headed a shadow government.[24]

According to the indictment, the SVU's *raison d'être* was to plan an armed revolt that would be coordinated with foreign powers. The conspiracy allegedly had armed men at its command at the time of its discovery. The SVU depended upon former bandits, the clergy of the Autocephalous Church, and the "kulak intelligentsia" for its cadres in the villages. Cells were organized in the high schools to bring young people up in an anti-Soviet frame of mind, as well as to recruit young peasants who would fight or serve as propagandists. A rising was supposedly planned for 1930–31, that would capitalize on kulak dissatisfaction with Soviet agricultural policies. The SVU leadership also approved of terror, advocated the killing of communists on a mass scale, and plotted to murder Party leaders, including Stalin, Voroshilov, Budennyi, and Skrypnyk.[25]

The indictment accused the hierarchy of the Ukrainian Autocephalous Church of being involved with the SVU since the conspiracy began in 1926. The clergy was portrayed as Petliurist, and the church was accused of openly demonstrating its solidarity with the SVU on a number of occasions. Rural cooperatives were allegedly infiltrated by the conspiracy, thereby causing a struggle between "Petliurist kulak"

---

[24] "Spilka Vyzvolennia Ukrainy (Z vynuvalnoho vysnovku v spravi 'SVU')," *Visti VUTsVK*, February 26, 1930, pp. 2–3; February 27, 1930, pp. 2–3.

[25] "Spilka Vyzvolennia Ukrainy (Z vynuvalnoho vysnovku...)," *Visti VUTsVK*, February 28, 1930, pp. 2–3; March 1, 1930, pp. 2–3.

cooperatives and those of the toilers for control of the cooperative movement, with the SVU hoping to get control of the cooperative apparatus
in order to help organize an uprising. The medical section of VUAN,
already active under Petliura, was accused of organizing itself as a conspiratorial force even before the alleged formation of the SVU, which
in turn received it and the Institute of Scientific Language in 1926. The
VUAN Scientific Pedagogical Society had supposedly joined the conspiracy at the very time of SVU's formation in 1925. VUAN as a whole
was portrayed as reactionary from the start, "a counterrevolutionary
island in a proletarian sea," around which anti-Soviet nationalist con-
spiracies had long been organized. SVU had allegedly tried to get complete control of VUAN and actually succeeded in controlling a number
of its sections. The SVU had members on the editorials boards of leading
journals, among the so-called fellow-traveller writers, and published
works of an anti-Soviet nature in the leading literary journals of the day,
Chervonyi shliakh and *Zhyttia i revoliutsiia.* It even had a youth organization, the Union of Ukrainian Youth (SUM), and was able to recruit
members from the old rural Prosvita intelligentsia and former bandits.[26]

The charges made in the official indictment make it apparent that the
SVU must have been quite a formidable organization, since it had supposedly controlled a large part of Soviet Ukrainian cultural life and
recruited on a massive scale in high schools and villages. It is absolutely incredible that it would have taken the GPU years to have
uncovered such an omnipresent movement. According to official Soviet
historiography, the SVU existed and was a dangerous counterrevolutionary organization. Those who were convicted for their alleged participation have never been rehabilitated. Works published in the West
even accept its existence.[27] The fact remains, however, that the conspiracy, as it was portrayed in the official indictment, could not have
existed undetected for years in the Soviet Union.[28] Even in the 1920s,
the *seksot* system of police spies was in place, and *seksoty* infiltrated

---

[26] "Spilka Vyzvolennia Ukrainy," *Visti VUTsVK,* March 2, 1930, p. 2; March 4,
1930, pp. 2–3; March 5, 1930, pp. 2–3; March 6, 1930, pp. 2–3; March 7, 1930, pp.
2–3; March 8, 1930, pp. 2–3; March 9, 1930, pp. 2–3.

[27] See, for example, V. Plushch, "The Union for the Liberation of the Ukraine,"
Ukrainian Review, no. 3, 1956, pp. 13–30. It was long taken as an article of faith among
a certain segment of the Ukrainian diaspora that the SVU did in fact exist, perhaps on
the grounds that if it did not, it should have.

[28] The best work on the SVU, which exposes the entire affair as a falsification is Gelii
Snigirëv, "Mama moia, Mama...," *Kontinent,* no. 11, pp. 11–53; no. 12, pp. 163–209;
no. 13, pp. 173–203; no. 14, pp. 152–192; no. 15, pp. 90–122 (1977–1978).

cultural organizations and even the villages.[29] No conspiracy, no plot existed; the trial was only an elaborate sham. Why, then, did it take place?

Of the forty-five defendants, almost half were Autocephalous priests or the sons of priests, the latter being common among Ukrainian intellectuals. About half had belonged to one of the Ukrainian socialist parties during the revolution; the rest seem to have been apolitical. Some had been ministers in various Ukrainian national governments and had returned from abroad to take advantage of the opportunities for cultural work which Soviet Ukraine offered after 1923. Among the accused were two historians: Osyp Hermaize, whose work on the Ukrainian socialist movement is still consulted by scholars, and Mykhailo Slabchenko, one of Ukraine's leading economic historians. Vsevolod Hantsov, Hryhorii Holoskevych, and Hryhorii Kholodnyi had all played prominent roles in standardizing the Ukrainian language. Oleksander Cherniakhivskyi, Arkadii Barbar, and Volodymyr Udovenko were prominent medical researchers. Fourteen of the defendants were either academicians or research associates at VUAN. A number of others were teachers or professors, activists in the rural cooperative movement, or priests in the Ukrainian Autocephalous Church.[30] In short, the SVU defendants represented the flower of the Ukrainian national intelligentsia, which as a group was branded counterrevolutionaries and "wreckers".

There would be other such trials. Hryhory Kostiuk lists fifteen alleged counterrevolutionary organizations "uncovered" by the secret police between 1930 and 1938.[31] The most prominent members of the intelligentsia would be liquidated.[32] The search for "class enemies" reached into every corner of the country; each show trial was preceded by a wave of arrests, and was followed by an even larger wave of arrests.[33] The Ukrainian cultural revival would be obliterated.

The SVU trial was in part a response to rural resistance to the collectivization of agriculture in Ukraine, a way of preventing nation-wide

---

[29] Plushch himself admitted that, "The widespread Soviet secret police apparatus of secret collaborators (*seksoty*) excluded any possibility of a definite form of underground activity." Plushch, "The Union for the Liberation of the Ukraine," p. 17.

[30] "Sprava 'Spilky Vyzvolennia Ukrainy'," *Visti VUTsVK*, March 11, 1930, p. 3.

[31] Kostiuk, *Stalinist Rule in the Ukraine*, pp. 85–86.

[32] See Viktor Petrov, *Ukrainski kulturni diiachi URSR, 1920–1940: Zhertvy bilshovytskoho teroru* (New York, 1959).

[33] Alexander Weissberg, *The Accused* (New York, 1951), p. 4; Vasyl I. Hryshko, *Moskva slozam ne viryt: Trahediia Ukrainy 1933 roku z perspektyvy 30 richchia (1933–1963)* (New York, 1963), p. 22.

organization of such resistance by cowing the sole group capable of leading it, the national intelligentsia. The trial was also a blow aimed at Skrypnyk, just as the Shakhty affair had been directed against Bukharin. Skrypnyk had been intimately involved in the standardization of the language with those who were now "exposed" as wreckers, but he could hardly have defended the Ukrainian Autocephalous Church or academicians who had been prominent in the struggle against the Bolsheviks before 1921. The targets were thus well chosen: national institutions that were by their nature suspicious to the Bolsheviks, institutions that it would have been impossible for Skrypnyk to even think of defending, but with which Skrypnyk had on occasion cooperated in ways that could now be viewed as counterrevolutionary. The show trial was thus a political master stroke, implicitly attacking Skrypnyk by discrediting actions with which he had been associated in the past, doing so in such a way that Skrypnyk himself had to go along with it. According to information published by Anton Antonov-Ovseenko, possibly apocryphal, Skrypnyk was Stalin's real target from the start, because in January 1930 Stalin called Ukrainian GPU chief Vsevolod Balytskyi into his office, told him that he should "look into" VUAN's "counterrevolutionary deal with Pilsudski" and that Skrypnyk was probably involved.[34]

Skrypnyk was able to defend himself from fallout from the SVU affair, even in the field of linguistics. This was only one of the fields alleged to have fallen under SVU influence, but the effect of the trial on Ukrainian linguistics was immediate and obvious. At the trial, Iefremov testified that linguistic purism had been one of the forms SVU wrecking had taken. As a result, the linguistics institutes of VUAN were closed down, and a number of prominent scholars were arrested.[35] Even more far-reaching than the catastrophe which befell individual linguists was the ultimate implication for the language itself. The allegation (and confessions) of "wrecking" in linguistics had linked linguistic purism with treason and counterrevolution, and Skrypnyk had both participated in linguistic discussions and gone on record in favor of purism.

Skrypnyk was able to contain the damage wrought by the SVU trial by condemning those accused of wrecking, while ignoring the substance

---

[34] Anton Antonov-Ovseenko, *The Time of Stalin: Portrait of a Tyranny* (New York, 1981), p. 109.

[35] "Sprava 'Spilka Vyzvolennia Ukrainy'," *Visti VUTsVK*, March 14, 1930, p. 4; Wexler, *Purism and Language*, p. 157.

of what the wreckers were accused of having done. He attempted to deal with the matter during the trial in a lecture on wrecking in culture:

> Our forces are growing, developing, making themselves manifest, and producing, but they are still insufficient and in some spheres completely absent as, for example, in linguistics. We need linguistics because for us language is a tool for a job that as to be done: raise the masses to culture and develop Ukrainian culture so that the new hundreds of thousands of Ukrainian workers coming from our villages to the factories can talk to our new engineering professionals and *vice versa*. A substantial number of our old linguists are now sitting in the camp of the SVU defendants because it has become evident that while they worked on the problems of terminology they were also carrying out their wrecking line. This situation regarding the new forces in certain fields of culture has hitherto made it possible for representatives of the old Ukrainian culture to occupy select positions both in VUAN and in the terminological commissions of the Institute of Scientific Language. This was the reason why Iefremov, Nikovskyi, and their ilk wrote introductions to editions of the Ukrainian classics which we need, and, taking advantage of it, they made statements with which the old intelligentsia expressed solidarity to the effect that they were *par excellence* the leading part of the Ukrainian intelligentsia (*holovna chilna ukrainska intelihentsiia*).[36]

What he said here is far less important than what he did not say. He said nothing about the substance of the alleged wrecking in linguistics, attempting to portray it merely as the intelligentsia of the pre-revolutionary generation disparaging the new "proletarian" intelligentsia trained after the revolution. He did not say what, if any, effects the supposed wrecking had on the Ukrainian language. What Skrypnyk said was intended to be vague and confusing.

Skrypnyk specifically addressed the issue of "Marxist-Leninist" linguistics in a lecture given in UIML in May 1931. On the surface his remarks constituted a strident call for ideological purity, the type that had by then become ubiquitous: insistence that a correct and precise Party line in linguistics was necessary. At the same time, his only criticism of linguistic purism was implied and indirect: he noted that "Arabization" and scouring old religious texts for new words in the Muslim republics had gone too far and shown itself to be the work of the adherents of the discredited Tatar national communist, Sultan-Galiev. He added that analogous phenomena existed in Belorussia and Ukraine,

---

[36] Mykola Skrypnyk, "Kontr-revoliutsiine shkidnytstvo na kulturnomu fronti," *Chervonyi shliakh*, 1930, no. 4, pp. 141–142.

but declined to elaborate on them. He defended the idea that a nation's language had to reflect the particular character of that nation. Lenin's dictum that culture should be national in form and socialist in content did not mean that a national language should be given an "international" content. The temptation to adopt international terms wholesale had to be resisted, he argued, referring to his earlier statements on the Karelian question, where he had noted that terminology must reflect a language's particular character. Besides, he added, so-called international terms were really Europeanisms and could not serve as the basis for a future international language, because such a language would have to draw on non-European sources as well as European ones. Lastly, he expressed mild disagreement—couched in terms emphasizing points of agreement—which Kaganovich, the former KP(b)U head who had come from Moscow and made a statement to the effect that the syntax of the Ukrainian language should be brought closer to Russian.[37]

Skrypnyk succeeded in holding back the attack on linguistic purism in Soviet Ukraine until his fall in 1933. He was still largely able to set the Party line in Ukrainian cultural affairs, and the linguists had little choice but to follow his lead. The new Party line in linguistics consisted mainly in praising the Japhetic theory of language advocated by N. Ia. Marr; those who dissented were attacked as class enemies (until 1952, when Marr's theory was itself declared to be counterrevolutionary).[38] Linguistic purism as such remained acceptable. A discussion article, published in 1932 in a leading Ukrainian journal of literary criticism, attacked certain associates of the Ukrainian Soviet Encyclopedia project who had suggested reversing some of the more controversial provisions of the Skrypnyk orthography such as the use of the soft L and a special letter, Г, to designate the hard G sound in foreign words.[39] In 1932, such suggestions were denounced as bourgeois,

---

[37] Mykola Skrypnyk, "Do pytannia borotby za markso-leninske movoznavstvo," *Chervonyi shliakh,* 1932, no. 1–2, pp. 88–92. The reference to linguistic national deviations in the Muslim republics was made because of a massive purge then going on in various cultural, scientific, artistic, and literary institutions in the Volga-Ural region. On this see Alexandre A. Bennigson and S. Enders Wimbush, *Muslim National Communism in the Soviet Union,* p. 91. On the Karelian question, see chapter four above.

[38] B. Iatsymirskyi, "Za marksystske ozbroiennia movoznavchykh kadriv," *Chervonyi shliakh,* 1931, no. 11–12, pp. 87–92, attacked those who favored the Indo-European theory over the Japhetic and emphasized that the old linguists had to be replaced by "proletarian" Marxist cadres.

[39] Volodymyr Boiko, "URE i zavdannia marksystskoho movoznavstva," *Za markso-leninsku krytyku,* 1932, no. 7–8, pp.73–82.

but in 1933, the use of the soft L and the letter Г were equated with counterrevolution.

When Pavel Postyshev, a former secretary of the Kharkiv Party committee who was sent back as KP(b)U Second Secretary and *de facto* dictator of Soviet Ukraine in 1933, denounced Skrypnyk for nationalistic deviations, one of Skrypnyk's alleged sins was that he had aided the "nationalistic wreckers" in linguistics by advocating the use of the letter Г.[40] Immediately thereafter, Andrii Khvylia, the former Borotbist who was rumored to have risen to prominence by betraying Shumskyi's plans to Kaganovich in 1926, attacked those who sought to preserve as many distinctions as possible between Ukrainian and Russian as Petliurists and wreckers aided by Skrypnyk. He condemned the 1928 orthography and Skrypnyk's role in its adoption. He even disinterred Skrypnyk's old proposal to add S and Z to the alphabet, charging that "Comrade Skrypnyk could not have failed to know that he had entered upon the path of isolating the Ukrainian language from Russian and bringing it closer to Polish." Khvylia announced that the Central Committee and the Commissariat of Education, no longer under Skrypnyk, were fighting "to purge the Ukrainian orthography of the counterrevolutionary rubbish put in it," and pledged to have a new orthography off the press in a month's time. The meeting which Khvylia addressed obligingly passed a resolution denouncing the 1928 orthography and Skrypnyk for having countenanced nationalistic errors in the Ukrainian language.[41] Soon the periodical press was carrying articles by Khvylia denouncing Skrypnyk's opposition to the adoption of international terms and his role in the adoption of the 1928 orthography as linguistic separatism "in a kulak-Petliurist spirit" and the kind of wrecking exposed as the SVU trial.[42] Despite the temporary rehabilitation of Skrypnyk after Stalin's death (he has been "derehabilitated" since 1972), linguistic purism in Soviet Ukraine, the 1928 orthography, and the whole legacy of Ukrainian linguistics in the 1920s have remained castigated as nationalistic.[43]

---

[40] "Mobilizuiemo masy na svoiechasnu postavku zerna derzhavi. Promova t. P. P. Postysheva na plenumi TsK KP(b)U 10–VI 1933," *Visti VUTsVK*, June 22, 1933, pp. 1–2.

[41] "Stan na movnomu fronti. Dopovid tov. Khvyli veleliudni zbory v budynku pratsivnykiv osvity," *Visti VUTsVK*, June 30, 1933, p. 3. Excerpts from the resolution appear beside Khvylia's remarks.

[42] A. Khvylia, "Vykorinyty, znyshchyty natsionalistychne korinnia na movnomu fronti," *Bilshovyk Ukrainy*, 1933, no. 7–8, pp. 42–56; A. Khvylia, "Na borotbu z natsionalizmom na movnomu fronti," *Za markso-leninsku krytyku*, 1933, no. 7, pp. 3–26.

[43] A post-Stalinist textbook on the history of the Ukrainian literary language declared

Khvylia's specific arguments consisted mainly of charges that linguistic purism and anything tending to make the Ukrainian language different from Russian were somehow counterrevolutionary.[44] This attack really meant that separate national development was no longer to be tolerated in Soviet life. What happened in linguistics is paralleled by events in every other sphere of Ukrainian culture.

Ever since the adoption of Ukrainization in 1923, Soviet rule in Ukraine had been based on a *modus vivendi* between the regime and the national intelligentsia as the leading stratum of the nation. Even after the SVU provocation, Skrypnyk was able to save a vestige of that *modus vivendi.* It ended because once the regime began to wage war against the rural majority of the Ukrainian nation, it could, and did, dispose of its intellectuals. According to Jurij Lawrynenko, nearly four-fifths of the Ukrainian cultural elite (*kulturni robitnyky*) were eliminated during the 1930s.[45]

The Collectivization of Agriculture and Ukrainian Famine of 1933

The Ukrainians were basically a nation consisting of a peasantry and a national intelligentsia. Although Ukrainization encouraged many Ukrainians to move into other social roles and to retain their Ukrainian identity, the vast majority of Ukrainians still worked the land in 1933. For Ukrainians, NEP and Ukrainization were but two sides of the same coin: both were concessions designed to placate social forces on which the Bolsheviks had been unable to inflict a decisive defeat. During the 1920s official statements in the Soviet Ukrainian press defined the Party's main task as winning over the "rural masses" in general and the rural intelligentsia in particular.[46] Ample evidence indicates that this approach enjoyed only limited success. For example, the village correspondents (*selkory*) who were encouraged to contribute to the Soviet press on village life were shunned by their neighbors, the vast majority of whom had little sympathy for the regime the *selkory* supported. Zatonskyi frankly admitted as much in a speech delivered to a 1926 *selkor* conference:

---

that the 1928 orthography as well as dictionaries, terminology, and grammars of the period all suffered "great harm" from "nationalistic deformities." *Kurs istorii ukrainskoi literaturnoi movy,* vol. 2, p. 104.

[44] For a fuller exposition of Khvylia's specific arguments and a convincing refutation of them, see Roman Smal-Stotskyi, *Ukrainska mova v Sovietskii Ukraini* (2 ed., New York, Toronto, Sidney, Paris, 1969), pp. 52–270.

[45] Jurij Lawrynenko, *Rozstriliane vidrodzhennia,* p. 965.

[46] V. N., "Do Vseukrainskoi naradi pro robotu na seli," *Visty VUTsVK,* April 16, 1924, p. 1.

But you are a minority. We know that it is difficult to work so actively in the villages as peasant correspondents. We are well aware of the attitude toward you that is expressed by the kulaks and even by some disgraceful (*hanebni*) representatives of Soviet power.[47]

Yet, if the regime had failed to win the hearts and minds of the Ukrainian peasantry, its representatives at least succeeded in penetrating the countryside they had confronted as something completely alien during the revolution. In addition to the newly-created *selkor* movement, the old *komnezamy* were retained, albeit in somewhat different form. Despite calls by a number of prominent leaders for the abolition of this rough and ready expedient held over from the days of War Communism, the 1925 "reorganization" of the *komnezamy*, worked out by Kaganovich and Petrovskyi in close consultation with Stalin, merely deprived them of political power and retained them as "voluntary social organizations."[48] Village soviets (*silrady*) were gradually established, and with the 1925 *komnezam* reorganization became the leading state organs in the countryside. In addition, the secret police established a system of residents on the *raion* (district) level who, as one account explains it,

disguised as instructors, statisticians, insurance agents, agronomists, and so on, worked ceaselessly to create a dense network of secret collaborators known as *seksoty*. The secret district residents of the OGPU did not directly involve the *seksoty* in subversion. When visiting villages they merely observed, noted and selected candidates as possible agents for the OGPU, and notified the authorities. A man who was earmarked for work as a future *seksot* or agent was called to the *okruh* department of the OGPU. There the chief of the *okruh* department had a "talk" with him, while a revolver lay on the table between them, and required him to sign an obligation. From that moment on the *seksot* was in touch with the district agent of the OGPU in the locality where he lived. Numbers varied from place to place depending on the size of the population, but everywhere the number of people thus recruited constituted a considerable part of the population.

The fact that the *seksoty* were not acquainted with one another greatly assisted the activities of the OGPU, especially in their control of the

---

[47] V. Zatonskyi, *Leninovym shliakhom (Promova na poshyrenii naradi selkoriv "Radianske Selo")* (Kharkiv, 1926), p. 21.

[48] M. D. Berezovchuk, "Zakhody Komunistychnoi partii Ukrainy po orhanizatsiino-politychnomu zmitsnenniu komnezamiv (1925)," *Ukrainskyi istorychnyi zhurnal, 1964,* no. 1, pp. 65–68.

seksoty themselves. Soon no one knew who could be trusted and mutual
confidence disappeared. Sons denounced fathers and brothers denounced
brothers. This was one of the most frightful measures of terrorism under
the Soviet regime.[49]

The district OGPU residents and their secret collaborators enabled
the regime to identify not only those who were openly hostile, but also
potential enemies. In contrast to the situation existing at the time it was
established, the Soviet Ukrainian regime now had a substantial network
in the village, greatly increasing its strength. Whenever the Party should
decide the time was right for the final reckoning of accounts, the regime
would be ready.

The regime always identified the kulaks as its main enemy in the countryside, an omnipresent foe whose role in the Bolshevik world view
was comparable to that of the Jews in Nazi ideology: evil incar-
nate. Since the kulaks were also perceived to be the basis of Ukrainian
nationalism, the regime seemed even more hostile to Ukrainian kulaks
than to their Russian counterparts. The retention of the *komnezamy* illus-
trates this hostility, as does the fact that these organizations were charged
with carrying out a program of dekulakization (that is, confiscation and
redistribution of ''surplus'' kulak land and property, not complete expropriation) until the end of 1923. Even after the program officially
ended, Ukrainian head of state Hryhorii Petrovskyi praised it, saying:
''Our revolution solved the land question, and with dekulakization we
only cut off the tail of what was left over from the revolution.''[50] The
final elimination of the kulaks as a class was, in fact, an ideological
imperative with which no communist could disagree in principle.

Who was a kulak? The basic definition of a kulak was a farmer whose
income was greater than that of a toiler, but the distinction between kulak
and middle peasant (*seredniak*) rested on the source of income. According to an official source published in 1926, a *seredniak* made his living exclusively from his own and his family's labor, while a kulak hired
others. The kulaks were estimated as constituting between four and five
percent of the rural population and, in some places, as low as one or
two percent.[51] The trouble arose from the flexibility of the allied

---

[49] P. Lutarewytch, ''A Resistance Group of the Ukrainian Underground, 1920–1926,''
Ukrainian Review, no. 2, 1956, p. 90.

[50] H. Petrovskyi, ''4-i zizd Nezamozhnykh selian Ukrainy,'' *Visty VUTsVK,* April
12, 1924, p. 1.

[51] B. S. Borev, *Kak izbiraiut Sovety na Ukraine* (Kharkiv, 1926), pp. 35–39.

category of "kulak henchmen, " *pidkurkulnyky, (podkulachniki* in Russian), a category which could be applied to any peasant who resisted official policies, and which during dekulakization was used to extend the repression of the kulaks to anyone considered suspect. During dekulakization, even poor peasants were often labeled kulak henchmen and deported—or worse.[52] The category of kulak henchmen rested on attitude rather than the material standing of the person to whom it was applied. The poorest individual in the village could be labeled a kulak henchman; the general Bolshevik mistrust of the "*petit-bourgeois* proprietary instincts" of the peasantry as a whole insured the broad application of both the rubric of kulak and that of kulak henchman. In addition, Bolshevik ideology identified the peasantry as the basic reservoir of nationality. As Stalin wrote, "The nationality problem is, *according to the essence of the matter,* a problem of the peasantry."[53] Thus, the mixing of the notions of class and nation made it possible for the ideology of class struggle to serve as justification for what was in essence a campaign to destroy the Ukrainian nation as a social organism and political factor.

The first preparatory salvo in the regime's war against the Ukrainian peasantry can be dated from 1926, with the first application of the so-called expert tax, an extraordinary levy first applied to farmers with ten hectares of land, later applied to anyone the local authorities wanted to drive off the land. A farmer declared an expert had to pay not only his tax in kind, an obligation amounting to 440–600 kilograms per hectare of arable land, but also an additional levy of 800–1000 kilograms per hectare, a levy often repeated. Once the resources of the "kulak" were exhausted, he would be "taken in tow," that is, special "tow brigades" (*buksyrni brygady*) consisting of local "activists" would expropriate his farm.[54]

The policy of "liquidation of the kulaks as a class" and forced total collectivization was announced by Stalin on December 27, 1929, in a speech to a conference of Marxist experts on agriculture and legalized by the VKP(b) Central Committee resolutions of January 5 and 30, 1930.[55] The various exactions preceding this final expropriation left little for the regime to take at the end. In one *okruh* where 4080 farms were

---

[52] M. Lewin, *Russian Peasants and Soviet Power: A Study of Collectivization* (New York, 1975), p. 249.

[53] I. V. Stalin, *Sochineniia,* vol. 7, p. 72.

[54] P. S. Lykho, "Sovetskaia vlast na mestakh," pp. 156–159.

[55] Stalin, *Sochineniia,* vol. 12, pp. 141–172; R. H. McNeal, ed., *Resolutions and*

expropriated in January-February 1930, these farms contained only 2367 buildings, 3750 horses, 2460 pigs, 1747 plows, and 125,743 poods of grain and millet.[56] A Ukrainian worker interviewed in the early 1950s told how it happened to his father, a fairly typical case:

> First they gave us a plan for grain collection which my father fulfilled. When he fulfilled this, they gave us a second plan for more grain to be delivered. He had to sell two horses in order to get the money to buy the grain for the collection. After this a third grain collection plan was given to him. . . This was in August 1928, right after the harvest. It all took four months. After the third plan was given to him, he said, "I will not fulfill it, because they will take everything, and it will never end." When he told them this, they said, "We will give you five days to fulfill the plan, and if the grain is not delivered, all your property will be confiscated," and this is what happened. They came after five days and took a complete inventory of our property down to the last knife and fork. They put a so-called boycott on our property, which meant that we did not have the right to sell any of it or to move away. . . This lasted about twenty days. One night in November, a wagon came from the village Soviet and took everything away, including our last cow and and pig. They took it all to the kolkhoz and left only one set of clothing for each of us; the rest was sent to the village store to be sold. Three days later the police came from the district and took my father away. He never returned, and we never heard of him again. All the inventory was given to the kolkhoz, and our personal things were sold at auction. We stayed in our home one month more, because the house was still considered ours. Then they came to us with a large quantity of state bonds. My mother said, 'How can we do this—we do not have a kopek?" They said, "Tomorrow, if you do not buy these bonds, we will have to sell your house." Then they came, appraised the house, and sold it to the cooperative. We were driven from our house, and we had to live in a small, one room hut which was on our land.
>
> In December, when the snow was already on the ground, they came one night and drove us out of the hut. "Where can we go?" my mother asked. "Anywhere," they said, "but you must get out." They loaded us on a wagon and left us there, my mother, and I, and my little sister.[57]

Others tell of being shunned by their neighbors because the word was

---

Decisions of the Communist Party of the Soviet Union (Toronto, 1974), vol. 3, pp. 40–43; Merle Fainsod, *Smolensk Under Soviet Rule* (New York, 1958), p. 242.

[56] I. I. Slynko, *Sotsialistychna perebudova i tekhnichna rekonstruktsiia silskoho hospodarstva Ukrainy (1927–1932 rr.)* (Kiev, 1961), p. 189.

[57] Harvard University Refugee Interview Project, Case 284.

spread that whosoever sheltered a kulak would be dekulakized as well.[58] Dekulakization, usually carried on simultaneously with the closing of the local church and removal of the village schoolteacher, if the latter were considered suspect, meant the removal of the village leadership, the best farmers, the most nationally conscious, in hopes of preventing resistance by denying it any individuals capable of leading it. Nearly 200,000 whole families were dekulakized.[59]

At the same time collectivization took place, and usually there was a facade of democracy such that the peasants themselves would be forced to vote to give up their farms. Another Ukrainian, interviewed by the Harvard project, gave this version of such a meeting:

> An authorized representative of the district executive committee was sent to each village. His job was to organize a kolkhoz or a number of kolkhozes in that village according to the number of people living there. He would hold a meeting in the village to give the appearance of democratic forms. I was at one such meeting, and I saw how the peasants voted. The Party representatives shouted, "Who is in favor of the socialization of agriculture?" No one answered. He shouted again, "Who is in favor of the socialization of agriculture?" Still there was no answer. Then he shouted, "Who is against the socialization of agriculture?" The peasants all raised their hands. Then he shouted, "And who is against the Soviet regime?" Then no one answered. From this you can conclude how willing the peasants were to join the collective system.[60]

They did join, however, and collectivization was forced on the peasants of Ukraine faster than elsewhere in the Union. The decree of January 5 singled out the predominantly non-Russian southern tier of the USSR for most rapid collectivization, the heavily Ukrainian North Caucasus and the Volga region.[61]

In Ukraine as well collectivization was more rigorously carried out than in Russia, as shown by the following figures on the percentage of the peasantry collectivized in Ukraine and Russia:

---

[58] See, for example, the eyewitness account in M. Verbytskyi, ed., *Naibilshyi zlochyn Kremlia* (London, 1952), pp. 68–69. These and similar collections published by Ukrainian groups in the West are broadly confirmed by materials in the above cited Harvard Project files.

[59] Hryshko, *Moskva slozam ne viryt,* p. 22.

[60] Harvard University Refugee Interview Project, Case 323.

[61] McNeal, ed., *Resolutions and Decisions,* vol. 3, p. 41. This resolution singles out the Volga region and North Caucasus as priority areas.

	Ukraine	Russia
Late 1929	8.6% of all peasants	7.4% of all peasants
Early 1930	65% of all peasants	59% of all peasants
Mid-1932	70% of all peasants	59.3% of all peasants

The trend continued for succeeding years: while 91.3% of Ukraine's peasants were collectivized as of 1935, Russian did not reach the 90% mark until late 1937.[62] The higher level of collectivization in Ukraine is only partially explained by the fact that the collectivization of the most important grain producing regions were given priority; collectivization in Ukraine had a special task which the Party organ *Proletarska Pravda* summed up on January 22, 1930: "to destroy the social basis of Ukrainian nationalism—individual peasant agriculture."[63]

Ukrainian peasants responded by fighting back. Even the Soviet sources make this clear. According to A. F. Chmyga, the number of "registered kulak terrorist acts" grew fourfold from 1927 to 1929, with 1,262 such acts known to have been committed during the latter year.[64] But in the first half of 1930 alone, more such acts of resistance occurred than during the entire preceding year, over 1,500.[65] Later figures are unavailable, perhaps because they became so numerous that officials could no longer keep count. There were even cases—many of them—where the women of a collective farm would take it upon themselves to expel the local Soviet administration, abolish the kolkhoz, and take back what had been taken from them. Such cases were so widespread that the popular parlance gave them their own special name, *babskyi bunt,* literally, the revolt of the village women.[66]

The regime quickly discovered that its forces in the countryside were inadequate to deal with the resistance. At first, the hope seemed to be that Ukraine might be able to put its own house in order; in November 1929, Moscow ordered the Ukrainians to purge the *komnezamy* of

---

[62] Hryshko, *Moskva slozam ne viryt,* p. 21.

[63] Quoted by F. Pigido, *Ukraina pid Bolshevytskoiu okupatsiieiu* (Munich, 1956), p. 107.

[64] A. F. Chmyga, "XV sezd VKP(b) o kollektivizatsii selskogo khoziaistva i nachalo osushchestvlenniia ego reshenii na Ukraine," *Vestnik Moskovskogo universiteta,* 1967, no. 6, p. 33; A. F. Chmyga, *Kolkhoznoe dvizhenie na Ukraine* (Moscow, 1974), p. 302.

[65] O. M. Krykunenko, *Borotba Komunistychnoi partii Ukrainy za zdiisnennia leninskoho kooperatyvnoho planu* (Lviv, 1970), p. 55.

[66] F. Pravoberezhnyi (Fedir Pigido), *8,000,000: 1933-i rik na Ukraini* (Winnipeg, 1951), p. 42.

"kulak" elements and strengthen them.[67] In truth, the *komnezamy* were able to play an important role in what was euphemistically known as "socialist construction" in the village, participating in collectivizing agriculture, procuring grain and in the sowing campaigns.[68] To guide them the regime sent outsiders into the village: brigadeers, thousanders, plenipotentiaries of the Central Committee, and so on. Most important of these outsiders were the so-called twenty-five thousanders.

At the November 1929 plenum of the all-Union Central Committee, the decision was made to send twenty-five thousand workers to the village to help carry out the Party's decisions of dekulakization and collectivization. By mid-February 1931, about 26,500 of them were spread over every corner of the Soviet Union. In early 1930, about 6,000 were working in Ukraine.[69] According to numerous accounts, the twenty-five thousander would come to a given village, take charge of the local activists, particularly the *komnezam,* and lead expeditions to expropriate kulaks, organize kolkhozes, or supervise grain levies. One Soviet account from the Stalinist era referred to them as the direct ancestor of the Political Section of the Machine Tractor Station.[70]

Whatever expectations the regime might have had that collectivization would raise agricultural output, the transition from individual to collective farms was extractive, not productive. Although the first Five Year Plan called for a growth in Soviet gross agricultural production of between 44 and 55%, gross output actually declined 23% from 1928 to 1932.[71] However, the greater control of the farmers' activities, which collectivization provided, meant that more produce could be "marketed," i.e., extracted from them. Thus, although the total Soviet grain harvest

---

[67] Z postanovy plenumu TsK VKP(b) pro silske hospodarstvo Ukrainy i pro robotu na seli," in *Komitety nezamozhnykh selian Ukrainy (1920–1933): Zbirnyk dokumentiv i materialiv* (Kiev, 1968), pp. 388–389.

[68] See, for example, M. D. Berezovchuk, "Rol komnezamiv u sotsialistychnoi perebudovy sela," *Ukrainskyi istorychnyi zhurnal,* 1960, no. 3, pp. 51–57. Ia. M., "Slavetnym shliakhom," *Visti VUTsVK,* May 9, 1930, p. 5.

[69] V. M. Selunskaia, "Rabochie-dvadtsatipiatitysiachniki—provodniki politiki partii v kolkhoznom stroitelstve (1929–1930 godu)," *Voprosy istorii,* 1954, no. 3, p. 21. E. Zombe, "Dvadtsatipiatitysiachniki," *Voprosy istorii,* 1947, no. 5, p. 19. A. N. Timofeev, "Dvadtsatipiatitysiachniki—provodniki politiki partii v kolkhoznom stroitelstve na Ukraine (1929–1930)," in *Iz istorii borby Kommunisticheskoi Partii Ukrainy za sotsialisticheskoe pereustroistvo selskogo khoziaistva* (Kiev, 1961), p. 84.

[70] E. Zombe, "Dvadtsatipiatitysiachniki," p. 21.

[71] Naum Jasny, *The Socialized Agriculture of the USSR: Plans and Performance* (Stanford, 1949), pp. 64–65.

in 1932 was at least 10% below that of 1927, grain marketings from the 1932 harvest were almost two and one-half times those of 1927–28.[72]

As economic depression deepened in the capitalist West, the prices of agricultural goods dropped steeply in relation to the prices of manufactured goods, and the Soviet Union, whose entire plan of development was predicated on paying for imported machinery with agricultural exports, found that the same number of machines as previously could be purchased only by substantially larger grain exports. Exploitation of the peasantry had to be stepped up.[73] The question arose: which peasants? An answer suggested itself by events which took place in Kazakhstan in 1930. The Kazakhs, primarily herdsmen, had responded to collectivization by the large-scale slaughter of cattle. So many of them starved in consequence, that the 1939 census shows 21.9% fewer Kazakhs in the Soviet Union than in 1926.[74] But the resistance of the Kazakhs to collectivization ended: Famine could be used as a weapon against those whom the regime found troublesome.

The most superficial observer of events in the Soviet countryside had to realize that the planned increases in agricultural output were fantasy. This is clear from in Khrushchev's later admission that the early kolkhozy consisted of nothing more than what happened to be in the village at the time.[75]

During the 1920s, Ukraine and the then heavily Ukrainian North Caucasus together supplied about half of all the grain procured by the state.[76] Moscow clearly expected this state of affairs to continue under the new regime of the collective farm. Before collectivization, the state procured only what the farmer himself could afford to sell; afterwards, however, the farmer had to give up a much greater amount. In 1930,

---

[72] *Ibid.*, p. 81.

[73] This point was made by the late Vsevolod Holubnychy in V. Holub (pseudonym), "Prychyny holodu 1932–1933 rr.," *Vpered: Ukrainskyi robitnychyi chasopys,* 1958, no. 10, p. 6.

[74] V. I. Kozlov, *Natsionalnosti SSSR (Etnodemograficheskii obzor)* (Moscow, 1975), p. 249.

[75] "...what did kolkhoz property consist in, say, in 1929–1930? It was simply the socialization of village property—horses, plows, *sokhas,* harrows, and some outbuildings. Of course, it played a progressive role at the time..." N. S. Khrushchev, *Pro dalnyi rozvytok kolhospnoho ladu i reorhanizatsiiu mashynno-traktornykh stantsii* (Kiev, 1958), p. 35. This statement was originally made on March 28, 1958 in the USSR Supreme Soviet, First Session, Fifth Convocation.

[76] G. Koniukhov, *KPSS v borbe s khlebnymi zatrudneniiami v strane* (Moscow, 1960), p. 62.

7.7 million tons of Ukrainian grain were procured, 33% of that year's 23 million ton harvest. In 1926, the best pre-collectivization year, 3.3 million tons or 21% of that year's harvest was procured. Thus, the burden placed on Ukrainian agriculture more than doubled. Ukraine's burden was also higher than that placed on other republics: although it accounted for only 27% of the total grain harvested in the USSR, it had to supply 38% of all the grain procured by the state. The 1930 harvest was a relatively bountiful one, despite the disorganization wrought by forced collectivization, but the 1931 harvest was only 18.3 million tons. Still, the procurement quota of 7.7 million tons was enforced.[77]

According to the Soviet historian I. I. Slynko, the lower harvest of 1931 was caused by a heat wave while the grain was maturing and hard rains during the harvest itself; in some areas, almost no grain remained after the state had taken its quota. In one village only 136 poods of grain were left, after the compulsory procurement, to feed 1230 collective farmers for a whole year.[78]

What happened in 1931 was nothing compared to what followed. The 1932 harvest was the worst since collectivization, but hardly of famine proportions. The 1928 harvest had been lower, and while the state suffered a procurement crisis, there was no mass starvation. At least, that is what Soviet historians claim.[79] Many who survived the famine remember the 1932 harvest as a bountiful one.[80] With changes in the methods of computing the harvest adopted in those years, Soviet crop statistics for the period are notoriously untrustworthy.[81] But we can safely conclude that any suffering that occurred in the countryside during those

---

[77] V. Holub(nychy), "Prychyny holodu 1932–1933 rr.," *Vpered: Ukrainskyi robitnychyi chasopis,* 1958, no. 1, p. 5.

[78] I. I. Slynko, *Sotsialistychna perebudova i tekhnichna rekonstruktsiia silskoho hospodarstva Ukrainy (1927–1932 rr.),* p. 288.

[79] *Ibid.,* p. 302.

[80] In the files of the Harvard University Refugee Project virtually all Ukrainian famine survivors describe the 1932 harvest as bountiful. So does the Soviet press of the period.

[81] "Furthermore, there are many reasons to doubt the reliability of the official statistics for crop acreage for 1930 and 1931 because the methods of estimating were again changed during these years, with the revolutionary reorganization of agriculture from small peasant farms to large collective farms. Moreover, the agricultural policy is now the party issue in Soviet Russia, and crop statistics are used to show the success of the new agricultural policy." Vladimir P. Timoshenko, *Agricultural Russia and the Wheat Problem* (Stanford: 1932), p. 175. Timoshenko was only the first of many in the West to doubt Soviet crop figures. See also Jerzy F. Karcz, "Thoughts on the Grain Problem," *Soviet Studies,* vol. 18, 1967, pp. 399–412.

years was due to a government policy of extraction, not to a failure of production. The regime could either have ameliorated its policy of extraction and let the peasants survive, or it could have carried out the policy ruthlessly and let them starve. The latter course was chosen. When the first collections were made in August 1932, most peasants in Ukraine met the quotas set for them. Then in October, a second levy was imposed to make up for those who had not met the earlier quota, and those who had met the old quota had to give half against as much. The brigades went around to the peasants' homes, searched, and took whatever they could find. At the beginning of 1933, a third levy was announced; this time everything edible was seized, leaving neither food nor seed.[82] Victor Kravchenko, a Soviet defector who took part in the campaign, told what it was like: urban communists were issued revolvers, assigned villages, and told to obtain 100% of the quota of grain; they proceeded to take whatever they could find.[83]

The official policy is quite clear from the regime's own decrees. A Union decree of October 20, 1931, forbade any distribution to collective farmers until after all state obligations had been fully met. A virtual reign of terror against local officials and the heads of collective farms who did not meet the quotas was instituted: an October 18, 1931, decree of the KP(b)U Central Committee removed from their posts and excluded from the Party leaders of four districts (*raiony*) for delaying or sabotaging the grain procurements campaign. Severe reprimands were issued to leaders in five other raiony. Other Party penalties were imposed on officials in 33 other raiony. Directors of several Machine Tractor Stations were also removed for "inaction" and "right opportunist practice," and severe reprimands were issued to heads and senior agronomists of others. According to figures covering the period up to January 10, 1932, for 146 raiony, the administrative boards of 250 kolkhozy were dissolved, 345 boards were "brought to justice," 355 kolkhoz chairmen were dismissed, 304 kolkhoz chairmen were brought to court, and 943 chairmen and members of kolkhoz administrative boards were issued Party penalties—all for "frustrating the grain procurements."[84] The most superficial reading of Soviet Ukrainian newspapers of the period will show countless diatribes against "opportunists" who "did not want to see the kulaks in their midst" (how could they, when they themselves

---

[82] Pravoberezhnyi (Pigido), *8,000,000*, pp. 51–54.

[83] Victor Kravchenko, *I Chose Freedom: The Personal and Political Life of a Soviet Official* (New York, 1946), pp. 91–131.

[84] Slynko, *Sotsialistychna perebudova*, pp. 289–290.

had participated in getting rid of the "kulaks" at the beginning of 1930?) and were "sabotaging" the procurements.[85] Although occasional editorials were written against "distortions," that is, excessive heavy handedness in dealing with the peasants, most Ukrainian collective farmers got nothing from the 1932 harvest; according to Soviet figures, by February 1, 1933, distribution of procedes from the 1932 harvest had been carried out in only 22.7% of all kolkhozy in Ukraine.[86]

Draconian legal measures were imposed on the peasants. On the Union level, the law of August 7, 1932, on the inviolability of socialist property, declared all collective farm property—including produce and animal fodder—"sacred and inviolate." Anyone who so much as gleaned an ear of wheat or broke the root off a sugar beet was declared an "enemy of the people" and could be shot or, in extenuating circumstances, imprisoned for not less than ten years in the Gulag and suffer confiscation of all property. A second part of the decree provided for five or ten years in a concentration camp for collective farmers who attempted to force others to leave the kolkhoz. During 1932, 20% of all persons convicted in Soviet law courts were sentenced under this decree, and Stalin himself called it "the basis of revolutionary legality at the present moment."[87]

---

[85] I. Kharchenko, "Shkidnytske keruvannia," *Visti VUTsVK*, October 10, 1929, p. 6; M. Popov, "Pravyi ukhyl na praktyki. Deiaki slozh. T-va Poltavshchyny," *Visti VUTsVK*, October 15, 1929, p. 5; "Posylyty natysk na na hlytaia," *Visti VUTsVK*, October 31, 1930, p. 1; "Postanova prezidii Vseukrainskoho Tsentralnoho Vykonavchoho Komitetu na dopovid narkomtorhu USRR pro khlibozahotivli," *Visti VUTsVK*, October 21, 1930, p. 1; "Khlib—mohutne znariaddia dlia pidnesennia vsioho Radianskoho narodnoho hospodarstva. Z Promovy holovu TsKK Narkoma RSI tov. Zatonskoho na zborakh raipartaktiv Berdianskoho raionu—3 zhovtnia," *Visti VUTsVK*, October 28, 1930, p. 4; M. Cherniak, "Bezhospodarnist na orhanizovane shkidnytstvo," *Visti VUTsVK*, October 29, 1930, p. 5; "Za iakist khliba," *Visti VUTsVK*, November 1, 1930, p. 5; "Bohuslavskyi raion na khvyli oportunizmu," *Visti VUTsVK*, November 1, 1930, p. 5; "Vyrishalni dni khlibozahotivel," *Visti VUTsVK*, November 23, 1930, p. 1; I. Plys, "Osnovni momenty khlibnoi kampagnii 1930-1931 roku," *Bilshovyk Ukrainy*, 1930, no. 13-14, pp. 17-25; "S.-H. kooperatsiia i soiuzkhlib ne hotovi do prynymannia khliba novoho vrozhaiu. Po-bilshovytskomu hotuvatys do nastupnykh khlibozahotivel," *Visti VUTsVK*, July 2, 1931, p. 6; "Oportunistiv vykliucheno z partii," *Visti VUTsVK*, November 5, 1931, p. 1; "De pokladaiutsia na samoplyv—tam khlib 'plyve' v kurkulski iamy," *Visti VUTsVK*, November 15, 1931, p. 1. Such references could be extended almost indefinitely.

[86] I. F. Ganzha, I. I. Slinko, P. V. Shostak, "Ukrainskoe selo na puti k sotsializmu," in V. P. Danilov, ed., *Ocherki istorii kollektivizatsii selskogo khoziaistva v soiuznykh respublikakh* (Moscow, 1963), p. 202.

[87] Robert Conquest, ed., *Agricultural Workers in the USSR* (London, Sidney, Toronto, 1968), pp. 24-25.

A Ukrainian decree of December 6, 1932, singled out six villages that had allegedly sabotaged the grain deliveries. They were placed on a blacklist (*chorna doshka*), which meant: 1) the immediate closing of state and cooperative stores, and the removal of all goods in them from the village; 2) a complete ban on all trade, including trade in essential consumer goods, by kolkhozy, collective farmers, and individual farmers; 3) the halting and immediate collection of all credits and advances; 4) a thoroughgoing purge of the local cooperative and state apparatuses; and 5) the purge of all "foreign elements" and saboteurs of the grain procurements from the kolkhozy.[88] A decree of December 13 extended roughly the same sanctions to 82 raiony for "criminal laxity in the task of procuring grain." In addition, the KP(b)U Central Committee ordered the Dnipropetrovsk and Kharkiv *obkomy* to seize all property belonging to 1500 private farmers in these areas who had not met their quotas.[89]

The year 1933 was difficult for all Soviet peasants, but mass death from starvation seems to have been confined to Ukraine, the North Caucasus *krai,* and parts of the Volga region, the latter perhaps in hopes of weakening the Volga Germans. Along the border with Russia proper (as distinct from the Kuban), the famine seems to have stopped right at the border. The conclusion seems inescapable that in Ukraine, as William Henry Chamberlin put it, "the government was determined to 'teach the peasants a lesson' by the grim method of starvation" which he found evident from the fact that "every village (he) visited reported a death rate of not less than ten percent."[90]

Many accounts by survivors narrate the horrors of life in the village during the terrible winter of 1932–1933. Survivors tell of mass death by starvation such that the number of bodies exceeded the capability of those who were left to bury them decently: they were either dumped in pits or piled up and covered with a little dirt. Hundreds of cases of cannibalism were reported. Whole villages were completely deserted.[91]

---

[88] "Pro zanesennia na chornu doshku sil, iaki zlisno sabotuiut khlibozahotivli: Postanova Radnarkomu USRR i TsK KP(b)U," *Visti VUTsVK,* December 8, 1932, p. 1.

[89] Slynko, *Sotsialistychna perebudova,* p. 298.

[90] William Henry Chamberlin, *The Ukraine: A Submerged Nation* (New York, 1944), pp. 59, 60.

[91] In addition to the files of the Harvard University Refugee Interview Project, the following works contain much valuable eyewitness testimony on the Ukrainian famine of 1933: *The Black Deeds of the Kremlin: A White book* (Toronto and Detroit, 1953, 1955); M. Verbytskyi, ed., *Naibilshyi zlochyn Kremlia;* Iur. Semenko, ed., *Holod 1933 roku v Ukraini: Svidchennia pro vynyshuvannia Moskvoiu ukrainskoho selianstva* (Munich, 1963); Dmytro Solovey, ed., *The Golgotha of Ukraine* (New York, 1953). Other materials

Starving peasants were common sights in the cities, and armies of homeless children, the *bezprizorni* or waifs, roamed the country seeking food.[92] The state ultimately declared the *bezprizorni* problem "liquidated" and carried out mass executions of such children.[93] Many went to Russia to try to get bread. Iwan Majstrenko, a former KP(b)U functionary and newspaper editor, recalled two villages, one on each side of the Russo-Ukrainian border, where the peasants from the Ukrainian side would nightly sneak across the border to get bread that was available only on the Russian side.[94] In order to limit the famine to Ukraine, GPU border checkpoints were established along the railroad lines. At these checkpoints, peasants going to Russia from Ukraine would be halted, and any food being taken from Russia to Ukraine would be seized.[95]

One account, no less valuable for being second-hand, comes from Khrushchev himself:

> Mikoyan told me that Comrade Demchenko, who was then First Secretary of the Kiev Regional committee, once came to see him in Moscow. Here's what Demchenko said: "Anastas Ivanovich, does Comrade Stalin—for that matter, does anyone in the Politburo—know what's happening in the Ukraine? Well, if not, I'll give you some idea. A train recently pulled into Kiev loaded with the corpses of people who had starved to death. It picked up corpses all the way from Poltava to Kiev. . ."[96]

Stalin, of course, did know. In 1932 Terekhov, a secretary of the KP(b)U Central Committee reported to Stalin on starvation in the Kharkiv region, and Stalin accused him of telling fairy tales.[97] Later Razkolnikov and General Iakir both protested to Stalin, and were rebuffed.[98]

---

are examined by Dana Dalrymple, "The Soviet Famine of 1932–1934," *Soviet Studies,* vol. 15, 1964, pp. 250–284; vol. 16, 1965, pp. 471–474. Useful bibliographies are: Alexandra Pidhaina, "A Bibliography of the Great Famine in Ukraine, 1932–1933," *The New Review: A Journal of East-European History,* vol. 13, 1973, no. 4, pp. 32–68; "Ukrainska literatura pro holod v 1932 i 1933 rokakh," *Vilna Ukraina,* no. 18, 1958, pp. 42–44.

[92] Kravchenko, *I Chose Freedom,* p. 63.

[93] Robert Conquest, *The Great Terror,* p. 129.

[94] I. M(ajstren)ko, "Do 25-richchia holodu 1933 r.," *Vpered: Ukrainskyi robitnychyi chasopys,* 1958, no. 7, pp. 1–2.

[95] Leonid Plyushch, *History's Carnival: A Dissident's Autobiography* (New York and London, 1977), p. 41; Verbytskyi, ed., *Naibilshyi zlochyn Kremlia,* pp. 89–90.

[96] N. S. Khrushchev, *Khrushchev Remembers* (Boston and Toronto, 1970), pp. 73–74.

[97] Medvedev, *Let History Judge,* p. 94.

[98] Plyushch, *History's Carnival,* pp. 40–41.

The 1939 Soviet census, itself suspect, shows that the number of Ukrainians in the Soviet Union dropped between 1926 and 1939 by over three million, 9.9%.[99] Even on the basis of these highly suspect figures, Janusz Radziejowski has calculated for this period a population deficit, that it, the failure of the population to reach a level projected on the basis of past trends due to a rise in the mortality and/or a decline in birth rates, of 9,263,000 for Ukrainians.[100] The true figure may well be higher. According to the KGB defector W. Krivitsky, the official Soviet census of 1937 found a total of 145,000,000 inhabitants of the Soviet Union instead of the 171,000,000 that had been calculated and expected on the basis of demographic trends. These data were never officially released; rather, the directors of the statistical bureau and their closest collaborators were arrested.[101] That the 1939 census lists a total Soviet population of 170.5 million would seem to indicate that their successors were eager to avoid the shortcomings found in the predecessors' work. Even this census could not conceal the literal decimation of the Ukrainian nation.

Certainly, the reversal of the Ukrainization policies increased assimilatory pressures on Ukrainians, but it is impossible to to attribute such a population loss to assimilation. This is so, because the Belorussians—closely related to Ukrainians in language and culture, subjected to the same assimilatory pressures, certainly no better equipped to resist these pressures, but unaffected by the famine of 1933—showed, during the same period, a population increase of 11.3%. The Soviet demographer V. I. Kozlov more realistically, if somewhat euphemistically, since the harvest did not in fact fail, refers to the "harvest failure of 1932" which "probably caused a very temporary rise in the mortality rate" in Ukraine.[102] The evidence is overwhelming that one of the worst famines in human history raged in Soviet Ukraine in 1932–1934, to a somewhat lesser degree also in the heavily Ukrainian and Cossack North Caucasus, largely non-Russian regions of the Volga, and that it claimed millions of victims.

We may never know precisely how many perished during the famine.

---

[99] Kozlov, *Natsionalnosti SSSR,* p. 249.

[100] Janusz Radziejowski, "Collectivization in Ukraine in Light of Soviet Historiography," *Journal of Ukrainian Studies,* no. 9, 1980, p. 17.

[101] Boris Souvarine, *Stalin: A Critical Survey of Bolshevism* (New York, 1939), p. 669. Anton Antonov-Ovseenko's account (205–209) may well have been largely borrowed from Souvarine.

[102] Kozlov, *Natsionalnosti SSSR,* p. 153.

Estimates from those claiming to have received them from Soviet officials are about ten million, with fifteen million appearing as a maximum
figure. According to Adam J. Tawdul, a Russian-born American citizen
who moved in the ruling circles thanks to a prerevolutionary acquain-
tance with Skrypnyk, Skrypnyk before his death told him that eight
million had perished in Ukraine and North Caucasus.[103] At that time,
the famine had not yet fully run its course. Another high official later
that year gave him the figure of eight to nine million in Ukraine alone,
while yet another told him that over a million also died in the Urals,
the Trans-Volga region, and western Siberia.[104] Tawdul's account contains ample internal evidence showing that he actually was there, although
it is impossible to confirm much of what he wrote. Dr. William Horsley
Gantt, a British psychologist who was in Russia studying with Pavlov
at the time, claimed to have received estimates from Soviet officials
that as many as fifteen million might have perished. This, however,
was considered a maximal figure.[105] On the other hand, the ten million
figure appears even in Stalin's conversation. In his history of World
War II, Winston Churchill records the following conversation he had
with Stalin during the war:

> "Tell me," I asked, "have the stresses of this war been as bad to you
> personally as carrying through the policy of the Collective Farms?"
> This subject immediately aroused the Marshal.
> "Oh, no," he said, "the Collective Farm policy was a terrible
> struggle."
> "I thought you would have found it bad," said I, "because you were
> not dealing with a few score thousands of aristocrats or big landowners,
> but with millions of small men."
> "Ten millions," he said, holding up his hands.[106]

Even if these figures did circulate among the Soviet elite, those who
circulated them had no way of knowing the precise extent of the loss

---

[103] Adam J. Tawdul, "10,000,000 Starved in Russia in Two Years, Soviet Admits,"
The New York American, August 18, 1935, pp. 1–2.

[104] Adam J. Tawdul, "Russia Warred on Own People," *The New York American,*
April 19, 1935, p. 2.

[105] Dana J. Dalrymple, "The Soviet Famine of 1932–1934: Some Further References,"
Soviet Studies, vol. 16, 1965, no. 4, p. 471. The Gantt account has recently been reex-
amined by Jaroslaw Sawka, "American Psychiatrist: Fifteen Million Died in the Thirties Famine," *Ukrainian Quarterly,* vol. 38, Spring 1982, no. 1, pp. 61–67. It was Dr.
Sawka who first brought the Gantt testimony to the attention of Dalrymple, and I am
grateful to him for allowing me to read an advance text of his article.

[106] Winston Churchill, *The Hinge of Fate* (Boston, 1950), p. 498.

of life. Regulations requiring the registration of burials could have made such knowledge possible, but all eye-witness accounts indicate that these regulations were widely ignored. Statisticians working in the West tend to offer figures of between five and seven million dead. Maksudov, the dissident Soviet demographer who recently emigrated to the United States, is currently completing a major study of Soviet population losses and has calculated the total "unnatural" population loss suffered by all the peoples of the Soviet Union from the beginning of collectivization to the culmination of the Great Purge, at over nine million, with 8.5 million of these deaths occurring before the 1934 Soviet elections and clearly attributable to collectivization and the famine. Most of the 8.5 million undoubtedly perished during the famine in Ukraine.[107]

This writer must leave to others the precise task of determining how many perished prematurely during the Ukrainian famine. Would the difference between, say, five and fifteen million victims diminish or augment in any meaningful way the horror of what occurred? At a very minimum, the Soviet Union suffered an absolute loss of 9.9% of its Ukrainian inhabitants between 1926 and 1939, at least five to seven million lives when natural population growth is factored in. The Ukrainian population of the Soviet Union was quite literally decimated.

The Fall of Skrypnyk

By 1933, Skrypnyk's policy of pursuing what he perceived to be Ukrainian national interests was in a shambles. The national intelligentsia was being discredited by means of show trials, and arrested wholesale. The peasantry was being decimated by a deliberately created famine. One can trace the process of chipping away Soviet Ukrainian sovereignty as far back as 1927 when an All-Union plan for agriculture was adopted, or to the 1928 regulations on republic budgets and land use. The budget regulation did not define the limits of the power of the Union or guarantee the rights of the republics. The land law made all land the property of the Union, thus leaving the republics in the position of governments without territory. Skrypnyk opposed both proposals; both times, he lost.[108] We have seen how ideology as well as economics came more and more under the purview of Union organizations, and how Ukrainian cultural distinctiveness was attacked in one sphere after another.

---

[107] S. Maksudov, *Dinamiki poter naseleniia SSSR v pervoi polovine XX veka* (unpublished manuscript, Harvard University, 1982), pp. 266, 270, 281.

[108] Sullivant, *Soviet Politics and the Ukraine,* pp. 149–153.

Skrypnyk was long a man under political siege, and the attack on him was an attack on his country.

On January 24, 1933, the VKP(b) Central Committee passed a special resolution, altering the leadership of the KP(b)U. Pavel Postyshev, who had formerly headed the Kharkiv Party organization before leaving for a stay in Russia, was returned to his old post in Ukraine and made Second Secretary of the KP(b)U.[109] During the following weeks, an extensive purge of Ukrainian cultural life was effected.[110] On February 28, a major governmental reshuffle was made in Soviet Ukraine. Skrypnyk was removed from his post as Commissar of Education and named head of the Soviet Ukrainian State Planning Commission and deputy head of Ukrainian Sovnarkom. Zatonskyi took over his education post.[111] On March 4, *Pravda* carried a self-critical letter from the leaders of Soviet Belorussia confessing to "errors in the nationality question."[112] A few days later, *Visti* published a lead editorial informing its readers that the letter was relevant to Ukraine as well.[113] At the end of April, the KP(b)U Central Committee held a conference on nationality policy at which Zatonskyi denounced national deviations in education, and Khvylia denounced them in linguistics.[114] The ground was being laid for the final assault.

On June 10, 1933, Postyshev delivered a speech at the June plenum of the KP(b)U and attacked Skrypnyk by name. According to Postyshev, Skrypnyk had sheltered national deviationists, wreckers, and counter-revolutionaries in his Commissariat of Education; his advocacy of the use of the letter Γ had served the Polish lords by helping to separate the Ukrainian and Russian languages.[115]

On June 27, Khvylia attacked Skrypnyk's policies in linguistics and held his "national deviation" responsible for the regime's difficulties in procuring grain:

---

[109] "Postanova TsK VKP(b) z 24 sichnia 1933 r. ta zavdannia bilshovykiv Ukrainy," *Bilshovyk Ukrainy,* 1933, no. 3, p. 3.

[110] Kostiuk, *Stalinist Rule in the Ukraine,* pp. 58–59.

[111] *Visti VUTsVK,* March 1, 1933, p. 1.

[112] N. Gikalo and N. Golodev, "Ob oshibkakh partiinikh i Sovetskikh organizatsii Belorussii v natsionalnom voprose," *Pravda,* March 4, 1933, p. 4.

[113] "Vyshche prapor proletarskoho internatsionalizmu," *Visti VUTsVK,* March 11, 1933, p. 1.

[114] "Narada z pytan natsionalnoho polityky partii," *Visti VUTsVK,* May 1, 1933, p. 2.

[115] "Mobilizuiemo masy na svoiechasnu postavku zerna derzhavi. Promova t. P. P. Postysheva na plenumi TsK KP(b)U 10–VI 1933 r.," *Visti VUTsVK,* June 22, 1933, pp. 1–2.

The fundamental cause of errors in the procurement of grain during the past year consists in the fact that many of Ukraine's party organizations did not exercise the desired Bolshevik vigilance and uncompromising attitude toward hostile elements, which is rooted in the very fact that they sabotaged us at every turn of our activity.

This, he added, included the cultural front, and those to blame were, above all, the national deviationists associated with Skrypnyk:

And our Commissariat of Education not only failed to expose wrecking, but, on the contrary, sheltered wrecking elements. Worse, the Commissar himself, Comrade Skrypnyk, enabled these elements to conceal their activities in linguistics... Comrade Skrypnyk could not have failed to understand that he himself had taken the path of alienating the Ukrainian language from Russian and bringing it closer to Polish.

This, he made clear, was Petliurist sabotage, and the present leadership was committed to a decisive struggle "to purge the Ukrainian orthography of this counterrevolutionary nationalistic rubbish."[116]

On July 6, *Visti* published a particularly savage attack on Skrypnyk by Panas Liubchenko, tying in Skrypnyk with the sort of wrecking exposed at the SVU trial and holding him responsible for "kulak Ukrainian nationalist" sabotage in linguistics, literature, and historical scholarship. Whereas Khvylia had connected Skrypnyk with now discredited Ukrainian linguists, Liubchenko took particular care to connect him with the historians Iavorskyi and Sukhyno-Khomenko, who had been purged in 1930. Liubchenko accused Skrypnyk of trying to create his own "national Bolshevism," putting the national struggle in place of the class struggle.[117]

Perhaps Liubchenko's attack was the last straw for Skrypnyk, removing any lingering illusions regarding the fate that awaited him. In any case, on the day it was published, Skrypnyk committed suicide.[118] Ukraine's quest for its own road to socialism came to its definitive end. Virtually everything Skrypnyk had ever done or been associated with was denounced as a "Skrypnykite deviation." By the end of 1933, Ukrainization was finished, as well the other indigenization policies—Belorussianization, Yiddishization, Tatarization, and so forth.

---

[116] "Stan na movnomu fronti. Dopovid tov. Khvyli," *Visti VUTsVK,* June 30, 1933, p. 3.

[117] "Pro deiaki pomylky na teoretychnomu fronti. Z promovy tov. P. P. Liubchenka na plenumi TsK LKSMU," *Visti VUTsVK,* July 6, 1933, pp. 2, 4.

[118] *Visti VUTsVK,* July 7, 1933, p. 1. Ironically, Liubchenko would also commit suicide five years later.

Skrypnyk had undoubtedly led the behind-the-scenes fight to convince Moscow to lower the amount of grain it demanded from Ukraine, and *Pravda* even published a lead editorial in January 1932 demanding that the Ukrainian officials overcome their backwardness in procuring grain for the Union.[119] The resolution of the Union Central Committee sending Postyshev to Ukraine, complained that Ukraine had failed to meet its procurement quota, despite the fact that it had been lowered three times (to 6.2 million tons, an amelioration largely cancelled out due to changed accounting procedures).[120] Three days after Skrypnyk died, Popov, with whose work as a historian the reader is already familiar, addressed the Kharkiv Party activists, connecting the struggle against the peasants for food with the one against Skrypnyk's ghost and against Ukrainian nationalism, defining the Party's goal as making Ukraine a model Soviet republic:

> The task of raising our agriculture cannot be accomplished without correcting the errors permitted in the national question, without purging our Party, our Soviet, cultural, agricultural, kolkhoz, and other institutions of bourgeois nationalists, without mobilizing the entire Party mass to fight nationalism, without strengthening our efforts to bring the masses up in the spirit of internationalism. . . . Bolshevik nationality policy, most closely bound up with all the tasks of our Party . . . will be a mighty weapon for the consolidation of Soviet Ukraine as an indivisible part of the Soviet Union. . .More acutely than ever before we face the task of making the Soviet Union into an impregnable fortress, ready to repel every assault from enemies both East and West. We face the task here and now in Soviet Ukraine . . . to make Soviet Ukraine into a model Soviet republic.[121]

Postyshev immediately set about making Ukraine "a model Soviet republic" with a frontal assault on Ukrainian culture. Not only was Russian imperialism rehabilitated, but even the visible reminders of Ukraine's rich heritage were destroyed, with the transfer of the Soviet Ukrainian capital from Kharkiv to Kiev in 1934. Buildings from the seventeenth-century Ukrainian hetmanate were particularly singled out; among the buildings that were demolished was the Uspenskyi sobor, built in the twelfth century and mentioned in *The Lay of the Host of Ihor*. Scholars

---

[119] *Pravda*, January 8, 1932, p. 1.

[120] "Postanova TsK VKP(b) z 24 sichnia 1933 r. ta zavdannia bilshovykiv Ukrainy," *Bilshovyk Ukrainy*, 1933, no. 3, p. 3. *Komunistychna Partiia Ukrainy v rezoliutsiiakh i reshenniakh*, I, p. 750. Bohdan Krawchenko, "The Great Famine of 1932–33 in the Soviet Ukraine," *One World*, vol. 20, 1982, no. 1, p. 20.

[121] M. M. Popov, "Pro natsionalistychni ukhyly v lavakh ukrainskoi part-orhanizatsii i pro zavdannia borotby z nymy," *Chervonyi shliakh*, 1933, no. 7, pp. 110, 125, 126.

who protested were labelled antiquarians; many of them were arrested. The buildings supposed to replace what was torn down were, in many cases, never built.[122]

The lives and positions of most of Skrypnyk's colleagues on the KP(b)U Central Committee were spared until the Great Purge of 1937–1938, but then perished almost to a man. Soviet Ukraine became a virtual fief of the NKVD. Only Petrovskyi was allowed to survive in obscurity; the former head of the Soviet Ukrainian state was allowed to work as a librarian until Stalin's death.[123]

For all their accomplishments in the cultural sphere before 1933, the gains made by the Ukrainians were too new and too fragile to survive the assault made upon them. With the abandonment of Ukrainization, Russian became once again the language of social mobility in the cities, and urban Ukraine was so thoroughly Russified that today one seldom hears the Ukrainian language spoken in the streets of Kiev.

*   *   *

The First Five Year Plan in Ukraine was accompanied by a calculated plan to destroy the Ukrainian nation as a political factor and as a social organism. The Ukrainian national intelligentsia, communist and non-communist, was virtually wiped out. What was left of it was cowed by repeated campaigns against "bourgeois nationalism" and harnessed to the state, merged with a new "Soviet intelligentsia" fashioned by the Stalinist regime in its own image. The Ukrainian communist leadership was destroyed, politically, with the fall of Skrypnyk, and physically, with the Great Purge. Ukrainian national culture was exiled from the cities to the farms, whence it had come; once again the peasants, the basic reservoir of nationhood, were attached to the land and turned into virtual serfs through the collectivization of agriculture, the internal passport system, and the introduction of compulsory labor duties indistinguishable from *corvée*.

Genocide is not too strong a word for what was done to the Ukrainians, but there were too many for the regime ever to entertain seriously the idea of their total physical liquidation. Rather, the attempt was made to break them, to destroy their culture, to decimate them through famine.

---

[122] B. Mikorskii, *Razrushenie kulturno-istoricheskikh pamiatnikov v Kieve v 1934–1936 godakh* (Munich, 1951).

[123] Conquest, *The Great Terror*, pp. 343–354, 627–631.

One Ukrainian dissident later coined the word "ethnocide" to describe what was done.[124]

Khrushchev once said that Stalin would have liked to deport all the Ukrainians to Siberia, as he had done with some of the smaller nationalities, only there were too many of them.[125] We have seen how the Ukrainian nation was decapitated by the destruction of its intelligentsia, decimated by man-made famine, and the last vestige of its independent political leadership destroyed.

---

[124] "Etnosyd ukraintsiv v SSSR," *Ukrainskyi vistnyk*, vol. 7–8, 1974, pp. 33–147.

[125] Nikita S. Khrushchev, *The Crimes of the Stalin Era: Special Report to the 20th Congress of the Communist Party of the Soviet Union* (New York, 1962), pp. 44–45.

Conclusion

THE 1930s WITNESSED a violent attempt to turn back the clock in Soviet Ukraine. The collective farms differed little from the old gentry estates: the collective farmer had to work there, could not leave, and received only what the master (in this case the state) gave him. If not enough remained to support life after the state had taken what it demanded, the peasant simply starved to death. The kolkhoznik's serf grandfather was well off by comparison.

All peasants in the Soviet Ukraine were forced to become kolkhozniki, but at least the Russian collective farmer could read Russian literature and history, be bossed by Russian overlords, and know that his sufferings were to build the might of a Russian state. Whatever types of oppression he might have suffered, national oppression was not among them. The Ukrainian collective farmer suffered all the social oppression of his Russian counterpart, as well as national oppression: the Ukrainian literary and historical works most avidly read in the 1920s were banned; the Russian bosses and Russocentric state for which he was forced to labor were foreign. Cities, which Ukrainization had seemed to be making theirs, once again became foreign bodies in which the Russian tongue regained its old supremacy.

A sometimes abused but nonetheless useful concept is the distinction between sociologically complete and incomplete nations.[1] A sociologically complete nation has mastery over the social division of labor in which it participates because both elites and masses are of the same nation. A sociologically incomplete nation lacks a full complement of

---

[1] For an interesting discussion of the concept, see Ivan L. Rudnytsky, ''Observations on the Problem of 'Historical' and 'Non-historical' Nations'' and George G. Grabowicz, ''Some Further Observations on 'Non-historical Nations' and 'Incomplete' Literatures: A Reply,'' *Harvard Ukrainian Studies,* vol. 5, 1981, pp. 358–388.

social classes as a result of having lost its elites through displacement or gradual assimilation. In 1800, the Czechs were a sociologically incomplete nation, a peasant folk. Over the course of succeeding decades, they succeeded in creating a national intelligentsia, a national bourgeoisie, a Czech working class; they gradually Czechized the cities of Bohemia, became sociologically complete, and in 1918 established an independent state.

In 1917, the Ukrainians were still overwhelmingly a nation of peasants to whom the city was alien. Since the peasantry was the only possible mass constituency for Ukrainian political parties, the Ukrainian groups with any hope of gaining a mass following were those that appealed to both the peasantry's social and national grievances. The Revolutionary Ukrainian Party, organized at the turn of the century, sought to reconcile socialism and nationalism, only to be rent by the seeming irreconcilability of the two doctrines. Nevertheless, the Ukrainian political parties and leaders who came to power in 1917 did so because they offered the peasants hope of social justice as well as national liberation. Indeed, their ultimate defeat can be attributed as much to their wavering on social issues as to their unfavorable geopolitical situation, for Ukrainian peasants continued fighting for years after their political leaders were expelled.

The protracted struggle between the Russian Bolsheviks, based in Ukraine on the Russified workers of the cities, and the Ukrainian socialists, based on the non-Russian countryside, led elements from both camps to seek some sort of *modus vivendi*. After all, both sides claimed to be fighting the same enemies: capitalism and imperialism. The Ukrainian Borotbisty and Ukapisty fought for a Soviet Ukraine that would be independent and Ukrainian by its national character, while even Petliura experimented with the semi-Soviet solution of the ''toilers' republic.'' Among the Bolsheviks, Mazlakh and Shakhrai were the first to argue for an independent Soviet Ukraine that would really be Ukrainian, and in 1920 Georg Lapchinskii led an organized opposition in the KP(b)U devoted to the same goal. The KP(b)U initially rejected those of its own who argued for taking Ukrainian aspirations seriously, while it saw the Ukrainian revolutionaries as untrustworthy allies at best, dangerous class enemies at worst. When change came, it was Moscow that forced it on the reluctant Ukrainian organization, and Ukrainian communists were dependent upon Moscow for their position in the KP(b)U.

Ukrainization was adopted because Moscow realized that the Ukrainian countryside could not be pacified without meeting its minimum demand, a government that would act Ukrainian and foster Ukrainian culture. Soon the Bolsheviks realized that Ukrainization had given them more than they bargained for. Led by Tiutiunyk and Hrushevskyi, many of the intellectual and political leaders of the Ukrainian Peoples Republic returned, eager to take part in the opportunities offered them to develop the nation's culture. Sixty-six of them signed a declaration saying that they would be good Soviet citizens now that the regime had corrected its past errors in nationality policy, implying that if the situation changed, they might not remain such loyal citizens. A national cultural rebirth of unprecedented depth and breadth took place. The regime felt the need to guide what it called the Ukrainian cultural process, and realized that communists had to participate before they could hope to lead it. The issue became not whether to Ukrainize, but how rapidly to do so, not whether to permit the expression of national distinctiveness, but how much. Ukrainian national consciousness was legitimized in the Party itself. Oleksander Shumskyi, Mykola Khvylovyi, and Mykhailo Volobuiev were all Bolsheviks who demanded that Ukrainization lead to real national liberation, and that meant ending Russian domination. They provoked a political crisis that went to the root of the *modus vivendi* on which Soviet rule in Ukraine was based.

Moscow insisted on their condemnation. Mykola Skrypnyk followed Moscow's orders, but at the same time he established a position of political dominance in Ukraine and a tremendous popular following. His personality cult, by the early thirties, was almost comparable to Stalin's. It took four full years for Moscow to bring him down.

Skrypnyk, the Ukrainian Old Bolshevik whom Lenin had sent to the country and who had been largely responsible for convincing Moscow of the need to take Ukrainian aspirations seriously, helped Kaganovich defeat Shumskyi's challenge, and became the leading spokesman for the official Party policy on the national question. When Stalin "bought" Skrypnyk's support against Bukharin by withdrawing Kaganovich, Skrypnyk came to see himself as a virtually independent national leader, pushing the Ukrainization policy with such vigor that Ukrainians were quickly becoming a sociologically complete nation: Ukrainians became a majority in the Party, the industrial proletariat, and were rapidly penetrating the elites of the society in which they had hitherto been confined to the bottom level of the social hierarchy. Skrypnyk developed his own theory of the nationality question, designed to justify his policy of pursuing what he construed to be his nation's interests, even demanding border revisions and seeking to establish a cultural protectorate over Ukrainians in Russia. Ukrainization was working, and even outside the USSR Ukrainians came to regard Skrypnyk as a national leader. Communism was indeed taking root in non-Russian national soil.

The Skrypnyk years witness the greatest quantitative successes in Ukrainization: numbers of books and newspapers published in Ukrainian, the Ukrainization of the cities and working class, and the recruitment of ethnic Ukrainians into the political and cultural elites of the country. Meanwhile, the quality of Soviet politics was changing. After Volobuiev, important political issues could only be discussed from only one point of view, the Party's official view. The Cultural Revolution which began with the Shakhty trial was manipulated in Ukraine in such a way as to discredit the national intelligentsia as a whole. Collectivization meant the forcible suppression of the primary constituency which Ukrainization was designed to placate, the Ukrainian peasantry. The Soviet Union, in short, became more regimented and centralized, thereby decreasing the value to Moscow of tolerating strong national leaders who could accord their regimes some veneer of national legitimacy.

At the basis of the political situation was the countryside. As Stalin put it, "The nationality problem is, *according to the essence of the matter,* a problem of the peasants." Ukraine was able to go its own way to the extent it was, because the regime never felt as secure in the Ukrainian village as in the Russian countryside. Thus, the *komnezamy,* a rough and ready expedient from the civil war without counterpart in Russia, was retained at Stalin's insistence and strengthened during forced collectivization on Moscow's orders. It was not until 1925, that Ukrainian *silrady* were given a position equal to that of the village Soviets in Russia. Collectivization in Ukraine implied a far more difficult struggle in Ukraine than in Russia, and required a complete change in the political situation. It took a deliberately created famine and cost the lives of millions for collectivization to be accepted and the Ukrainian people to be cowed.

Moscow's attack on Skrypnyk was protracted and carried on with considerable subtlety. It included chipping away his bureaucratic bailiwick in the Commissariat of Education, attacking his intellectual clients, such as the historian Matvii Iavorskyi, and indirectly implicating his policies at the show trial of the Union for the Liberation of Ukraine. The final assault on Skrypnyk could take place only within the context of an undeclared but nonetheless real war against the Ukrainian countryside, a war no less genuine because the major weapon with which it was fought was food.

The final defeat of the Ukrainians in 1933, and the end of Ukrainization, can be seen at the end of a process which began at the turn of the century with the formation of the first Ukrainian political parties in imperial Russia. This suppression of Ukrainian politics in the Soviet

Union paved the way for the revival of Russian centralism, chauvinism, and imperialism. Beginning in 1934, historians were ordered to emphasize the "historically progressive role" of the tsars and their conquests; journalists, to extol Moscow as the capital of the fatherland of the workers of the whole world. Only then did the Soviet Union truly become what it remains to this day, a totalitarian regime attempting to control all spheres of life and a revived Russian Empire in all but name.

In 1933, the Ukrainians were broken as a political factor and social organism. Ukrainian nationality was exiled from the cities to the countryside whence it came. But recurrent campaigns against Ukrainian "bourgeois nationalism" and the limited return to some of Skrypnyk's policies by Petro Shelest in the 1960s, show that even in the Communist Party itself, Ukrainian national aspirations persist.[2]

Implicit in this study is a question of the specific versus the general. What was unique about the events described and what is analogous to similar events elsewhere? While indigenization was applied to all non-Russian peoples in the Soviet Union, the Ukrainian experience was unique in the scope of its achievements, the depth of the strains it produced, and the harshness of the measures required to suppress it. The cultural revival of the 1920s, and the breadth of the discussions that took place, would have been inconceivable outside the environment of limited toleration characteristic of the NEP period of Soviet history. The political situation that produced and shaped Ukrainian communism was one in which the regime recognized its inability to conquer strong forces in society and tried instead to placate them. All such forces were destroyed during the Five Year Plans when the regime settled its accounts with those to whom it had earlier deferred. Nationality policy was linked with the situation in the countryside, and forced collectivization subjugated the peasants as never before.

Yet parallels are not far to seek: they abound not in the USSR but in the so-called Peoples Democracies of the Warsaw Pact. There nations are more developed than the Ukrainians were in 1917, and they never experienced immense traumas undergone by the peoples of the Soviet Union before World War II. Civil society there is far stronger than it ever was in Ukraine, and has never really been subdued in the

---

[2] An interesting essay comparing Skrypnyk and Shelest within the continuing problem of Ukrainian communism's approach to Ukrainian national aspirations is Yaroslav Bilinsky, "Mykola Skrypnyk and Petro Shelest: An Essay on the Persistence and Limits of Ukrainian National Communism," in Jeremy R. Azrael, ed., *Soviet Nationality Policies and Practices* (New York, 1978), pp. 105–143.

manner of Soviet society during the Five Year Plans. The regimes, unpopular in themselves and unable to rely solely on brute force, have been unable to remain isolated from the influence of those they rule. They are caught between Moscow and their own subjects, and they have on occasion shown a degree of independence quite discomforting to Moscow. Sometimes, as with Tito and partially with Gomulka, the quest for national roads to socialism has been successful. Other times, as with Dubček, it has ended in tragedy. Unlike Ukraine, the nations of Eastern Europe have retained control over their national armies and police, crucial levers of power allowing them to succeed where Skrypnyk failed. National communism might have been defeated in Ukraine where it was first attempted, but it persists in Eastern Europe, and even in Ukraine its hopes have not yet perished.

Bibliography

Adams, Arthur E. *Bolsheviks in the Ukraine: The Second Campaign, 1918–1919* (New Haven and London: Yale University Press, 1963).

Alatortseva, A. I. and Alekseeva, G. O., compilers. *50 let Sovetskoi istoricheskoi nauki: Khronika nauchnoi zhizni* (Moscow: Mysl, 1971).

Antonov-Ovseenko, Anton. *The Time of Stalin: Portrait of a Tyranny* (New York: Harper and Row, 1981).

Babii, B. M. *Ukrainska radianska derzhava v period vidbudovy narodnoho hospodarstva (1921–1925 rr.)* (Kiev: Vydavnytstvo Akademii Nauk Ukrainskoi RSR, 1961).

Babko, Iu. and Bilokobylskyi, I. *Mykola Oleksiiovych Skrypnyk* (Kiev: Vydavnytstvo politychnoi literatury Ukrainy, 1967).

Bachynskyi, P. *Panas Petrovych Liubchenko* (Kiev: Vyd. politychnoi literatury Ukrainy, 1971).

Bahalii, D. I. *Narys istorii Ukrainy na sotsiialno-ekonomichnomu grunti* (Kiev: Ukrainska Akademiia Nauk, 1928).

———. "Persha sproba nacherku istorii Ukrainy na tli istorychnoho materiializmu," *Chervonyi shliakh*, 1923, no. 9, 145–161.

———. "Z pryvodu antykrytyky prof. M. I. Iavorskoho," *Chervonyi shliakh*, 1924, no. 6, pp. 149–160.

Baikar, Oleksa. "Krymsko-ukrainska pravnycha mova," *Chervonyi shliakh*, 1930, no. 1, pp. 135–156.

Bailes, Kendall E. *Technology and Society under Lenin and Stalin: Origins of the Soviet Technical Intelligentsia, 1917–1941* (Princeton: Princeton University Press, 1978).

Barber, John. *Soviet Historians in Crisis, 1928–1932* (New York: Holmes and Meyer, 1981).

Bennigsen, Alexandre A. and Wimbush, S. Enders. *Muslim National Communism in the Soviet Union: A Revolutionary Strategy for the Colonial World* (Chicago and London: University of Chicago Press, 1979).

Berezovchuk, M. D. "Borotba komnezamiv za rozvytok narodnoi osvity na seli v 1921–1925 rr." *Naukovi pratsi z istorii KPRS*, no. 5, 1965, pp. 61–71.

————. "Rol komnezamiv u sotsialistychnii perebudovi sela," *Ukrainskyi istorychnyi zhurnal*, 1960, no. 3, pp. 46–57.

Biletskyi, L. "Umovy literaturnoi pratsi na Ukraini (1919–1926)," *Nova Ukraina*, 1927, no. 10–11, pp. 66–82.

Bilinsky, Yaroslav. "The Communist Takeover of the Ukraine," in Hunczak, ed., *Ukraine, 1917–1921*, pp. 104–127.

————. "Mykola Skrypnyk and Petro Shelest," in Jeremy R. Azrael, ed., *Soviet Nationality Policies and Practices* (New York: Praegar, 1978), pp. 105–143.

The Black Deeds of the Kremlin: A White Book (Toronto and Detroit: DOBRUS, 1953–1955).

Blackstock, Paul W. and Hoselitz, Bert F. eds. *The Russian Menace to Europe* (Glencoe, Ill.: Free Press, 1951).

Bloom, Solomon F. *The World of Nations: A Study of the National Implications in the Work of Karl Marx* (New York: Columbia University Press, 1942).

Bociurkiw, Bohdan R. "Ukrainization Movements within the Russian Orthodox Church and the Ukrainian Autocephalous Orthodox Church," *Harvard Ukrainian Studies*, vol. 3–4, 1979–80, part 1, pp. 92–111.

Boiko, Volodymyr. "URE i zavdannia marksystskoho movoznavstva," *Za markso-leninsku krytyku*, 1932, no. 7–8, pp. 73–82.

Bolshevitskie organizatsii Ukrainy v period ustanovleniia i ukrepleniia Sovetskoi vlasti (noiabr 1917 - aprel 1919 gg.) (Sbornik dokumentov i materialov) (Kiev: Gospolitizdat USSR, 1962).

Borev, B. S. *Kak izbiraiut Sovety na Ukraine* (Kharkiv: Iuridicheskoe Izdatelstvo narkomiusta USSR, 1926).

Borys, Juryj. "Political Parties in Ukraine," in Hunczak, ed., *The Ukraine, 1917–1921*, pp. 128–158.

————. *The Sovietization of Ukraine 1917–1923: The Communist Doctrine and Practice of National Self-Determination* (Edmonton: Canadian Institute of Ukrainian Studies, 1980).

————. "Who Ruled the Soviet Ukraine in Stalin's Time?" *Canadian Slavonic Papers*, vol. 14, 1972, no. 2, pp. 213–233.

Bosh, Evgeniia. *God borby: Borba za vlast na Ukraine s aprelia 1917 g. do nemetskoi okupatsii* (Moscow and Leningrad: Gosizdat, 1925).

————. *Natsionalnoe pravitelstvo i sovetskaia vlast na Ukraine* (Moscow: Kommunist, 1919).

Boshyk, George Y. *The Rise of Ukrainian Political Parties in Russia, 1900–1907: With Special Reference to Social Democracy* (D. Phil. thesis: University of Oxford, 1981).

Bottomore, Tom and Goode, Patrick, eds., *Austro-Marxism* (Oxford: University Press, 1976).

Bovanenko, Dm. "Naukovyi tsentr marksystskoi dumky na Ukraini," *Chervonyi shliakh*, 1929, no. 5–6, pp. 184–196.

Brown, Edward J. *The Proletarian Episode in Russian Literature, 1928–1933* (New York: Columbia University Press, 1953).

Bryl, Hnat. "Do likvidatsii zrady v KPZU," *Bilshovyk Ukrainy,* 1929, no. 4, pp. 88–101; no. 5, pp. 80–101.

Budivnytstvo Radianskoi Ukrainy (Kharkiv: Derzhvydav Ukrainy, 1928).

Carr, E. H. *Socialism in One Country, 1924–1926* (Baltimore: Penguin, 1970).

———. and Davies, R. W. *Foundations of a Planned Economy, 1926–1929* (Baltimore: Penguin, 1974).

Carrère d'Encausse, Hélène. *Decline of an Empire: The Soviet Socialist Republics in Revolt* (New York: Newsweek Books, 1979).

Chamberlin, William Henry. *The Ukraine: A Submerged Nation* (New York: Macmillan, 1944).

Chaplenko, Vasyl. *Propashchi syly: Ukrainske pysmenstvo pid komunistychnym rezhymom, 1920–1933* (Winnipeg: Nakladom Ukrainskoi Vilnoi Akademii Nauk, 1960).

Cherez pryzmu marksivskoi krytyky (Lviv: Kultura, 1928).

Chlebowczyk, Jósef. "Marks i Engels a problem małych narodów w Europie środkowo-wschodniej (W kwestii genezy i rozwoju tzw. narodów niehistorycznych)," *Z pola walki,* 1970, no. 2, pp. 15–43.

Chmyga, A. F. *Kolkhoznoe dvizhenie na Ukraine (1917–1929 gg): Ocherki istorii* (Moscow: Izdatelstvo Moskovskogo universiteta, 1974).

———. "XV sezd VKP(b) o kollektivizatsii selskogo khoziaistva i nachalo osushchestvleniia ego reshenii na Ukraine," *Vestnik Moskovskogo univer-siteta,* 1967, no. 6, pp. 19–33.

Churchill, Winston S. *The Hinge of Fate* (Boston: Houghton Mifflin, 1960).

Chyrko, V. A. *Kommunisticheskaia partiia—organizator bratskogo sotrud-nichestva narodov Ukrainy i Rossii v 1917–1922 gg.* (Moscow: Mysl, 1967).

———. "Krakh ideolohii ta polityky natsionalistychnoi partii Ukapistiv," *Ukrainskyi istorychnyi zhurnal,* 1968, no. 12, pp. 24–35.

Conquest, Robert. *The Great Terror: Stalin's Purge of the Thirties* (New York: Collier, 1973).

———, ed. *Agricultural Workers in the USSR* (London, Sidney, and Toron-to: The Bodley Head, 1968).

———, ed. *Soviet Nationalities Policy in Practice* (New York and Washington: Praeger, 1967).

Crossman, Richard, ed. *The God that Failed* (New York, Toronto, and Lon-don: Bantam, 1965).

Czajkowskyj, Melanie. "Volodymyr Vynnchenko and His Mission to Moscow and Kharkiv," *Journal of Ukrainian Graduate Studies,* no. 5, 1978, pp. 6–24.

Dalrymple, Dana. "The Soviet Famine of 1932–1934," *Soviet Studies,* vol. 15, 1964, pp. 250–284.

———. "The Soviet Famine of 1932–1934: Some Further References," *Soviet Studies,* vol. 16, 1965, pp. 471–475.

Daniels, Robert V. *The Conscience of the Revolution: Communist Opposition in Soviet Russia* (New York: Simon and Schuster, 1960).

Davis, Horace B. *Nationalism and Socialism: Marxist and Labor Theories of Nationalism to 1917* (New York and London: Monthly Review Press, 1967).

Desiatyi sezd RKP(b), mart 1921 goda: Stenograficheskii otchet (Moscow: Gospolitizdat, 1963).

Deutscher, Isaac. *Stalin: A Political Biography* (New York and London: Oxford University Press, 1966).

Diadchenko, V. A., Los, F. E., Sarbei, B. G. "Razvitie istoricheskoi nauki na Ukraine (1917–1963 gg.)," *Voprosy istorii,* 1964, no. 1, pp. 3–26.

Dimanshtein, S. M., ed. *Revoliutsiia i natsionalnyi vopros: Dokumenty i materialy po istorii natsionalnogo voprosa v Rossii i SSSR v XX veke* (Moscow: Izdatelstvo Kommunisticheskoi akademii, 1930).

Djilas, Milovan. *Lenin on the Relations Between Socialist States* (New York: Yugoslav Information Bureau, n. d.).

Dmytryshyn, Basil. *Moscow and the Ukraine, 1918–1953: A Study of Russian Bolshevik Nationality Policy* (New York: Bookman Associates, 1956).

———. "National and Social Composition of the Membership of the Communist Party (bolshevik) of the Ukraine, 1918–1928," *Journal of Central European Affairs,* vol. 17, 1957, pp. 243–258.

Dolengo, M. "Kyiv ta Kharkiv—literaturni vzaiemovidnoshennia," *Chervonyi shliakh,* 1923, no. 6–7, pp. 151–157.

Doroshenko, Dmytro. "A Survey of Ukrainian Historiography," *Annals of the Ukrainian Academy of Arts and Sciences in the U.S.,* vol. 5–6, 1957, pp. 3–304.

———. "Die Entwicklung der Geschichtsforschung in der Sowjetukraine in den letzten Jahren," *Mitteilungen des ukrainischen wissenschaftlichen Instituts in Berlin,* Heft 2, 1928, pp. 35–56.

———. *Istoriia Ukrainy, 1917–1923 rr.* (New York: Bulava, 1954).

———. *Moi spomyny pro davnie-mynule (1901–1914 roky)* (Winnipeg: Tryzub, 1949).

———. *Moi spomyny pro nedavnie-mynule (1914–1920)* (Munich: Ukrainske vydavnytstvo, 1969).

———. "Ukrainische Akademie der Wissenschaft in Kyjiv," *Mitteilungen des ukrainischen wissenschaftlichen Instituts in Berlin,* Heft 1, 1927, pp. 11–20.

———. "Voina i revoliutsiia na Ukraine," *Istorik i sovremennik,* vol. 1, pp. 207–245; vol. 2, pp. 180–205; vol. 4, pp. 178–209; vol. 5, pp. 73–205 (1922–1924).

———. *Z istorii ukrainskoi politychnoi dumky za chasiv svitovoi viiny* (Prague: Fr. Herman, 1936).

Dovhan, Kost. "Ukrainska literatura i masovyi chytach," *Krytyka,* 1928, no. 8, pp. 26–45.

Dovzhenko, Alexander. *The Poet as Filmmaker: Selected Writings* (Cambridge, Massachusetts and London: MIT Press, 1973).

Dva roky roboty. Zvit Tsentralnoho Komitetu Komunistychnoi Partii (bilshovykiv) Ukrainy (Kharkiv: TsK KP(b)U, 1927).

Dvenadtsatyi sezd RKP(b), 17–25 aprelia 1923 goda: Stenograficheskii otchet (Moscow: Gospolitizdat, 1968).

"Dyskusiia z pryvodu shkemy istorii Ukrainy M. Iavorskoho," *Litopys revoliutsii,* 1930, no. 2, pp. 264–324.

Ellan, Vas. *Poezii* (Kharkiv: DVU, 1927).

Elwood, Ralph Carter. *Russian Social Democracy in the Underground: The RSDRP in the Ukraine, 1907–1914* (Assen: Internationaal Institut voor Geschiedenis, 1974).

Entsiklopedicheskii slovar russkogo bibliograficheskogo instituta Granat: Deiateli SSSR i Oktiabrskoi revoliutsii (Moscow: Granat, n.d.)

Fedenko, Panas. *Ukrainskyi rukh u 20 stolitti* (London: Nashe slovo, 1959).

Fedyshyn, Oleh S. *Germany's Drive to the East and the Ukrainian Revolution, 1917–1918* (New Brunswick: Rutgers University Press, 1971).

Fitzpatrick, Sheila. "Cultural Revolution in Russia, 1928–1932." *Journal of Contemporary History,* IX: 1 (1974), pp. 33–52.

———. "Culture and Politics Under Stalin: A Reappraisal," *Slavic Review,* vol. 25, 1976, no. 2, pp. 211–231.

———. *The Commissariat of Enlightenment: Soviet Organization of Education and the Arts Under Lunacharsky, October 1917–1921* (Cambridge: Cambridge University Press, 1970).

———, ed. *Cultural Revolution in Russia, 1928–1931* (Bloomington and London: Indiana University Press, 1978).

Frid, D. "Do pytannia pro korinnia KPU," *Bilshovyk Ukrainy,* 1927, no. 10, pp. 39–50; no. 14, pp. 27–38.

Ganzha, I. F., Slinko, I. I., Shostak, P. V. "Ukrainskoe selo na puti k sotsializmu," in V. P. Danilov, ed. *Ocherki istorii kollektivizatsii selskogo khoziaistva v soiuznykh respublikakh* (Moscow: Gospolitizdat, 1963), pp. 151–223.

Gitelman, Zvi. *Jewish Nationality and Soviet Politics: The Jewish Sections of the CPSU, 1917–1930* (Princeton: Princeton University Press, 1972).

Grabowicz, George G. "Some Further Observations on 'Non-historical' Nations and 'Incomplete' Literatures: A Reply," *Harvard Ukrainian Studies,* vol. 5, 1981, pp. 369–388.

Graham, Loren R. *The Soviet Academy of Sciences and the Communist Party, 1927–1932* (Princeton: Princeton University Press, 1967).

"Grigorevskaia avantiura (mai 1919 goda)," *Letopis revoliutsii,* no. 3, 1923, pp. 152–159.

Gurevitz, Baruch. *National Communism in the Soviet Union, 1918–1928.* UCIS Series in Russian and East European Studies, no. 3 (Pittsburgh: University of Pittsburgh Center for International Studies, 1980).

Guski, Andreas, "Zur Entwicklung der sowjetischen Arbeiter- und Bauernkorrespondentenbewegung 1917-1932," in Eberhard Knödler-Bunte and Gernot Erler, eds. *Kultur und Kulturrevolution in der Sowjetunion* (West Berlin: Aesthetik und Kommunikation Verlags, 1978), pp. 94-104.

Guthier, Stephen. "The Popular Base of Ukrainian Nationalism in 1917," *Slavic Review*, vol. 38, 1979, no. 1, pp. 30-47.

Hak, Anatol. "Ne tak Khvylovyi, iak ti Khvylovyniatka," *Ukrainski visti*, May 23, 1971, p. 5.

Halahan, M. "Likvidatsiia U. K. P.," *Nova Ukraina*, vol. 4, 1925, no. 1, pp. 26-38.

Halushko, E. M. *Narysy ideolohichnoi ta orhanizatsiinoi diialnosti KPZU v 1919-1928 rr.* (Lviv: Vydavnytstvo Lvivskoho universytetu, 1965).

Han, O. *Trahediia Mykoly Khvylovoho* (n.d.: Prometei, n.d.).

Hantsov, Vsevolod. "Problemy rozvytku literaturnoi movy," *Zhyttia i revoliutsiia*, 1925, no. 10, pp. 61-65.

Harin, M. "Iak ne treba pysaty istorii," *Litopys revoliutsii*, 1928, no. 6, pp. 321-332.

Harvard University Refugee Interview Project. A Schedule, File 12.

Hermaize, Osyp. "Desiatylittia Zhovtnevoi revoliutsii i ukrainska nauka," *Ukraina*, 1927, no. 6, pp. iii-vii.

―――. "Iuvilei ukrainskoi nauki: Sorok rokiv diialnosty akad. M. S. Hrushevskoho," *Zhyttia i revoliutsiia*, 1926, no. 10, pp. 93-99.

―――. *Narysy z istorii revoliutsiinoho rukhu na Ukraine. Tom I. Revoliutsiina Ukrainska Partiia (RUP)* (n. p.: Knyhospilka, 1926).

Hirchak, Ie. F. *Na dva fronta v borbe s natsionalizmom* (Moscow-Leningrad: Gosudarstvennoe izdatelstvo, 1930).

―――. "Platforma ukrainskoho natsionalizmu," *Bilshovyk Ukrainy*, 1928, no. 6, pp. 28-50.

Hoetzsch, Otto, ed. *Aus dem historischen Wissenschaft in der Sovet-Union: Vorträge ihrer Vertreter während der "Russischen Historikerwoche" veranstaltet in Berlin 1928 von der deutschen Gesellschaft zum Studien Osteuropas* (Berlin: Ost-Europa Verlag, 1929).

Holubenko, Petro. "Khvylovyi i Shpengler," *Suchasnist*, vol. 3, 1963, no. 5, pp. 53-70.

Holubnychy, Vsevolod. "Outline History of the Communist Party of the Ukraine," *Ukrainian Review*, no. 6, 1958, pp. 68-125.

―――. "Prychyny holodu 1932-1933 rr.," *Vpered: Ukrainskyi robitnychyi chasopys*, 1958, no. 10, pp. 1, 5-6.

―――. "The views of M. Volobuyev and V. Dobrohaiyev and Party Criticism," *Ukrainian Review*, no. 3, 1956, pp. 5-12.

Horak, Stephen M. "Michael Hrushevsky: Portrait of a Historian," *Canadian Slavonic Papers*, vol. 10, 1968, no. 3, pp. 341-356.

Horlach, M. I. "Rol profspilok Ukrainy u zdiisnenni kulturnykh peretvoren u period pobudovy sotsializmu (1925-1937 rr.)," *Naukovi pratsi z istorii KPRS*, no. 10, 1966, pp. 57-62.

————. "Uchast profspilok Ukrainy v borotbi za rozvytok narodnoi osvity v period dovoiennykh piatyrichok," *Naukovi pratsi z istorii KPRS*, no. 5, 1965, pp. 113-124.

Hrushevskyi, Mykh. "Mizh Moskvoiu i Varshavoiu," *Boritesia-poborete! Zakordonyi organ Ukrainskoi Partii Sotsiialistiv-Revoliutsioneriv*, no. 2, 1920, pp. 1-18.

————. "Perspektyvy i vymohy ukrainskoi nauky," *Ukraina*, 1926, no. 1, pp. 3-15.

————. *Pochatky hromadianstva (Genetychna sotsiologiia)* (Vienna: Ukrainskyi sotsiologichnyi instytut, 1921).

————. "The Traditional Scheme of 'Russian' History and the Problem of a Rational Organization of the History of the Eastern Slavs," *Annals of the Ukrainian Academy of Arts and Sciences in the U. S.*, vol. 2, 1952, no. 4 (6), pp. 355-364.

————. "V dvadtsat piati rokovyny smerty O. M. Lazarevskoho: Kilka sliv pro ioho naukovu spadshchynu ta ii doslidzhennia," *Ukraina*, 1927, no. 4, pp. 3-17.

————. "V pravopysnii spravi," *Ukraina*, 1926, no. 5, p. 191.

————, ed. *Z pochyniv ukrainskoho sotsiialistychnoho rukhu: Mykh. Drahamanov i zhenevskyi sotsiialistychnyi hurtok* (Vienna: Ukrainskyi sotsiologichnyi institut, 1922).

Hrynko, H. "Narys ukrainskoi ekonomiky," *Chervonyi shliakh*, 1926, no. 5-6, pp. 120-136.

————. "Zapadnyi upor SSSR (Ukraina)," *Khoziaistvo Ukrainy*, 1925, no. 10, pp. 3-8.

Hryshko, Vasyl I. *Moskva slozam ne viryt: Trahediia Ukrainy 1933 roku z perspektyvy 30 richchia (1933-1963)* (New York: DOBRUS, 1963).

Hunczak, Taras. "The Ukraine Under Hetman Pavlo Skoropadskyi," in Hunczak, ed., *The Ukraine, 1917-1921*, pp. 61-81.

————, ed. *The Ukraine, 1917-1921: A Study in Revolution* (Cambridge, Massachusetts: Harvard Ukrainian Research Institute, 1977).

Humenna, Dokiia. "Mii borh Serhiievi Pylypenkovi," *Ukrainski visti*, February 20, 1972, pp. 2-7.

Humesky, Assya. "Pamiati Serhiia Volodymyrovycha Pylypenka," *Novi dni*, January 1976, pp. 18-20; February 1976, pp. 11-14.

Hurevych, Z. "Psevdomarksyzm na sluzhbi ukrainskoho natsionalizmu (Do ostannikh vystupiv O. Hermaize)," *Bilshovyk Ukrainy*, 1929, no. 9, pp. 55-69.

Hutianskyi, S. K. *V. I. Lenin i kulturne budivnytstvo na Ukraini* (Kiev: Naukova dumka, 1965).

Iakubskyi, B. "Ukrainska literatura za desiat rokiv revoliutsii," *Hart*, 1927, no. 6-7, pp. 124-141.

————. "Zhyttia molode: Sproba literaturnoi kharakterystyky 'kyivskykh pluzhan'," *Chervonyi shliakh*, 1925, no. 9, pp. 111-119.

Ialovyi, Mykh. "Pershi khorobri," *Chervonyi shliakh,* 1923, no. 9, pp. 111–119.

Ianata, Prof. O. "Do orhanizovanoho rozvytku nauky na Ukraini," *Chervonyi shliakh,* 1923, no. 2, pp. 173–182.

Iatsymirskyi, B. "Za marksystske ozbroiennia movoznavchykh kadriv," *Chervonyi shliakh,* 1932, no. 11–12, pp. 87–92.

Iavorskyi, M. I. "De shcho pro 'krytychnu' krytyku, pro 'obiektyvnu' istoriiu ta shche i pro babusynu spidnytsiu," *Chervonyi shliakh,* 1924, no. 3, pp. 167–182.

———. "Die Ergebnisse der ukrainischen Geschichtsforschung in den Jahren 1917–1927," in Hoetzsch, ed. *Aus dem historischen Wissenschaft in der Sovet-Union,* pp. 98–105.

———. "K istorii KP(b)U," in *Oktiabrskaia revoliutsiia: Pervoe piatiletie* (Kharkiv: Gosizdat Ukrainy, 1922), pp. 93–130.

———. *Narysy istorii Ukrainy* (Kiev: DVU, 1923).

———. *Narysy z istorii revoliutsiinoi borotby na Ukraini* (Kharkiv: DVU, 1927–1928).

———. "Problema ukrainskoi natsionalnoi-demokratychnoi revoliutsii u 1917 r., ii istorychni osnovy ta ii rukhovi syly," *Chervonyi shliakh,* 1927, no. 2, pp. 93–116; no. 4, pp. 96–116.

———. "Suchasni techii sered ukrainskoi istoriohrafii," in *Kryza suchasnoi burzhuaznoi nauky ta marksyzm: Zbirnyk* (Kharkiv: DVU, 1929), pp. 18–38.

———. "Westeuropäische Einflüsse auf die Ideengestaltung der sozialen Bewegung in der Ukraine im zweiten und dritten Viertel des XIX. Jahrhunderts," in Otto Hoetzsch, ed., *Aus dem historischen Wissenschaft in der Sovet-Union,* pp. 88–97.

Ilnytskyi, Roman. "Shistdesiat dniv ukrainskoi polityky (Lystopad-hruden 1917)," *Suchasnist,* vol. 12, 1972, no. 7–8, pp. 120–132.

———. "Tsentralna Rada i bolshevyky voseny 1917 roku. Chomu Tsentralna Rada ne vyznala uriadu Lenina," *Suchasnist,* vol. 12, 1972, no. 10, pp. 57–66.

"Instytut Naukovoi Movy Vseukrainskoi Akademii nauk," *Chervonyi shliakh,* 1923, no. 1, pp. 245–246.

Iuditskyi, A. "Bund v Cherkasskom raione v 1904–5 gg.," *Letopis revoliutsii,* no. 5, 1923, pp. 136–146.

Iugov, M. "Polozhenie i zadachi istoricheskogo fronta v Belorussii," *Istorik-marksist,* vol. 17, 1930, pp. 42–50.

Iurchenko, O. *Chetverta konferentsiia KP(b)U* (Kiev: Derzhpolitvydav Ukrainy, 1961).

Izvestiia (Moscow: 1917–1933).

Jasny, Naum. *The Socialized Agriculture of the USSR: Plans and Performance* (Stanford: Stanford University Press, 1949).

Johanson, Mexajlo. "Prystosuvannia latynytsi do potreb ukrainskoi movy," *Chervonyi shliakh,* 1923, no. 9, pp. 167–169.

K. "Klasova borotba y natsionalna solidarnist," *Ukrainska khata*, 1909, no. 7–8, pp. 376–390.

Kachinskii, V. "Zemelnaia politika sovvlasti na Ukraine v 1919 g.," *Litopys revoliutsii*, 1929, no. 1, pp. 7–51.

Kagan, S. *Agrarnaia revoliutsiia na Kievshchine: K voprosu o sotsialnykh i politicheskikh protsessakh na sele* (Kiev: Gosizdat Ukrainy, 1923).

Kaganovich, L. "Rozlam v KPZU i natsionalna polityka KP(b)U," *Bilshovyk Ukrainy*, 1928, no. 6, pp. 12–21.

Kak i pochemu Ispolkom Kominterna rasputil UKP (Kharkiv: Proletarii, 1925).

Karcz, Jerzy F. "Thoughts on the Grain Problem," *Soviet Studies*, vol. 18, 1967, pp. 399–434.

Kasianenko, E. "Kriza movy i shliakh ii rozvytku skriz sotsiializmu," *Komunist*, no. 1, August 1920, pp. 9–11.

Khmil, I. V. *Trudiashche selianstvo Ukrainy v borotbi za vladu Rad* (Kiev: Naukova dumka, 1977).

"Khronika: Zovnishia i vnutrishnia rabota 'Vaplite'," *Vaplite: Zoshyt pershyi*, 1926, pp. 97–98.

Khrushchev, Nikita S. *The Crimes of the Stalin Era: Special Report to the 20th Congress of the Communist Party of the Soviet Union* (New York: New Leader, 1962).

———. *Khrushchev Remembers* (Boston and Toronto: Little, Brown, 1970).

———. *Pro dalnyi rozvytok kolhospnoho ladu i reorhanizatsiiu mashynno-traktornykh stantsii* (Kiev: Derzhpolitvydav URSR, 1958).

Khrystiuk, Pavlo. *Zamitky i materiialy do istorii ukrainskoi revoliutsii, 1917–1920 rr.* (Vienna: Ukrainskyi sotsiologychnyi instytut, 1921–1922).

Khvylia, Andrii. "Burzhuazno-natsionalistychna trybuna," *Bilshovyk Ukrainy*, 1931, no. 5, pp. 46–58.

———. *Do rozviazannia natsionalnoho pytannia na Ukraini* (Kharkiv: DVU, 1930).

———. "Na borotbu z natsionalizmom na movnomu fronti," *Za markso-leninsku krytyku*, 1933, no. 7, pp. 3–26.

———. *Vid ukhylu u prirvu* Kharkiv: 1928), reprinted as *Vid natsionalnoho komunizmu do ukrainskoho antykomunistychnoho natsionalizmu* (New York: DOBRUS, 1954).

———. "Vykorinyty, znyshchyty natsionalistychne korinnia na movnomu fronti," *Bilshovyk Ukrainy*, 1933, no. 7–8. pp. 42–56.

Khvylovyi, Mykola. "Chym prycharuvala 'Nova Generatsiia' tov. Sukhyno-Khomenka," *Prolitfront*, 1930, no. 3, pp. 229–269.

———. *Dumky proty techii* (Kharkiv: Derzhvydav Ukrainy, 1926).

———. *Kamo hriadeshy: Pamflety* (Kharkiv: DVU, 1925).

———. "Krychushche bozhestvo," *Prolitfront*, 1930, no. 1, pp. 158–173.

———. "Otvertyi list do Volodymya Koriaka," *Vaplite*, 1927, no. 5, pp. 158–173.

———. *Tvory v piatokh tomakh* (New York, Baltimore, Toronto: Smoloskyp, 1978–).

————. "Valdshnepy," *Vaplite*, 1927, no. 5, pp. 5–69.

Koch, Hans. "Mychajlo Hruševskyj (1866–1966): Zum 100jährigen Geburtstag," *Ukraine in Vergangenheit und Gegenwart*, vol. 13, 1966, no. 37, pp. 151–158.

Kolasky, John. *Education in Soviet Ukraine: A Study in Discrimination and Russification* (Toronto: Peter Martin Associates, 1968).

Komarenko, N. V. *Ustanovy istorychnoi nauky v Ukrainskii RSR* (Kiev: Naukova dumka, 1973).

————. *Zhurnal "Litopys revoliutsii": Istoriohrafichnyi narys* (Kiev: Naukova dumka, 1970).

Komitety nezamozhnykh selian Ukrainy (1920–1933): Zbirnyk dokumentiv i materialiv (Kiev: Naukova dumka, 1968).

Kommunisticheskaia Partiia—Vdokhnovitel i organizator obedinitelnogo dvizheniia ukrainskogo naroda za obrazovanie SSSR: Sbornik dokumentov i materialov (Kiev:Gospolitizdat Ukrainy, 1962).

Komunistychna Partiia Ukrainy v rezoliutsiiakh i reshenniakh zizdiv, konferentsii i plenumiv TsK (Kiev: Politvydav Ukrainy, 1976).

Koniukhov, G. *KPSS v borbe s khlebnymi zatrudneniiami v strane (1928–1929)* (Moscow: Sotsekgiz, 1960).

Korduba, Myron. *La littérature historique soviétique-ukrainienne: Compte-rendu 1917–1931* (Munich: Fink, 1972).

Koriak, V. "Iak marksyst Sukhyno-Khomenko 'vziav' marksysta Lenina," *Krytyka*, 1928, no. 6, pp. 99–110.

Koropeckyj, Ivan Swiatoslaw. *The Economics of Investment in Ukrainian Industry, 1928–1937* (Ph.D. Dissertation: Columbia University, 1964).

Kostiuk, Hryhory, "Mykola Khvylovyi: Zhyttia, doba, tvorchist," in Khvylovyi, *Tvory u piatokh tomakh*, vol. 1, pp. 15–106.

————. "M. Zerov, P. Fylypovych, M. Drai-Khmara," *Ukrainska literaturna hazeta*, vol. 15, 1959, nos. 11, 12, vol. 6, 1960, nos. 1, 2.

————. "Ostanni roky zhyttia akademyka M. Hrushevskoho (Za Sovietskoiu presoiu i spohady suchasnykiv, 1934–1954)," *Ukrainskyi zbirnyk*, no. 1, 1954, pp. 73–84.

————. *Stalinist Rule in the Ukraine: A Study in the Decade of Mass Terror (1929–1939)* (London: Atlantic Books, 1960).

————. *Volodymyr Vynnchenko ta ioho doba: Dozlidzhennia, krytyka, polemika*, (New York: Ukrainska Vilna Akademiia Nauk, 1980).

Koszeliwec, Iwan. *Mykola Skrypnyk*, (Munich: Suchasnist, 1972).

Kovalevskyi, Mykola. *Pry dzherelakh borotby: Spomyny, vrazhennia, reflektsii* (Innsbruck: Mariia Kovalevska, 1960).

Kozlov, V. I. *Natsionalnosti SSSR (Etno-demograficheskii obzor)* (Moscow: Statistika, 1975).

Kravchenko, Victor. *I Chose Freedom: The Personal and Political Life of a Soviet Official* (New York: Garden City Publishing, 1946).

Krawchenko, Bohdan. "The Impact of Industrialization on the Social Structure of Ukraine," *Canadian Slavonic Papers,* vol. 22, 1980, no. 3, pp. 338–357.

―――. "The National Renaissance and the Working Class in Ukraine During the 1920s" (unpublished paper: Canadian Institute of Ukrainian Studies, 1982).

Krupnytskyi, Borys, "Die ukrainische Geschichtswissenschaft in der Sowjetunion, 1921–1941," *Jahrbücher für Geschichte Osteuropas,* vol. 6, 1941, no. 2/4, pp. 125–151.

―――. *Ukrainska istorychna nauka pid Sovietamy (1920–1950 roky)* (Munich: Institute for the Study of the U.S.S.R., 1957).

Krykunenko, O. M. *Borotba Komunistychnoi partii za zdiisneniia leninskoho kooperatyvnoho planu (1929–1931)* (Lviv: Vydavnytstvo Lvivskoho universytetu, 1970).

Krylov, I. *Systema osvity na Ukraini (1917–1930)* (Munich: Institute for the Study of the U.S.S.R., 1956).

Kucher, O. O. *Rozhrom zbroinoi vnutrishnoi kontrrevoliutsii na Ukraini u 1921–1923 rr.* (Kharkiv: Vydavnytstvo Kharkivskoho Universytetu, 1971).

Kulichenko, M. I. *Bolsheviki Kharkovshchiny v borbe za vlast Sovetov (1918–1920 gg.)* (Kharkiv: Izdatelstvo Kharkovskogo universiteta, 1966).

―――. *Borba Kommunisticheskoi partii za reshenie natsionalnogo voprosa v 1918–1920 godakh* (Kharkiv: Izdatelstvo Kharkovskogo universiteta, 1966).

Kulik, I. Iu. "Kievskaia organizatsiia ot fevralia do Oktiabria 1917 goda," *Letopis revoliutsii,* 1924, no. 1, pp. 189–204.

Kulish, Mykola. "Krytyka chy prokurorskyi dopyt?" *Vaplite,* 1927, no. 5, pp. 146–157.

―――. *Tvory* (New York: Ukrainska Vilna Akademiia Nauk, 1965).

Kultura i pobut (see *Visty VUTsVK*).

Kulturne budivnytstvo v Ukrainskii RSR: Vazhlyvishi rishennia Komunistychnoi partii i Radianskoho uriadu, 1917–1959 (Kiev: Derzhpolitvydav Ukrainy, 1959).

Kurbas, Les. "Shliakhy Berezolia," *Vaplite,* 1927, no. 3, pp. 141–157.

Kurs istorii ukrainskoi literaturnoi movy (Kiev: AN URSR, 1958, 1961).

Kyrychenko, N. "Apolohety kurkulstva," *Prolitfront,* 1930, no. 7–8, pp. 269–290.

Kyryliuk, Ievhen. "Zhovten i literaturna spadshyna ukrainskoho narodu," in *Zhovten i ukrainska kultura: Zbirnyk materialiv z mizhnarodnoho sympoziumu* (Prešov: 1968).

Lapchinskii, G. "Gomelskoe soveshchanie (vospominaniia)," *Letopis revoliutsii,* 1926, no. 6, pp. 36–50.

―――. "Z pershykh dniv vseukrainskoi Radianskoi vlady," *Letopis revoliutsii,* 1927, no. 5–6, pp. 46–66.

Larin, Prof. B. "Movnyi pobut mista," *Chervonyi shliakh,* 1928, no. 5–6, pp. 190–198.

Lawrynenko, Jurij. "Ukrainska sotsiial-demokratiia (hrupa USD) i ii lider Lesia Ukrainka," *Suchasnist*, vol. 11, 1971, no. 5, pp. 68–81; no. 6, pp. 56–71; no. 7–8, pp. 132–150.

————, ed. *Rozstriliane vidrodzhennia: Antolohiia, 1917–1933* (Paris: Instytut Literacki, 1959).

————, ed. *Ukrainian Communism and Soviet Russian Policy Toward the Ukraine: An Annotated Bibliography* (New York: Research Program on the U.S.S.R., 1953).

Leites, A. and Iashek, M., eds. *Desiat rokiv ukrainskoi literatury (1917–1927)* (Kharkiv: Derzhvydav Ukrainy, 1928, 1930).

Lenin, V. I. *Collected Works* (Moscow: Progress Publishers, 1960–1970).

————. *Polnoe sobranie sochinenii* (Moscow: Gospolitizdat, 1960–1965).

————. *V. I. Lenin pro Ukrainu* (Kiev: Derzhpolitvydav Ukrainy, 1959).

Levynskyi, V. *Iedyna nedilyma Sovitska Rosiia? (Na pravakh rukopysu)* (Kiev-Vienna: Nova doba, 1920).

Lewin, M. *Russian Peasants and Soviet Power: A Study of Collectivization* (New York: Norton, 1975).

————. "Society, State, and Ideology During the First Five Year Plan," in Shiela Fitzpatrick, ed., *Cultural Revolution in Russia, 1928–1931*, pp. 41–77.

Liubchenko, Arkadii. "Ioho taiemnytsia," *Novi dni*, vol. 2, 1943, no. 5, pp. 4–5, 10–12.

Loburets, V. E. *Formuvannia kadriv radianskoho robitnychoho klasu Ukrainy (1921–1932 rr.)* (Kharkiv: Vyshcha shkola, 1974).

Low, Alfred D. *Lenin on the Question of Nationality* (New York, Bookman Associates, 1958).

Lozynskyi, Mykhailo. *Halychyna v rr. 1918–1920* (New York: Chervona kalyna, 1970).

Luckyj, George S. N. *Literary Politics in the Soviet Ukraine, 1917–1934* (New York: Columbia University Press, 1956).

————, ed. *Modern Ukrainian Short Stories* (Littleton, Colorado: Ukrainian Academic Press, 1973).

————, ed. *Vaplitianskyi zbirnyk* (Toronto: Mosaic Press, 1977).

Lutarewytch, P. "A Resistance Group of the Ukrainian Underground, 1920–1926," *Ukrainian Review*, no. 2, 1956, pp. 86–120.

Luxemburg, Rosa. *The Industrial Development of Poland* (New York: Campaigner Publications, 1977).

————. *The National Question: Selected Writings*, Horace B. Davis, ed. (New York: Monthly Review Press, 1976).

Lykho, P. S. " 'Sovetskaia vlast na mestakh': Robota komunistychnoi partii Chornuskoho raionu na Poltavshchyni (1921–1941)," *Ukrainskyi zbirnyk*, no. 8, 1957, pp. 99–172.

M., O. "Ukrainska istorychna nauka v 1920-kh rokakh," *Suchasnyk*, vol. 1, 1948, no. 1, pp. 76–84.

Majstrenko, Iwan. *Borot'bism: A Chapter in the History of Ukrainian Communism* (New York: Research Program on the U.S.S.R., 1954).

———. "Do 25-richchia holodu 1933 r.," *Vpered: Ukrainskyi robitnychyi chasopys,* 1958, no. 7, pp. 1-2.

———. *Natsionalnaia politika KPSS v ee istoricheskom razvitii* (Munich: Suchasnist, 1978).

———. *Storinky z istorii Komunistychnoi partii Ukrainy* (Munich: Suchasnist, 1969).

Maksudov, S. *Dinamika poter naseleniia SSSR v pervoi polovine XX veka* (unpublished manuscript: Harvard Ukrainian Research Institute, 1982).

Mamet, L. "Otrazheniia marksizma v burzhuaznom vostokovedenii," *Istorik-marksist,* no. 17, 1930, pp. 69–96.

Manilov, V., ed. *1917 god na Kievshchine: Khronika sobytii* (Kiev: Gosizdat Ukrainy, 1928).

Marx, K., Engels, F., Lenin, V. *On Historical Materialism* (Moscow: Progress Publishers, 1972).

Mazepa, Isaak, *Bolshevyzm i okupatsiia Ukraina* (Lviv-Kiev: Znattia to syla, 1922).

———. *Ukraina v ohni i buri revoliutsii* (n.p.: Prometei, 1950).

Mazlakh, I. and Shakhrai, V. *Do khvyli: Shcho diietsia na Ukraini i z Ukrainoiu* (New York: Prolog, 1967).

———. *On the Current Situation in the Ukraine* (Ann Arbor: University of Michigan Press, 1970).

Medvedev, Roy A. *Let History Judge: The Origins and Consequences of Stalinism* (New York: Knopf, 1972).

Meisel, James H. and Kozera, Edwards S., eds. *Materials for the Study of the Soviet System: State and Party Constitutions, Laws, Decrees, Decisions and Official Statements of the Leaders in Translation* (2nd ed., Ann Arbor: George Wahr, 1953).

Melnyk, Zinowij Lew. *Soviet Capital Formation: Ukraine, 1928/29–1932* (Munich: Ukrainian Free University Press, 1965).

Memorandum Ukrainskoi Komunistychnoi Partii (borotbystiv) do Vykonavchoho Komitetu III-ho Komunistychnoho Internatsionalu (Kiev: Chervonyi prapor, 1920).

Memorandum Ukrainskoi Komunistychnoi Partii Kongresovi III. Komunistychnoi Internatsionalu (Vienna-Kiev: Nova doba, 1920).

Mikorskii, B. *Razrushenie kulturno-istoricheskikh pamiatnikov v Kieve v 1934–1936 godakh* (Munich: Institute for the Study of the U.S.S.R., 1951).

Motyl, Alexander J. *The Turn to the Right: The Ideological Origins and Development of Ukrainian Nationalism, 1919–1929* (Boulder: East European Monographs, 1980).

Nakai, Kazuo. "The Election to the Ukrainian Constituent Assembly" (unpublished paper: Harvard Ukrainian Research Institute, 1982).

Narodnyi kommissariat prosveshcheniia USSR. *Narodnoe prosveshchenie na Ukraine* (Kharkiv: Chervonyi shliakh, 1924).

"Natsionalne pytannia na Ukraini ta opozytsiia," *Bilshovyk Ukrainy*, 1927, no. 10, pp. 3–11.

Nettl, J. P. *Rosa Luxemburg* (London: Oxford University Press, 1966).

The New York American (New York: 1935).

Nikolaienko, V. Iu. "Zhovtneva revoliutsiia i dokorinna perebudova narodnoi osvity na Ukraini," *Naukovi pratsi z istorii KPRS*, no. 5, 1965, pp. 13–29.

Nove, Alec. *An Economic History of the U.S.S.R.* (Baltimore: Penguin, 1972).

Oberländer, Erwin. *Sowjetpatriotismus und Geschichte: Dokumentation* (Cologne: Verlag Wissenschaft und Politik, 1967).

"Oblastnoi sezd RSDRP (b-ov) (Pervoe vseukrainskoe soveshchanie bolshevikov)," *Letopis revoliutsii*, 1926, no. 5–6, pp. 64–92.

Observator. "Dumky pro molodu beletrystyku," *Vaplite*, 1927, no. 4, pp. 194–201.

Ohloblyn, Olexander. "Ukrainian Historiography, 1917–1957," *Annals of the Ukrainian Academy of Arts and Sciences in the U.S.*, vol. 5–6, 1957, pp. 307–456.

Okhrymovych, Iuliian. *Rozvytok ukrainskoi natsionalno-politychnoi dumky (Vid pochatku XIX stolittia do Mykhaila Drahomanova)* (New York: Vydavnytstvo Chartoryskykh, 1965).

Oslikovskaia, E. S. and Snegov, A. V. "Za pravdivoe osveshchenie istorii proletarskoi revoliutsii," *Voprosy istorii*, 1956, no. 3.

Ovcharov, H. "Z pryvodu vysvitlennia pytannia pro borotbyzm" *Komunist Ukrainy*, 1958, no. 2, pp. 36–47.

Perchyk, L. "Nainovisha 'teoriia' Radianskoi ekonomiky," *Bilshovyk Ukrainy*, 1928, no. 8, pp. 51–59.

Peremoha Velykoi Zhovtnevoi sotsialistychnoi revoliutsii na Ukraini (Kiev: Naukova dumka, 1967).

"Pervaia vsesoiuznaia konferentsiia marksistko-leninskikh nauchno-issledovatelskikh uchrezhdenii (Iz stenograficheskogo otcheta)," *Vestnik Kommunisticheskoi akademii*, 1928, no. 2 (26), pp. 239–294; no. 3 (27), pp. 289–316.

Petrov, Viktor. *Ukrainski kulturni diiachi URSR, 1920–1940: Zhertvy bilshovytskoho teroru* (New York: Prolog, 1959).

Pidhainy, Oleh S. *The Formation of the Ukrainian Republic* (Toronto and New York: New Review Books, 1966).

Pigido Fedir. *Ukraina pid bolshevytskoiu okupatsiieiu* (Munich: Institute for the Study of the U.S.S.R., 1956).

———. *8,000,000: 1933 rik na Ukraini* (Winnipeg: Kultura i osvita, 1951).

Pikulyk, Roman Bahrij. "The Expressionist Experiment in Berezil': Kurbas and Kulish," *Canadian Slavonic Papers*, vol. 14, 1972, no. 2, pp. 324–344.

Piontkovskii, S. "Velikoderzhavnye tendentsii v istoriografii Rossii," *Istorik-Marksist*, vol. 17, 1930, pp. 21–27.

————. "Velikorusskaia burzhuaznaia istoriografiia poslednego desiatiletiia," *Istorik-marksist,* vol. 18–19, 1930, pp. 157–176.

Pipes, Richard. *The Formation of the Soviet Union: Communism and Nationalism, 1917–1923* (New York: Atheneum, 1968).

Pivtoradni, V. I. *Ukrainska literatura pershykh rokiv revoliutsii (1917–1923 rr.): Posibnyk dlia studentiv-zaochnykiv filolohichnykh fakultetiv pedahohichnykh instytutiv i universytetiv* (Kiev: Radianska shkola, 1968).

"Plan raboty Istparta TsK KP(b)U i Gub-Istpartov na 1925 god," *Letopis revoliutsii,* 1925, no. 4, p. 233.

"Platforma ideolohychnoi i khudozhnoi spilky selianskykh pysmennykiv 'Pluh,' " *Chervonyi shliakh,* 1923, no. 2, pp. 211–215.

Plushch, V. "The Union for the Liberation of the Ukraine," *Ukrainian Review,* no. 3, 1956, pp. 13–30.

Plys, I. "Osnovni momenty khlibnoi kampanii 1930–1931 roku," *Bilshovyk Ukrainy,* 1930, no. 13–14, pp. 17–25.

Plyushch, Leonid. *History's Carnival: A Dissident's Autobiography* (New York and London: Harcourt Brace Jovanovich, 1977).

Pohrebinskyi, M. *Stanislav Vikentiovych Kosior* (Kiev: Derzhpolitvydav Ukrainy, 1967).

Pokrovskii, M. N. *Izbrannye proizvedeniia* (Moscow: Mysl, 1965–1967).

————, ed. *Ocherki po istorii Oktiabrskoi revoliutsii: Raboty istoricheskogo seminariia Instituta Krasnoi professury* (Moscow-Leningrad: Gosizdat, 1927).

————, ed. *Russkaia istoricheskaia literatura v klassovom osveshchenii* (Moscow: Izd. Kommunisticheskoi akademii, 1927, 1930).

Polonska-Vasylenko, Natalia. *Two Conceptions of the History of Ukraine and Russia* (London: The Association of Ukrainians in Great Britain, 1968).

————. *Ukrainska Akademiia Nauk (Narys istorii)* (Munich: Institute for the Study of the U.S.S.R., 1955, 1958).

Popov, M. M. *Narys istorii Komunistychnoi Partii (bilshovykiv) Ukrainy* (Kharkiv: Proletarii, 1928).

————. "Pro natsionalistychni ukhyly v lavakh ukrainskoi part-ohranizatsii i pro zavdannia borotby z nymy," *Chervonyi shliakh,* 1933, no. 7, pp. 109–126.

Popov, O. "Narodne hospodarstvo Ukrainy ta Radianskyi Soiuz," *Zhyttia i revoliutsiia,* 1925, no. 8, pp. 59–67.

Porsh, Mykola. "Vidnosyny Ukrainy do ynskykh raioniv Rossii na robit-nychomu rynku na osnovi materialiv pershoho vseliudskoho perepysu," *Literaturno-naukovyi vistnyk,* 1912, no. 2, pp. 313–327; no. 3, pp. 521–545.

"Postanova TsK VKP(b) z 24 sichnia 1933 r. ta zavdannia bilshovykiv Ukrainy," *Bilshovyk Ukrainy,* 1933, no. 3, pp. 3–20.

Posternak, S. "Stan i perspektyva naukovoi pratsi na Ukraini ta pokhodzhen-nia ii z pratsiieiu naukovykh ustanov S.R.S.R.," *Zhyttia i revoliutsiia,* 1925, no. 1–2, pp. 37–38.

Presniakov, A.E. *The Formation of the Great Russian State* (Chicago: Quadrangle Books, 1970).

"Protibolshevytski povstannia na Ukraini v 1921 (Na osnovi ofitsiialnykh bolshevytskykh zvidomlen i inshykh nepublykovanykh materiialiv sot. N. P-pa)," *Litopys chervonoi kalyny,* vol. 4, 1932, no. 6, pp. 19–23; no. 9, pp. 6–7.

Prohrama Ukrainskoi Komunistychnoi Partii (Vienna-Kiev: Nova doba, 1920).

Puti narodno-khoziaistvennogo razvitiia USSR. Materialy k postroeniiu piatiletnego plana (Kharkiv: Ukrhospilka, 1928).

Pylypenko, S. "Odvertyj lyst do vsix, xto cikavyts'ja cijeju spravoiu," *Chervonyi shliakh,* 1923, no. 6–7, pp. 267–268.

Radkey, Oliver H. *The Election to the Russian Constituent Assembly of 1917* (Cambridge, Massachusetts: Harvard University Press, 1950).

Radziejowski, Janusz. "Collectivization in Ukraine in Light of Soviet Historiography," *Journal of Ukrainian Studies,* no. 9, 1980, pp. 3–13.

————. *Komunistyczny Partia Zachodniej Ukrainy, 1919–1929: Węzłowe problemy ideologiczne* (Cracow: Wydawnictwo Literackie, 1976).

————."Kwestia narodowa w partii komunistycznej na Ukrainie radzieckiej (1920–1927)," *Prezgląd historyczny,* 1971, no. 3, pp. 477–498.

Rakovskii, Kh. G. *Borba za osvobozhdenie derevni* (Kharkiv: Isdatelstvo Politotdela Ukrsovtrudarma, 1920).

————. "Relations Between Soviet Republics: Russia and Ukraine," *The Communist International,* vol. 1, 1920, no. 11–12, columns 2321–2323.

Ravich-Cherkasskii, M. *Istoriia Kommunisticheskoi partii (b-ov) Ukrainy* (Kharkiv: Gosizdat Ukrainy, 1923).

————. "Ukrainska khudozhna literatura ruskoiu movoiu," *Krytyka,* 1930, no. 3, pp. 27–38.

Redkina, I. "Do pytannia pro osoblyvosty proletarskoi revoliutsii na Ukraini," *Litopys Ukrainy,* 1928, no. 6, pp. 333–350.

Reshetar, John. *The Ukrainian Revolution, 1917–1920: A Study in Nationalism* (Princeton: Princeton University Press, 1953).

"Resolution on the National Question in Central Europe and the Balkans," *The Communist International,* no. 7, December 1924-January 1925, pp. 93–99.

Revoliutsiia v nebezpetsi! (Lyst Zak. Grupu U.K.P. do komunistiv i revoliutsiinykh sotsiialistiv Ievropy ta Ameryky) (Vienna-Kiev: Nova doba, 1920).

Revutsky, Valerian. "The Prophetic Madman: *The People's Malakhiy*—A Play by Mykola Kulish," *Canadian Slavonic Papers,* vol. 1, 1956, pp. 45–48.

Richytskyi, Andrii. "Do problemy likvidatsii perezhytkiv koloniialnosty ta natsionalizmu (Vidpovid M. Volobuievu)," *Bilshovyk Ukrainy,* 1928, no. 2, pp. 73–93; no. 3, pp. 64–84.

————. "Iak Hrushevskyi 'vypravliaie' Engelsa," *Chervonyi shliakh,* 1924, no. 3, pp. 183–190.

————. *Natsionalne pytannia doby nastupu sotsiialyzmu v svitli XVI zizdu VKP(b)* (Kharkiv: Proletar, 1931).

324   Communism and the Dilemmas of National Liberation

Rish, Arnold, "Ocherki po istorii 'Spilki', *Letopis revoliutsii*, 1925, no. 2, pp. 125–173; no. 3, pp. 77–107.

Rivosh, E. Iu. *P. P. Postyshev (Biograficheskii ocherk)* (Moscow: Gospolitizdat, 1962).

Robitnycha hazeta (Kiev, 1917).

Rosdolsky, Roman. *Zur nationalen Frage: Friedrich Engels und das Problem der "geschichtlosen" Völker* (Berlin: Olle und Wolter, 1979).

Rubach, M. A. "Burzhuazno-kurkulska natsionalistychna ideolohiia pid mashkaroiu demokratii 'trudovoho narodu'," *Chervonyi shliakh*, 1932, no. 5–6, pp. 115–135; no. 7–8, pp. 118–126; no. 11–12, pp. 127–136.

———. "Federalisticheskie teorii v istorii Rossii," in M. N. Pokrovskii, ed., *Russkaia istoricheskaia literatura v klassovom osveshchenii*, vol. 2, pp. 3–120.

———. "Reviziia bilshovytskoi skhemy rukhomykh syl i kharakteru revoliutsii 1905–1917 r.r. (Prava pliatforma na istorichnomu fronti)," *Bilshovyk Ukrainy*, 1929, no. 17–18, pp. 20–41.

———, ed. *Shliakhamy zaslan ta borotby (Dokumenty do zhyttiepysu t. Skrypnyka)* (Kharkiv: Proletar, 1932).

Rudnytskyi, Ivan L. *Mizh istoriieiu i politykoiu: Statti do istorii ta krytyky ukrainskoi suspilno-politychnoi dumky* (Munich: Suchasnist, 1973).

———. "Observations on the Problem of 'Historical' and 'Non-Historical' Nations," *Harvard Ukrainian Studies*, vol. 5, 1981, no. 3, pp. 358–368.

Rybalka, L. (pseudonym of Lev Iurkevych). *Rosiiski sotsiial-demokraty i natsionalne pytannia* (Munich: Suchasnist, 1969)

Sadovskyi, V. *Natsionalna polityka Sovitiv na Ukraini*. Pratsi Ukrainskoho naukovoho instytutu, vol. 5 (Warsaw: Ukrainskyi naukovyi instytut, 1937).

Sawka, Jaroslaw. "American Psychiatrist: Fifteen Million Died in the Thirties' Famine," *Ukrainian Quarterly*, vol. 38, 1982, no. 1, pp. 61–67.

Savchenko, Fedir. "Instytut Ukrainskoi Naukovoi Movy Ukrainskoi Akademii Nauk,"*Ukraina*, 1926, no. 5, pp. 179–186.

———. "Vseukrainska konferentsiia v spravi uporiadkuvannia ukrainskoho pravopysu," *Ukraina*, 1927, no. 3, pp. 203–205.

———. *Zaborona ukrainstva 1876r.* (Kharkiv-Kiev, DVU, 1930).

Sedmaia (aprelskaia) vserossiiskaia konferentsiia RSDRP (bolshevikov), aprel 1917 goda: Protokoly (Moscow: Gospolitizdat, 1958).

Selunskaia, V. M. "Preodolenie Kommunisticheskoi partii levatskikh oshibok v stroitelstve pervykh kolkhozov i sovkhozov," *Vestnik Moskovskogo universiteta*, 1965, no. 6, pp. 3–19.

———. "Rabochie-dvadtsatipiatitysiachniki—provodniki politiki partii v kolkhoznom stroitelstve," *Voprosy istorii*, 1954, no. 3, pp. 19–35.

———. "Vedushchaia rol proletarskikh tsentrov v ustanovlenii vlasti Sovetov na mestakh (oktiabr 1917 - vesna 1918 g.)," *Vestnik Moskovskogo universiteta*, 1967, no. 5, pp. 20–43.

Semenko, Mykh. "Mystetstvo iak kult," *Chervonyi shliakh*, 1924, no. 3, pp. 222–229.

Semenenko, Oleksander. *Kharkiv, Kharkiv...* (Munich: Suchasnist, 1977).

———. "Narkomiust Skrypnyk," *Suchasnist,* vol. 1, 1961, no. 6, pp. 91-101.
Serge, Victor, *Memoirs of a Revolutionary, 1901-1941* (London and New York: Oxford University Press, 1963).
Sh(apoval), M. "Chudo sv. Antoniia i Oleksander Shumskyi," *Nova Ukraina,* 1927, no. 8-9, pp. 71-75.
Sherekh, Iurii. *Ne dlia ditei: Literaturno-krytychni statti i esei* (New York: Prolog, 1964).
Shkandrij, Myroslav. *The "Literary Discussion" in Soviet Ukraine, 1925-1928* (Ph.D. dissertation: University of Toronto, 1980).
Shliakhy rozvytku suchasnoi literatury: Dysput 24 travnia 1925 r. (Kiev: Kultkomisiia mistskomu UAN, 1928).
Shlikhter, Aleksandr. "Borba za khleb na Ukraine v 1919 godu," *Litopys revoliutsii,* 1928, no. 2, pp. 96-135.
Shteppa, Konstantin. "The Lesser Evil Formula," in C. E. Black, ed., *Rewriting Russian History: Soviet Interpretations of Russia's Past* (New York: Vantage Books, 1962).
———. *Russian Historians and the Soviet State* (New Brunswick: Rutgers University Press, 1962).
Shumskyi, Oleksander, "Ideolohichna borotba v ukrainskomu kulturnomu protsesi," *Bolshovyk Ukrainy,* 1927, no. 2, pp. 11-26.
———. "Stara i nova Ukraina," *Chervonyi shliakh,* 1923, no. 2, pp. 91-110.
Silnický, František. "Lenin i borotbisty," *Novyi zhurnal,* no. 118, 1975, pp. 228-235.
———. *Natsionalnaia politika KPSS v period s 1917 po 1922 god* (Munich: Suchasnist, 1978).
Skorovstanskii, V. (pseudonym of Vasyl Shakhrai). *Revoliutsiia na Ukraine* (2nd Russian edition, Saratov: Borotba, 1919).
Skrypnyk, Mykola. "Do pytannia borotby za markso-leninske movoznavstvo," *Chervonyi shliakh,* 1932, no. 1-2, pp. 88-92.
———. *Do teorii borotby dvokh kultur* (2nd ed., Kharkiv: DVU, 1928).
———. "Khvylovyzm chy Shumskyzm?" *Bilshovyk Ukrainy,* 1927, no. 2, pp. 26-36.
———. "Kontr-revoliutsiine shkidnytstvo na kulturnomu fronti," *Chervonyi shliakh,* 1930, no. 4, pp. 138-150.
———. "Pomylky ta vypravlennia akademyka M. Iavorskoho," *Bilshovyk Ukrainy,* 1930, no. 2, pp. 12-26.
———. "Proty zaboboniv," *Krytyka,* 1929, no. 6, pp. 16-23.
———. *Statti i promovy* (Kharkiv: Proletar, 1930-1931).
———. *Statti i promovy z natsionalnoho pytannia* (Munich: Suchasnist, 1974).
———. "Z pryvodu ekonomichnoi platformy natsionalizmu," *Bilshovyk Ukrainy,* 1928, no. 6, pp. 45-50.
———. "Za leninsku filosofiiu," *Bilshovyk Ukrainy,* 1931, no. 6, pp. 18-35.
Skubitskii, T. "Klassovaia borba v ukrainskoi istoricheskoi literature," *Istorik-marksist,* vol. 17, 1930, p. 28-40.
Sluchevska, S. Ia. "Do pytannia pro homelsku naradu partiinykh orhanizatsii

pravoberezhnoi Ukrainy ta okremykh vidpovidalnykh pratsivnykiv (25–26 listopada 1919 r.)," *Ukrainskyi istorychnyi zhurnal*, 1965, no. 10, pp. 77–83.

Slynko, I. I. *Sotsialistychna perebudova i tekhnichna rekonstruktsiia silskoho hospodarstva Ukrainy (1927–1932 rr.)* (Kiev: AN URSR, 1961).

Smal-Stotskyi, Roman. *Ukrainska mova v sovietskii Ukraini* (2nd ed., New York, Toronto, Sidney, Paris: Shevchenko Scientific Society, 1969).

Smerechynskyi, S. "Kudy ide ukrainska mova (Do pytannia pro predykatyvnyi nominatyv ta 'predykat.' instrumental v ukrainskii movi)," *Chervonyi shliakh*, 1928, no. 5–6, pp. 172–189.

Smolych, Iurii. *Rozpovid pro nespokii* (Kiev: Radianskyi psymennyk, 1966–1972).

Snegirev, Gelii. "Mama moia, Mama...," *Kontinent*, no. 11, pp. 11–53; no. 12, pp. 163–209; no. 13, pp. 173–203; no. 14, pp. 152–192; no. 15, pp. 90–122 (1977–1978).

Sobranie Uzakonenii i Rasporiazhenii Raboche-Krestianskogo Pravitelstva Ukrainy (Kiev: 1919).

Soiuz Sovetskikh Sotsialisticheskikh Respublik. Tsentralnyi ispolnitelnyi komitet, 3 sozyva, I sessiia. Stenograficheskii otchet (Moscow: Izdatelstvo TsIK SSSR, 1925).

Soiuz Sovetskikh Sotsialisticheskikh Respublik. Tsentralnyi ispolnytelnyi komitet, 3 sozyva, 2 sessiia. Stenograficheskii otchet (Moscow: Izd. TsIK SSSR, 1926).

Solchanyk, Roman. *The Communist Party of Western Ukraine, 1919–1938* (Ph.D. dissertation: University of Michigan, 1973).

Souvarine, Boris. *Stalin: A Critical Survey of Bolshevism* (New York: Longman, Green and Co., 1939).

Stalin, I. V. *Sochineniia* (Moscow: Gospolitizdat, 1946–1950).

———. *Statti i rechi ob Ukraine: Sbornik* (Kiev: Partizdat TsK KP(b)U, 1936).

"Statut Vilnoi Akademii Proletarskoi Literatury 'Vaplite'," *Vaplite: Zoshyt pershyi*, 1926, pp. 94–99.

Sukhyno-Khomenko, V. "Na marksystskomu istorychnomu fronti," *Bilshovyk Ukrainy*, 1929, no. 17–18, pp. 42–55; no. 19, pp. 40–56.

———. "Problemy istorii KP(b)U (M. M. Popov—Narys istorii Komunistychnoi Partii (bilshovykiv) Ukrainy)," *Bilshovyk Ukrainy*, 1928, no. 13, pp. 69–78.

———. "Z pryvodu osoblyvostei proletarskoi revoliutsii na Ukraini," *Litopys revoliutsii*, 1928, no. 4, pp. 79–119.

Sullivant, Robert S. *Soviet Politics and the Ukraine, 1917–1957* (New York and London: Columbia University Press, 1962).

Tereshchenko, Iu. I. "Polityka 'voiennoho komunizmu' na Ukraini," *Ukrainskyi istorychnyi zhurnal*, 1980, no. 10, pp. 75–85.

Tillett, Lowell. *The Great Friendship: Soviet Historians on the Non-Russian Nationalities* (Chapel Hill: University of North Carolina Press, 1969).

Timofeev, A. N. "Dvadtsatipiatitysiachniki—provodniki politiki partii v kolkhoznom stroitelstve na Ukraine," in *Iz istorii borby Kommunisticheskoi partii Ukrainy za sotsialisticheskoe pereustroistvo selskoho khoziaistva* (Kiev: Izdatelstvo Kievskogo universiteta, 1961), pp. 77–107.

Timoshenko, Vladimir P. *Agricultural Russia and the Wheat Problem* (Stanford: Stanford University Press, 1932).

Tkachuk, I. "Nevidkladne zavdannia (Do spravy zavedennia latynskoho alfabitu v ukrainskim pysmi)," *Chervonyi shliakh,* 1924, no. 4–5, pp. 245–247.

"T-vo Dopomohy Rozvytku ta Poshyrenniu Ukrainskoi Naukovoi Movi," *Chervonyi shliakh,* 1924, no. 6, pp. 248–249.

Trudy Pervoi Vsesoiuznoi konferentsii Istorikov-marksistov (2nd ed., Moscow: Izd. Kommakademii, 1930).

Tymchenko, E. "Ustalennia ukrainskoho pravopysu," *Ukraina,* 1925, no. 4, pp. 187–191.

Ukrainskaia Kommunisticheskaia Partiia (borotbistov), *K razresheniiu natsionalnogo voprosa* (Kiev: Borotba, 1920).

Ukrainska Partiia Samostiinykiv-Sotsiialistiv. *Ukrainska Revoliutsiia (1917–1919): Diialnist partii S.-S. v zviazku z politychnymy podiiamy na Ukraini za chas 1901–1919: Ideologiia, prohram i statut partii* (Kiev-Vienna: Ukrainska Partiia Samostiinykiv-Sotsiialistiv, 1920).

"V bahni natsionalizmu," *Bilshovyk Ukrainy,* 1929, no. 4, pp. 3–11.

Vedmitskyi, Ol. "Literaturnyi front (1919–1931): Materiialy do skhemy rozvytku literaturnykh orhanizatsii na Radianskii Ukraini," *Literaturnyi arkhiv,* 1931, no. 4–5, pp. 104–147.

Verbytskyi, M. *Naibilshyi zlochyn Kremlia: Stvorennyi sovietskoiu Moskvoiu shtuchnyi holod v Ukraini 1932–33 r.* (London: DOBRUS, 1952).

"Vid redaktsii," *Chervonyi shliakh,* 1923, no. 1, pp. iii–vi.

Visti VUTsVK (Kharkiv, 1924–1933).

Vlasenko, E. "Finansy Ukrainy," *Nova Ukraina,* 1927, no. 12, pp. 3–20.

Volobuiev, M. "Do problemy ukrainskoi ekonomiky," in *Dokumenty ukrainskoho komunizmu* (New York: Prolog, 1962), pp. 132–250.

―――. "Proty ekonomichnoi pliatformy natsionalizmu (Do krytyky volobuivshchyny)," *Bilshovyk Ukrainy,* 1930, no. 5–6, pp. 54–69; no. 7, pp. 28–40.

VIII sezd RKP(b): Stenograficheskii otchet (Moscow: Izd. TsK RKP, 1919).

"Vseukrainskoe Soveshchanie Istpartov," *Letopis revoliutsii,* 1925, no. 3, 225–236; no. 4, 165–174.

"Vtoroe vseukrainskoe soveshchanie Istpartov," *Letopis revoliutsii,* 1926, no. 3–4, pp. 269–297.

Vtoroi sezd Kommunisticheskoi Partii (bolshevikov) Ukrainy (protokoly) (Second ed., Kharkiv: Proletarii, 1927).

Vynnychenko, V. *Ukrainska derzhavnist* (Vienna-Kiev: Nova doba, 1920).

―――. *Vidrodzhennia natsii* (Kiev-Vienna: Dzvin, 1920).

―――. Archive of Volodymyr Vynnchenko, Ukrainian Academy of Arts and Sciences in the U.S.

Vyshnia, Ostap. *Tvory v semy tomakh* (Kiev: Derzhvydav Ukrainy, 1963).
Weissberg, Alexander. *The Accused* (New York: Simon and Shuster, 1951).
Wexler, Paul N. *Purism and Language: A Study in Modern Ukrainian and Belorussian Nationalism (1940–1967)*. Language Science Monographs, vol. 11 (Bloomington: University of Indiana Press, 1974).
Wolfe, Bertram D. "The Influence of Early Military Decisions Upon the National Structure of the Soviet Union," *American Slavonic and East European Review,* vol. 9, 1950, no. 3, pp. 169–179.
Wynar, Lubomyr. "Ukrainian-Russian Confrontation in Historiography: Michael Hrushevsky versus the Traditional Scheme of 'Russian' History," *Ukrainian Quarterly.* vol. 30, 1974, no. 1, pp. 13–25.
Zabarevskyi, M. *Viacheslav Lypynskyi i ioho dumky pro ukrainsku natsiiu i derzhavu* (Kiev-Vienna: O. Zherevka, 1920).
Zahorskyi, P. S. and Stoian, P. K. *Narysy istorii komitetiv nezamozhnykh selian* (Kiev: Vydavnytstvo Akademii Nauk Ukrainskoi RSR, 1960).
Zaikin, Viach. "Ukrainskaia istoricheskaia literatura poslednikh let," *Na chuzhoi storone,* vol. 10, 1925, pp. 236–251.
Zatonskyi, V. *Leninovym shliakhom (Promova na poshyrenii naradi selkoriv hazety "Radianske Selo")* (Kharkiv: Radianske Selo, 1926).
———. *Natsionalna problema na Ukraini* (Kharkiv: DVU, 1927).
Zerov, Mykola. *Do dzherel: Istorychno-literaturni ta krytychni statti* (reprint: State College, Pa.: Dr. Vasyl Lutsiv, 1967).
Zhyvotko, Ark. "Do istorii Ukr. Partii Sotsiialistiv-Revoliutsioneriv," *Vilna Spilka: Neperiodychnyi organ UPSR,* no. 3, 1927–1929, pp. 128–132.
Zombe, E. "Dvadtsatipiatitysiachniki," *Voprosy istorii,* 1947, no. 5, pp. 3–22.

Index

330 *Communism and the Dilemmas of National Liberation*

HARVARD UKRAINIAN RESEARCH INSTITUTE

Monograph Series

Ievhen Sverstiuk, *Clandestine Essays,* translated with an introduction by G.S.N. Luckyj. Littleton, Colo.: Ukrainian Academic Press, 1976.

Taras Hunczak (ed.), *The Ukraine, 1917–1921: A Study in Revolution.* Cambridge, Mass.: Harvard Ukrainian Research Institute, distributed by Harvard University Press, 1977.

Paul R. Magocsi, *The Shaping of a National Identity: Subcarpathian Rus',* *1947–1948.* Cambridge, Mass., and London: Harvard University Press, 1978.

Ivan Zilyns'kyj, *A Phonetic Description of the Ukrainian Language,* translated by W.T. Zyla and W.M. Aycock. Cambridge, Mass.: Harvard Ukrainian Research Institute, distributed by Harvard University Press, 1979.

George G. Grabowicz, *Toward a History of Ukrainian Literature.* Cambridge, Mass.: Harvard Ukrainian Research Institute, distributed by Harvard University Press, 1981.

Omeljan Pritsak, *The Origin of Rus',* Vol. I. Cambridge, Mass.: Harvard Ukrainian Research Institute, distributed by Harvard University Press, 1981.

George G. Grabowicz, *The Poet as Mythmaker: A Study of Symbolic Meaning in Taras Ševčenko.* Cambridge, Mass.: Harvard Ukrainian Research Institute, distributed by Harvard University Press, 1982.

Andrei S. Markovits and Frank E. Sysyn (eds.), *Nationbuilding and the Politics of Nationalism: Essays on Austrian Galicia.* Cambridge, Mass.: Harvard Ukrainian Research Institute, distributed by Harvard University Press, 1982.

Paul R. Magocsi, *Galicia: An Historical Survey and Bibliographic Guide.* Toronto and Buffalo: University of Toronto Press, 1982.

John-Paul Himka, *Socialism in Galicia: The Emergence of Polish Social Democracy and Ukrainian Radicalism (1860–1890).* Cambridge, Mass.: Harvard Ukrainian Research Institute, distributed by Harvard University Press, 1983.

Sources and Document Series

Proceedings of the Conference on Carpatho-Ruthenian Immigration, transcribed, edited and annotated by Richard Renoff and Stephen Reynolds. Cambridge, Mass.: Harvard Ukrainian Research Institute, 1975.

Nonconformity and Dissent in the Ukrainian SSR, 1955–1975: A Select Bibliography, compiled by George Liber and Anna Mostovych. Cambridge, Mass.: Harvard Ukrainian Research Institute, 1978.

The Cossack Administration of the Hetmanate, 2 vols., compiled by George Gajecky. Cambridge, Mass.: Harvard Ukrainian Research Institute, 1978.

An Early Slavonic Psalter from Rus': St. Catherine's Monastery, Mt. Sinai, Volume I: Photoreproduction, edited by Moshé Altbauer and Horace G. Lunt. Cambridge, Mass.: Harvard Ukrainian Research Institute, distributed by Harvard University Press, 1978.

The Ukrainian Experience in the United States: A Symposium, edited by Paul R. Magocsi. Cambridge, Mass.: Harvard Ukrainian Research Institute, 1979.

Occasional Papers

Omeljan Pritsak, *The Origin of Rus',* Inaugural Lecture delivered at Harvard University, October 1975. Cambridge, Mass.: Harvard Ukrainian Research Institute, 1976.

HARVARD SERIES IN UKRAINIAN STUDIES

Eyewitness Chronicle (Litopys Samovydcja), Part I, edited by Orest Levyc'kyj. Munich: Fink Vlg., 1972.

George S.N. Luckyj, *Between Gogol' and Ševčenko.* Munich: Fink Vlg., 1971.

Myron Korduba, *La littérature historique soviétique ukrainienne.* Munich: Fink Vlg., 1972.

Oleksander Ohloblyn, *A History of Ukrainian Industry.* Munich: Fink Vlg., 1971.

Fedir Savčenko, *The Suppression of Ukrainian Activities in 1876* (Zaborona ukrajinstva 1876 r.). Munich: Fink Vlg., 1970.

The Galician-Volynian Chronicle, translated and annotated by George Perfecky, Munich: Fink Vlg., 1973.

Dmitrij Tschiževskij, *Skovoroda: Dichter, Denker, Mystiker.* Munich: Fink Vlg., 1974.